ART TREASURES OF THE VATICAN

ART TREASURES OF
THE VATICAN

EDITED BY
D. REDIG DE CAMPOS

CONTRIBUTORS:

MARIA DONATI BARCELLONA
GEORG DALTROP
GIOVANNI FALLANI
GERMANO GUALDO
ENRICO IOSI
GIANFRANCO NOLLI
CECILIA PERICOLI
FRANCESCO RONCALLI
NELLO VIAN

ART TREASURES OF THE VATICAN

Architecture · Painting · Sculpture

WITH 410 COLOR ILLUSTRATIONS

PARK LANE

NEW YORK

ART TREASURES OF THE VATICAN
Redig de Campos, Editor

© 1974 by Smeets Offset B.V., for text and illustrations
Translated by J. Gerber

This edition is published by Park Lane, a division of Crown Publishers, Inc.

a b c d e f g h

Library of Congress Catalog Card Number: 81-4017

Produced and Printed in the Netherlands by Royal Smeets Offset.

CONTENTS

INTRODUCTION

To observe is not enough; one would also like to understand what the eyes perceive. This rule of thumb for travelers is especially applicable to the Vatican. Archaeologists, historians, authors and artists have all delved into the history of each individual edifice there. Yet another aspect, much more important than those which have been the subjects of scientific investigation, remains to be characterized—especially so, since it escapes such precise academic definition. It is an omnipresent sense of living history that has made the Vatican the city of the soul. The visitor who cannot detect the features of this secret countenance, who cannot discover the real life of the Vatican, will never have a satisfactory explanation for the power it exerts. Here, for almost 2,000 years, has been the center of a spiritual communion; in countries all over the world, Christians aspire to achieve a community of spirit with the successor to St. Peter. By comprehending this significance of the Vatican, one can also understand what it was that led Roman Catholicism to embellish the center of its spiritual power with the diversity of human knowledge, including the arts. Thus it is that both the architecture and the art treasures of the Vatican are joined by bonds of divine wisdom. It is certainly true that anyone making his initial pilgrimage to this all-encompassing city of the spirit spends much time trying to organize the innumerable impressions which dog his every footstep. When he crosses a courtyard, enters a chapel, climbs a staircase, or visits a loggia, he is, actually and physically, participating in the history of epochs, both long past and recent—even if his eyes see nothing more than the many Latin inscriptions on the walls or the papal coats of arms on the doors.

Each and every visitor will try to imagine what this area must once have looked like. In the age of classic Rome, the imperial gardens were in the environs of the city; located therein were Nero's arena, the Naumachia (the site of mock-seafights), Hadrian's mausoleum and the large Egyptian obelisk of red granite. The "ager vaticanus," which was neither fertile nor pretty, became hallowed Christian ground between 64 and 67 A.D. For it was here that the cross was erected upon which the apostle Peter, the first bishop of Rome, was crucified at his own wish, with his head downward. The venerated corpse of St. Peter was buried in the vicinity of the Via Triumphalis, not far from the site of his martyrdom. Later, Emperor Constantine's basilica was built here—a large holy edifice with several aisles. The basilica remained standing, despite the damage and destruction brought about during the invasions of the Goths, the Vandals and the Saracens. It was around the year 1000 that pilgrims began flocking to Rome to revere the burial site of the apostolic prince; they often climbed the 35 steps leading to the portico-surrounded atrium on their knees. It is in the portico, which was called "paradise," that more than thirty Popes found their last resting-place. Within sight of the city, the pilgrims used to sing *O Roma nobilis* as they paid homage to their Christian faith in the basilica where emperors and kings were consecrated and crowned at the tomb of the Fisher from Galilee.

Both Pope Nicholas V and, following him, Pope Julius II, wished to have the old basilica—whose foundations were no longer secure—demolished; and the latter Pope pursued this plan with great resolve. Employing old Roman prototypes, Donato Bramante conceived a bold new design; it was in the form of a Greek cross, with apses, rotundas, domes and towers; and towering over it all was a gigantic dome supported by huge columns. "In St. Peter's I learnt what it meant for art, as well as nature, to set aside all the standards of proportion," wrote Goethe.

What then is the Vatican? Pope Paul VI has written, "The Vatican is not only a visible entity. The realization of an idea, a design, a plan, its intention is to unite mankind; and yet, for this very mankind, it contains the secret of immanent youth, of an abiding immediacy. Over the centuries, it has spoken of the everlasting rather than of that which is fleeting; and, with no spatial limitation upon it, the appeal is made to the entire world. As far as the imperfection of our knowledge is concerned, one talks here of infallibility. In contrast to the repeated faultiness of human institutions, an indelible rule holds sway here, one which is the inexhaustible hope of the world: it is extant, and yet in a process of eternal self-realization and perfection. Here is the Church: church, ecclesia, comprehensive and visible communion of the spirit, authentic and free, not only for the individual soul, but also for whole nations."

For everyone who comes to Rome, there is a church to provide a connecting link with the homeland, a house of worship in which each nationality can celebrate the Catholic rites in its own tongue. Frenchmen gather in the church of S. Luigi dei Francesi, on the square of the same name in Campo Marzio, or in S. Claudio and S. Andrea dei Borognoni at the Piazza S. Claudio al Tritone. North Americans attend services in the Via XX Settembre in the Church of S. Susanna, whose beautiful façade stems from Carlo Maderna; Germans, in the 16th century church of S. Maria dell'Anima in the Via della Pace, in which there is a monument to Hadrian VI based on a design by Peruzzi. English worshippers go to the church of S. Silvestro in Capite (Piazza S. Silvestro) and in the church of S. Tommaso di Canterbury (Via di Monserrato 45). Argentinians gather in the church of S. Maria Addolorata (Piazza Buenos Aires); Belgians, in S. Giuliano dei Belgi (Via del Sudario 40); Canadians, in the modern church of Santissimo Sacramento e dei Martiri Canadesi (Via G. B. Rossi); the Irish, in the old church of S. Clemente (Via di S. Giovanni in Laterano), which contains a famous 13th century mosaic of the school of Rome, depicting the triumph of the cross—they also worship at S. Patrizio a Villa Lodovisi (Via Boncampagni), or at S. Isidoro a Capo le Case (Via degli Artisti). Yugoslav churchgoers attend services at the church of S. Girolamo degli Schiavoni (Via Ripetta); Mexicans, at N. S. di Guadalupe a S. Filippo (Via Aurelia 675); Poles, at S. Stanislao (Via delle Botteghe Oscure); Portuguese, at S. Antonio in Campo Marzio (Via dei Portoghesi); Spaniards, at the church of S. Maria di Monserrato (Via Giulia) and in SS. Quaranta Martiri e di S. Pasquale di Babylon (Via S. Francesco a Ripa); Swedes, at S. Brigida (Piazza Farnese). Rumanians celebrate mass in the Rumanian-Byzantine rite at the church of S. Salvatore (Piazza delle Coppelle); Russians, in the Russian-Orthodox rite, at S. Antonio all'Esquilino (Via Carlo Alberto); Greeks, in the Greek-Orthodox rite, at the church of S. Atanasio al Babuino (Via dei Greci). It should also be mentioned that, in the church of S. Nicola da Tolentino agli Orti Sallustiani (Via S. Nicola da Tolentino), mass is celebrated in the Armenian rite; while in the chapel of the Ethiopian College in the Vatican, the Ethiopian rite is observed. The church of S. Maria in Cosmedin (Piazza Bocca della Verità) is now Melkite; S. Maria in Campo Marzio (Piazza Campo Marzio) adheres to the Antiochene-Syrian rite; and in the Lebanese church of S. Giovanni Marone (Via Aurora), mass is sung according to the Maronite-Syrian rite.

It is especially the association each pilgrim and tourist has to his own church, to the Vatican and to the city of Rome, which has given rise to some of the most moving testimonials in travel reports, memoirs and diaries, many of which are in private archives; these spontaneous utterances, stemming from none other than the traveler himself, contain extensive conversations held with friends and acquaintances. But unfortunately there is no book on Rome that offers, alongside a resumé of the historical edifices, a listing of private letters and literary excerpts, thus permitting a correlation of thought and feeling in both arts and letters. How can we re-awaken the feelings Dante experienced when, as a pilgrim looking at the old Papal palace, he was moved to write that the Lateran "rises above all that is transitory"? Many of the written comments are of coincidental nature and cursory, but the pilgrims of the Middle Ages have handed down to us Latin distichs and hymns, which have served as ample expressions of their faith. Thus it was that, on December 21, 1336, in Avignon, Petrarch wrote to the Bishop of Lompez, Giacomo Colonna, telling him of his desire to see the city, this image of heaven on earth, which had been erected upon the hallowed bones of the martyrs and sprinkled with the precious blood of the witnesses of truth! On April 18, 1341, Petrarch, having been crowned poet laureate by Senator Arso dell'Anguillara, went with his retinue to St. Peter's to let his crown hang from the altar.

In the 15th and 16th centuries, it was artists like Michelangelo, Raphael and Bramante who, with works of great religious intensity, won for Rome a reputation as a city of the arts. Antiquity was re-discovered and given new life by artists who emulated the past, thus themselves becoming "classic." This was not achieved consciously, or through imitation, but spontaneously, by means of an expressiveness comparable only to the Greek and Roman prototypes. The conception which the Renaissance artists had of Rome's Christianity is an aspect of the city's history with which one must be acquainted if one wants to discern its universality and fascination.

The Catholic Counter-Reformation in the second half of the 16th century led to an inner renewal—not in the Church as an institution, nor in its dogma, but with respect to people and discipline. This conformed with the admonition of the gospel that man must base his life on those of the great saints. Michelangelo, in the Sistine Chapel, and Raphael, in the "stanze" of the Vatican, created the outward signs of a view of mankind and of an apologetic conception of the Christian faith.

In the 17th century, Borromini, Caravaggio and Bernini continued the work of the Renaissance, using forms which suited their own age. They re-formulated a triumphal concept, which had developed out of tradition and which is clearly visible in baroque architecture and many other brilliant creations.

In Rome in 1786, Goethe admired the basilica, and wrote of the "Last Judgment" in the Sistine Chapel that he could only gaze at it in wonderment. "The inner sureness and masculinity of the master, his magnitude, surpass all forms of expression." In 1829, Chateaubriand wrote feelingly of Rome: "I have just come from the Sistine Chapel, where I participated in the liturgy of the passion and heard the miserere.... The sun went down; the shadows gradually spread out over the frescoes in the chapel, and one was able to see only the broad strokes of Michelangelo's brush. One after another the candles went out, and their smothered light exuded soft, white smoke, an... image of life.... The cardinals were on their knees, the new Pope was prostrate in front of the self-same altar at which I had seen his predecessor only a few days earlier. The wonderful prayer of penitence and compassion was heard in the intervals of tranquillity and night... the great mystery of a God who died to redeem man's sins. Rome is a magnificent place to forget everything, to despise everything, and to die."

The great poet Shelley said of St. Peter's Square: "It is huge, in all of Europe there is nothing to compare with it." Contemporary students could benefit from the notes made by Veuillot, Chesterton and Herman Melville. In his "Journal up the Straits," after a visit to the museums, the loggias and the Sistine Chapel, Melville wrote: "I stayed until closing time. Exhausted, I sat down next to the obelisk to try to recover from the dizzying effects of my first visit to the Vatican."

In addition to the impressions of travelers and artists, one ought to turn for a moment to those of the poets. As an elucidation of the city's significance, the *Hymn to Rome*, by Giovanni Pascoli, is worthy of mention. The poet tries to illustrate the characteristic landmarks of the holy city. He creates the allegory of the boat laden with refugees in search of their homeland—it is the ever-recurring myth of Aeneas. He anchors the ship near the Lido, for it is there that the vision has taken shape: a shepherd, a dove, a cross and an anchor. He stops the ship and drops anchor. Here the seekers on Roman soil find the synthesis of truth, the connection between the human and the divine, between time and eternity.

In St. Peter's and the Vatican one can experience simultaneously an earthly and heavenly reality—both the mystery of the spiritual Church of Christ and the visible Church. In a single volume it is not possible to do justice to such a subject, both complex and worthy of veneration. Instead, this book will seek to act as a guide, a connecting link between artists, authors and those who, if only for artistic considerations alone, want to become acquainted with these cultural and historical relics.

GIOVANNI FALLANI

ST. PETER'S AND ITS HISTORY

THE ORIGINAL STRUCTURE. OLD ST. PETER'S

The basilica was originally built by Emperor Constantine, following both his victory over Maxentius at the Milvian Bridge (312) and the Edict of Milan (313). It was to honor St. Peter, and had the announced purpose of containing the shrine that was to signify to the faithful the tomb of the Apostle. The church kept its original architectural form until the beginning of the 16th century, when the west section was razed.

The priest Tiberio Alfarano, prebendary of St. Peter's, described the church in "De Basilicae Vaticanae antiquissima et nova structura" down to the last detail, including a ground plan. Recent investigation and research have confirmed that this work is one of the best sources of information on Old St. Peter's. The belfry, with a golden globe and a bronze cock at the top, was not built until the 8th century (the sketch by Jacopo Grimaldi depicts it with the gothic alterations); it became the model for an entire series of belfries.

In front of the basilica there was an atrium (with the famous mosaic, the "Navicella," which has been attributed to Giotto) bordered by a portico; in the center of this there was a fountain in which the faithful used to bathe. At the end of the 4th century, Pope Damasus built a fountain to which he joined all the springs of the Vatican hills; the uncontrolled flow of water emanating from these springs had caused serious damage to many of the tombs of the Popes and other famous persons which were located in the portico. The activities of this Pope are preserved in an inscription which he designed himself and which is to be found in the grottoes. The Damasus fountain, surrounded by columns of porphyry on which there rested a bronze dome, was adorned toward the end of the 5th and the beginning of the 6th centuries by Pope Symmachus. He erected the bronze pine cone ("pigna"), which is today in the Belvedere courtyard, and decorated it with dolphins and peacocks. Pope Damasus also used the water of this fountain to fill the font of the Vatican baptistery, which at that time was in the center of the transept, at the site where St. Peter's chair was supposed to have stood.

The façade of the basilica was faced with mosaic; a second mosaic, which had been commissioned by Leo the Great, was renovated by Gregory IX (1227–1241). The work consisted of two parts: above was the Saviour, flanked by the apostles; at his feet on the left was Gregory IX, kneeling.

On the side of the façade bordered by the atrium there used to be five portals, the central one of which was known as the "silver portal," because it had been decorated with silver-leaf.

The interior of the church was divided by four rows of columns into a five-aisled nave. The transept extended beyond the walls of the nave, thus giving the structure the form of a Latin cross. In front of the apse was the shrine above St. Peter's tomb; marble ornamentation covered its surface, and it was noticed immediately by all who entered the hallowed spot. It was covered by a baldachin supported by four serpentine columns embellished with cruciform-patterned vine branches. A pendant-lamp beneath the baldachin had the shape of a crown.

Gregory the Great (590–604) raised the floor of the apse, and above the shrine placed a table, on which he celebrated Mass; in addition, next to the altar, he erected a tabernacle, supported by four silver columns. The semicircular passage along the interior of the apse, offering direct access to the altar, is also the result of his initiative. This deserves particular attention, since it was the first example of a semicircular crypt; as likely as not, it was also the first example of a raised choir. The mosaic of the apse appears to have been a depiction of a festive "traditio legis." It was completely

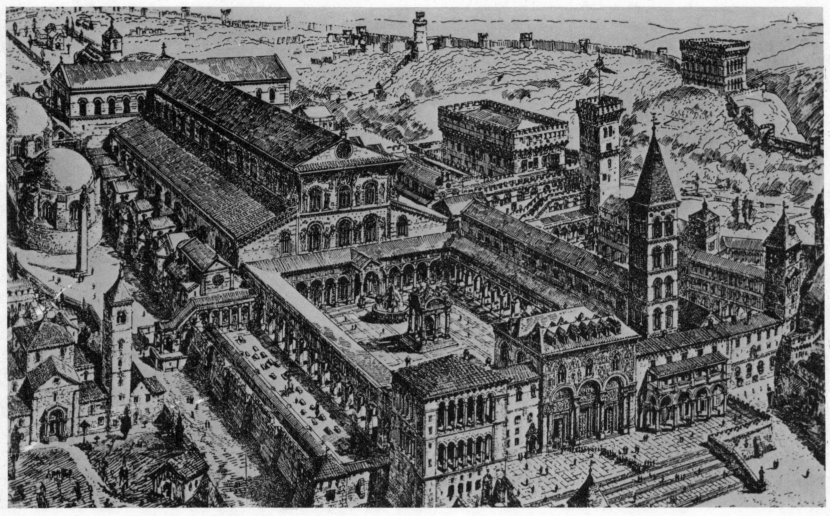

A view of Old St. Peter's. Reconstruction

re-done under Innocent III (1198–1216). On the basis of Grimaldi's sketch, made while the basilica was being demolished, and by referring back to the painting in the grottoes, we know what the mosaic looked like. The top portion contained the figure of Christ on a throne between Saints Peter and Paul; the lower portion depicted the throne with cross and mystical lamb; the side panels contained a portrait of Innocent III and a female figure representing the "Ecclesia Romana." The work was completed by a depiction of the cities of Bethlehem and Jerusalem, which had produced the mystical lamb, as well as several small trees and two palm trees with the phoenix between the branches.

The central nave was decorated with a cycle of frescoes showing scenes from both the Old and the New Testaments; this was a model for many other such fresco cycles in central Italy. Although at first attributed to Pope Formosus, the cycle was in reality commissioned by Leo the Great (440–461), as is indicated by a letter from Hadrian I to Charlemagne. Between the windows, there were figures of the prophets, and beneath this, in two sections, were episodes from the New Testament, on the left, and from the Old Testament, on the right. Then came a section with medallions of the Popes and, in the narthex, the vestibule, twelve episodes from the life of St. Peter.

Grimaldi's sketch of the portico indicates some of the extraordinary monuments which that venerated site contained. There was, for example, the oratory, built by John VII in 705 and dedicated to the Mother of God, as one can conclude from the inscription on the back, beneath the depiction of the "Virgin Queen." Adjacent to, and above, the figure of Mary were scenes from the life of Jesus; on the walls were scenes of Peter preaching in Antioch, Jerusalem and Rome. A conception of what the decoration of the oratory looked like can be gotten from the remains of the

11

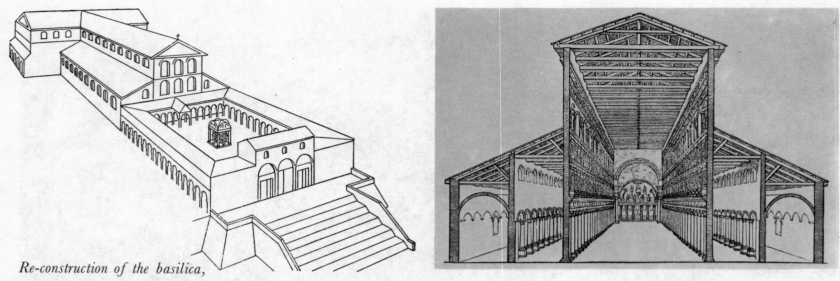

Re-construction of the basilica,
Old St. Peter's, built in 326 under Emperor Constantine. — A cross-sectional view of the five-aisled nave of the basilica.

mosaics, which are now in the church of Santa Maria in Cosmedin (perhaps the most beautiful and certainly the least restored of the fragments); in Orte; and in the Vatican grottoes. In front of the oratory stood the altar, with the "sudarium of St. Veronica," a relic highly venerated in the Middle Ages. Behind the Ravegnana portal was the tapered "chapel" of Boniface VIII (1295–1303), which contained his tomb. A statue of this Pope by Arnolfo di Cambio is now in the grottoes. Although the most revered bronze statue of St. Peter (illustration 15) has been attributed to a variety of artists, for example, Arnolfo di Cambio or his followers, the statue's signs of workmanship have led contemporary experts to conclude that it was made in the late Middle Ages.

Martin V (1417–1431), who was always ready to contribute to Rome's beautification, restored the basilica's portico, which was at that time in very poor condition. Cultural matters and the arts of humanism were never matters of indifference to Eugenius IV (1431–1447), despite the happenings of his eventful pontificate and his own monastic views. Not only did he restore Old St. Peter's; he also commissioned Antonio Averlino, known as Filarete, with the design for the bronze doors (illustration 14), which were intended to replace the old "silver" portal. Florentine artists worked on the new doors from 1433 to 1445, years that were especially bitter for the Pope, since he was forced to leave Rome. Each of the doors is divided into three panels; the bottom panel is quadratic in form, while the others have rectangular shapes. The panels represent (looking from top to bottom) Christ enthroned, the Virgin enthroned, and Saints Peter and Paul, with Eugenius IV kneeling at the feet of the former; beneath this is a depiction of the martyrdom of the two Apostles. The panels of the doors are surrounded by foliage decoration framing a variety of motifs: animals, scenes from mythology and Roman history, and medallions of the emperors and other leading figures. These are further divided into four pictorial reliefs, which represent scenes from Eugenius' IV pontificate: Eastern Emperor John Palaeologos' journey to Italy and his reception by the Pope; the Council of Florence and the departure of the Greeks from Venice; the coronation of Emperor Sigismund and his ride with the Pope; Abbot Andrew of the St. Anthony Brotherhood in Egypt receiving the formal certificate of the union of the two churches, and the abbot's arrival in Rome to visit the tombs of the Apostles. At the back of the doors, low down on the right one, Filarete portrayed himself and his assistants with names; two further self-portraits and a signature are on the front. Although criticized by Vasari, this work nevertheless possesses a certain artistic justification, especially in the small reliefs and in the foliage decoration. The gilding and the enamel-work, of which there are still fragments, must certainly have contributed toward making the doors an impressive sight. Also still in existence is a replica in miniature of the interior of the basilica as it was during the reign of Eugenius IV. This, contained in a copy of the "Grandes Chroniques de France" (Paris, Bibliothèque

Nationale) by Jean Fouquet (the coronation scene of Charlemagne), is a historical document of special significance. Fouquet, who is assumed to have worked with Filarete on the bronze doors of St. Peter's, was in Rome during the reign of Eugenius IV; he was influenced by Fra Angelico, who was working in the Vatican at the same time.

Nicholas V (1447–1455) was the first to plan a replacement for the old basilica, although his plan was not executed; and, on the basis of the notes and analyses of Leone Battista Alberti, in 1452 he commissioned Bernardo Rosselino with the project. Rosselino designed a church in which existing Gothic elements harmonized with those of classicism. The ground plan was a Latin cross with two lateral towers and, infelicitously, a dome above the central crossing—the intersection of nave, transepts, and choir.

Pius II (1458–1464) had the tombs transferred from the central nave to the aisles, commissioned the restoration of the atrium steps and began the construction of the "benediction loggia," work on which continued under his successors and was completed by Alexander VI (1492–1503). This loggia, consisting of three rows of four arches each, connected with the papal palace; all this is indicated in a drawing by Maarten van Heemskerck (circa 1533), which also has a view of the vestibule with considerable differences in elevation. On the right, one can make out the fountain of Innocent VII, later demolished by Paul V.

Of the many sculptural works which graced the basilica in the 15th century, the tombs of Sixtus IV and Innocent VIII by Antonio del Pollaiuolo deserve special mention. The former, signed by the artist and bearing the date 1493, has on the plate a bas-relief figure of the prostrate Pope, surrounded by the theological and cardinal virtues; the base bears figures representing the various arts. The tomb, which originally stood in the choir chapel of the old basilica, was moved first to the adjacent Rotonda Santa Andrea and, finally, after many other migrations, to the grottoes. The tomb of Innocent VIII is the only monument which survived the transition from the old basilica to the new one, and it is the first to show a Pope sitting on the throne. In niches on the sides are the four cardinal virtues, and, above them, the theological virtues. These wonderfully relaxed and elegant female figures exhibit Pollaiuolo's unusual talent for modeling and dramatic expression. In 1499, Michelangelo completed his marble Pietà; he obtained the commission for it, through the good offices of Jacopo Galli—who guaranteed that it would become the most beautiful work of art in all of Rome—from Cardinal Jean de Villiers da la Grollaye. This piece of sculpture by the young Michelangelo Buonarroti is full of strong dramatic sensibility, and it not only reveals elements of the 15th century Florentine tradition but also discloses the influence of the school of Ferrara and of Leonardo da Vinci. The Pietà was placed on the southern side of the old basilica, in the chapel of St. Petronilla, the "chapel of the French kings." After having stood at various other locations, it was placed in 1749 in the first chapel of the right-hand aisle, where it stands today (illustration 17).

THE CONSTRUCTION OF THE NEW BASILICA

Julius II (1503–1513) decided to carry out the plan devised by Nicholas V, and he commissioned Bramante, whose design he had selected, with the construction of the new basilica. Bramante designed a building in the form of a Greek cross with a cupola supported by mighty piers, four galleries and four belfries. Julius II, who had contemplated placing his tomb (for which Michelangelo already received the commission) under the dome of Bramante's basilica, on April 18, 1506, laid the foundation stone for one of the four piers. So hurried was the architect with the work, that he had the western portion of the old basilica demolished, with no consideration paid to mosaics, tombs, statues and other works of art; this won him the designation as "master of the ruins." Nevertheless, Julius II instructed him to erect a provisional stone structure for the protection of St. Peter's grave; known as the "holy house," it remained standing until 1592. The work made speedy progress, although, at the same time, Bramante designed, with Peruzzi's help, additional plans, in which the two arms of the cross would be connected up by broad choir passages, thus giving

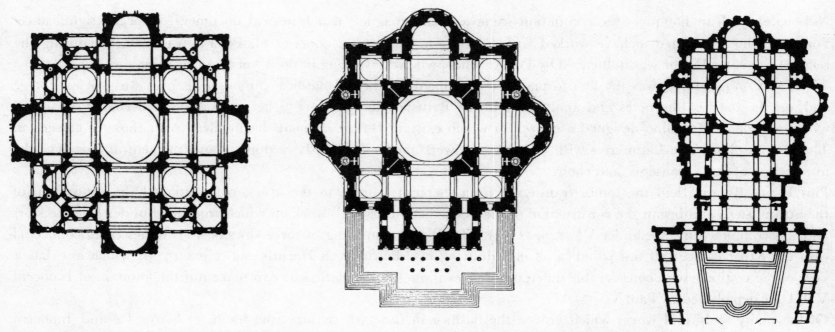

Ground plan of St. Peter's, based on Bramante's design (1506) – Ground plan, based on Michelangelo's design (1547) –
Actual ground plan of St. Peter's today, based on Michelangelo's design, as altered by Maderna (1606/15).

the whole an almost quadratic form. Piers, columns, niches, vault and dome would thus have united to form an image of bright amplitude and picturesque liveliness. In one important sketch he also illustrated his ideas of what the area immediately surrounding the basilica should look like, and in this he revealed his native sense of greatness. This area was to be quadratic and, like the church itself, it was to consist of a harmonious arrangement of architectural forms. The work continued until Bramante's death in 1514, and those who carried on beyond that date did so in light of his conception.

In August, 1514, Bramante was succeeded by Fra Giocondo, Giuliano da Sangallo (his assistants) and by Raphael. Liturgical considerations caused Sangallo and Raphael to be commissioned with the design for an elongated structure. When Fra Giocondo died and Giuliano da Sangallo returned to Florence, Raphael took as his assistant Raffaello Antonio da Sangallo junior, who, together with Baldassare Peruzzi, assumed control of the project, following Raphael. As his sketches reveal, Sangallo drew up several designs; the last of these relies basically on Bramante's conception, although Sangallo enlarged upon it by adding a nave that ended in a broad façade, flanked by two belfries. A wooden model in the Vatican Museum makes clear the artist's idea, which was severely criticized by Michelangelo.

After Sangallo died, 1546, Michelangelo yielded to the wishes of Paul III (1534–1549), who insisted that he become chief architect of St. Peter's. Paying no attention at all to the liturgical exigencies, which had determined the ideas of his predecessor, he returned to Bramante's project, which he characterized as "clear and pure, full of light," adding that "whoever distances himself from Bramante, also distances himself from the truth." He took over the form of the Greek cross without Sangallo's additions; the ground plan called for a quadrate, out of which the galleries protruded. From 1547 to 1548, he personally supervised the preparation of a model for the dome, and, from 1558 to 1561, he worked on another, a larger model. The wooden model in the Vatican Museum clearly indicates his immense conception of a spherical dual dome; however, also there are the changes wrought by Giacomo della Porta and Domenico Fontana, who raised the curvature of the sphere. Both Michelangelo and Bramante had conceived of a huge, encompassing space, which would give the basilica a sense of near isolation. A fresco in the Vatican Library shows the façade, the vestibule and the columns surrounding it. It conveys an impression of Michelangelo's total conception, which was supposed to beautify the architectural complex that was dominated by the dome.

Sixtus V (1585–1590) insisted that Michelangelo's project be brought as quickly as possible to a conclusion; perhaps he had a premonition of the brevity of his pontificate, during which he was nevertheless in a position to give the city the general plan it still has today. On November 1, 1589, as the Pope was announcing that he hoped soon to celebrate Mass under the dome of St. Peter's, work was still going on with "unbelievable care." On May 12, 1590, there appeared this triumphant proclamation: "It is to his everlasting honor and to the humiliation of his predecessors that Sixtus V has completed the magnificent edifice, the dome of St. Peter's." Exactly one week later, a High Mass was sung and the last stone was added to the dome. On August 9th of the same year the lantern was placed upon the dome, "on whose 36 columns work was still going on... the interior is being faced with mosaics, the exterior with lead and the groins with gold-leaf." This was the jubilant conclusion of the majestic structure of the great Pope, who died on the 27th of that same month. Della Porta deserves credit for having carried out Michelangelo's design and for the ingenious solution of the static and structural problems inherent in Bramante's brilliant project; credit is also due to Fontana, who completed the work.

In November, 1593, under Clement VIII, the sphere and the cross for the top of the dome were cast. It was under Sixtus V that the monumental and hazardous task was accomplished of removing the obelisk from its previous location, where the Sacristy is today, to the square (the idea had already occurred to Nicholas V and Paul III). Domenico Fontana was justifiably proud of this feat; he himself described it in his book, *Della Trasportazione dell'Obelisco Vaticano*, which was illustrated with engravings by Giovanni Guerra.

Following the monumental work involved in building the dome, the completion of Michelangelo's house of worship became ever more urgent over the years, for the remaining parts of the old basilica were in a state of advanced decay. Clement VIII (1592–1605), under whose pontificate the mosaic facing of the dome was begun, had Maderna renovate the Confessio and ordered the Clementine chapel to be richly decorated; he also appointed, in 1603, Carlo Maderna and Giovanni Fontana as the architects of St. Peter's. Paul V (1605–1621) wanted to accomplish this difficult task, which was resumed with the demolition of the old basilica; thus it was that, in 1607, he announced a competition, in which, in addition to Maderna and Fontana, all the prominent architects of the day were to participate. It was Maderna who won this competition, and, although he tried to avoid making considerable alterations in the Greek cross ground plan, he was forced to accede to the wishes of the cardinals, who gave priority to cultic and sacred considerations. As a result, Maderna had to change over to the form of the Latin cross—both because of its symbolic significance, and to conform to the prevailing taste of the day. Thus was the harmonious Renaissance design, calling for a church with the altar in the center—a concept both Bramante and Michelangelo had embraced—rejected.

In works like the façade of Santa Susanna, Maderna had had the opportunity to express, untrammelled, his talents and he had given proof of his unbridled originality. Here, however, he was dependent upon Michelangelo's creation and, although he tried to do justice to this conception, he ended up interpreting it quite differently. He planned at first a façade without bell towers; at the Pope's request, however, he included two towers in his scheme, which resulted in the façade appearing less spacious and lighter. But this project had to be rejected, since the foundations did not offer sufficient support. Later on, Bernini courageously faced this task, though he had to abandon the project after many attempts to accomplish it. Maderna's travertine façade, with its gigantic proportions, is one of sober elegance. His extension of the basilica exerted a positive influence, as far as the interior is concerned, on the development of sacred baroque architecture. The work was completed in 1614.

Whereas Michelangelo had conceived of a pillared vestibule, what eventually developed was a large atrium, the walls of which were divided by piers and ionic columns; this was the most striking example of Maderna's ability; he also designed and supervised the especially beautiful stuccowork. Scenes from the Acts of the Apostles are depicted on the ceiling vaults. The central portal is Filarete's door; to accommodate it to the new entrance to the basilica, it was restored and, by adding pictorial bands above and below, enlarged.

It is certainly true that the contrast inside the basilica between Michelangelo's construction and Maderna's transformation is there evident—and it has perhaps been subjected too often to criticism; equally visible, however, is the honest effort to tone down this contrast by means of the architectural relationship of vault and chapels. There develops, in addition, a feeling of unity, which is also caused by the wide angle of aperture of the dome (illustration 13) and by Bernini's baldachin, the magnitude of which represents a harmonious element connecting the two parts of the church. Bernini did not simply create a conventional tabernacle, but rather a gigantic "machine" for the everlasting glory of St. Peter's tomb. Bernini spent much time on the form of this work of art in relation to its location, as many sketches indicate. The artist knew that here a kind of architecture was necessary that contained elements of painting—of movement, in other words. On four large serpentine columns (which relate to those in the Confessio of the old basilica) there rests an adorned canopy, from which imitation fabric fringes are suspended (illustration 12). Bernini began work in 1624; it went ahead slowly and was not completed until 1633. He had many assistants, for whom he was a strong influence, and under his direction, excellent artists were trained.

In accord with the baldachin and its adornment, Bernini planned a new arrangement of the dome piers, and to this purpose he fitted them out with niches and galleries. This brought him a storm of criticism, especially so when a crack appeared in Michelangelo's dome. This was attributed to the niches, which are supposed to have greatly weakened the dome's stability. Urban VIII desired statues in these niches. Accordingly, Bernini made the figure of St. Longinus; although this was typical of his theatrical kind of art, he endowed the statue with such an elegant bearing and a surprising freshness of style that it gives one the impression of great harmony. Andrea Bolgi made the statue of St. Helena with a noble face, but with ponderous drapery which, rather than wreathing the figure, merely hung down from it. St. Veronica is a remarkable and original work by Francesco Mochi (although Bernini, as well as other contemporaries, criticized it); its diagonal bearing and mobile drapery accorded with baroque taste. Francesco du Quesnoy's St. Andrew displays an absolutely spiritualized facial expression and, although its bearing is somewhat conventional, the workmanship is very beautiful, including the drapery. Above the statues Bernini fashioned four relics galleries—for the Holy Lance, a part of the Cross, the Sudarium of St. Veronica and the head of St. Andrew—for all of which he employed the spiral columns of the old baldachin.

Maderna had already begun to transform the interior of the church by creating facing made up of precious marble works of art. Bernini continued along these lines, bringing his marked painting talents to the fore. Thus it was that the piers were adorned with Papal likenesses in marble medallions held by "putti" who bear palm branches, lilies and other symbols. This decorative work was carried out according to Bernini's designs by Andrea Bolgi, Niccolò Sale, Niccolò Menghini and Ercole Antonio Raggi.

In August, 1656, the foundation stone for the colonnades of St. Peter's was laid. Bernini's design for the rows of columns was intended not only for Christians, but for all the peoples of the world; this is made clear by a sketch attributed to him in which a figure extends his arms in exactly the same form which Bernini gave his colonnades. The gigantic plan originally called for an additional arm extending toward the Piazza Rusticucci, but the artist finally decided upon a more distinct ground plan, one which would allow an unimpeded view of the church.

While he was working on this huge project, he also created the famous Cattedra of St. Peter, the bishop's chair of the Apostle, on which he labored for more than ten years and which formed the logical conclusion to his decorative and plastic conceptions: it was a clear and systematic synthesis of imposing effects. For the Cattedra he made many sketches and designs and he included the old ivory ornamented wooden chair, allegedly St. Peter's throne. In carrying out this project, he was aided by artists like Raggi, Ferrata, Morelli and the German, Johann Paul Schor.

The tomb of Alexander VII, with which the Pope had commissioned Bernini, is a product of the artist's later period; it was not begun until 1672, and was completed in 1678. Here, too, Bernini had several collaborators, including Lazzaro Morelli, Giulio Cartari, Michele Maglia, Giuseppe Baratta, the metal caster Girolamo Lucenti and Giuseppe Mazzuoli, who had made the figure of *Charity*. It was because of his advanced age that Bernini required so many co-workers, although he was still able to supervise the work. His other late works were created in the same manner—like the chapel of the Holy Sacrament, for the execution of which he had the assistance of such specialists as Girolamo Lucenti and Carlo Mattei. The small cupola-shaped chapel, flanked by the figures of two praying angels, appears especially magnificent, as the result of the bronze, gold, lapis lazuli and marble adornment.

In the 17th century, the basilica was furnished with additional remarkable works of sculpture and painting. Alessandro Algardi built Leo XI's tomb, the elegant and cheerful Papal statue of which he created himself, whereas he left the execution of the figures of *Dignity* and *Generosity* to Ercole Ferrata and Giuseppe Peroni. In 1650, the artist completed a large marble altar-piece depicting *Attila's Meeting with Leo the Great*. For the tomb of Clement X, which was designed by Mattia de Rossi, Ferrata executed the Papal statue, whereas the lateral figures, *Forbearance* and *Mercy* are by Giuseppe Mazzuolo and Lazzaro Morelli, respectively. For the Clementine chapel, Andrea Sacchi painted the *Miracle of Gregory the Great;* Cardinal Francesco Barberini presented the basilica with the large painting, *The Martyrdom of St. Erasmus*, with which he had commissioned Nicholas Poussin; Valentin de Boulogne painted Saints Processus and Martinian; Guercino painted *Burial and Glorification of St. Petronilla,* a masterpiece of his early style; and Lanfranco painted the *Triumph of the Cross,* in the so-called "Chapel of the Crucifixion."

At the end of the 17th century, work began on the completion of the baptismal font chapel; in charge was Carlo Fontana, and here he was able to give clear proof of his extraordinary talent as a decorator. For the font he used the porphyry lid from the tomb of Otto II that had stood in the Constantinian basilica; he fitted it with a beautiful and richly ornamented fastener made of shell-gold. The lid bore two "putti" holding a bas-relief trinity on high, and it was rounded off with the Agnus Dei. The sides, which bear the coat of arms of Innocent XII, are faced with porphyry panels, and these have wonderful bronze ornamentation.

At the outset of the 18th century, the tombs of Queen Christina of Sweden and Innocent XI were completed; the latter was designed by Maratta and displays the direct elegance and fineness which marks the style of Pietro Stefano Monnot. It was in this century that the following Papal tombs were created: that of Alexander VIII, with a bronze statue by Angelo de' Rossi; that of Gregory XIII, by Camillo Rusconi; that of Innocent XIII, executed by Filippo della Valle, who worked with a design prepared by Ferdinando Fuga; and, finally, the tomb of Benedict XIV: a noteworthy work by Pietro Bracci, in collaboration with Gaspare Sibilla.

It was also in the 18th century that many a prominent artist took a hand in sculpting the statues of the founders of the religious orders, and these were set up in the niches of the nave, the transept and the galleries.

Plans for the construction of a sacristy were drawn up under Alexander VII (1655–1667) and, later, during the pontificate of Innocent XII (1691–1700). In 1715 a competition was announced, and among those participating were Filippo Juvarra, Niccolò Michetti, Domenico Paradisi, Antonio Canevari and Antonio Valeri. Although Juvarra won the competition, it was not his design that was carried out. After having studied many of the plans that had been entered, Pope Pius VI selected, in April, 1776, Carlo Marchionni's design, and, on September 22nd of that same year, he laid the foundation stone. To make room for the new structure, completed in 1784, the old sacristy, the Porta Fabbrica, and the church of Santo Stefano degli Ungari had to be torn down. It was a massive building which Marchionni erected, richly decorated but yet practical. It included the usual sacristy and that of the canons and prebendaries, as well as providing for the chapter room, quarters for treasury and archives, and the canons' residence.

At the end of the 18th century, Antonio Canova was commissioned by Clement XIII's nephews to create a tomb for the deceased Pope; when it was finished, Pope Pius VI expressed his ecstatic admiration of the work's impressive similarity to his predecessor.

Twenty-five years later, Canova designed the monument to mark the spot in the grottoes below which lie buried the last three members of the royal House of Stuart. On it are portrait busts of the *Old Pretender* and *Bonnie Prince Charlie* in armour, as well as Henry of York in his cardinal's robes. The entire project was commissioned by Britain's King George IV, as a generous tribute to the last pretenders to the throne. The last work by the great sculptor from Possagno is the statue of Pius VI, in the Confessio of the basilica. He portrayed the Pope kneeling and lost in prayer. The statue is similar to that of Clement XIII; here, however, Canova designed merely the expressive head and the hands, leaving the remainder to Adamo Tadolini.

Subsequently, to this day, Papal monuments and statues of the saints have been placed in the church—in the nave, the transept and the galleries.

CECILIA PERICOLI

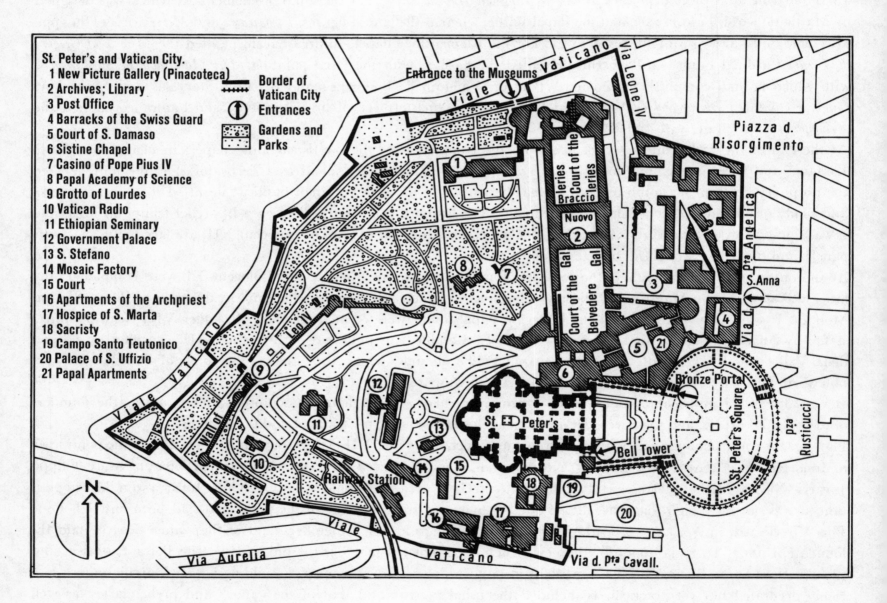

St. Peter's and Vatican City.

St. Peter's and Vatican City.

BUILDINGS AND PALACES

Following the Edict of Milan in the year 313, by which Constantine the Great had sanctioned the freedom of the Church within his empire, his second wife, Fausta, gave the Pope the buildings which had originally belonged to the Lateran on the Caelian hill for use as his official residence. St. Peter's basilica, which Constantine had had erected over the tomb of the Apostle Prince, remained for many centuries merely a cemetery church in the open fields, surrounded by a monastery and several structures for the priests and custodians of the hallowed site. This area, which was on the other side of the Tiber and was considered to be unhealthy, offered the Popes a secure sanctuary during the many upheavals of the Middle Ages. Pope Symmachus, taking advantage of this during the Laurentian schisma, lived there from 501 to 506, and on the sides of the basilica he built two "escopia." To these Charlemagne, in the year 781, added a "palatium Caroli"; additional buildings arose in the 8th and 9th centuries, under Leo III and Gregory IV. By constructing a turreted wall, Leo IV (847–855) gave this area the security of a fortified city, creating the pre-requisites for its decisive development in the years to come. Thus it was that the so-called Leonine city took shape, as part of which, between 1145 and 1153, Eugene III built a "palatium novum."

Of these old structures, all of which later on fell victim to the new St. Peter's basilica, Franz Ehrle wrote extensive reports in the three chapters of his unfinished *History of the Vatican Palaces,* a work which was published after the author's death by his pupil, Egger. Their mention here serves only as a topographical introduction to what must be noted about the structures that developed during the subsequent period on the hill north of St. Peter's.

We now come to Innocent III, a Count Segni who became the Pope of Saints Dominic and Francis and who reigned from 1198 to 1216, significantly increasing the political power of the Holy See. He was the Lord of Christendom, but not of Rome, which, although divided into various rival factions and interest groups, guarded its freedom jealously. Local unrest often forced the Pope to exchange his residence in the Lateran for the safety of the Leonine city, where he enlarged the palace of Eugene III by adding quarters for the clergy, as well as erecting administrative buildings. In order to increase the security of the Vatican as a sanctuary, he surrounded it with a second turreted wall within that built by Leo IV. We know this from the *Gesta Innocenti,* and it has been confirmed by recent discoveries. In fact, parts of this fortification came to light during the restoration of the exterior of the Nicholas chapel; it was connected to the residential palace which had been built around 1278 by Nicholas III and, with additions and alterations, it has survived almost in its entirety. It has been determined that the famous chapel was located between the fourth and fifth storey of a turret at the northeast edge of the Sala Ducale, about 27 meters high. Studies of the limestone wall have indicated that what we are dealing with was originally a single military structure (perhaps a small fortress), bounded by the first section of the room ("aula tertia"), whose second section ("aula secunda") had been added by Nicholas III. In the small room beneath the chapel, window recesses with seats for the guards were found, as well as embrasures and niches, the latter having been decorated once the tower had lost its martial significance and had been attached to the palace. It is the oldest building on the hill north of St. Peter's, an elevation known in those days as "Mons Saccorum." After eleven pontificates had elapsed without having left any traces worth mentioning at the Vatican, Nicholas III Orsini (1277–1280) was elected Pope, and he made the Vatican his permanent residence (there are no documents of his from the Lateran). In the three years of his short but eventful reign, he began the construction of a fortified residence upon the hill. One can characterize this as the citadel of the Leonine city. It appears to have been planned as a quadratic building fitted out with battlements, guarded by angle-turrets and surrounding the "Cortile del Pappagallo." Equipped with cisterns and granaries, it was a castle which could be defended even in the face of an attack upon the city. Nicholas III was unable to complete his "palatium novum," but he did build a part of the east wing and the entire south wing, the first section of which consists of the "small barracks," or the fortification of Innocent II with the tower belonging to it. It was to this earliest section that he attached the "aula secunda" of the "Sala Ducale," which leads to the large "aula prima" (now the royal hall), and it is through the latter which one had to go to reach the old "Capella Magna." This chapel is mentioned in the famous inscription on the Capitol, but it was razed in the second half of the 15th century to make room for the Sistine Chapel. The main façade of the palace, which faced Rome, bordered on a garden—now the Court of S. Damaso, known then as "hortus secretus"—and since its construction it had been adorned with two rows of loggie; later on these were replaced by the loggie of Bramante and Raphael which are in existence today. The palace of the Orsini Pope had only two storeys (above the portico in the ground-floor); that means it extended up to the floor-level of Raphael's loggie. Among the new buildings of the 16th century, its masonry has been almost completely preserved.

The explorations which were carried out during the various restorations—conditions are then ideal for such investigatory studies—often led to discoveries which were basic for determining historical dates. In almost all the rooms which have been described up to this point, significant fragments of friezes painted in fresco were found on each floor. These are very decorative and it is certain that they originate from the 13th century—thus, in all probability, from the period of Nicholas III. They were found, for example, in the old hall of the Swiss Guard, in the adjoining hall of the Chiaroscuri, in the Nicholas chapel, in the hall below and on the ground-floor of the loggie of San Damaso. In the latter structure, also were found several capitals of columns in Roman style; from this one can deduce that Bramante did not completely raze the medieval portico, but simply erected his above that on the ground-floor.

Nicholas III also bought all the vineyards north of his palace up to the hill known as "Mons sancti Aegidii," where Innocent VIII later had his famous Belvedere built. He transformed this tract of land into a garden, on the surrounding wall of which he had the capitoline inscription affixed, so as to remind posterity of the work of this great builder among the Popes. We do not know the name of his architect, but we do know that, at the Vatican of that time, Fra Ristoro dei Campi and the lay brother Fra Sisto were active—both of them Florentines, who had come to Rome in the final year of the pontificate (1280).

Three other buildings of the Vatican are of a later date, although before Nicholas V (1447–1455): the "turris scalarum" at the southwest corner of the "Cortile del Maresciallo," where the stairs lead to the buildings at the foot of the hill; the "capella parva sancti Nicolai"; and the extension of the east wing of the palace (the product of two different periods) and the wing's loggia. Belonging to this new section were, on the first floor, the Papal hall ("Sala dei Pontefici") in the Appartamento Borgia (to use today's designations) and, on the second floor, the "Sala di Constantino," one of Raphael's "stanze." Both of these were originally paneled. The wing was attached to a massive tower, as indicated in the well-known drawing by Heemskerck, and the lower portion of this tower has been re-discovered. The "turris scalarum" and the "capella parva sancti Nicolai" were demolished under Paul III (1534–1549)—the latter, merely to widen the Scala del Maresciallo and with no consideration paid to the decorative frescoes by Fra Angelico! The chapel and the second section of the east wing were probably built by Boniface VIII Caetani (1294–1303), who often spent time in the Vatican, where he also died.

During the long years of exile at Avignon (1309–1377) and the great schism (1378–1417), little or nothing transpired in the Papal residence adjacent to St. Peter's. However, with the election of Nicholas V Parentucelli (1447–1455), a pious priest and educated humanist, a new and magnificent chapter began in the history of the Vatican palaces, and one in which the Renaissance made a victorious entry. Vespasiano da Bisticci wrote of him: "He always said that if he had money, he would spend it on books and buildings." When he became Pope, he did both: he gave impetus to the establishment of the Vatican Library and he drew up a magnificent plan for the construction of the

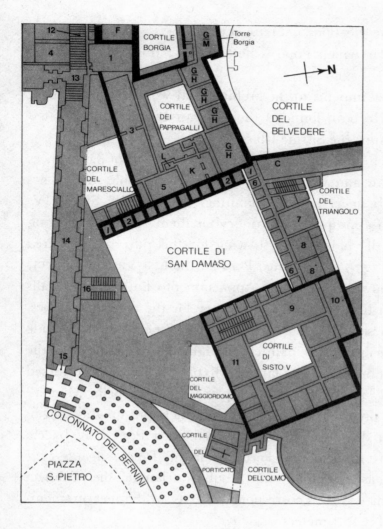

Plan of the Papal Palace — at the top is the medieval palace (Nicholas III – Alexander VI).

1. Sala Regia. – 2. The Loggie of Bramante and Raphael. – 3. Sala Ducale. – 4. Cappella Paolina. – 5. Sala dei Paramenti. – 6. North wing of the loggie of Pirro Ligorio. – 7. Cappella Matilde. – 8. Sala dei Foconi. – 9. Sala Clementina. – 10. Sala del Concistro. – 11. Private library of the Holy Father. –. 12. Scala Regia. – 13. Equestrian statue of Constantine, by Bernini. – 14. Portico di Constantino. – 15. Portone di Bronzo. – 16. Scala di Pio IX.

L Chapel of Fra Angelico – K Sala dei Chiaroscuri. – G Appartamento Borgia; above, H Stanze di Raffaello. – F Sistine Chapel. – M Sala dell'Immocolata. – C Galleria Lapidaria. – I Loggia di Raffaello.

Leonine city; this plan, initiated by Leon Battista and drawn by Manetti, had only a small portion carried out. There were two motives for this project: the significance of the Holy See's reputation and apprehension about the safety of the Popes, for whom the aged walls of Leo IV were no longer sufficient protection. The new city was to be protected by a ring of massive walls with round artillery towers; and another wall, in front of and similar to the first one, was to protect the Papal residence from enemies coming from the north and the east. It was only this latter wall that was built and it is still standing today with its imposing main tower, in the vicinity of the St. Anna gate.

Nicholas V also had to leave unfinished his other dream, the new palace. He was limited to finishing the half-completed north wing. He kept the (by then) archaic style, even as far as the battlements (something unusual for the Renaissance), and to such an extent that the new section can hardly be distinguished from the old one. However, if the exterior bore the characteristics of the 14th century, the ceilings and the proportions of the interior—Appartamento Borgia and Raphael's stanze—reveal the taste of a new century in its highest and greatest realization: the Florentine style. The "palace engineer" was known as Antonio da Firenze, and, after 1451, Bernardo Rosselino.

Of special significance is one of the painted frescoes, which Nicholas V commissioned for the embellishment of the rooms in the medieval residence; this work, by an unknown successor to Pisanello, was discovered several years ago in the old hall of the Swiss Guard. In addition, the discovery was made of the painted wooden ceiling of the Papal bedroom, on which the hook for the canopy can still be seen. It was for Pope Nicholas V that Fra Angelico, in the chapel of Nicholas V, made frescoes based on the lives of Saints Stephen and Lawrence.

In the period between the death of Nicholas V, in 1455, and the election of Sixtus IV, in 1471, the wing which closes off the "Cortile del Pappagallo" to the west was built (under which Pope is not known); thus the quadratic structure, as originally planned by Nicholas III, was complete.

The pontificate of Sixtus IV della Rovere (1471–1484) imparted new impetus to the architectural work in the Vatican. Like Nicholas V, Sixtus had a weakness for books and buildings. He both founded the Vatican Library and created the incomparable collection of masterworks which was named after him: the Sistine Chapel.

The Papal Library, founded by Nicholas V (largely with books which he himself had donated), consisted of 824 codices (manuscripts); these were kept in an unknown room in the Vatican and were not to be made accessible to scholars until the extensive library of which he dreamed had been built. It never left the planning stage. Under Sixtus IV, the number of manuscripts had increased to 2,527, and the lack of an appropriate repository for them became a pressing problem. The Pope thus decided to set aside the ground-floor of the palace's north wing for this purpose, this area having previously been used as a granary and a wine cellar. In July, 1475, Bartolomeo Platina, the first Vatican prefect, began supervising the transformation of the rooms beneath those known today as the Appartamento Borgia. Four halls were furnished with the Latin library, the Greek library, the secret library, the Papal library for the church archives, and the "Regesta." Of those painters who painted frescoes in these halls, four are known: Domenico and Davide del Ghirlandajo, Antoniazzo Romano and Melozzo da Forli. The latter also painted the famous fresco, now in the Vatican Picture Gallery (Pinacoteca), *Installation of Plantina* (illustration 359). The fame of Sixtus IV, however, is linked especially to the construction and decoration of the Sistine Chapel; this was built to replace the "Cappella Magna" of Nicholas III which, in a condition of deterioration, had stood on that site. The work, which presumably began in the year of the indulgences, 1475, was supervised by Giovanni de' Dolci and was based on a design by Baccio Pontelli, whom Vasari mentions as the architect. Both of them are depicted by Perugino in his fresco, *Apostle Peter Receiving the Keys to the Kingdom of Heaven* (illustration 160); the master-builder with a square-triangle, the architect with a pair of compasses. The central nave measures 40.23 X 13.41 meters; this corresponds exactly to the measurements of Solomon's Temple in the Bible (Battisti). The height of the chapel is 20.7 meters.

The 15th century decorative paintings consist of portraits of the first Popes; these are in the niches between the windows. Two fresco cycles along the walls deal with episodes from the lives of Moses and Christ. They are all the work of a group of artists who were under Perugino's direction and to which Cosimo Rosselli, Botticelli, Ghirlandajo and, later, Luca Signorelli belonged. The continuing restoration work brought to light on the cornices the Latin "tituli" to various scenes, and this was something that had until then been unknown.

But the Sistine Chapel did not only fulfill a religious function as a Papal chapel. Located as it is at the southeast corner of the palace, it is an essential section of the comprehensive plan formulated by the architects of Nicholas III; this called for four defensive towers, one at each of the corners of the complex of buildings surrounding the "Cortile del Pappagallo." Mention was already made of the two towers which faced Rome. This is the third one, and it is more of a fortification than a tower. The fourth—the Borgia tower—was built during the rule of Alexander IV (1492–1503) at the northeast corner, opposite the Sistine Chapel, thus strengthening the defense of the hillside ascent at its most accessible and most sensitive point. It is conceivable that this was also the purpose of the earlier medieval chapel. There thus developed a conspicuous contrast between the outward appearance of the plain brick wall with the battlement-studded breastwork and the building's interior, whose nave from the very beginning was intended to contain the largest project of early Renaissance painting.

A new chapter in the architectural history of the Vatican begins with the successor to Sixtus IV, the Genoese, Innocent VIII Cibo (1484–1492). The complex extends beyond the old center of the residence, expanding to the north into the far reaches of the garden enclosed by the walls of Nicholas III. In 1484, Innocent VIII launched the construction of the so-called Belvedere (the name originated at that time and became an accepted architectural term) on the second

View of Old St. Peter's and the Vatican Palace. Drawing (circa 1535) by Maarten van Heemskerck.

hill north of St. Peter's, on the "Mons sancti Aegidii." Vasari attributes the design of the Belvedere to Antonio del Pollaiuolo, although he also says that "it was carried out by others, since he (Pollaiuolo) had little building experience." According to documents in the archives, the name of at least one "other" is Jacopo da Pietrasanta, a well known master-builder of the day. The development of the Sistine Chapel repeats itself here, with the one difference that, in this case, the initiator of the plan is a painter with no architectural knowledge. This explains certain peculiarities of the project, like the incongruity of the 14th century top storey with the battlements, on the one hand, and the peaceful loggia in pure Tuscan style, on the other hand; the latter originated more as a figurative than as an architectural conception, somewhat like the background to a picture. The building was originally thought of as a covered walk for the Pope, allowing him to enjoy a wide view of the area around Rome, as far as Soratte. As a matter of fact, Pollaiuolo's plan included only the north wing. It was to be a vaulted loggia, consisting of eight arches between Doric columns with cornice and attic, and flanked by two small towers. Innocent VIII decided later to transform the covered walk into a modest summer villa. The two eastern arches were turned into two closed rooms, and to the other side was added a small chapel with sacristy; it was Pietrasanta who, by himself, drew up all the designs. This chapel, which was ruthlessly demolished at the end of the 18th century in order to make room for the Pio-Clementine Museum, was furnished completely by Mantegna with frescoes. On the main wall of the loggia there were several views of the city, framed within imitated arches, and all by Pinturicchio; during recent restoration work, some poorly preserved fragments were found, among them a view of the Belvedere itself. Also part of the second stage of construction was the east wing of the building, with the Papal suite and the rooms for the domestics, kitchen, etc. In the 16th century, the first antique statues of the Vatican collection were placed in the inner courtyard (*the Apollo Belvedere*, the *Laocoön* group and others), and the villa was used as quarters for those artists working in the Papal residence, among them Bramante and Leonardo da Vinci.

We are also indebted to Innocent VIII for the sacristy of the Sistine Chapel, which, incomprehensibly, was neglected during the construction of St. Peter's; later on, it was enlarged by Gregory XIII and, under Clement VII, completed.

23

In 1492, Alexander VI Borgia (1492–1503) was elected Pope—an unpleasant recollection for the Church, although not so for the history of art. In the Vatican, his fame is justified especially by the frescoes, by Pinturicchio and his pupils, which are in the apartments on the first floor of the north wing, where the Pope lived. However, the only structures bearing his coat of arms are St. Peter's gate and the Torre Borgia—typical for a man, perhaps, who mistrusted everything and everyone. St. Peter's gate, at the entrance to the barracks of the Swiss Guard (illustration 8), was recently carefully restored; its plain strength and elegance reveal the style of Giulio da Sangallo, although reports do not mention his name in connection with the gate. This is, all in all, a structure of secondary rank, whereas the Torre Borgia had great significance for the development of the Vatican complex of buildings.

By the time Innocent VIII died, the ideal plan for the Papal residence, as drawn up by Nicholas III and carried out by his successors, had been almost completely realized. Indeed, opposite the citadel-chapel of Sixtus IV there was not yet a similarly fortified structure, which could safeguard the entrance to the palace from the west. Many details of the masonry allow one to conclude that Nicholas V had intended to add to the west side of the north wing which he had had built. This could only have been the still missing fourth tower, since the converging axes of the wing and the chapels (old and new) made the continuance of the Nicholas wing impossible. Alexander VI carried the plan through to its logical conclusion by building the Torre Borgia, which towered some eight meters above the Belvedere court.

Alexander VI died in 1503 and his successor, Pius III Piccolomini, died after a reign of only 26 days. Thereafter, the conclave elected Julius II della Rovere (1503–1513), nephew of Sixtus IV and a truly imperial Pope, who recognized genius and who was the deserving patron of Bramante, Michelangelo and Raphael. More than 60 years old, the aged Pope drew up plans for Rome's urban renewal for years into the future, as well as far-seeing plans for the Vatican and St. Peter's. So comprehensive were these projects that they kept the successors to Julius II busy for the next century. It was in Bramante that he found the man capable of building the new basilica and of turning the Papal palace into that splendid residence of which he dreamed. He installed Bramante at the Belvedere and together they drew up a plan which included three basic projects (as far as the Vatican was concerned): the demolition and re-construction of St. Peter's, the creation of the Belvedere court and the construction of a new and more magnificent façade on that side of the medieval residence that faced the city of Rome. Any one of these projects would have sufficed to endow his reign with fame and glory.

The Belvedere court extends over a great deal of the garden of Nicholas III, between the Mons Saccorum, the site of the Papal palace, and the Mons sancti Aegidii, with the villa of Innocent VIII. Until 1503, this area had been given over to agricultural pursuits, with orchards and vineyards which ascended from south to north. The Pope and his great (and equal) architect decided to make Belvedere more accessible by connecting the residence and the villa with two very long, straight corridors, running parallel to one another; aside from a portico-like ground-floor, each was to consist of two storeys covered, not by a roof, but by a terrace. The slope's incline was compensated for by three terraces—a large one along the street and two others further up, all joined together by broad steps and corresponding to the three storeys of the corridors. Thus, the ground-floor merges into the first flight of stairs, the second storey merges into the next flight, and it is only the top storey which leads to the Belvedere and the famous garden of statues. How the interior of Bramante's corridor looked, before the buttresses were added in the 17th and 18th centuries, can be clearly seen in a drawing at the Sloane Museum in London. Its ornamentation and elegance are in contrast to the plain and almost martial outer façade. The edifice was actually conceived for the defense of the Papal palace and was thus called "moenia Belvidere," whereas the courtyard, in which performances and jousts took place, bore the unusual name of "atrium of pleasure." The low north façade faced the garden of Innocent VIII's villa and had only one storey. In the center of it, there was an exedra and a staircase with semi-circular steps—the one half convex, and, further up, the other half concave.

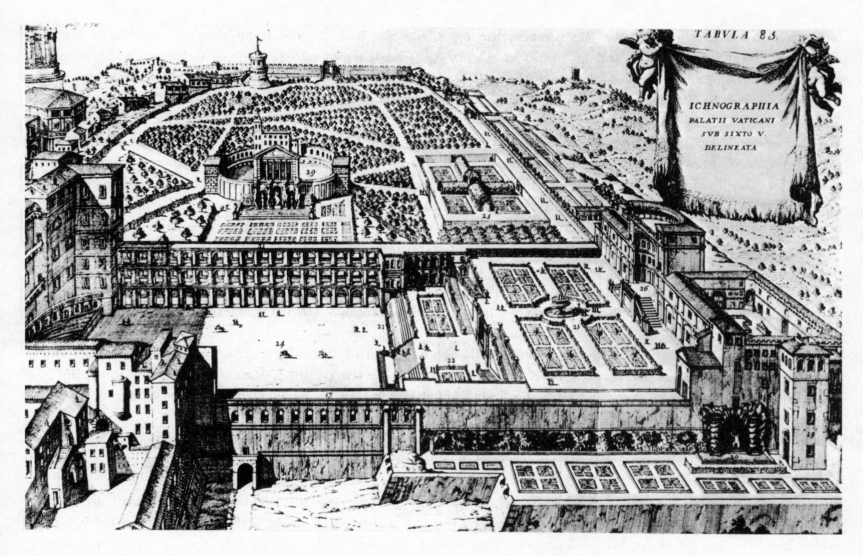

View of the Vatican Palace, the Belvedere court and the Belvedere Palace at the time of Pope Sixtus V (1585–1590). In the background, the Vatican gardens with the Casino of Pius IV.

The low south façade presented the difficult architectural problem of getting the 16th century style of the corridor to conform with the completely different style of those buildings which had been constructed under Boniface VIII, Nicholas V and Alexander VI. From a sketch in the Sloane Museum one can see that Bramante wanted to endow the various buildings with a certain unity of style by constructing an enclosing wall, flanked by two frontispieces. In addition, he got rid of the martial, and by then useless, battlements, which he replaced with a balustrade; and he had the unusual idea of crowning the Torre Borgia with a modern dome, which was later destroyed by fire. Bramante died in 1514, leaving unfinished the grandiose Belvedere court, which Pirro Ligorio completed in 1565 under Pius IV.

Another admired work of Bramante is the famous spiral staircase in a rustic quadratic tower on the east side of Innocent VIII's Belvedere. This staircase, which offered easier access to the garden (illustration 41), rises in a perfect spiral from right to left, the walls merging without a cornice into the barrel vault. The columns are arranged in the classical sequence of the three Vitruvian orders: 16 Doric, eight Ionic and 12 Corinthian, all of the same height but becoming more and more slender the further up they climb.

The spiral staircase, begun in 1512, was not finished until 1564.

Bramante solved in magnificent manner the problem which had been given him by Julius II: that of adapting the old palace to the new ideas of the Renaissance. Razing it, like the basilica, and re-building it would have been the simplest solution for the Pope, and he would have done so if he had not had to live in it. However, if the palace could not be re-done, it at least had to give the appearance of it—to the Roman populace and to the pilgrims who looked at it from St. Peter's square below. It was to be new, larger and more splendid, worthy of a Pope. Bramante fell back upon the plan of Nicholas III's architect, who had called for several rows of loggie for the façade of the Papal residence, and it was from these loggie that one would have a view of the city. He enclosed the portico in the ground-floor; above this, he built two galleries with 13 arches each, flanked on the first floor by Doric and on the second floor by Ionic columns. He extended the new façade by 22 meters over the southeast corner of the old palace, thereby giving it a total length of 65 meters. The proportion of this length to the height—26.3 meters to the architrave of the second loggia—is unequal, and one can only assume that Bramante had intended adding a third row, according to the classical orders, in Corinthian style and, presumably like the others, furnished with arches. Death kept him from carrying this out, and it was under Leo X that Raphael completed the project by crowning the new façade with a colonnade with a raftered-ceiling. Behind the section protruding to the south, Bramante built the covered Papal staircase which led to the first gallery. Of this staircase Marcantonio Michiel remarked with awe, "all ascended, even horses!"

Eventually, Julius II was satisfied with a new façade, although he did furnish his living quarters—the famous stanze—sumptuously. He commissioned the very young Raphael of Urbino with the painting. Raphael worked at this from 1508 until his untimely death in 1520, and with the frescoes of the "Segnatura" he created the most significant document of Western humanism.

In this context one cannot overlook the decoration on the ceiling of the Sistine Chapel, a work which the Pope urged upon an unwilling Michelangelo. The sculptor learned the difficult art of fresco painting and created the most magnificent painting of the Renaissance.

Julius II was followed by Leo X de' Medici (1513–1521). This Pope was the dominant art patron of his century, and yet his contribution to the history of the Vatican buildings was limited basically to the continuance of those projects which had been started under his predecessors—with several variations and additions. He also continued the painting projects within the Papal residence, especially the stanze. His architect was Raphael (whom Bramante, on his death bed, had recommended to the Pope), who prepared for his new assignment by studying thoroughly the works of Vitruvius; Marco Fabio Calvo, the physician and humanist from Ravenna, had translated them into Italian for him. His most important works in the Vatican are: the completion of the San Damaso loggie and the adjoining staircase; the third floor of the Papal palace, with the "loggette" and the so-called "stufetta" (bath) of Cardinal Bibbiena; the second gallery of the Belvedere corridor (as far as the arch).

Vasari says of Raphael that "he resumed work on the Papal staircase and loggie, which Bramante had begun so well, death having forced him to leave them unfinished, and Raphael continued the projects with his new design and according to his architecture; he made a wooden model, of greater regularity and ornamentation than Bramante." When Bramante died, the second loggia was not yet finished, and Raphael completed it without any single alteration in the design of his master. With the exception of the differing architectural arrangement and the form of the balusters, it is actually identical to the first design. However, when Vasari writes of the "imperfection" of the structure, he is not only referring to the fact that it was incomplete; he was also alluding to the lack of a third, a Corinthian, order which in all probability had been foreseen in the plan and which, presumably, was to have been similar to the other two orders—in other words, with arches flanked by pilasters. It is stylistically justified to assume that Raphael rejected this plan; to loosen the somewhat monotonous strictness of Bramante's design he ended the loggie with a Corinthian portico, finished in wood. This is why Vasari insists upon the "novelty" of Raphael's architectural style, this structure illustrating the contrast to his master's style. The portico consists of 14 granite columns; because of the weight, the architrave is wooden and was not installed until after Raphael's death. The raising of the loggia would have been absurd, if, at the same time, a third storey had not been added to the palace; the office of the State Secretary is quartered here. Here, too, are two important works by Raphael, although Vasari does not mention them: the "loggetta" and the "stufetta" in the private apartment of Cardinal Bibbiena, the secretary of Leo X. Until the first was discovered in the year 1943, it had been completely forgotten (although there is mention of it in a letter Bembo wrote to Bibbiena); the second was known, but it was not easily accessible.

The façade of the loggetta facing the "Cortile del Maresciallo" consists of three arches with four bay windows each, and flanked by Doric columns, which support the classical raftered-ceiling. What we have here is a repetition, with no basic alterations, of Bramante's design for the portico on the east side of the "pigna" court. The elegant grotesques, with which they, like those of the second loggia, are adorned, were painted betwen 1516 and 1519 by Raphael's pupils under the artist's direction.

Bibbiena's stufetta is a small room, 2.5 meters wide and 3.2 meters high; it has a groined vault, a small window and, in the walls on the side, two decorative marble niches with beautifully formed socles, which are probably by Lorenzo Lotti, who was known by the name of Lorenzetto. The entire room is covered with grotesques and mythological frescoes, all of them designed by Raphael and partially painted by him; they revert to the painting of Nero's "domus aurea," a style which had just been re-discovered. This tiny work of art indicates that, in architecture, greatness is less a matter of dimensions than of "the highest proportion."

Following the short period of transition of the Dutch Pope, Hadrian VI (1522–1523), whose pontificate left no traces in the Vatican, the conclave elected Clement VII de' Medici (1523–1534), the hapless Pope of the apocalyptic sack of Rome (1527). He appointed Antonio da Sangallo the younger as his architect, and we are indebted to him for the vault of the Sala Ducale, the tapered windows of the "aula tertia" (at that time, the hall in which the public consistory met) and the upper storeys of this palace wing. The stufetta, decorated with a fresco bearing the Medici coat of arms, is worth mentioning because of its originality and its excellent state of preservation. It was discovered during the restoration work from 1949 to 1953 in a room above Bramante's Papal staircase. It was under Clement VII that most of the paintings in the hall of Constantine, which were executed by members of the school of Raphael, were completed.

The splendor, boldness and magnificence of his projects make the reign of the last humanist Pope, Paul III Farnese (1534–1549) comparable to that of Julius II; each of them also had a propensity for fame and strove to attain it. Paul III fetched Baldassare Peruzzi from Siena and commissioned him with the restoration and re-inforcement of Bramante's corridor, which was in a partial state of collapse (the portion above the doors). However, the architect with whose name that of Paul III is inseparably joined was Antonio da Sangallo the younger, who succeeded Peruzzi in 1536 and whose work on the corridor was completed with the construction of the second storey. In addition, he renewed almost the entire foundation of the old palace—a task which, according to Vasari, was "more dangerous than honorable" (by which he meant that it brought him more responsibility than prestige). His fame also does not rest upon these indisputable, although inconspicuous, accomplishments, but rather upon another project which was as worthy of the architect as it was of his patron: the almost complete re-construction of the southeast section of the Vatican, whose renovation until then had proceeded slowly and without any system.

To this section of the residence belonged the Sala Regia, both parts of the Sala Ducale, the "capella parva sancti Nicolai," the Cortile del Maresciallo and the old staircase, which led from that point to the Sala Regia. These were public, or reception, rooms, while the eastern and northern sections of the palace were reserved for the private lives of the Popes. Early in 1538, the work was begun; it proceeded systematically and made speedy progress.

Until then, the Sala Regia had been a large room with arbitrarily arranged doors and windows; it had a raftered-ceiling, which was lower than it is today, and above which was both an additional storey and an attic. They were torn down, the 13th century wall was re-inforced, and the hall was then covered with an impressive, semi-cylindrical barrel-vault 5.9 meters in diameter; this rested upon a magnificent cornice 13 meters above the floor and was decorated with wonderful stuccowork by Perin del Vaga, a pupil of Raphael. Perin del Vaga also started work on the graphically powerful wall dividers, bordered by allegorical figures—a project which Daniele da Volterra completed.

On the back, which faced the south, lay the door to the "Capella Paolina," which stands on the site of the 14th century "capella parva sancti Nicolai"; paying no consideration to Fra Angelico's decorative frescoes, Sangallo had it brutally demolished in order to widen and straighten the old, narrow "Scala del Maresciallo." The new rectangular chapel, with a quadratic area in the center and a narrow, rectangular choir, is graced by Michelangelo's final frescoes, *Conversion of Saul* (illustration 229) and *Crucifixion of St. Peter* (illustration 230).

The Farnese Pope died at the end of 1549, about three years after the death of Sangallo. With their demise, there set in, in art and religion, the gradual decline of the Renaissance, whose place in art was taken by mannerism—which preceded the baroque—and in religion by the new awareness resulting from the Council of Trent.

Julius III Giovanni del Monte (1550–1555), the successor to Paul III, was elected Pope after a very long conclave. His architects were Girolamo da Carpi and Jacopo Vignola, and we are indebted to them for the construction of several rooms located behind Bramante's exedra (until then, the façade had been merely a facing for a wall which shored up the garden of statues higher up), and for the addition of a second storey to the façade, with the resultant raising of the exedra. At the same time, Bramante's pleasant spiral staircase was replaced by the present one, whose conception goes back, originally, to a design by Michelangelo which was later altered. This exchange, although regrettable, can be explained by the necessity of creating a connection between the old rooms and the new west section; the last circular landing, too (today, the semi-circle of the Etruscan and Egyptian Museum), was transformed into a passage by the construction of a second, concentric and thinner wall, whereby, without an upper landing, the staircase would have remained.

Julius III also raised the level of the palace by extending Sangallo's construction of the fourth floor, at the southern end of Bramante's corridor. He created here an apartment for himself (until recently, the quarters of the Guard of the Nobility) and had it furnished with frescoes by Daniele da Volterra and Taddeo Zuccari. In order to use the rooms, which were arranged in a row, a seven-storey building with a quadratic wing had to be built on the eastern side of the corridor, above the wall of Nicholas V; this had purely practical rather than artistic value.

The reign of Pope Marcellus II Cervini (1555) lasted only 22 days and left no traces in the Vatican. However, it was then that a wonderful masterwork of sacred music was composed, the *Missa Papae Marcelli*, by Pierluigi da Palestrina, written in memory of the Pope. Marcellus was followed by Paul IV Carafa (1555–1559), who restricted himself chiefly to the continuation, improvement and decoration of those projects which had been launched under Julius III. However, two events during his pontificate are of decisive importance in the history of the palaces: the appointment of the excellent Neapolitan architect Piero Ligorio, and the start of construction on the Casino of Pius IV in the Papal gardens. This villa was completed under his successor, Pius IV de' Medici, through whose activities the Vatican assumed a new appearance.

A sketch by Dosio, dating back to the mid-16th century, clearly indicates how much work was necessary to carry out Bramante's plan for the Belvedere. From the corridor east of the court only the foundation was still standing; work on the two monumental staircases between the three ascending "Curias" had barely begun; and the difficult problem of the south side, with buildings of various epochs and styles, was still unsolved. Since the execution of the plans of his predecessors was not enough for him, Pius IV added two works of his own to the Belvedere: he constructed the famous "Nicchione" above the exedra of the north wing, and he extended the so-called Casino (shelter), built by Julius III, by adding a wing which enclosed the statuary garden of the Belvedere, by Innocent VIII, to the west. For the sake of brevity, we shall pass over this edifice, which is especially interesting because of its paintings. We turn instead to the "Nicchione" (illustration 28), the highest point of the Vatican from where all Rome can be seen. It is a structure that remained unique in 16th century architecture, and so impressive is it that Frey assumed that Pirro had taken the idea from a lost sketch of Michelangelo's; however, it must have been a product of his own imagination. Girolamo da Carpi had added another story to Bramante's exedra and to the two adjoining buildings; that is to say, he had solved a practical problem (that of living quarters), but at the same time he created an architectural problem which he did not solve. The exedra resembled an incomplete apse and had no half-cupola. Pirro Ligorio decided to build a cupola and he executed it with the boldness and simplicity worthy of a master-builder of imperial Rome: he followed the structural logic with an appreciative perception that was strongly influenced by ancient laws. Above the unfinished exedra he erected a new edifice, and one that was large enough to enclose a perfect quarter-sphere with the considerable diameter of 15 meters at the height of the cornice, 17.4 meters from the ground. In order to reduce the weight of the gigantic construction, he fell back on an ancient method of setting empty earthenware jugs into the masonry. In one such jug was found a shard with an inscription indicating that the structure had originated in the second year of the pontificate of Pius IV, in other words, in 1561. The Nicchione originally had a roof; however, in 1564 work was begun on the construction of the present terrace, with its colonnade and semi-circle and, on the façade, two graceful, small porticos with tympanum-like front gables. Some critics have remarked that the additional section is too delicate in proportion to the extent of the structure. If, however, the dimensions of the two sections do not conform to the rules of genuine classical architecture, they do reflect—as other authors have noted—the fanciful architecture depicted in Roman frescoes; and we believe that just this was the intent of the "antiquary," Ligorio. In addition, the strong contrast in the proportions of portico and hemisphere serve to create a false perspective, whereby the large niche seems to be taller than it really is. During the construction of the west wing of the Belvedere court, Ligorio conformed more exactly to Bramante's design, as indicated in a plan and a relief (both of them originals) in the Institute for Archaeology and Art History in Rome. The new wing differed from the old one only by means of the "serlio" windows of the third order and a roof-ridge bordered with a balustrade, which had ancient statues. According to Ligorio's design for the difficult south side of the court, the windows of the Appartamento Borgia would have been masked by a two-storey exedra with niches and statues. In a comparison of the plans of Ligorio and Bramante, Ackermann has determined that the former places decoration over architecture, in a style which has nothing to do with the strict classicism of the first half of the 16th century but which is nevertheless based on ancient models. On March 5, 1565, the new "atrium of pleasure" was inaugurated with a memorable tournament, on the occasion of the wedding of Annibale Altemps and Ortensia Borromeo, both related to Pius IV.

In the above-mentioned works, Ligorio's fantasy was both supported and restricted by the pre-requisites which Bramante had created. However, in the construction of the Casino of Pius IV he had complete creative freedom and he produced a masterpiece which, in Italian mannerism, has no equal. The small rustic palace stands about 100 meters west of the west corridor in the garden on slightly ascending terrain. It consists of two sections, the loggia and the villa, both of which are joined by a courtyard, surrounded by a wall, with a fountain in the middle, and two porches at the back. Their interiors have a form in conformity with that of the courtyard—a novelty which heralds the onset of the baroque. The villa itself is merely a two-storey building, small in scope and with clear, simple lines, although it boasts of rich ornamentation; the latter is especially noticeable on the ceilings of both ground-floor rooms and on the façade, which is faced with stuccowork executed by Rocco da Montefiascone. Among those artists who helped to decorate the villa, Federico Zuccari and Barrocci ought to be mentioned. Here it is evident that Ligorio treated ancient art as did Erasmus the Latin language—not like Cicero, but unaffected and in his own way (illustrations 30–34).

It is also to a design by Ligorio that we are indebted for the conversion of the so-called Secret Garden to the San Damaso court of today. Bramante's and Raphael's loggie, until then the façade of the Papal palace, were supported by the northern angle-turret. It was also at this turret that the eastern corridor of Innocent VIII began, leading to the Belvedere. The architectural problem was a consequence of the diversity of these three buildings, which, although they were independent of one another, stood all in a row. Ligorio's solution was to raze the turret and to extend the loggie by means of a second "Braccio" in vertical line; thus began the transformation of the court, in that the corridor was hidden from sight. The "Secondo Braccio" is identical with the first; here, too, as in the case of the Nicchione, Ligorio allowed himself to be inspired by the structure itself. The work on the new loggie has been documented from June, 1563, to the death of Pius IV in the year 1565, but it did not extend beyond the first three arches, including the corner arch.

The new Pope, Pius V Ghislieri (1566–1572), did not actually display an unfriendly attitude toward the arts, but his behavior was so distrustful that he even presented many of the ancient statues his predecessors had collected to the Capitoline Museum. Immediately after his election, he ordered that work be resumed on the west corridor, now on the first floor, and on the so-called "Torre Pia," which had also been started under Pius IV. This building links the "Torre Borgia" with the new corridor and in this way forms an impressive front. The only project that was entirely his is the church of St. Martin and Sebastian, which was built by an unknown architect, and which is now hidden by Bernini's colonnades.

Gregory XIII Boncompagni (1572–1585) appointed Martino Longhi senior and Ottaviano Mascherino as his architects. The former continued the work which Ligorio had started on the "Secondo Braccio" of the San Damaso court and he completed it without any alterations. This supplementary structure, richly decorated with stuccowork and frescoes, borders on the palace of Gregory XIII, which contains some of the most splendid rooms of the Vatican, such as the Bologna and the Foconi halls.

Longhi disappeared after 1577 and Mascherino replaced him as Papal architect. We are indebted to him for the Gallery of Geographic Maps, which was added to Pirro Ligorio's corridor as the third storey. The name refers to the 34 maps of the regions of Italy, in accordance with a design by the renowned cosmographer Ignazio Danti, which were painted between the windows. The closely woven painting on the barrel-vault, however, is the work of a large group of manneristic artists, who were under the direction of Girolamo Muziano and Cesare Nebbia. At the north side of this magnificent gallery there rises ponderously the so-called "Torre dei Venti" (illustration 39); 73 meters high, it descends in three terraces from west to east and served the Pope, who reformed the calendar, as an astronomical observatory. It was here, in 1655, that Queen Christina of Sweden was the guest of Alexander VII. The tower was built between 1578 and 1585. And it was between 1582 and 1585 that the colonnade east of the highest point of the Belvedere court (today, the Cortile della Pigna) took shape; its form is a repetition of that by Bramante, which lies opposite it. Gregory XIII died in 1585. His contribution to the history of Vatican architecture is, because of its range and the significance of the construction undertaken, remarkable; however, from the artistic point of view, it does not go beyond an impersonal mediocrity. Ottavio Mascherino was neither a Bramante nor a Pirro Ligorio.

The successor to Gregory XIII, Sixtus V Peretti (1585–1590), who altered the face of Rome in the five years of his reign, is the last of the series of architecturally inclined Popes of the Renaissance, which at that point had attained the late manneristic phase. He was responsible for the new site of the Vatican Library and for the present Papal residence.

Because of the ever greater number of manuscripts and printed books which had been collected by the Vatican Library, the modest site which had been established by the Library's founder, Sixtus IV, was no longer large enough. Gregory XIII had intended to transfer it—as we know from Vasari—"illustriori loco." Sixtus V decided to accommodate it in an appropriate site in a building which would be erected specifically for this purpose. He entrusted Domenico Fontana from Lugano with this task and decided to have the building put up on the site of the tiers of seats in the Belvedere theater, that is, on the level of the first steps in the court. At the same time, it was decided to incorporate the side-sections of the two corridors into the new building. The court was thus unfortunately divided in two, and the three adjoining "curie" designed by Bramante were destroyed. Aside from this severe loss, however, it is clear that the site for the new library had been well selected; it was dry, bright and had an already existing foundation (the old staircase), which was a welcome saving for Pope Sixtus.

At the end of 1588, after little more than a year of construction, the structure was consecrated. Since the 18th century, five ugly buttresses have disfigured the façade, which originally consisted of a colonnade, within which there were the windows of a mezzanine and two further storeys with rectangular windows. Thus, in every way it resembled the architecture of the western corridor, whose "rules it follows," as Fontana puts it. Because of the differing ground height, the north side had only three storeys and the wall was decorated with graffiti, hardly any of which can be seen today. The luxurious painting of the so-called "Salone Sistino" above the mezzanine was carried out just as speedily; earlier a reading room, this is now an exhibition room for special library specimens (illustration 115).

Fontana's most important work in the Vatican is the new Papal palace, still the Papal residence today, towering over St. Peter's square. The quadratic building with an inner court covers an area of 2,809 square meters. The façade to the San Damaso court is the "Terzio Braccio" of the loggie, which was begun by Martino Longhi the elder and Mascherino, but finished by Fontana; its construction is identical with the two others, although it is shorter so as to detract as little as possible from the view of the city. The three galleries correspond to the three storeys of the building (above the ground-floor). The ceiling of the first two is arched, whereas the third has a flat ceiling. To the north, the palace of Gregory XIII was lengthened and it abuts on the wall of Nicholas V. According to Fontana, the palace contained 85 rooms. The work began in 1589 and was almost finished in 1590, shortly before Sixtus V died.

Following three short pontificates, none of which left much of a mark in the Vatican (Urban VII, Gregory XIV and Innocent IX), Clement VIII Aldobrandini (1592–1605) ascended the Papal throne. His reign came at a time when the baroque was replacing mannerism. Domenico Fontana had left Rome, and his place was taken by his brother, Giovanni, and by the architect Taddeo Landini; they had been assigned the task of completing the Sistine palace. Thus it is that the cornice is adorned with the emblems of the new Pope. It is very probable that Landini built the "Sala Clementina," whereby he removed the ceiling between the second and third floors, thus successfully and decisively altering Fontana's original plan, which had called for two small halls rather than one. The Sala Clementina forms a worthy ante-chamber to the Papal reception room. It measures 23 by 14.4 meters, is covered by an unencumbered vault and, because it originally had two storeys, it has two rows of windows. The walls and the ceiling are painted with frescoes in ascending perspective, and these are by Giovanni and Cherubino Alberti, who worked in collaboration with Paul Bril; the latter was responsible for the landscape of the painting over the south door, the *Martyrdom of St. Clement*. Under this Pope, the first four buttresses took shape in the western corridor, in an effort to offset the weight of the storey which had been added by Gregory XIII. Later on, the entire Belvedere court was equipped with these ugly architectural accessories, and they destroyed completely the clear harmony of Bramante's design.

The growth of the Vatican's architectural complex did not come to a full stop following the building of the Sistine palace at the threshold to a new century, but it did slow down considerably until the end of the 18th century, when the Museo Pio-Clementino was built. The reason for this is, in part, the fact that the Popes since Clement VIII preferred the residence on the Quirinal, built by Gregory XIII in 1574, claiming that it was healthier.

Following the 26-day-long pontificate of Leo XI de' Medici di Ottaiano (1605), Paul V Borghese (1605–1621) was elected Pope. He was the first Pope of the baroque, which was dominated by Gianlorenzo Bernini in the fields of both architecture and sculpture, and it is a tribute to Paul that he recognized the artist's genius and helped him to achieve renown. Paul V preferred the Quirinal, which he enlarged and decorated, and thus he added only three structures to the Vatican, none of them residential. The oldest of them provided a direct connection from the Torre Pia to the garden. It extends beyond the avenue of the museums and has an unusual quadratic groundplan: east-west and south-north; the latter section consists of three buildings which, conforming to the staircase within, have a descending character. It is possible that Flaminio Ponzi was the architect (according to Ackermann).

The other two buildings abutted onto the façade of St. Peter's (the name of the Pope appears on the front gable); the Pope had commissioned Carlo Maderna, Domenico Fontana's nephew, with the construction of the façade and it was consecrated in 1612. After the old problem had been solved (in a manner which did not win general acclaim), a new problem presented itself immediately: how could one soften the contrast between the stylistic unity of the new façade and the confusion of the structures to the right of it, with their varying styles and epochs? Part of this historical and architectural medley was the entrance to the Vatican. Built by Paul II, re-designed by Innocent VIII and modernized in 1607 by Carlo Maderna, it still made a somewhat modest impression. Among the plans for a new entrance which had been set before the Pope, that by Marino Ferrabosco and Hans van Xanten (Giovanni Vansanzio), both of whom worked for Maderna, was selected. In a print by Bonanni one can see this structure, which later fell victim to Bernini's colonnades. The "Porta Horaria," as it was called, consisted of a gallery (which was never built) over an elevation, upon which is now the Braccio of Constantine. Toward the east, the gallery merged into a broader front gable, above which there rose the small tower with the large bell, crowned by an elegant little belfry. The chief initiator of this project must have been Vansanzio, a Dutchman who designed furniture, since it displays more of a Nordic "Italianized" style than that which prevailed in Rome at the time. Part of this complex was the third Vatican structure for which Paul V was responsible: the building that towers up against Bramante's loggia, protruding diagonally in the direction of St. Peter's square. Judging from its style, it ought certainly to be attributed to Maderna. Remains of a gallery which Giulio Romano had built for Leo X were found inside.

The short pontificate of Gregory XV Ludovisi (1621–1623) was followed by those of two Popes, who, although leaving few marks on the complex of the Vatican palaces, helped baroque architecture in Rome and in St. Peter's to achieve its decisive breakthrough: Urban VIII Barberini (1623–1644) and Innocent X Pamfili (1644–1655). Urban VIII, who spent much time in the Vatican, created a new connection between the old and the new apartments behind the loggie of Gregory XIII (Secondo Braccio); this ran through a gallery with an arched ceiling and was decorated with stuccowork and frescoes by Romanelli, by whose name it is known. In addition, Urban built the Consulata palace (seat of a Church tribunal); appended to the loggie on the south, it was largely demolished when Pius IX had the area re-built. During a recent renovation, the large reception hall with the chiaroscuro frescoes from the 18th century was restored.

Pope Innocent X, whose interest was riveted mainly on the construction of the magnificent family palace on the Piazza Navona, turned his attention at the Vatican only to the charming fountain by Algardi, located in the San Damaso court. It was at his request that Bernini made the equestrian statue of Constantine (illustration 20), which, in 1609, was erected on the first landing of the Scala Regia.

Alexander VII Chiqi (1655–1667) showed almost as little interest in the Vatican as his predecessor, with reference not only to the quantity of his architectural activity but also to its quality. Only two Vatican structures are by him: the Mint, which was completely re-built under Pius VI and otherwise not worth mentioning—and the Scala Regia (illustration 27), which Gianlorenzo Bernini finished in the summer of 1665.

In contrast to the modest architectural monuments of his predecessors, this stair represents a turning-point in the development of baroque architecture in Italy and the rest of the world, and it displays a close relation to the colonnades in St. Peter's square, which were also created by Bernini for Alexander VII. Bernini was fond of saying, "If you want to discover what an eminent personality is capable of, you have got to place him in a difficult position" (thus anticipating Baudelaire's maxim, *"l'art ne danse que dans les chaines"*). So it was with the history of the Scala Regia, which was rich in unavoidable difficulties; and yet, like a magician, Bernini transformed seemingly insurmountable hurdles into the very requisites of his architectural project. Here was the task with which the Pope burdened Bernini: to replace the old, narrow and dark stair which Sangallo had built between the Sala Regia and the basilica with a new one—wider, brighter and more beautifully decorated. (Bonanni had called the old stair *tenebricosum transitum*.)

Let us go through the various individual sections of the Scala Regia as if we were descending it. It was not possible to widen the upper landing, since the right-hand wall was the external wall of the Sistine Chapel; to move the left wall would have resulted in placing Sangallo's entrance in an unfavorable location (and the sculpture and painting in the hall would have been damaged if the door had been moved). Bernini thus limited himself to illuminating the entrance by means of two windows in the roof of the barrel-vault; he decorated this further with stucco panels and columns entirely in bas-relief, so as not to narrow the already limited space even further. Another problem cropped up with the first landing: although the stair could have been widened at this point, the arcades at the end of the first ramp and at the outset of the second ramp, which lay side by side, could not be allowed to be different sizes. Therefore, the second segment of the stair had to be widened gradually (from 4.8 meters at the top to 8.3 meters at the bottom and this accounts for the unusual trapezoid form. A further problem was the obligatory barrel-vault, which in part had to extend beneath the Scala Regia and the Cappella Paolina. As Bonanni writes, it had to be shored up during the construction by an entire "forest" of buttresses. The preservation of these walls, says Bernini, was his boldest achievement, and he previously would not have believed it possible. In addition, it was not feasible at the greatest possible height to install a barrel-vault on walls which were so wide apart; the consequence would have been a flattened vault, which would not have been able to carry the weight of both the Scala Regia and the Cappella Paolina. Bernini solved the two-pronged problem (technical and artistic) by means of a single idea which was commensurate with his ingenuity as an architect. He introduced two rows of columns which support the prescribed barrel-vault. They thus serve to strengthen the construction while, at the same time, "correcting" the structural irregularities present. An extraordinarily impressive perspective is evoked, and this is re-inforced by the gradually diminishing height of the vault and the smaller and narrower appearance of the columns. One has the illusion of a long sweeping stair, while in reality, it is steep and irregular.

Bernini was also commissioned by Alexander VII to make one room out of the two into which the Sala Ducale of today had previously been divided, the axes of which were not completely congruous. With his sublime sense of effect, Bernini corrected (or, better, hid) this irregularity by maintaining on the sides one section each of the old dividing wall; this gave the effect of wings, which he joined with another irregular element: heavy drapes held by winged putti (illustrations 213, 214).

Alexander VII died in 1667 and more than a century (eleven Papal reigns) passed without anything new being built in the Vatican. However, with the accession of Clement XIV Ganganelli (1769–1774) a new chapter in the history of the Papal residence began; and, because of the creation of one of the largest and most important museum complexes in the world, the Museo Pio-Clementino, this was a period of great importance. This museum developed under the influence of Johann Joachim Winckelmann, the founder of modern archaeology.

From the time of Julius II, the statuary garden in the Belvedere court had been the only "Vatican Museum"; and because of the aversion of many of the Popes to "pagan gods," this garden contained only a few—although highly valuable—works. Those statues which had been found during the many excavation projects, or which had been purchased by the Popes, usually either were turned over to the Capitoline Museum or served to decorate buildings and gardens.

However, space also became scarce in the Capitol, and the purchase of the important Fusconi and Mattei collections in the year 1770 made the immediate creation of a joint museum imperative. Thus it was that the Museo Clementino took shape in the loggia of the Belvedere, the sculpture gallery of today. Work on this, which began in 1771, was under the supervision of the architect Alessandro Dori.

Clement XIV died in September 1774; his successor, Pius VI Braschi (1775–1799), was the last great architecturally minded Pope before the end of the worldly power of the Church. As his contemporaries noted, he was a man who was born to rule, and who was a sovereign and generous ruler. He completed the Museo Clementino. Because of the many various marble figures that had enlarged the art collection of the Holy See—the result of successful excavations, as well as purchases from art dealers—, the museum had already become too small. Another museum had to be constructed, one that was connected to the first but that was much larger; an impressive complex with magnificent rooms thus developed—the Museo Pio-Clementino.

The construction of the Museo Pio-Clementino began in 1776 with an act which today is inconceivable: the chapel by Mantegna, and the sacristy which belonged to it, were completely demolished for the sole purpose of widening the statuary gallery by some ten meters! Since the time of Paul III nothing had changed in the attitude toward art—the "primitives" were not only from the past, they were outdated, and there was every justification in sacrificing their works to more "mature" art. A short time later, in the year 1780, the cabinet of the masks (from the very beginning, the prostrate figure of Arianna, called Cleopatra, had been located here) received its present form and name (derived from an ancient mosaic of tiny pieces of stone which was set in the floor). The new section of the statuary gallery was joined to the hall of the animals; having developed in part from already existing buildings, it had a vaulted ceiling and was divided by a colonnade which Clement XIV had begun. It is from here that one comes into the octagonal museum hall, which boasts of a faceted dome with frescoes painted by Tommaso Conca. Adjoining this is the "Rotonda," a late 18th century version of the Pantheon; done in strict, although not cold, classic style, it is Simonetti's masterwork. Behind the "Rotonda," the southwest section of the Museo Pio-Clementino makes a right-angle turn to the south, where one arrives at the "Sala a Croce Greca" and the very elegant stairway by Simonetti; the latter leads to the axis of the corridor by Pirro Ligorio, in which are the Museo Profano and the Museo Sacro of the Vatican Library. In designing the Sala a Croce Greca, Simonetti had apparently allowed himself to be influenced by the architecture of the Roman baths, whose majestic sober grandeur he imitated "with the sensitivity for ancient construction which marked his character" (De Rinaldis). An unusual and significant detail are two Egyptian Atlases which flank the monumental entrance to the Rotonda. Contrary to appearances, they are not modern imitations, but are originals, having been found at Hadrian's villa (Tivoli) during excavations at the beginning of the 16th century. Indeed, the fact that although they are displayed because of their archaeological importance, they serve merely as an architectural and decorative element for this large hall, is indicative of the insecurity in matters pertaining to museums still dominant in the 18th century. Less classical, but certainly more original, is the distinguished stair with which Simonetti's fame is closely linked. He took eight years to build it, from 1780 to 1788. The first section leads from the atrium to the floor containing the Sala a Croce Greca. From this point, two lateral and overlapping sections lead to the floor of the gallery of the candelabra, whence a third section, parallel to the first, leads to the landing and to the entrance to the Etruscan Museum. This very elegant construction, as seen from the Sala a Croce Greca, reminds one of the setting of a baroque court theater.

The impressive museum complex was ultimately given an entrance worthy of its grandeur in the atrium with the screens—an architectural jewel. Giuseppe Campore built it between 1792 and 1793. The ground-floor reflects the structure of the Sala a Croce Greca in miniature, whereas the first floor (Sala della Biga), with its louvered cupola—in the form of an "eye"—and the two tall niches, resembles the "Rotonda." Under Pius VII Chiaramonti (1800–1823), the "Braccio Nuovo" was built in order to make more room for the collection of ancient sculpture.

In adherence to Antonio Canova's suggestion, the Roman architect, Raffaele Stern, was given the commission for this building, and he began work in 1817. The new structure closes off the "Pigna" court to the south by joining the two Belvedere corridors with one another; it runs parallel to the Braccio of the Vatican Library by Sixtus V. Stern died in 1820, but Pasquale Belli took up his plan and brought it to conclusion; thus it was that the new hall could be opened to the public in 1822. The edifice, a perfect example of classical style, is marked by extraordinary cold solemnity. It is a long corridor, whose barrel-vault is perforated by louvers. The barrel-vault is supported by a cornice beneath which, and running its entire length, is a classically inspired stuccowork bas-relief by Massimiliano Laboureur. Into the side walls, 28 niches for statues have been sunk, while the busts stand on truncated columns or on consoles. The long gallery is interrupted in the middle by a hall, whose groined vault, like that of the Sala a Croce Greca, is borne by four arches. The façade faces the "Pigna" court, and it is just as subdued—a pronaos supported by eight columns and adorned with Roman statues.

The "Braccio Nuovo" is not only a remarkable example of classical architecture, in a certain respect it is a museum devoted to the science of maintaining museums. In contrast to the halls of the Museo Pio-Clementino, its architecture is without importance of its own. Its special structure can only be understood in the light of its chief function: namely that of displaying sculpture in the best possible way. This conception, although obvious today, was at that time completely new.

Let us pass over the Chiaramonti Museum, which is not an architectural work but merely a disorderly gallery of ancient busts set up in a section of Bramante's corridor. Let us also pass over the pontificates of Leo XII della Genga (1823–1829) and Pius VIII Castiglioni (1829–1830), neither of whom contributed anything remarkable to the Vatican buildings (Leo XII was only responsible for the barracks of the Swiss Guard, at the St. Anna gate). We come, then, to Gregory XVI Capellari (1831–1846).

The name of this Pope is inseparably connected with the creation of the Gregorian-Etruscan and Gregorian-Egyptian Museums, which were opened in 1837 and 1839, respectively. These were not really new buildings but simply the result of the transformation of both the two floors of the wing bordering the huge niche by Pirro Ligorio, and the semi-circular corridor that connects them. To carry out this plan, Gregory XVI appointed a group of scholars, artists and architects—a combination typical of the time. The material contained in the Egyptian Museum was assembled by the learned Barnabite father, Luigi Ungarelli; in so doing, he employed a method which, for that day and age, was daringly new. Following a design by the former director-general of the Vatican Museums, Giuseppe de Fabris, he reconstructed a building dating back to the age of the Pharaohs. Parts of it, which are reminiscent of opera scenery, were retained during a thorough re-organization of the museum carried out by the present Pope; he felt that it was a historical document of the taste prevailing in that period.

Gregory XVI died in 1846, and his successor was Pius IX Mastai-Ferretti (1846–1878), who for the first time exceeded the 25 years of St. Peter's pontificate. Pius led the Church for 31 years and seven months. The struggle of the Risorgimento took place during his reign, and that resulted, in 1870, in the occupation of Rome and the end of the Church's secular power.

At this period, as far as architectural art is concerned, there is a kind of pause. It is only the late classical style of Filippo Partinucci that has consequence. His was the design for the magnificent stairway of Pius IX, which leads from the portico of Constantine to the San Damaso court. It consists of three sections set out with balusters, and two landings. The walls are faced with artistic marble, the ceiling is decorated with stucco and has a large sky-light. The stairway was consecrated in 1860. It ends in the San Damaso court in a single-story portico, which consists of nine segments to the south and four to the east. It reaches as far as the "Consulta" of Urban VIII, which was partially demolished by Martinucci. The arcades, identical to those on the ground-floor of the north wing, are without any architectural adornment; an exception is the middle arch in the south wing, which is furnished with a portal on each of the other three sides of the court and a balcony above. It is a tribute to the modest architect that he solved, in the simplest manner imaginable, the difficult problem of the south and east sides of the court; it was a problem that had troubled many of his famous predecessors. He maintained the stylistic unity of the court by resuming the forms of the oldest arches and by limiting his portico to the ground-floor; he thus left untouched the incomparable view of Rome from Raphael's loggie.

It is with Pius IX that we come to the end of this survey of the architectural history of the Vatican palaces. We have pursued the gradual and systematic development from the medieval core of Nicholas III, to the enlargement by Bramante under Julius II, to the realization of many of the possibilities Bramante indicated during the period from Gregory XIII to Sixtus V and Clement VII. There then followed, in the second half of the 18th century, the creation of the renowned museum complex under the name of Museo Pio-Clementino. And, last but not least, there was Pius IX with his modest, but not unimportant task of making a new entrance to the Vatican, as well as enclosing the San Damaso court.

This has necessarily been a concise survey. Those readers who are interested in further details and historical information are invited to read my monograph: "The Vatican Palaces" (I Palazzi Vaticani, published by Cappelli, Bologna, 1967). Following this general historical outline of what one could term the "historical center" of the Vatican complex of buildings, one should, for the sake of thoroughness, turn here to the more important structures that have been built since the death of Pius IX.

The unsolved "Roman question" certainly did not contribute to a strengthening of the Popes' construction activities. However, the coat of arms of Leo XIII Pecci (1878–1903) graces the gallery of the candelabra, which he added to the Museo Pio-Clementino, and the ceiling of which he had decorated, in 1884, by Lodovico Seitz and other painters. Pius X, the saint, constructed the underground passage between the Belvedere court and the Vatican gardens, so as to avoid stepping on Italian territory. He also constructed the stairway, named after him, between the Viale di Belvedere and the court of the Holy Office. Pius X built quarters for the civil servants and employees of the Vatican in the vicinity of the St. Anna gate. He also created new rooms for the picture gallery (Pinacoteca) with a new entrance in the Avenue of the Museums.

Little happened under Benedict XV della Chiesa (1914–1922). On the other hand, Pius XI Ratti (1922–1939), the Pope of reconciliation, undertook an ambitious construction program, much of which was a consequence of the new situation resulting from the signing of the Lateran treaties (1929). He erected the radio station (Marconi, 1931) and the present site of the Pinacoteca, with its entrance formed of a double spiral ramp (Momo, 1932). He added a wing to the Casino of Pius IV, in which he later quartered the Papal Academy of Sciences, which he founded in 1936. He also provided his state with a number of buildings necessary for its administration, such as the governor's palace, the railroad station, the post office, the tribunals and workshops.

Pius XII Pacelli (1939–1958) continued the work of his predecessor. We are indebted to him for the new offices of the secretariat of state and, especially, for the thorough and intelligent restoration of most sections of the old palaces. John XXIII Roncalli (1958–1963) deserves our appreciation for the careful restoration of the halls of the library of Sixtus IV. In conclusion, it is fair to say that the pontificate of Paul VI Montini, the present Pope, will be recorded in the annals of architectural history as a result of the auditorium (Nervi) and the new modern quarters which the Vatican has created for the collections from the Lateran Museums.

D. REDIG DE CAMPOS

right: 1) A View of the dome of St. Peter's

above: 2) The fountain in St. Peter's Square.
right: 3) The façade of St. Peter's.

left: 4) Statues on the colonnades of St. Peter's Square.
below: 5) The obelisk in the center of St. Peter's Square.
right: 6) Columns at the base of St. Peter's dome.

right : 7) Saint Peter's Square and
the Vatican Palace.

above: 8) Gate in the courtyard of the Swiss Guard.

below: 9) The Canonica.

left: 10) The east apse of St.
Peter's. To the right, columns
of the tabernacle above the
papal altar.
right: 11) The barrel-vault of
the nave of St. Peter's.

above: 12) The main altar below the dome, with the baldacchino.
right: 13) The dome of St. Peter's.

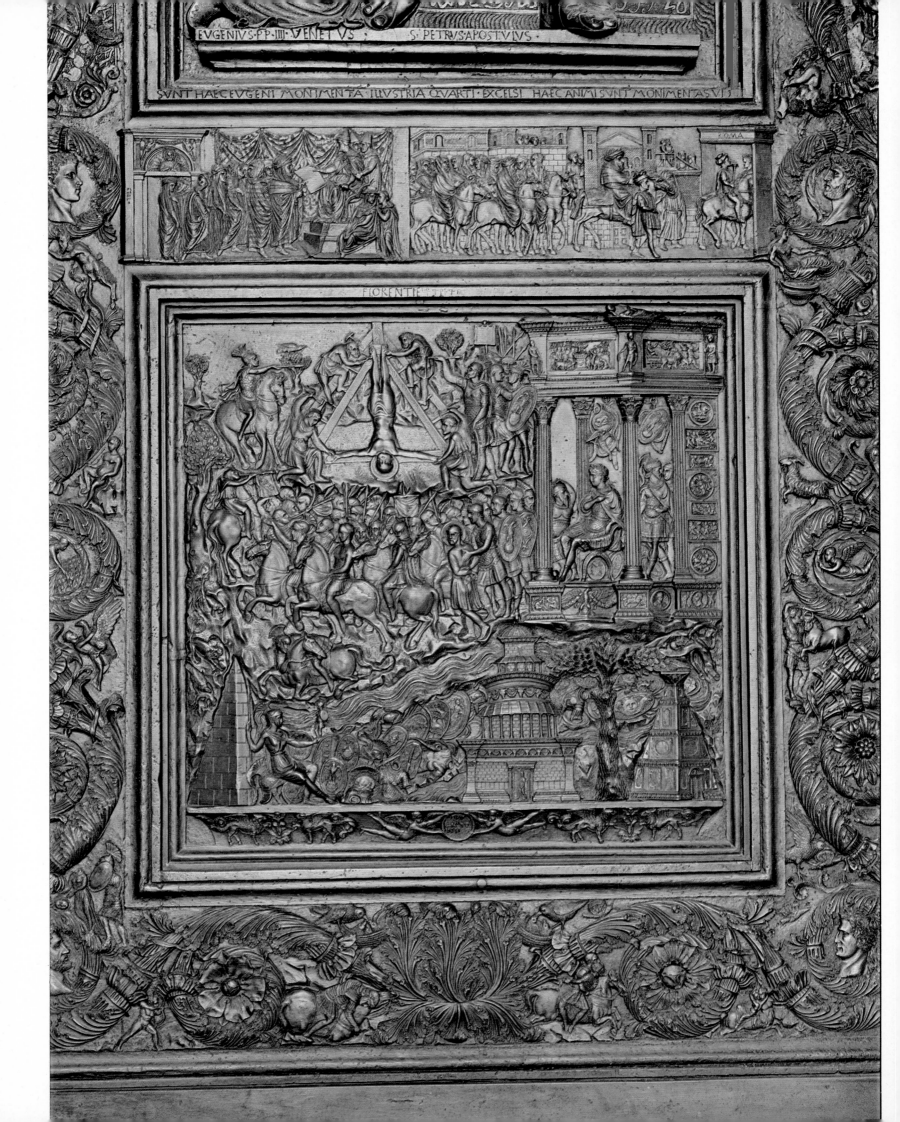

left: 14) *The Crucifixion of St. Peter*. Bronze relief from the center door of the portico.
below: 15) Bronze statue of the Apostle Peter.

above: 17) Michelangelo's *Pietà*.

above: 18) The tomb of Pope Alexander VII by Bernini.

left: 19) *Love*. A figure from the tomb of Pope Alexander VII.

right: 20) *Emperor Constantine*. An equestrian statue by Bernini.

left: 21) Façade in the San Damaso Court.

lower left: 22) The arched gateway, by Bramante, in the San Damaso Court.
lower right: 23) The Belvedere Court.
below: 24) A view of the Vatican Museums from St. Peter's.

below: 25) Portone di Bronzo, the entrance to the Vatican Palace.

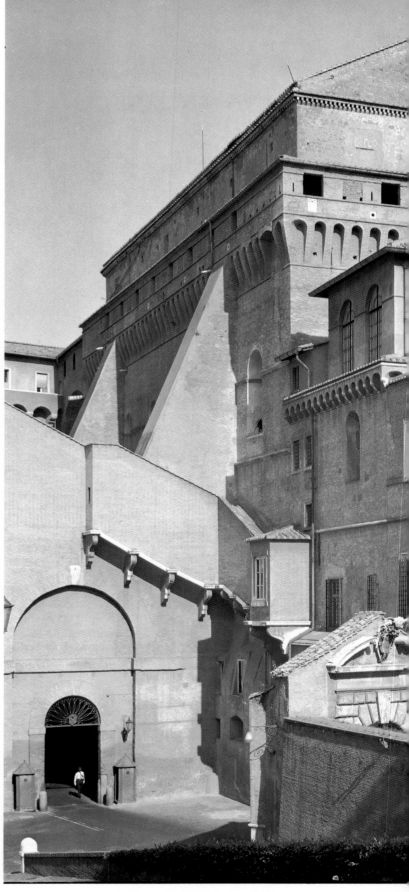

above: 26) An exterior view of the Sistine Chapel.

below: 27) The Scala Regia by Bernini.

left: 28) Large niche in the Belvedere Court, with the pine-cone.
below: 29) A view of St. Peter's dome from the Vatican Gardens.

far left: 30) The interior façade of the residence of Pope Pius IV.

left: 31) The lower façade of the residence of Pius IV.

left: 32) A view of the buildings of the residence of Pius IV in the Vatican Gardens.

above: 33) The upper façade of the residence of Pius IV.

left : 34) The ceiling in the residence of Pius IV.

right : 35) The throne-room in the Papal apartments.

below : 36) The library in the Papal apartments.

upper left: 37) The gate of the Swiss Guard's chapel.

lower left: 38) Façade in the library courtyard.

right: 39) The Torre dei Venti.

below: 40) A section of the mural decoration in the library courtyard.

left : 41) Bramante's
spiral staircase in the
museum building.

THE BORGIA APARTMENTS

Following the death of Innocent VIII on August 11, 1492, Cardinal Rodrigo Borgia was elected Pope and took the name of Alexander VI. He immediately took pains to continue the work on the "palatium novum" of the Vatican. Nicholas V had added a north wing to the early section of Nicholas III. Further sections were added by the succeeding Popes so that, as far as the fortification was concerned, the structure was finished by the time Innocent VIII died. Toward the west, however, a fortified section that had been called for in the plan of Nicholas V was missing. Thus it was that Alexander VI eventually built this still-missing fortified section along the western entrance. He annexed it to the north wing of Nicholas V, although not in a straight line, and he gave it the name of "Torre Borgia." Among those apartments which were chosen by the new Pope were, in addition to the first floor of the Torre Borgia, the rooms in the palace of Nicholas V and one room that belonged to the palace of Nicholas III. The rooms which made up this section of the Vatican palaces are, to take them in order, the Sala delle Sibille and the Sala del Credo (in the Torre Borgia); the Sala delle Arti Liberali, the Sala dei Santi and the Sala dei Misteri (in the palace of Nicholas V); and the Sala dei Pontefici (in the palace of Nicholas III). They were not actually living quarters for the Pope, but rather reception rooms, the so-called "secret cabinets." His living area consisted of a number of small rooms, to which access was gained from the Sala delle Arti Liberali. Alexander VI commissioned Pinturicchio, or Bernadino di Betto, from Perugia with the decoration of these rooms, and, as we know, he began work as early as November, 1492. Documents which report on the latter-day doings of the artist indicate that the decoration of the apartments must have been completed by the beginning of 1494—at least for those sections for which he and his assistants were responsible. During this pontificate the apartments flowered; but shortly after the death of Alexander VI, in August, 1503, the rooms were completely abandoned. They were given the role of a kind of "damnatio memoriae" in unpleasant remembrance of the Pope who had adorned and resided in them, and they were allowed to be forgotten. In the 17th and 18th centuries, they occasionally served as lodging for those cardinals who were in Rome during conclaves (at one time, they were divided into cells); or they served as dining rooms for junior palace civil servants during Holy Week—and this certainly did not keep the rooms from deteriorating even further.

It was not until the reign of Pius VII (1800–1823) that the Appartamento found new use as a depot for those pictures which the French had stolen and which had been ordered returned by the Congress of Vienna. On this occasion, in 1816, they suffered for the first time a radical restoration. Suffering is the correct word here, for, as was usual at that time, the restorers went to work with great vigor, displaying little consideration for the artist's personality. A second restoration was undertaken under Leo XIII in an effort to make good at least some of the misplaced zeal of the earlier restoration. It was during the former occasion that the pictures in the Pinacotheca Vaticana were housed elsewhere, and the Appartamento Borgia harbored the "Museo Miscellanee." A large number of varied objects were brought together here, among them frescoes, marble sculptures, terra cottas and modern books, for which no other room had been found. Even after most of the objects had been transferred to the "Gregoriano Etrusco" and "Gregoriano Egizio" museums, as well as to the "Lateranese" and to the room "Nozze Aldobrandini," the books were allowed to remain here; and, by request of Pius IX, they were supplemented by the library of Cardinal Mai.

When Leo XIII (1878–1903) re-organized the Secret Archives and the Vatican Library, the Appartamento was emptied so that that the rooms could be restored. The architect, Francesco Vespignani, was responsible for the architecture, while Ludovico Seitz was in charge of the frescoes. Once the original splendor had been restored, the Appartamento was appended to the museums and, in March, 1897, it was opened to the public. Following the outbreak of the Second World War, it was closed again and was not re-opened until December, 1947.

As has already been mentioned, Pinturicchio and his assistants began their work toward the end of 1492, according to some reports, in the Sala dei Misteri (others, e.g. Carli, maintain that this room was not painted until after Pinturicchio had left Rome). The Sala dei Santi and the Sala Arti Liberali followed. The Sala del Credo and the Sala della Sibille were decorated last, the two of them being in the by then completed "Torre Borgia" (1494). The Sala dei Pontefici, in which the Pope mainly granted audiences, was furnished with frescoes at a later time.

Among Pinturicchio's assistants on this project were Pastura (Antonio da Viterbo), Tiberio d'Assisi, Pier Matteo d'Amelia and others whose names we still do not know. The experts have attempted to mark off each artist's work against those of the others, and they have not always achieved agreement. There is no doubt, though, that in each of the most important rooms, the personality of the painter responsible for the entire artistic work is dominant. One finds here a unity of style and purpose: at times a decorative taste, a "coarseness" in the "unfolding of the elegant Umbrian style"; elsewhere, one perceives an understandable, occasionally naïve, but always joyful and rich language, with much gold—something that accorded astonishingly well with the Pope. He placed great value on this form of expression which was already ridiculed as being backward and provincial—especially in contrast to the then prevailing Tuscan style of painting. He liked the "false use of gold," which Vasari condemns as being the "greatest heresy," since its luster corresponded to his desire for splendor and pomp.

In the Sala dei Misteri one finds the *Annunciation, Nativity, Epiphany, Resurrection* (with the famous and astonishingly realistic portrait of Alexander VI), the *Ascension,* the *Pentecost* and the *Assumption.* The Sala dei Santi contains *St. Catherine Disputing, St. Anthony and St. Paul the Hermit,* the *Visitation,* the *Martyrdom of St. Sebastian, Susanna and the Elders, St. Barbara,* and, in the roundel above the door, *Madonna and Child.* In the next room, which is dedicated to the "Arti Liberali," and which the Pope chose to have furnished as his study, there are throned figures in niches; they represent rhetoric, geometry, music, astronomy, grammar, arithmetic and dialectic. The Sala del Credo and the Sala delle Sibille have group pictures depicting, respectively, the Prophets and the Apostles, and the Prophets and the Sibyls. In addition to these main frescoes, the fan-vaulting of the ceiling contains frescoes or gilded pastel pictures enclosing individual figures or scenes, which, in contrast to the main theme, relate episodes from Egyptian (Isis, Osiris) and classical (Io and Argus) mythology.

The Borgia coat of arms—a red bull on a field of gold—appears again and again and is repeated many times on the priceless marble frieze that winds its way beneath the frescoes in the Sala dei Misteri; it is attributed to a disciple of Mino da Fiesole.

This painter and his school must have executed the decoration of the private rooms. Proof of this is the discovery of sections of a fresco (a landscape behind arches), which resembles one by Pinturicchio in the palace of Domenico della Rovere.

The present ceiling vault in the 13th century Sala dei Pontefici was erected in the period of Alexander VI in place of a wooden ceiling, which collapsed on June 29, 1500, almost killing the Pope. Under Leo X (1513–1521), Giocanni da Udine decorated the ceiling in stucco with astrological motifs. Next to the twelve signs of the zodiac, one sees the constellations of the Great Dipper, the Swan, Argus and the Dog Star. Perin del Vaga was responsible for the grotesques and angels in the central roundel.

Of the architectural and landscape scenes with which the walls were decorated when St. Carlo Borromeo, the Secretary of State to his uncle, Pius IV, lived here, very few remain. Nor is anything left of the Papal portraits in the lunettes. According to Vasari, Giotto painted them, and the room was named after him during the second half of the 16th century. The ten lunettes now contain only painted shells and panels, which are fitted out with white stucco lettering on a blue field. These inscriptions refer to various Popes and their activities, including Stephen II, Hadrian I, Leo

III, Sergius II, Leo IV, Urban II, Nicholas III, Gregory XI, Boniface IX and Martin VI. Vasari links the inscriptions to the purported portraits by Giotto, which may have been destroyed when the ceiling collapsed. Today, experts are of the opinion that these hymns of praise to the Popes refer to a number of tapestries which were to have been hung beneath the frescoes, a project which was never carried out. The 17th century Flemish tapestries which now hang there, and which relate the tale of "Cephalus and Procris," have no relation to the frescoes and serve merely as decoration. In the Sala dei Santi there hangs another Flemish tapestry, which depicts the "mystical grape." This room also contains the inlaid benches which Giovanni de Dolci made for the secret library of Sixtus IV.

MARIA DONATI BARCELLONA

RAPHAEL'S STANZE AND LOGGIE

The rooms in which Julius II—he was elected Pope in 1503—resided are generally known as "Stanze di Raffaello" (Raphael's Stanze). Like the Appartamento Borgia on the floor below, these rooms were built at various periods of time. The Sala di Constantino belongs to the palace of Nicholas III; the Stanza dell'Incendio, the Stanza della Segnatura and the Stanza dell'Eliodoro were built by Nicholas V. Julius II intended to complete the palace, but when he died, only the north wing had been finished. It is to this wing—work on which had been interrupted in the 14th century—that the stanze belong; they are on the second floor, which was really supposed to have been the top storey of this section. This was revealed by recent investigations, indicating that the present rib-vaulting is an alteration planned during the lifetime of Nicholas V. He wanted to construct yet a third storey, which would have necessitated replacing the original ceiling with an arch; however, the project was not completed until the pontificate of Leo X (1513–1521), based possibly on designs by Raphael. As we have already mentioned, Alexander VI resided on the first floor of this wing, in adjoining rooms. Sixtus IV had already installed the Bibliotheca Apostolica in the ground-floor and had intended to make it accessible to the public. This intention has been preserved in the famous fresco by Melozzo da Forlì, which he painted for the library. It has since been removed and now hangs in the picture-gallery.

Colored fragments of plaster which were found under *The School of Athens* prove that the decoration of the Stanze had already begun under Nicholas V. We know that at the end of the 15th century, in addition to Bartolomeo della Gatta and Luca Signorelli, Piero della Francesca worked here. It was not until after 1507, however, that work began in earnest. Until then Julius II had been willing to take up temporary residence in the Appartamento Borgia. But he could no longer endure the constant reminder of his unloved predecessor, as presented to him by Pinturicchio's decoration of the Sala dei Misteri. He therefore decided to have this section of the "palatium novum" re-done. Perugino, who had worked on the ceiling of the Stanza dell'Incendio, was commissioned with the painting, as well as Sodoma, Peruzzi, Lotto and Bramantino.

According to Vasari, Raphael was summoned to Rome in the autumn of 1508. By obeying the summons of Julius II, he was forced to leave behind in Florence several unfinished works. Vasari also surmises that it could have been Bramante, a distant relative of Raphael, who recommended his young compatriot to the Pope. Raphael first proved his artistic capabilities in the Stanza della Segnatura, and Julius II was so satisfied that, without hesitation, he entrusted the entire decoration of all the rooms to the painter from Urbino, ordering the immediate removal of the work of the other artists. Although the rooms are known as "Stanze di Raffaello," it is only in the Stanza della Segnatura and the Stanza dell'Eliodoro that Raphael's full power is visible. The last fresco executed in the Stanza dell'Eliodoro already exhibits a predominance of his assistants; this is even more noticeable in the Stanza dell'Incendio, and completely dominates the frescoes of the Sala di Constantino, which was completed between 1517 and 1524, following Raphael's death.

The frescoes in the Stanza della Segnatura illustrate the Neoplatonic conception of Truth, Goodness and Beauty. The room, originally intended as the Papal library, gets its name from an ecclesiastical court which met there. The frescoes in the Stanza dell'Eliodoro represent incidents illustrating the intervention of Providence in defense of the Church. The frescoes in the Stanza dell'Incendio are in praise of the ruling Pope—Julius II had been succeeded by Leo X—with episodes from the lives of two Popes with the same name. The Sala di Constantino, finally, serves to glorify the Church, employing historical scenes which depict the eventual and decisive victory of Christianity over paganism.

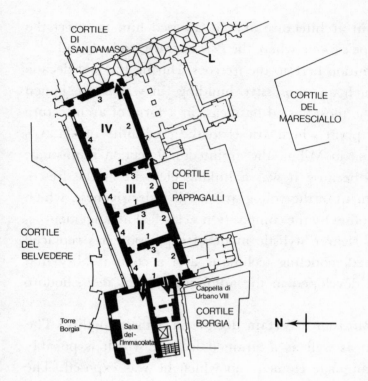

CORTILE DI SAN DAMASO

L

CORTILE DEL MARESCIALLO

CORTILE DEI PAPPAGALLI

IV

III

II

CORTILE DEL BELVEDERE

Torre Borgia

Cappella di Urbano VIII

CORTILE BORGIA

N

Sala dell'Immacolata

Raphael's Stanze. I. Stanza dell'Incendio, with the frescoes *The Oath of Purgation of Leo III* (4), *Coronation of Charlemagne* (1), *Fire in the Borgo* (2) and *Naval Victory of Leo IV over the Saracens at Ostia* (3). – II Stanza della Segnatura, with the frescoes *Disputa* (1), *The Cardinal Virtues* (2), *School of Athens* (3) and *Parnassus* (4). – III Stanza dell'Eliodoro, with the frescoes *Leo Meets Attila* (1), *Miraculous Mass of Bolsena* (2), *Expulsion of Heliodorus* (3) and *Deliverance of St. Peter* (4) — IV Sala di Constantino, with the frescoes *Baptism of Constantine* (1), *Battle of the Milvian Bridge* (2), *Constantine and the Apparition of the Cross* (3) and *Constantine's Donation of Rome to the Pope* (4).

Raphael began work in the first Stanza; and because of the artist's theme, the decoration of this room afforded the greatest amount of zeal. Many of the humanists at the Papal court had participated in preparing the thematic program for the decorations; among them were Baldassare Castiglione, Inghirami, Caleagni and Ariosto. According to Giovio, the Pope himself had chosen the theme. This is a glorification of Truth—both in its supernatural implication as Theology, and in its natural form as Philosophy—, Goodness in the form of Virtue, and Beauty as Poetry.

The allegorical frescoes on the upper section of the ceiling are linked to the scenes of the wall frescoes by rectangular ceiling panels. On the wall is *The Disputa*, which is below *Theology* and is linked to it by *The Fall of Man*. Beneath *Philosophy*, and linked to it by *Astronomy*, is *The School of Athens*. *Poetry* is brought into association with *Parnassus*, which is beneath it, by *Apollo* and *Marsyas*. Beneath *Justice*, and linked to it by the *Judgment of Solomon*, is a lunette containing the *Cardinal Virtues*. To the left of the door is a depiction of *Justinian Receiving the Pandects*, and to the right of the door is a representation of *Gregory IX Delivering the Decretals*. In this task of expressing pictorially abstract philosophical concepts, Raphael was aided by his training in Urbino, which, through Ficino's influence, had become a well known center of Neoplatonic culture. The artist's own concepts robbed the Neoplatonic conception of the original scheme of much of its intellectual ponderousness; in addition, they made it possible for his extraordinary sensitivity to prevail over the dogmatism of his advisors. They also permitted him to transform purely abstract concepts into genuine poetry. The setting itself is proof of the young artist's ability. *The Disputa* takes place in the out-of-doors, under blue skies, and this serves to underline the mysticism of the theme. Raphael falls back here on a scheme that he had already employed in 1505, in the church of San Severo in Perugia: a projecting semi-circle, dominated by a figure of Christ enthroned in the clouds, and this figure sits beneath a wide heaven that appears to extend beyond the edge of the vaulted lunette. This fresco in the Vatican, however, displays different sentiments. The width of the room is emphasized as well by the vaulting of the lunette and the double semi-circle of the militant and victorious Church as by the curved, rhombic golden rays, which emanate from the arch surrounding God the Father and the chorus of angels. This is completely 16th century and is, in many ways, reminiscent of Bramante. Bramante's influence, indeed the influence of his work, can be seen on the opposite wall in *The School of Athens*: a glorification of knowledge and human intellect. The setting of this fresco is an edifice which is supposed to represent the earthly significance of Truth.

Vasari reports that Bramante "taught Raphael of Urbino much about architecture and he advised him to insert the buildings, for which he had prepared the perspective sketches, in the Pope's room, where the *Parnassus* was to be found...." Art historians are today in complete agreement on Bramante's contribution here to the frescoes. During the first decade of that century there was no one else who could have portrayed such an impressive building, in which are joined together elements of classical Roman edifices, from the Pantheon to the most varied basilicas, in a form of architecture that is, at the same time, traditional and new. There is yet another point which attests to the credibility of Vasari's words. In the cartoon for this fresco, still preserved in the Ambrosiana in Milan, the architectural section is missing; and this was indispensable—not only for aesthetic reasons, but also because it was a linking element in the fresco. This is Raphael's second painting, and it indicates the rapid development of the young artist. All indecisiveness, which close examination reveals to be present in *The Disputa*—although this is offset by the composition's classical arrangement—, have disappeared here. In this fresco it now becomes evident that a clearer stylistic mode of expression has replaced those initial weaknesses; more powerful forms disclose a more marked modeling technique and a color quality that point to an increasing interest in painterly craftsmanship—and this developed in the adjoining Stanza dell'Eliodoro to complete beauty.

In contrast to these two main frescoes, many art critics see in the *Parnassus* a certain decline in artistic quality. The emphasis on classical guidelines allows a theoretical bias to creep in as well as a strained feeling, which is possibly a result of the artist's attempts to integrate all the new style and language elements to which he was exposed. The decoration of this wall facing the Belvedere court was fraught with great difficulties, since the fresco had to be painted around a window. Raphael tried to achieve a unified and wide-ranging composition by raising the figures on the left side and lowering those on the right side; however, he did not completely achieve this goal.

The same problem presented itself on the wall opposite, but he was able to solve it here by dividing up the fresco into three scenes, all of which were linked to the allegorical figure of *Justice* on the ceiling vault, hovering over the wall. Three of the four Cardinal Virtues are portrayed in the lunette over the window: *Fortitude, Prudence* and *Temperance*. *Justice* is located above them, "... as if, with the figures of the lunette, to form the apex of a triangle." Redig de Campos sees in this solution not only "a necessity dictated by the given situation," but primarily the affirmation of the Platonic and Augustinian conception, "according to which Justice is not only a virtue, but is the greatest of all the virtues and the mentor of the others."

Justice appears on both sides of the window—in the form of civil law: *Justinian Delivers the Pandects to Tribonian*—and in the form of canonical law: *Gregory IX Delivering the Decretals*. The arrangement of these two scenes creates a link to the compositions on the main walls; for the scene with civil law, to the right of the window, borders the wall with *The Disputa*, while on the left side, adjacent to *The School of Athens*, is the scene devoted to canonical law. Although the arrangement of the scenes is by Raphael, and the cartoons—especially that of Justinian—are probably his, it is unthinkable that he participated in their execution, which is certainly of poorer quality. On the basis of certain stylistic peculiarities, it has been presumed that Guglielmo di Marcillat was the artist. A French glass-stainer, very active in the Vatican, his works were destroyed during the sack of Rome. Two very beautiful windows in the church of S. Maria del Popolo are his. It appears more improbable that Raphael took any part in the adjoining panels, to the right of the window.

The ceiling vault was attributed to artists who worked on the Stanze prior to Raphael's appearance. The division of this fresco, typical of the 15th century, consists of eight framed sections, painted and embellished with grotesques. Alternately rectangular and circular, they are joined to an octagon in the center of which a group of putti prance around the coat of arms of Nicholas V; the putti have been attributed to both Sodoma and Bramantino. Many art critics are of the opinion that sections of the painting in the rectangulars can definitely be attributed to these two artists. However, there is no doubt that the allegorical figures of *Theology, Philosophy, Justice* and *Poetry*, in the four roundels corresponding to the wall scenes, are by Raphael. Off the Stanza della Segnatura, Vasari tells us that "the Pope was very satisfied with this work and appointed Giovanni da Verona from Monte Oliveto Chisuri to make a suitable wall-molding for the paintings; at that time, he was a master of the wood-relief, and in addition to a wall-molding he also made marvelous doors and chairs in wood-relief…." This wall-molding was presumably destroyed during the sack of Rome and the plaster socle was exposed. Paul III commissioned Perin del Vaga with a monochrome decoration; this consists of scenes of alternately imitated statues, all enclosed by simulated frames.

In connection with this and the other Stanze, one should bear in mind that a number of restorations have been undertaken. These began with one commissioned by Clement VII, and carried out by Sebastiano Veneziano, to remove the damages which had been caused by the plundering of the Bourbons. Another restoration was carried out by Maratta, who had been appointed by Clement IX as curator of the paintings. These activities extend to those undertaken by the restorers of the Laboratorio Vaticano, who, during the past few years, have performed their work according to the most modern points of view and methods.

It was probably toward the middle of the year 1511 that Raphael completed the fresco cycle in the Stanza della Segnatura; he then started with the decoration of the Stanza dell'Eliodoro and this lasted from 1512 to 1514. It was also for this second Stanza, used as a secret ante-chamber, that Julius II chose the motif for the painting. Through the central theme, that of the intervention of Providence in defense of the Church, the Pope wished to glorify the events of his own pontificate. The illustrated episodes have been taken from the Bible: *The Expulsion of Heliodorus* from the Old Testament, *The Deliverance of St. Peter* from the Epistles of the Apostles. *The Meeting of Attila with St. Leo the Great* and *The Miraculous Mass of Bolsena* stem from medieval incidents. In these pictures, Raphael's artistic mode of expression has been enriched by new experiences and the resumption of earlier influences—the latter having either been newly reflected upon, or strengthened through renewed contact. His interest in light and color is already evident toward the end of his stay in Florence, and it makes itself clearly evident in *The Disputa* (the portrait of Dante contains subtleties of color that bring the Venetians to mind).

In this period, his contact to the world of the Venetians was strengthened by collaboration with, or the influence of, painters like Giovanni da Udine, Dossi Dossi, Lorenzo Lotto (Longhi or Zanetti), and Sebastiano del Piombo. Nevertheless, the fresco which gives the Stanza its name—*The Expulsion of Heliodorus*—is not so much dominated by the desire to unite Florentine design with Venetian color as it is by the wish to express the grandeur of the image-rich style. In this painting, as well as in *The Deliverance of St. Peter*, it is light which is the chief effect, and this is the stylistic element which connects up the scenes. It is especially in *The Expulsion of Heliodorus* that the alternation between shadows and gleaming areas of light forms a powerful unit, together with the lively figures gathered in the basilica, which encloses the scenes. There are certainly hints here, too, of Venetian color gradation, especially in the group on the left; however, it is not until the next fresco that Raphael's artistic expression reaches its culmination.

The Miraculous Mass of Bolsena is one of the most significant examples of Raphael's expressive strength. In this fresco, he succeeded in achieving an equal accentuation of the basic elements; this he did by uniting perfectly the color tonality of the Venetians and the restrained representational technique of the Tuscans. One should not forget that here, too, as in the case of the wall with *Parnassus*, the difficulty of composition was complicated yet further by a window which was not centered in the wall. However, in contrast to the previous room, Raphael not only solved the problem here in a coherent manner, he also turned this shortcoming to his artistic advantage. The painting refers to an incident from the year 1263. A Bohemian priest on his way to Rome interrupted his journey in order to read Mass at the church in Bolsena. At the moment of transubstantiation, and as if in answer to his doubts, he found the Host bleeding in his hands. This miracle is the basis of both the Feast of Corpus Christi as well as the construction of the cathedral of Orvieto, in which the precious relic of the blood-stained cloth is supposed to be reposited.

On the next wall is *The Meeting of Attila with St. Leo the Great*. This encounter, more legendary than factual, is supposed to have taken place near Mantua. During the discussion which then took place, the armed figures of St. Peter and St. Paul appeared behind the Pope, and this vision is supposed to have kept the dreaded king of the Huns from engaging in further wars of conquest. This refers apparently to Julius II, whose warlike undertakings aimed at defending the rights of the Church to its own territory as well as newly defining the extent of that area; it refers especially to the Pope's efforts to drive the French out of Italy, which aim he achieved in 1512. To indicate this association, Raphael transferred the event from the banks of the Mincio to the gates of Rome—in the background one can make out the walls and a number of buildings—and he gave the figure of St. Leo the facial features of Julius II; this is revealed by two sketches, one of which is in the Louvre, and the other at Oxford. In the fresco, however, the new Pope, Leo X, personifies St. Leo, and the meaning of the work was transformed into an allegory of the Battle of Ravenna. The fresco was still being painted when Julius II died; Cardinal Giovanni de'Medici was elected his successor in March, 1512. The new Pope had Raphael continue with the work, although he wished to have certain alterations carried out.

The experts are in agreement that this fresco is not on a par with Raphael's masterworks. It is largely the work of his assistants, as indicated especially by the unevenness on the left and the right edges. The predominance of his assistants is noticeable in other works that were painted at the same time. Raphael was so overburdened with commissions that he was forced to rely more and more on his pupils and assistants.

The experts do not agree on the exact year in which the fresco on the wall facing the Belvedere court was painted. It also appears that there was an earlier fresco by Piero della Francesco on that wall. There are those who agree with Vasari, believing that *The Deliverance of St. Peter* was executed prior to the death of Julius II. On the other hand, a great many experts are of the opinion that this fresco, like *The Meeting of Attila with St. Leo the Great,* was commissioned by Leo X. In the case of the former, the Pope wished to have reference made to his own escape from imprisonment by the French in 1513, whereas the reference in the latter work was to the Battle of Ravenna. In *The Deliverance of St. Peter,* Raphael's famous color tonality has returned, and the light effects have a marked significance which one might well term avant-garde.

As in the previous Stanze, the artist provided a link in the Stanza dell'Eliodoro between the decoration on the ceiling vault and the wall frescoes. The four trompe l'oeil tapestries on the ribbed ceiling vault (the ornamental work was done earlier) contain repetitions of the basic theme of the main frescoes: that of the intervention of divine Providence. The works in question are episodes taken from the Old Testament: *The Sacrifice of Isaac, The Burning Bush, Jacob's Ladder* and *God Appearing Before Noah.* Here, too, the artist sought a direct reference of the ceiling scenes to those on the walls, even if only as an allegory.

Although the final design and those cartoons now maintained in private and public collections are undoubtedly by Raphael, these paintings nevertheless reveal stylistic peculiarities which can be attributed to Guglielmo di Marcillat, whose collaboration on the Stanze della Segnatura has already been mentioned. Another painter who worked on the aforementioned room makes a reappearance here: Perin del Vaga, who did the monochrome figures of the socle, based on designs by Raphael.

The Stanza dell'Incendio, already mentioned, takes its name from the fresco of the great fire which occurred in the Borgo in 847. According to *The Liber Pontificalis* its progress was arrested by Leo IV making the sign of the cross. The other fresco, *The Battle of Ostia,* also refers to Leo IV, under whom—as the fresco illustrates—the Saracens landing on the shore near Rome were defeated by the Papal troops. Two further frescoes illustrate events in the life of Pope Leo III: *The Crowning of Charlemagne* in the basilica of the Vatican on Christmas Eve in the year 800; and *The Vindication of Leo III,* who, in St. Peter's basilica and in front of the Emperor and the clergy, was acquitted of the charges brought against him by the nephews of Hadrian I. The connecting element in all these scenes is the name of the depicted Pope, a name which the reigning Pope also bore at the time these frescoes were painted.

It has already been noted that, as work progressed on these paintings, the school of Raphael came to play an increasingly great role. This room, which was painted from 1514 to 1517, indicates a limited participation by Raphael in the frescoes *Fire in the Borgo* and *Battle of Ostia;* although he made the cartoons for them, he did not work on the painting itself. For the other scenes, he most probably prepared only drawings or sketches, upon which his assistants, notably Penni and Giulio Romano, based the work. The further lowering of artistic standards in the frescoes in these rooms did not escape the critics—contemporary or later. While some saw in this a falling-off in the expressive power of the artist, others attributed it to the fact, already mentioned, that increasing demand for his works caused Raphael to rely more and more upon the help of his assistants; in fact, he often allowed them to work on their own. Many critics, like Camesasca, maintain that "around the year 1514, if not earlier," Raphael "underwent a change, developing from a painter of tradition... to a producer of paintings; and his share of the work often did not extend beyond the making of general suggestions." This view applies, of course, not only to the Stanze, but for all those works which came after 1514. Perugino had already painted the ceiling of the Stanza dell'Incendio before Raphael commenced work, and it was his express wish that, out of respect for his master, the ceiling remain untouched. The socle, however, was painted by Giulio Romano.

The last room of the Papal apartment, the Sala di Constantino, was painted from 1517 to 1524, with a short interruption during the reign of Hadrian VI. It is entirely the work of the school of Raphael. His assistants and pupils apparently obtained the commission after having announced that they possessed the designs. However, there is nothing in this room that could even be indirectly attributed to Raphael. As in the Stanze, the theme here—the glorification of the Church and its victory over paganism—was chosen by humanists at the Papal court. The painting was accomplished chiefly by Giulio Romano and Penni, with the help of a large staff of assistants. The tapestry-like frescoes illustrate *Constantine's Apparition of the Cross, The Battle of the Milvian Bridge, The Baptism of Constantine* and *The Donation of Constantine*. These main scenes alternate with the coats of arms of Leo X and Clement VII, who commissioned the works, and with figures of the Virtues and the Popes. Most deserving of notice in this room are the clear signs of a change in taste. The striving for balance and rhythm, so peculiar to the Renaissance, has given way to a more artificial and decorative style—perhaps because this style is associated with motifs and conceptions which are the fore-runners of mannerism.

Of the four paintings already mentioned, it is *The Apparition of the Cross* and *The Battle of the Milvian Bridge* that are, in the main, attributed to Giulio Romano, for they display a very clear stylistic unity. The former portrays that moment when, during a solemn speech by Emperor Constantine to his followers prior to the battle against Maxentius, a cross appeared in the sky with the words: "in hoc signes vinces." The latter is a representation of the battle and the victory in the year 312. Giulio Romano also had a big share in the execution of the *Donation*. The most beautiful figures are attributed to him, especially those in the foreground. These exhibit impressive contrast of light and shadow, often in connection with metallically luminous colors or with a certain hardness of contour. Its form, rather than being composed of classical proportions, is indicative of a turning toward manneristic techniques. Of inferior artistic expressiveness is the *Baptism;* this is set in an architectural framework reminiscent of the baptistery at the Lateran and has Clement VII in place of St. Sylvester. Pale, chalky colors in moderate gradations reveal the weaker personality of Penni. Among those Virtues alternating with these scenes, the figure of *Comitas* deserves notice. Hess is of the opinion—not shared by other experts—that it could be by Raphael.

While looking at this room, we ought not to forget that its present appearance differs from the original. During the reign of Pius IV, the plain raftered-ceiling to which the artist referred when preparing his design was replaced by an imitative vaulted ceiling. This was painted toward the end of the 16th century by Tommaso Laureti and his school. Among the tasks with which Julius II entrusted Bramante was a façade on the side of the old palace facing the city; it was to conform to the taste and the concepts of the time. It consisted of a round-arched portico on the ground-

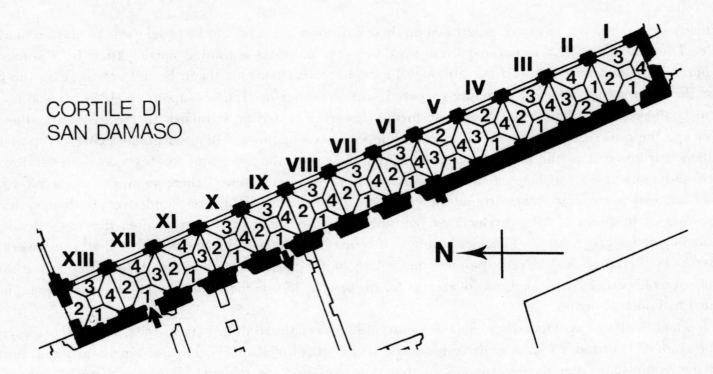

CORTILE DI SAN DAMASO

The ceiling frescoes in the arcades of Raphael's loggia.

I. arcade: *Separation of Light and Darkness. Separation of Land and Water. Creation of the Sun. Creation of the Moon and the Animals.* – II. arcade: *Creation of Eve. The First Fall of Man. Expulsion from Paradise. Adam and Eve with their Children.* – III. arcade: *Construction of Noah's Ark. The Flood. Leaving the Ark. Sacrifice of Noah.* – IV. arcade: *Abraham and Melchisedech. God's Promise to Abraham. Abraham and the Three Angels. The Destruction of Sodom.* – V. arcade: *God Forbids Isaac to Travel to Egypt. Abimelech Secretly Beholds Isaac and Rebecca. Isaac Blesses Jacob instead of Esau. Isaac Blesses Esau.* – VI. arcade: *The Vision of Jacob's Ladder. Jacob and Rachel Meet at the Fountain. Jacob Chides Laban. Jacob Returns to Canaan.* – VII. arcade: *Joseph Tells his Brothers of his Dreams. Joseph is Sold by his Brothers. Joseph and Potiphar's Wife. Joseph Interprets the Pharaoh's Dream.* – VIII. arcade: *Moses is Found in the Nile. The Burning Bush. Crossing the Red Sea. Moses Smites the Rock and Draws Water.* – IX. arcade: *Moses Receives the Ten Commandments. Worshipping the Golden Calf. God Speaks to Moses from the Pillar of the Cloud. Moses Gives the People the Ten Commandments.* – X. arcade: *Passing Over the Jordan with the Ark of the Covenant. The Taking of Jericho. Joshua Makes the Sun Stand Still. Dividing the Land of Canaan Among the Twelve Tribes of Israel.* – XI. arcade: *David is Anointed King. David Slays the Giant, Goliath. David's Triumph. David's Sin.* – XII. arcade: *Solomon is Anointed King. The Judgment of Solomon. Solomon and the Queen of Sheba. The Building of the Temple.* – XIII. arcade: *Birth of Christ. Adoration of the Magi. Baptism of Christ. The Last Supper.*

floor and two corresponding loggias on the two floors above. Bramante kept to this plan, left the portico on the ground-floor (it was closed later for structural reasons) and extended it beyond the old palace to a total length of 65 meters. It was upon this that he built two loggias with vaults; they were supported on the first floor by Doric, and on the second floor by Ionic columns. Work on this edifice began in 1512 and, under Leo X, was continued until the death of the architect in March, 1514, by which time only the second loggia had begun to take shape. Raphael, on the advice of Bramante, had replaced the old architect as director of the work in the palace, and he completed the structure according to the designs of his predecessor.

Corresponding to the third floor of the palace of Nicholas III—an addition to that structure—he built a third loggia with Corinthian columns. Raphael devoted himself to his architectural work with great enthusiasm; and at the same time he threw himself into an intensive study of ancient Rome and its buildings. Various literary sources and several remaining sketches indicate that he planned an archaeological map of Rome and its architectural monuments.

The result of these studies is recognizable not only in the works stemming from that period, like the Stufetta of Cardinal Bibbiena and the Loggetta, but also in the decoration of the second Loggia; not only did he design it, but his studio carried it out. Here, the theme of the "grotesques" was jubilation, enlivened by an inexhaustible fantasy. His tireless imagination sought out a profusion of subjects; flowers, fruit, vegetables, bizarre animal figures and lively winged putti soaring through stucco and fresco. Although there is an exact artistic order to all this, a narrative sequence is missing; there is absolutely no connection with the cycle of painted frescoes on the ceiling vault, which is known as the "Bible of Raphael." This fresco is devoted basically to the Old Testament. Raphael both planned and directed the work, although the decoration of the loggia was a collective undertaking by his assistants, notably Giuliano Romano and Penni, in addition to Perin del Vaga and Giovanni da Udine (who did the stuccowork); mention also ought to be made of such lesser artists as Raffaelino del Colle, Tommaso Vincidor da Bologna, Polidoro da Caravaggio, Pelligrino da Modena and Vincenzo da S. Gimignano.

Also worth mentioning is the fact that the original floor, consisting of many-colored Majolica tiles, was executed by Luca della Robbia the younger. In 1869, the tiles were removed and portions of them were used for the floor of the Fra-Mariano-Fetti-Chapel in the church of S. Silvestro in Monte Cavallo. Aside from the architecture, this is the only part of the loggia whose creator is known for certain. In the case of the painting decoration, it is extremely difficult to determine which portions were done by which artist. It is indeed tempting to try to attribute this or that section of the frescoes to various of Raphael's assistants and in many cases this is not even difficult to do. However, clear and unequivocal is the dominating personality of Raphael, under whose direction the work was designed and carried out. We know that, at the time, he was engaged in a thorough study of ancient art, as the Stanza dell'Incendio indicates. And as has been written of his work, "in none of the works which wished to recall the classical style—this theoretical dream of the Renaissance—did the dream ever come so close to reality as in the second loggia."

MARIA DONATI BARCELLONA

above : 43) Part of the ceiling decoration in the Sala delle Arti Liberali.

left : 44) *Apostle and Prophet*. Painting in a lunette of the Sala del Credo.

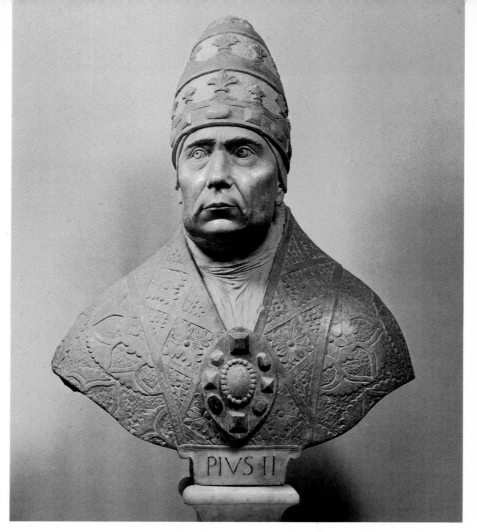

right: 45) Bust of Pius II.

below: 46) *Arithmetic*. Painting by Pinturicchio in the Sala delle Arti Liberali.

below: 47) *St. Catherine Disputing with the Philosophers Before the Emperor Maximian*. Painting by Pinturicchio in the Sala dei Santi.

right: 48) *Barbara Fleeing From her Father*. Painting in the Sala dei Santi.

lower right: 49) *Susanna and the Elders*. Painting in the Sala dei Santi.

below : 50) *Madonna and Child, with Angels*. Painting in the Sala dei Santi.

upper right : 51) Marble frieze with a medallion portrait of Pope Alexander VI. in the Sala dei Santi.

lower right – left corner : 52) *The Prophet Isaiah*. Painting in the Sala dei Misteri.

lower right – right corner : 53) A mythological scene. A painting in the Sala dei Santi.

below: 54) *Pope Alexander VI*. Painting (a section) in the Sala dei Misteri.

right: 55) *Adoration of the Magi*. Painting in the Sala dei Misteri.

following pages:
left: 56) *Saturn*. Painting in the Sala delle Sibille.

right: 57) Ceiling painting in the Sala dei Pontefici.

SATV
RNO

THE LOGGIA AND THE STANZE BY RAPHAEL

below: 59) View of Raphael's Loggia.

STANZA DELLA SEGNATURA

right: 60) *Disputa dei Sacramento – Triumph of the Christian Faith*.

below: 61) "A group with Pope Julius II". A section from the *Disputa*.

below: 62) "God the Father". A section from the *Disputa*.

upper right: 63) "St. Peter's while under construction". A background section from the *Disputa*.

lower right – left corner: 64) A group on the left side of the *Disputa*.

lower right – right corner: 65) A group on the right side of the *Disputa*.

left: 66) *The School of Athens*.

below: 67) Center group, with Plato and Aristotle.

left: 68) A group of geographers, from *The School of Athens*.

right: 69) A group of astronomers, from *The School of Athens*.

below: 70) A group of natural philosophers from *The School of Athens*.

STANZA DELLA SEGNATURA

right: 71) *Parnassus – The Triumph of Poetry*

below: 72) The poetess Sappho. A section from *Parnassus*.

left: 73) The poet Dante. A section from *Parnassus*.

below: 74) Apollo with the Muses and the poets of antiquity.

right: 75) The Muses (to Apollo's right).

STANZA DELLA SEGNATURA

below: 76) *The Cardinal Virtues:* "Prudence between Fortitude and Temperance".

upper right: 77) "Prudence".

lower right: 78) "Fortitude".

below: 79) *Astronomy*. A ceiling fresco.

right: 80) *Adam and Eve – the Fall of Man*.

STANZA DELL'ELIODORO

left: 81) *The Expulsion of Heliodorus from the Temple in Jerusalem.*

above: 82) The "High Priest prays for succor". A section from *The Expulsion*.

below: 83) The
*Miraculous Mass of
Bolsena*.

right: 84) "Members
of the Swiss Guard".
A section.

below: 85) *The Deliverance of St. Peter*.

left: 86) The "Angel and the Apostle". A section.

LEO·PP·III

NEPHAS

AISTVLP

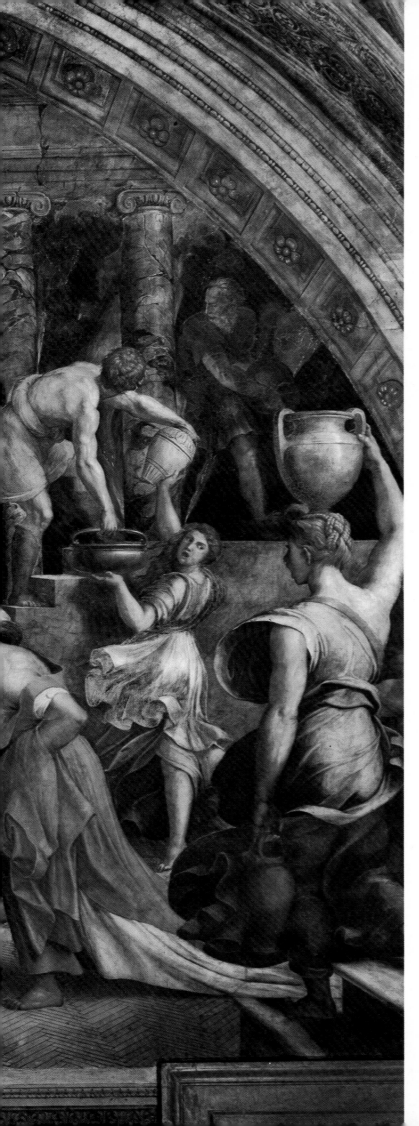

left: 87) *The Great Fire in the Borgo.*

below: 88) *Moses and the Burning Bush.*

THE STUFETTA OF CARDINAL BIBBIENA
AND RAPHAEL'S LOGGETTA

These two rooms on the third floor of the Papal palace face the portico of the loggie on the San Damaso court; they are today the seat of the Secretary of State. They form part of an apartment which Pope Leo X (1513–1521) had built over the Papal apartment for his secretary and former teacher, Cardinal Bernardo Dovizi. Known as "il Bibbiena," he was a celebrated author and playwright. The architecture and the rich adornment are mostly the work of Raphael (1483–1520), but a major section was accomplished by his pupils working under his direction. The result is a perfect harmony of architecture and decoration; created by one spirit, each complements the other. Although this is one of the rare examples of Raphael's architectural style—decisively influenced by Bramante, but not without its own mature grace—both these works are little known. One of the rooms was soon forgotten after it had been subjected to several whitewashings; the other chamber fell into neglect because of its inaccessibility.

Vasari does not mention either room, but many other documents—especially the correspondence between Cardinal Bembo and Cardinal Bibbiena—make a re-construction of its history possible. Both cardinals were friends of Raphael, and Cardinal Bembo kept the future tenant informed of the progress of the work on his apartments in the Vatican. From his letters one can see that the Loggetta and the Stufetta were built and painted at the same time: approximately between the end of 1515 and the summer of the following year. On May 6, 1516, Bembo wrote: "…the Stufetta is almost finished and it will really be very beautiful—the new rooms and the Loggetta have been completed; we miss your Eminence and you ought to come soon…." However, on July 19, 1517, Bembo informed him that the structure of the wall had to be altered somewhat: "Your Eminence's Loggetta is being rebuilt and it will be very beautiful…." And if a notation from that period by Michiel refers to this structure (which is probable), then it was still being painted in May, 1519. Cardinal Bibbiena was unable to enjoy his little realm for long, for, like Raphael, he died in the year 1520. Some time prior to the year 1721, the arches were closed and windows were inserted, and a wall-chest was built between the small arches. It was probably about the same time that the frescoes were whitewashed and the room was partitioned off by new walls into three small rooms. These walls were removed in 1906. This was the condition of the "Corridor of the Secretary of State" prior to its restoration, which lasted from 1943 to 1945 and returned to Raphael's neglected Loggetta at least some of its former splendor. This graceful little gallery has interior dimensions of 15.74 meters in length and 3.12 meters in width, and in the center of the barrel-vault it is 4.64 meters high. The window frames are of travertine. On the exterior wall facing the "Cortile del Maresciallo" are three wide arches with Corinthian columns, steps and a balustrade with small columns—all in travertine. The remains of the old floor-covering of Spanish-Moorish majolica tiles were re-assembled in small panels in a terra-cotta base. In the wall parallel to the façade are three niches in chiaroscuro; they have been painted with female figures, probably the Four Seasons, by Francesco Penni. Between them are three small paintings, with black background, by Giuliano Romano; copied from an old columbarium (now destroyed), they represent the scenes of the contest between Apollo and Marsyas. In some of the small figures one can recognize the hand of this painter as well as the especially fine brush-work of Perin del Vaga. The figures cover the walls and the ceiling, both by Giovanni da Udine. He was an unrivalled imitator, or, rather, reviver, of the decorative style of Nero, "domus aurea," which was re-discovered at that time; his name has been found scratched into the stucco as "Zuan da Udene firlano."

As in the case of the "Seconda Loggia," which was reserved for the Pope and his art collection, Raphael designed the entire decoration and directed the work of his pupils. He divided up the sections, gave each assistant that section which corrresponded best to his style, prepared designs and sketches, made corrections and supervised everything. It does not appear that he himself ever took a hand in painting the frescoes in Cardinal Bibbiena's Loggetta, yet he was everywhere at once, and his presence is more than evident. After his death, his pupils were never able to do anything that compared to this creation.

Raphael participated much more directly in the decoration of the Stufetta (small bath), which he also built in this apartment. This is a tiny room, measuring 2.5 meters by 2.5 meters, and 3.2 meters at the vertex of the cross vault. It was lit by a solitary window, set into the wall opposite the original entrance. At some unknown later date, this entrance was walled up and was replaced by another; this entailed the sacrifice of a large number of frescoes. The walls on the side are decorated with niches on marble socles, which contain gilded satyr heads enclosed in shells. These are flanked by cornucopiae with sheaves of wheat—a symbol of plenty ("dovizia"), which is a clear allusion to the Cardinal's name. Out of the metallic cornucopia of the satyr on the right (now missing) water used to flow into a basin. The floor-covering of inlaid many-colored marble resembles that in the "Stanza della Segnatura."

The walls and the ceiling are covered with elegant grotesques, and impressionist brush-work painted them onto an underpainting of "Pompeiian red" in an intended and very successful imitation of the frescoes done in the ancient style known as Nero's "domus aurea." Flanking the small door, the niches and the window are small framed pictures. One of them depicts an episode from the myth of Venus; another is a representation of some Greek myth, not clearly identifiable. The rest of the pictures—from Greek mythology, Ovid, or other sources—are arranged in an alternating sequence. On the wall in which the original door had been located there is, to the left, *Vulcan* and *Minerva;* to the right is *The Birth of Venus*. In this direction, to the right and flanking the niches, one finds *Galatea on a Sea Monster* accompanied by *Eros Riding a Dolphin,* and *The Wounded Venus* who is complaining to Amor. Flanking the small window to the left are *Pan and Syrinx;* to the right had been *Venus Removing a Thorn from her Foot,* but this picture has been removed and is now lost. When this happened is not known, but this picture's existence is documented by a print by Marcantonio and by an 18th century copy now in the Hermitage in Leningrad. Finally, to the left of the second niche is a picture of *Ariadne and Bacchus; The Myth of Venus,* which had been to the right, must remain unknown since it fell victim to the new door. The socle of this small room is adorned with charming frescoes, painted onto a black underpainting. Framed in red, and standing upright in sea-shells, tubs and other fanciful receptacles are winged putti, drawn by doves, snakes, swans and butterflies. The frames are decorated with fish and other creatures of the sea, all very realistically depicted against antique red underpainting. The state of repair of the frescoes varies considerably; some of them, especially the grotesques, are in excellent condition, whereas the others vary from medium quality to very poor. This applies especially to the vault, which is in the style of a classical Roman coffered ceiling, on which the motif of many scenes can barely be made out.

The correspondence between Cardinal Bembo and Cardinal Bibbiena reveals a great deal of reliable information about the way the work proceeded. On May 16, 1516, "the new rooms and the Loggetta" were finished, and the Stufetta was almost completed. Another letter, written on June 20, notes that it was finally finished. "I am pleased to inform you that… the Loggetta, the Stufetta, the rooms and the leather curtains are ready for your Eminence and that everything awaits you." In contrast to the Seconda Loggia and the Loggetta, in the case of the Stufetta one cannot exclude the possibility that Raphael himself took a hand in the decoration, especially certain sections of the grotesques. What one sees here is a standard of painting never again achieved by his pupils; in addition to that, one is aware of an atmosphere of classical art that this eclectic genius summons up with the same credibility with which he "imitated" the Umbrian grace of a Perugino, the sculptural art of a Michelangelo and the color-magic of a Titian. Moreover, he also incorporated these styles into his own individual mode of work. This is the model which Giulio Romano,

Penni, Perin del Vaga and Giovanni da Udine used as the basis for the work they later carried out, under the supervision of their master, on the loggia of Leo X, the Loggetta of Cardinal Bibbiena and on several other sections of the Stufetta. And although the extremely poor condition of the frescoes makes a critical judgment difficult, it does appear possible to attribute at least two of the six pictures to Raphael: namely, *The Birth of Venus* and *The Wounded Venus*.

In conclusion, I would like to quote from two additional letters from the Bembo-Bibbiena correspondence. The first of them gives a lively account of Raphael during the work on the frescoes for the Stufetta; at the same time, it relates information about the initiator of the learned iconographic "program." The second letter is typical of the guileless humanistic thought processes of a Renaissance cardinal. Cardinal Bembo wrote on April 19, 1516: "Just now, as I am writing this letter, Raphael came to me—it is as if he had known that I was writing about him—and he asks me to tell you this: you should send him the rest of the stories, i.e., a written précis of the stories which your Eminence wishes to have painted in the Stufetta, since the painters will be finished this week with those which you had already sent." The other letter is from April 25 of that year and it deals with a small statue of Venus that Cardinal Bembo wanted as a present since it could not be installed in one of the niches, as Cardinal Bibbiena had wished. "I beg of you, dear, good Monsignore—what am I to do? I would like to ask you for a big favor, and I fear that it is presumptuous of me.... I ask you to be so kind as to give me the little marble figure of Venus which you got from Signor Giangiorgio Cesarino and for which Raphael could find no room in the Stufetta, as had been intended. I would take it lovingly into my household, placing it in my dressing room, between Jupiter and Mercury, her father and brother; with great enthusiasm, I would delight in it daily—more, in fact, than your Eminence could, because of your many obligations. And, finally, you could come at any time to reclaim it, which would not be possible if it fell into other hands; and that would certainly come to pass if it is not conveyed to me...." The extent of damage which the valuable frescoes have suffered during the past centuries was too great to have been repaired by the restoration in 1942. All that could be accomplished was a strengthening of the layers of color, a cleaning of the painted surfaces and a treatment of certain missing sections with local color. However, even in this incomplete condition, the Stufetta represents perhaps the most valuable example of the affinity between the art of the Renaissance and its classical prototype.

D. REDIG DE CAMPOS

below: 90) A view of the Stufetta.

right: 91) *Venus Wounded by Love*. Fresco on the south wall.

upper left: 92) *Cupid in a Tub, Drawn by a Seaserpent.* Fresco on the pedestal of the east wall.

above: 93) *The Birth of Venus.* Fresco on the east wall.

left: 94) *Venus and Cupid.* An example of grotesque painting.

right: 95) *Pan and the Nymph.* Fresco on the west wall.

upper left: 96) An example of grotesque painting, with a depiction of the river deity of the Nile.

lower left: 97) Grotesque painting: depiction of a river deity.

below: 98) *The Crane and the Wild Boar*. Fresco on the ceiling of the Stufetta.

left: 99) A view of the Loggetta.

above: 100) A woman spinning, with child and cat.

101) A winged spirit donning a helmet.

102) A woman spinning, with child. Three frescoes on the windowed wall.

right: 103) *The Contest Between Apollo and Marsyas.* Painting along the niched wall.

right: 104) A decorative grotesque painting on the ceiling of the Loggetta.

next page, above: 105) Figures of Eros in Vulcan's forge. Painting on the frontal wall.

next page, below: 106) A philosopher with a lantern.

previous page: 107) A grotesque painting on the windowed wall.

left: 108) Decorative grotesque figures between two niches.

below: 109) "The Judgment in the Musical Contest on Olympus". A section from the above composition.

right: 110) An allegorical niche-figure.

left: 111) "Minerva". A section from the ceiling decoration.

below: 112) Part of the Majolica floor tiles in the Loggetta.

THE VATICAN LIBRARY

The Vatican Library is an ideal repository for a series of unrelated old archives and Papal libraries; in its present form it is a creation of the most lavish period of Italian humanism, the 15th century. Its founding can be precisely accounted for. On June 15, 1475, Pope Sixtus IV della Rovere (1471–1484) signed the Papal decree "Ad decorem militantibus Ecclesie," which made the Library accessible to scientists, determined its location and regularized its funds, and named the humanist Bartolomeo Platina as librarian. This historic moment has been documented in a painting by Melozzo da Forlì and is now in the Vatican's collection of paintings.

The foundations, however, were laid by others. Thus, since an epoch is judged more by the works which resulted than by the wishes of an individual, Nicholas V Parentucelli (1447–1455), in fourth place before Sixtus IV, is usually designated as founder of the Library. In the estate of Eugene IV he discovered 350 Latin manuscripts, plus several in Greek and Hebrew. He significantly increased this amount through his own manuscripts. In addition, he ordered a number of purchases in the European and Asian market and employed a group of copyists to prepare transcripts. From the inventory listing at the time of his death on March 25, 1455, and from other records, one can conclude that he left behind about 1,500 manuscripts. This collection was thus the largest of its kind in Europe. He also planned a site for it which, according to the rules of the time, would have been a long room with side windows. But he did not have enough time to carry out his plan, and neither did his successors. Callistus III (1455–1458) used the financial resources of the Holy See to finance a war against the Turks; Pius II Piccolomini (1458–1464) and Paul II Barbo (1464–1471) devoted themselves entirely to their private libraries and family possessions. Sixtus IV took up the idea of a permanent library again and carried it out. The number of volumes grew to about 3,700, and 1,475 were prepared for a suitable location. Initially a special building was to be erected. But then it was decided to locate the library on the ground-floor of Nicholas V's palace, formerly used for grain storage and as a cellar. This very central location lay between the "Cortile dei Pappagalli," where the entrance was also located, and the Belvedere Courtyard. There were four rooms of differing sizes. Appropriate to their contents, they were designated the "Latin Library," the "Greek Library" (for the works in these two languages), the "Secret Library" (for the most valuable volumes), and the "Papal Library" (for the Archives and regesta). In the first two rooms the manuscripts lay on benches with inclined surfaces, as can be seen in a fresco in "Ospedale di Santo Spirito in Sassia." In addition, there also was a room available for the librarian, his three assistants, and a book-binder. Famous painters such as Domenico and Davide Ghirlandajo, Melozzo da Forlì, and Antoniazzo Romano decorated the rooms with frescoes. In the "Latin Library" a number of philosophers of antiquity and church fathers were presented through an eclecticism characteristic of the time (the preserved decorations were uncovered through modern restorations). Julius II della Rovere (1503–1513) added on several more rooms, and the Library remained here for more than a century. It was finally known as the Vatican Library, a name which it still bears today.

Because of its site, the Library remained a palace library. It belonged to the residence and possessions of the ruler. But it was never clearly limited to that, and Sixtus IV intended to do away with that restriction and to expand the library. In the Papal Bull *(Officii nostri debitum* of August 27, 1487) is found the following paragraph: "Bibliothecae... palatii nostri pro communi curialium et aliarum personarum quarumlibet ad Romanum curiam pro tempore confluentium commodo et utilitate ordinatae." Thus the Library was open not only to the members of the Curia, but also to all who, for any reason, applied to the Curia. The loan figures for the years 1475 until 1547 *(Codices Vaticani Latini* 3964 and 3966) are found in two preserved lists. They show that even external loans were made. In this way foreigners, such as French, English, Spanish, and Germans, were in a position to borrow manuscripts in order to study them at leisure; for this they left a deposit (money or valuable objects such as plates, rings, or candy dishes). Because of losses, the policy of lending books out was later discontinued.

The collection was constantly enlarged in the 16th century, primarily through the increasing number of printed books. Like other princely libraries in Italy, the Vatican at first accepted these books only hesitantly, although one of the librarians, Bishop Giovanni Andrea de'Bussi (d. 1475), was a very ardent editor of books published by Rome's first book publishing house, Sweynheim and Pannartz. It is known that a number of books sent to the Library by Sixtus IV on November 26, 1483, were put into a special department "insuper armario," that is, for "printed books." In the first years of the 16th century, librarian Tommaso Inghirami, called Fedro, arranged a sale of printed books which were found in the study of Sixtus IV and which, on directions from Innocent VIII, were sent to the Library in 1490. Eventually printed books were saved and formed into a special collection, today the "Prima Raccolta" (8,304 works, almost all 16th century editions).

The shortage of space and poor conditions prompted Sixtus V Peretti (1585–1590) to let a contract for construction of a new site. This was erected between 1587 and 1598 and was the work of architect Domenico Fontana. The structure was erected above the divided steps in the Belvedere Courtyard. Fontana connected the two long corridors by Bramante which border the courtyard and thus divide it. The south façade, which faces the original site, consists of three floors: the ground-floor, originally used as a cellar; the second floor, in which the rooms "Scholars and Librarians" are located on two mezzanines; and the third floor, entirely taken up by the large hall, the "Library," with two aisles 70 meters long and 15 meters wide. A group of painters decorated this room with frescoes which glorify the victory of Truth through books. As in the library of Sixtus IV, the books lay on benches and on shelves, but after 1605 they were stored in closed cabinets which ran the length of the hall. This hall, called "Salone Sistino" became the model for other historical libraries.

At this time the Vatican Library also devised regulations concerning the arrangement of its collection. The manuscripts on hand were carefully ordered and given an enumeration still valid today. Then the contemporary material—the Regesta—was grouped according to languages, which had increased to 17. Regularly appearing catalogues and inventory lists were also preserved from this period, a still-incomplete, tedious and difficult task.

In the 17th century, the Vatican Library was increased through additional collections, which are generally separated from the original collection and carry their own designation or numbers. This development has continued to the present time.

The first library that came into Vatican possession was war booty; it was the princely German library in Heidelberg. At the beginning of the 30 Years War, when the Duke of Bavaria, Maximilian I, attacked Heidelberg, Emperor Ferdinand II gave the Holy See the library out of gratitude for the economic assistance offered him by Gregory XV. Fifty wagons, under military protection, brought the crates of printed books and manuscripts to Rome. This collection, in part because of the importance of its volumes about the Reformation, was enriched by the Electors with additions from various private and church libraries. In 1816, 847 of the German, 26 Greek, and 16 Latin manuscripts were returned. Today the collection consists of 2,037 Latin, 432 Greek, and numerous Hebrew manuscripts (which were added to the works in this language already available in the Vatican), and about 3,000 printed books.

The next significant additions were manuscripts from the library of the Dukes of Urbino. The collection was begun about the middle of the 15th century under the protectorate of Federico di Montefeltro, the "optimus princeps" of the Italian Renaissance. It was constantly enlarged by his successors, primarily the last prince, Francesco Maria II della Rovere. After the dukedom was annexed by the Papal States, Alexander VII brought the library to Rome through a resolution of expropriation which absolved the city of responsibility. The manuscripts, incorporated into the Vatican

Library in 1653, included 1,776 Latin (later another 300 were added), 165 Greek, and 59 Hebrew manuscripts. Among them were works of important and lesser important Latin humanists, humanistic translations from Greek, and commentaries of the classicists. Manuscripts in the national language also were included, among them the *Divine Comedy*, and numerous historic documents sent to the court of Urbino by various countries, as well as those addressed to the Augsburg banker Ulrich Fugger by German publishers in Venice. These constitute an extraordinary source of information.

The collection which bears the name of Queen Christian of Sweden ("Reginensi") was at first a war booty of her father, King Gustav Adolf, who died in battle in 1632. Between 1647 and 1649, 1,208 manuscripts were brought to Stockholm. The educated Queen increased the collection and, through careful searching throughout Europe, finally could add the libraries of Hugo Grotius, Alexander Petau, Gerardus Johannes Vossius, and Jean Bourdelot. After the abdication of the Queen in the year 1654, the library was brought first to Antwerp and then to Rome. It remained, separately stored in the Riario Palace, where further works were added. After the death of the Queen, on April 19, 1689, it was bought by Cardinal Pietro Ottoboni, who on October 6 of the same year, ascended the Papal throne as Alexander VIII. In 1690 he gave the manuscripts to the Library, after deciding to retain about 450 for his family library and 72 for the Vatican Archives. About 1,900 remained, but the collection was increased through additional works of various origins, including the extremely significant manuscripts of S. Andrea della Valle (including several of the Piccolomini manuscripts of Pius II and Pius III). The "Reginensi" now numbers 2,121 Latin and 190 Greek manuscripts, plus 55 Greek manuscripts of Pius II. The last member of an important Roman family, the Marchese Alessandro Gregorio Capponi (1683–1746), was an enthusiastic archaeologist and book lover. From the beginning of the 18th century he dedicated himself to collecting manuscripts and printed books, above all Italian editions with literary content. In addition, he collected historical writings, chronicles, reports of ambassadors, political letters, biographies of princes and statesmen, Papal memoirs, libel documents, etc., in addition to his own extensive private correspondence with important scholars of his time. In 1745, he willed 286 manuscripts and 3,210 printed books to the Vatican Library. Pope Benedict XIV Lambertinni, in 1749, bought the manuscripts from the above-mentioned Ottoboni Library for the Vatican Library. These included primarily the collection compiled by Cardinal Pietro, later Alexander VIII, his personal archives and that of his family, as well as gifts and items willed to him. Above all, it also included the acquisition of excellent collections, such as the already mentioned "Reginensi," and a large part of the Altemps manuscripts (a summary of the codices of Colonna, Sirleto, Cervini, among others). The Ottoboni collection now includes 3,396 Latin and 473 Greek manuscripts, plus a number of others of various origins.

THE LIBRARY'S ART COLLECTION

The development of various art collections in the 18th century was significant in the history of the Library. The Museo Sacro arose out of the compilation of diverse art collections (Carpegna, Buonarroti, and Vettori) and became increasingly valuable as various objects of early Christianity were added, for the most part from the Roman catacombs. The objects were of ivory, enamel, bronze, glass, terracotta, etc.

Through the order of Clement XIII (1758–1769) to separate secular from religious objects, the Museo Profano came into being. It contained objects from antiquity and various cultures, sheltered in cabinets of unusual wood and placed in rooms appropriately decorated for the epoch represented. The collection also included medals and coins.

The French invasion of 1798 caused great damage throughout the Library. In connection with the armistice of Bologna and the Treaty of Tolentino, the Library had to hand over 500 manuscripts. After the murder of General Duphot, another 5 manuscripts, 120 incunabula and other valuable printed materials were confiscated. The collections of smaller objects suffered especially heavy losses, for many items were stolen and distributed. After the war, the collections had to be rebuilt. At that time the well-known coin collection, the Medagliere, was detached. It had developed from practically nothing and continued to increase until it became what it is today: not only the largest existing collection of Papal coins, but one renowned for its series of Roman, Greek, Italian, Oriental and other coins.

The Vatican Library resumed its function as palace library, with limited access, after the fall of the Napoleonic Empire. At that time representatives of the Holy See intervened in Paris, and almost all manuscripts and valuable objects were returned to Rome. An extensive renovation of the furnishings was undertaken toward the end of the 19th century, during the pontificate of Leo XIII Pecci (1878–1903), who made the Vatican Archives available to scholars. Not only was the department for reference works enlarged, but the number of scholars admitted for research purposes was also increased. Important librarians, such as Franz Ehrle, Achille Ratti (Pius XI), Giovanni Mercati, Eugène Tisserant and Anselmo Albareda supported the building and the organization and began to increase its scientific reputation through publications. In 1891, 387 Borghese manuscripts were acquired by purchase. For the most part, they came from the old Papal library in Avignon. In 1902, a number of manuscripts from the Museo Borgiano di Propaganda Fide, consisting of works in 19 languages, was accommodated in the Library. In the same year, the purchase of the Barberini library also took place. Regarded as the second largest library in Rome, it contained 19,041 Latin, 595 Greek, and 160 Oriental manuscripts and more than 36,049 printed books. (Later the Barberini family also bequeathed its valuable archive.) After the Italian government acquired the Chigi Palace in 1922, it gave the palace library, consisting of 3,916 manuscripts and 22,497 printed books, to the Vatican Library (in 1944, the family added the archives). In 1922, the Jesuit Order gave the Library its collection, consisting of 1,204 manuscripts, 2,508 incunabula, and 5,624 rare books which Giovanni Franceso de'Rossi had willed to the Order. Similarly, the Vatican Library received as a gift the manuscript collection of two historical church choirs—in 1935 that of the Sixtinian and in 1942 the Julianian. Finally, the Cathedral Chapter of St. Peter's donated its manuscript collection and a part of its archives (including several hundred printed books) to the Vatican Library. The jurisprudence scholar, Federico Patella, left a large heterogenous collection of manuscripts, papers and documents to the Library after his death, and their transfer followed in 1945.

As the ocean absorbs the waters of all rivers, so has the Vatican Library—expressed in the metaphorical language of an old epigram—for the past 500 years collected objects and historical relics from all over the world, making it possible for scholars to seek and find meaningful knowledge, thus contributing to the intellectual development of humanity.

NELLO VIAN

right: 113) Bronze door to Vatican Library

right: 114) The Salone Sistina in the Library.

below: 115) The inaugural inscription by Pope Sixtus V in the Library.

SIXTI · V · PONT · MAX
PERPETVO HOC DECRETO DE LIBRIS VATICANAE
BIBLIOTHECAE CONSERVANDIS
QVAE INFRA SVNT SCRIPTA HVNC IN MODVM
SANCITA SVNTO
INVIOLATEQ · OBSERVANTOR
NEMINI LIBROS CODICES VOLVMINA
HVIVS VATICANAE BIBLIOTHECAE
EX EA AVFERENDI EXTRAHENDI
ALIOVE ASPORTANDI
NON BIBLIOTHECARIO NEQ CVSTODIBVS
SCRIBISQ · NEQ · QVIBVSVIS ALIIS
CVIVSVIS ORDINIS ET DIGNITATIS
NISI DE LICENTIA SVMMI ROM · PONT
SCRIPTA MANV
FACVLTAS ESTO
SI QVIS SECVS FECERIT LIBROS
PARTEMVE ALIQVAM ABSTVLERIT
EXTRAXERIT CLEPSERIT RAPSERITQ
CONCERPSERIT CORRVPERIT
DOLO MALO
ILLICO A FIDELIVM COMMVNIONE EIECTVS
MALEDICTVS
ANATHEMATIS VINCVLO
COLLIGATVS ESTO
A QVOQVAM PRAETERQVAM ROM · PONT
NE ABSOLVITOR

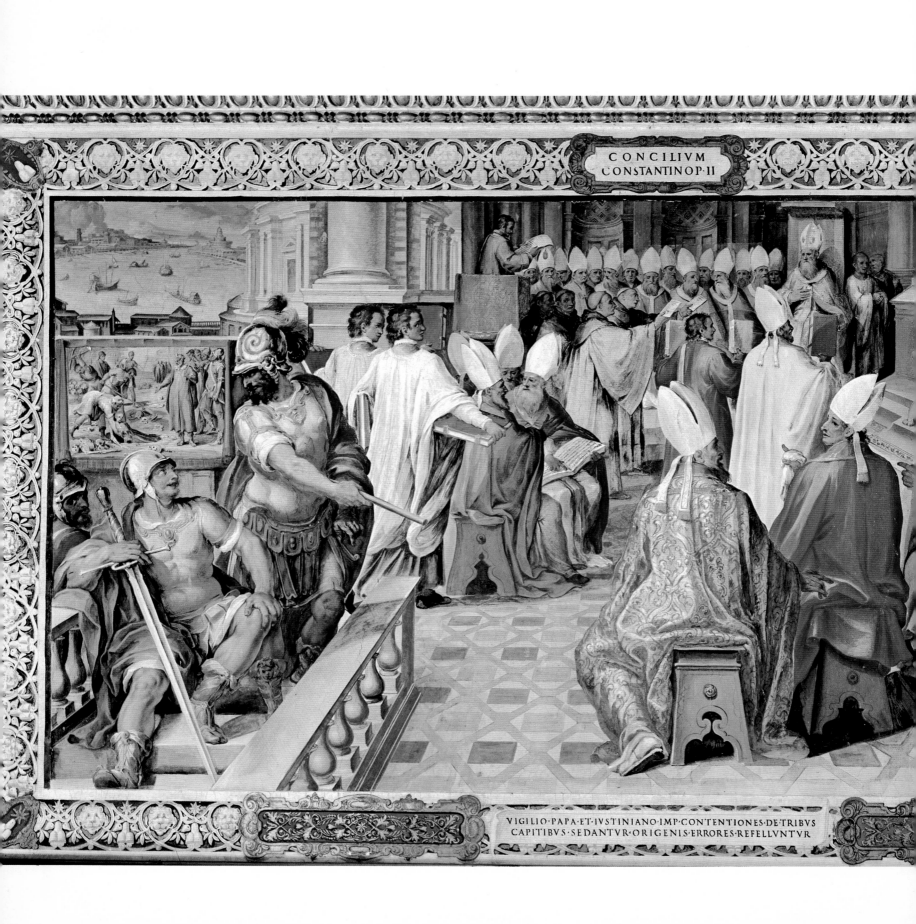

CONCILIVM
CONSTANTINOP·II

VIGILIO·PAPA·ET·IVSTINIANO·IMP·CONTENTIONES·DE·TRIBVS
CAPITIBVS·SEDANTVR·ORIGENIS·ERRORES·REFELLVNTVR

below: 116) *The Second Council of Constantinople*. Fresco in the Salone Sistina.

right: 117) A Vergil manuscript, with illustration.

lower right: 118) A Greek Bible.

upper left: 119) Cicero: *De re publica.*

lower left: 120) Terence: *Codex Bembinus.*

below: 121) Frederick II, Holy Roman Emperor: *De Arte venandi cum Avibus.*

right: 122) A Livy manuscript.

bottom of page: 123) A parchment scroll of the Book of Joshua.

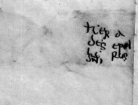

left: 124) The library vestibule – Sala degli Scrittori.

right: 125) An illustration from the *Vatican Vergil*.

lower left: 126) A Dante manuscript from Urbino.

lower right: 127) An illustration by Botticelli of Dante's *Divina Commedia*.

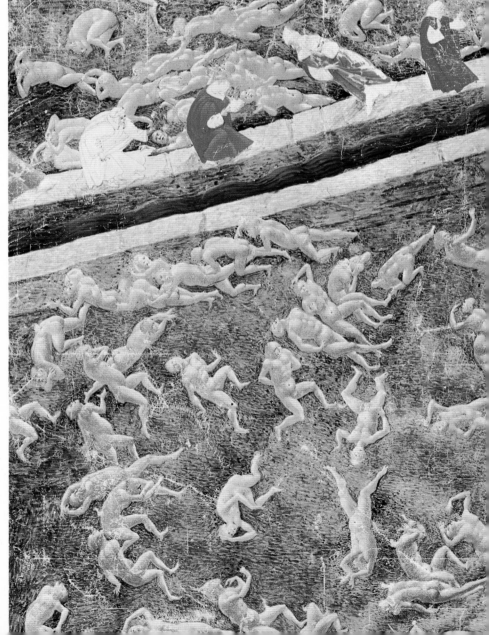

HAEC·SVNT·NOMINA

filioz ifrl qui ingreffi funt in egyptū cū Iacob
finguli cū domib fuif introeruūt. Ruben Syme
on Leui Iudaf Yfachar zabulon et Beniamin
Dan et Neptalim Gad et Afer Erant igitur
omēf anime eoz q egreffi fūt de femore Iacob
feptuagita Iofeph aūt in egypto erat Quo
mortuo et uniuerfif frib eiuf omni q cognatio
ne fua filii ifrl creuerūt et quafi germinātef
multiplicati fē ac roborati nimif impleuerūt
terrā Surrexit interea rex nouuf fuper egyptū
qui ignorabat Iofeph Et ait ad pplm fuū Ec
ce populuf filioz ifrael mltuf et fortior nobif é
Venite fapient opprimamuf eū ne forte mul
tiplicetur et fi ingruerit contra nof bellū ad
datur nrif inimicif expugnatifq nobif egreci
atur de terra Prepofuit itaq magiftrof operū
ut affligerēt eof onerib edificaueruūt q urbef
tabernaculoz Pharaoni Phiton et Rameffef
quātoq opprimebant eof tanto magif multi
plicabantur et crefcebat Oderant q filiof ifrl
egyptii et affligebāt illudentef eif atq ad a
maritudinē perducebant uitā eoz operibuf
durif luti et lateriſ omniq famulatu quo in
terre opibuf premebātur Dixit aūt rex e
gypti obftetricibuf hebreoz quarū una uoca
batur Sephora altera Phua precipif eif Qñ

obftetricabitif hebreaf et partuf tēpuf aduene
rit fi mafculuf fuerit interficite eū fi femina
referuate Timuerunt obftetricef deum et nō
fecerunt iuxta preceptū regif egypti fed con
feruabāt maref Quib ad fe accerfitif rex ait
Quid nā eft hoc quod facere uoluiftif ut puez
feruaretif Que rīderūt Non fut hebree fi
cut egyptie mulieref Ipe enim obftetricādi
hēt fcientiā et priufq ueniamuf ad eaf pa
rūt Bene ergo fecit deuf obftetricibz Et cre
uit ppluf cōfortatuf q eft nimif Et qa timue
rūt obftetricef deū edificauit illif domof Pre
cepit aūt Pharao omni pplo fuo dicēf Quicqd
mafculini fexuf natū fuerit in flumē proicite
quicqd feminei referuate · C II
Greffuf eft poft hec uir de domo leui accepta
uxore ftirpif fue q cōcepit et peperit filium
Et uidef eum elegantē abfcōdit menfib trib
cū iam celare non poffet fumpfit fifcelam
fcarpeā et liniuit eā bitumine ac pice pofu
it q intuf infantulū et expofuit eū in carep
to fluminif ftāte procul forore eiuf et cōfi
derate euentū rei Ecce aūt defcēdebat fi
lia Pharaonif ut lauaretur in flumine et pu
elle eiuf gradiebātur p crepidinē aluei Que
cū uidiffet fifcellā in papirione mifit unā de

left: 128) A Bible page from Urbino.

below: 129) A letter from King Henry VIII of England

right: 130) A manuscript by St. Thomas Aquinas.

lower right: 131) A letter by Martin Luther.

left: 132) A sonnet handwritten by Michelangelo.

lower left: 133) A sketch by Raphael.

right: 134) A Petrarch manuscript.

Junto egia Corso della vita mia
Cō tempestoso mar p fragil barca
al Comū porto ouarender si uarca
Cōto eragiō dognioprā falsa e via
ndr̄ laffectuosa fantasia
che larte mi fece idole monarca
Conosco orbē Comera derror carca
e quel camalsuo grado ognuō desia
hamorosi pēser gia uani eheti
che funor Sadūo morte mauicino
duna sol certo elaltra mimnaccia
e pigēr nescolpir fu piu che qūeti
sanima uolta aquellamor diuino
Caperse aprender noincroce lebraccia

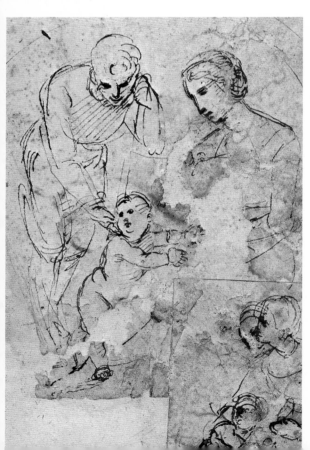

above: 135) A page from Giuliano da Sangallo's sketch-book.

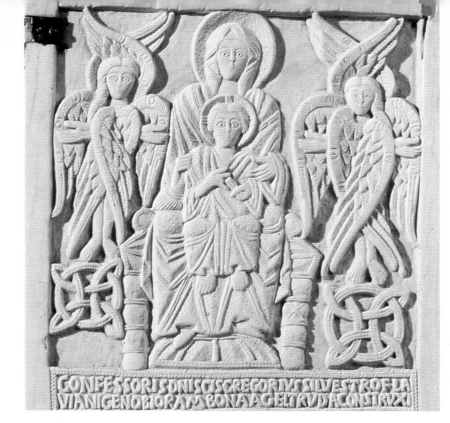

upper left: 136) *The Aldobrandini Wedding Scene*. A section of the fresco.

lower left: 137) *A Landscape From the Odyssey*. A fresco.

right: 138) *Madonna and Child with Cherubim*. On ivory.

below: 139) *The Annunciation*. Silk emroidery.

left : 140) An emalled cross
with scenes from the life of
Jesus.

THE SECRET ARCHIVES

The Vatican Archives are considered to be the central archives of the Holy See. Here have been compiled the archives of numerous departments and ministries of the Roman Curia, and of representatives of the Vatican to various states. Even today, important material from time to time is added, and so the valuable documentary repository will continue to grow.

The rooms in which the Archives are housed belong to the Palazzi Apostolici. They include almost all rooms between the Torre Borgia and the Torre dei Venti. On the one side, they extend out to the Vatican Garden; on the other side, they turn toward the small Cortile della Biblioteca (or della Libreria) and Bramante's Belvedere Courtyard.

The main function of the Archives is, "in the first place, and above all, to serve the Pope and his Curia, that means the Holy See," as it is stated in the May 1, 1884, "motu proprio" of Leo XIII. Accordingly, their arrangements fulfill clearly outlined tasks of religious, juridical, administrative, political, and social importance. With their stored documents of great historical value, today open to the public, the Archives also fulfill cultural needs.

The establishment of the Secret Archives of the Vatican in their present form can be dated back to the year 1610 and was the work of Paul V Borghese (1605–1621). To designate the Archives as "secret" fitted the custom of that time, for it emphasized that the archives were intended by the rulers to be for their private use. In the second half of the 16th century, it had already been recognized that it was necessary to create central archives in which all Church documents stored in various places could gradually be brought together. It is to the credit of Paul V that he carried out this plan, although it was not completed until much later.

He chose as a site for the new archives the rooms which had served as a residence for those cardinals who worked as librarians. The rooms had been unused since the death of Cesare Bormio. The entry to them lay in the "Salone Sistino" of the Vatican Library. After the rooms were renovated and decorated, the Pope (between 1611 and 1614) began to transfer to them regesta and volumes out of the Biblioteca Vaticana, the Guardaroba Papale, the Castel Sant'Angelo, and, above all, from the Camera Apostolica. It is known that before the founding of the Vatican Archives the documentary material of the various ministries of the Holy See were stored in numerous offices and in special depots.

In the beginning, the church manuscripts—that is, books and documents—had a common origin. Thus it is difficult to make a clear separation between archives and library. In the Middle Ages and until the end of the 12th century—as probably also in previous periods—the *Scrinium Sanctae Romanae* surely was located in the Lateran, the Papal residence, since the Pontiff is also Bishop of Rome. However, it is known that especially important documents were stored in other places, as, for example, in St. Peter's basilica at the Apostle's tomb, in the Byzantinian "chartularium," and the Palatine Cliffs. Nevertheless, the stock of documents from the time of Innocent III (1198–1216), still preserved today, is rather sparse. The serious losses probably were caused by the frequent displacement of archival materials resulting from the Popes' numerous changes of residence. In addition, war, theft, and, above all, the stirring history of these epochs took their toll.

In the 13th century, the Popes showed a growing interest in the Vatican, where they spent increasingly long periods of time and which they considered a secure area because of the Wall of Leo IV. This situation had a positive effect on the Papal archives which, like all important departments of the Curia, gradually found a home in the Vatican Palace. It also is shown that from the time of Innocent III a series of Papal regesta were acquired, in addition to a number of documents based on the life and organization of the Church and its relations to the rulers and peoples of the West and Middle East.

Thereafter, the Archives of the Curia, seen by the Popes as a "Church treasure," continued their wanderings, the significant stock of documents thereby suffering considerable losses. In 1245, Innocent IV took the Archives, or at least part of them, to the first Council of Lyon. Later they were in Viterbo and, during the rule of Boniface VIII Caetani (1294–1303), in Anagni. Little by little, the Archives were transferred to Perugia and finally—after stop-overs in Assisi and Carpentras—they came to Avignon, the city in the Provençe where the Popes lived for about 70 years.

An extraordinary situation arose through the relocation of the Papal seat to Rome by resolution of Gregory XI (1377), the election of an Italian Pope, Urban VI, in the following year, and the outbreak of the schism. The Papal Archives, since they could not be brought back to Rome quickly enough, remained in the Curia of the oppositional Pope, Clement VII, in Avignon. On the other hand, as the ministries of the Curia were re-organized, the Archives were re-built in Rome on the basis of the documentary material of the past 40 years. This took place primarily after the end of the schism and the election of Martin V (1417–1431). Meanwhile it had become possible to regain part of the material left behind in France. Together with new books and documents of Sixtus IV della Rovere (1471–1485), it was then methodically put in order. In the Vatican Library founded by him, he made a room, called "Biblioteca pontificale," available for the recording of Papal correspondence. Imperial records and most valuable documents were stored in the Castel Sant'Angelo for security reasons, while the ministries and courts of the Curia (Camera Apostolica, Cancelleria, Penitenzieria, etc.) took care of their archives independently.

The following Popes, above all Julius II and Leo X, agreed with the decision of Sixtus IV. This care proved its worth in the year 1527, during the sack of Rome. The regesta of the Camera and the Segretari suffered considerable damage, but the material stored in the Biblioteca pontificale and in Castel Sant'Angelo remained for the most part untouched. Pius IV and Clement VIII proved to be highly interested in the Archives, although often with barely perceptible results. But it became increasingly clear that unified, comprehensive archives were absolutely necessary for the international administration, and for the establishment of a modern Church history. A first step in this direction, during the rule of Clement VIII Aldobrandini (1592–1605), was the final ordering of the books, letters, and documents stored in Castel Sant'Angelo. This storehouse took on archival character; a custodian was made available, as well as special cabinets created to house the materials.

As already mentioned, the pontificate of Paul V was a decisive turning point for the history and organization of the Papal Archives. It was he who founded the Secret Archives, which fulfilled the purpose of a central archive; and he ordered brought there all documents of historical significance, resolutions and legal documents concerning the rights of the Holy See, in addition to manuscripts and books about the government of the Church and the administration of the Papal States. After Paul V, a period of constant expansion followed, as the registers and collected volumes of the ministries of the Roman Curia were introduced into the Vatican Archives by the successive Popes. During the pontificate of Urban VIII Barberini (1623–1644) and Alexander VII Chigi (1655–1667), the Archives were expanded to the floor above. There, new space was prepared and decorated for the introduction of diplomatic manuscripts. They concerned correspondence of the state secretaries with rulers, princes, secular and church agencies, and, above all, with the Papal Nuncios in the main European states and with the administrators of the Papal States. The compilation of all archival material in the Vatican Archives continued in the following centuries. Of primary importance was the return in the 18th century of materials still remaining in Avignon (including the collection of Papal letters, labeled "Avignonesi," which was of special importance) and the transfer of the entire archives of Castel Sant'Angelo to the Vatican Archives. However, the Vatican and other archives stored outside the Palazzi Apostolici suffered further damage, the extent of which can be estimated only with difficulty. This occurred chiefly during the French occupation of Rome in 1798 and during the transport of the archives to France, as ordered by Napoleon and carried out in 1810 in accordance with the Treaty of Tolentino. The material was brought back to Rome between 1815 and 1817, but with considerable losses. In the course of the 19th and in the first ten years of the 20th century, the development of the Vatican Archives was increased and enriched through addition of such important materials as the Borghese Collection, numerous regesta of Papal briefs from the Lateran, petitions, and archives of communities, ministries, and courts.

In connection with this construction, an expansion of space was necessary. Pius XI Ratti (1922–1939), more concerned with this problem than all others, annexed to the Archives the rooms built under contract for Gregory XIII (1572–1585), "Torre dei Venti," and the gallery which until 1930 had housed the painting collection. This gallery, brightened by the big windows looking out onto the Belvedere Courtyard, was equipped with two levels of utilitarian book shelves made of metal, with a total area of several thousand square meters.

In the last twenty years the Archives have expanded even more rapidly because they had to store multitudinous material resulting from the extension of the Church into the secular world and from the increased activity of the ministries and departments of the Holy See. The use of the top floor above the "Galleria della Carte Geografiche" in the Vatican Museum is a consequence of the intervention of Pius XII Pacelli (1939–1958). This floor extends for nearly 200 meters and connects the Torre dei Venti with the Torre Borgia. Because of the interest of John XXIII and Paul VI, the Archives have been expanded even further in recent times. Reception rooms and work rooms (including a modern photo laboratory and a restoration workshop) were created, as well as a new direct entry from the Belvedere Courtyard. The Archives of the Vatican are among the greatest of their kind in the world. The religious and political significance of the Holy See since the Middle Ages has made the Archives an excellent source of information, not only for Church history but also for the history of many lands and peoples.

In a short survey of the material from the 13th to the 19th centuries, the well-known collections of Papal letters (Papal decrees and briefs) should also be mentioned. From the time of Innocent III, they cover a total span of 700 years: the extensive collection of petitions (from Clement VI to Leo XIII); the archives of the Camera Apostolica, the Sacro Collegio, and the numerous congregations of the Roman Curia. From the 16th century until today, the series of the state secretaries and the reports of the Papal nuncios have an important place next to the church tribunals (Sacra Romana Rota and Segnatura Apostolica). The collection of decrees and documents of the Council of Trent and the Archives of the first Vatican Council should also be mentioned, together with Fondo Pio IX and other special collections of unusual historical importance from the 19th century. The Archives of Castel Sant'Angelo are the most valuable collection of documents. They were rightly called the "trésor des chartes" of the Church. They include thousands of historically unusual and valuable documents, especially those sent to the Popes or the Roman Church by rulers, government offices, civil and religious alliances in West and East, from the 9th century to the second half of the 19th. In addition, all letters of political or personal content, public decrees, international agreements and documents issued by the Popes relating to their legal and administrative tasks are found here. Further, the world's greatest collection of gold seals belongs to these archives.

Since 1600, many men have made important contributions to the construction, development and furnishing of the Vatican Archives: Bartolomeo Cesi, who stimulated and carried out the measures of Paul V; Michele Lonigo, who put together the first valuable inventory directory; and, later, G. Battista Confalonieri, Felice Contelori, Silvio de Paoli, the brothers de Pretis and Filippo Ronconi. In the second half of the 18th century came Guiseppe Garampi, scholar, historian, diplomat, enthusiastic collector of documents, Prefect in 1751, and then Nuncio and Cardinal. He organized the Archives anew and introduced the big card index named after him and consulted daily by scholars. Another man of great significance was Gaetano Marini, who, as Prefect, experienced the misfortunes of the Archives, from the last years of the 18th century to 1815. After him, his nephew, Marino Marini, assumed the position as Prefect and then Agostino Theiner, an untiring editor of documents. The activities of Cardinal Hergenröther, Pater Denifle, and Monsignore Angelo Mercati in the last ten years of the 19th and the first half of the 20th century should also be mentioned—they were men who, in addition to other matters, earned great credit for their support and stimulation of research in the Archives. As early as the 16th and 17th centuries, the Vatican Archives were a valuable aid in the creation of important historical works: the first work, *Annales ecclesiastici*, edited by Baroni and his successors, was created not only through use of the Vatican Archives' sources of information, but also made their abundance widely known. In the 18th and 19th centuries, famous scholars were granted access by the Popes to the documents, but the opening of the archives to the public first came about in 1900, thanks to an especially insightful Pope, Leo XIII (1878–1903). Thereby historical research, in the context of the renewal of Catholic science and culture, received new impetus. Since this time, the rooms of the Vatican Archives have been visited by an ever-increasing number of scholars. They come from all countries and races and are peacefully and creatively unified in their search for truth through the analysis of documents, which are valuable evidence of the distant and recent past. For better or worse, these are a significant part of our civilization. To support this research, numerous historical institutions have been founded in Rome since the last century, with the assistance of the big European nations. Their task is to accommodate groups with special tasks, as well as representatives of the various governments and research groups devoted to the study and publication of historic documents concerning specific nations. Thus, in the course of the centuries, and chiefly in the past 90 years, the Vatican Archives have fulfilled an especially important task. They will continue, too, to make an indispensable contribution to the further development of historical science.

GERMANO GUALDO

right: 141) Portrait of Paul V, founder of the Secret Archives, above a door in the rooms of the Secret Archives.

GREGORIO·VI·PONT·MAX·CASIMIRVS·POLONIA·REX·DEBELLATIS
HOSTIBVS·REGNVM·SVVM·B·PETRO·EX·VOTO·VECTIGALE·FECIT

VII

PAVLVS·V·PONT·MAX·
ANNO·IX

HA

left: 142) A frescoed room in the Secret Archives.

lower left: 143) A room of diplomatic correspondence in the archives.

below: 144) A letter by the Byzantine Emperor.

upper right: 145) A document confirming the privileges of the Bishopric of Tivoli.

lower right – left corner: 146) Two letters from the Khan of Persia in the Mongolian language addressed to the Holy See.

lower right – right corner: 147) Three documents from Holy Roman Emperors.

ottor dñi nri ihu xpi. eterni incendii supplicio
concremandu sit deputatu. nequaqa apfatis
anathematis nexibz absolutur. Ad uo q pio
intuitu. obseruator omnibz exitterit. custo
diens huiˀ nri aptica constituta. ad cultu di
respicientus. benedictione. Gratia Amiseri
cordissimo dño deo nro conseq mereatur. Atq
mtis Beati martyris apli laurentii. eter
ne uite particips effici mereatur.
Scriptu pmanˀ Stephanu scriniaru sce ro
mane eccle. In mse februario Indictione sexta.

✝ **BENE VALE TE.**

Datu septimo kł martias pmanu iohis epi
sce nepesine eccle. et bibliothecarii sce sedis
aptice. Anno pontificatus domni nri iohˀ
scissimi quarti decimi pape sexto. In mse
et Indictione suprascripta Sexta.,

OTTO SECUNDO.

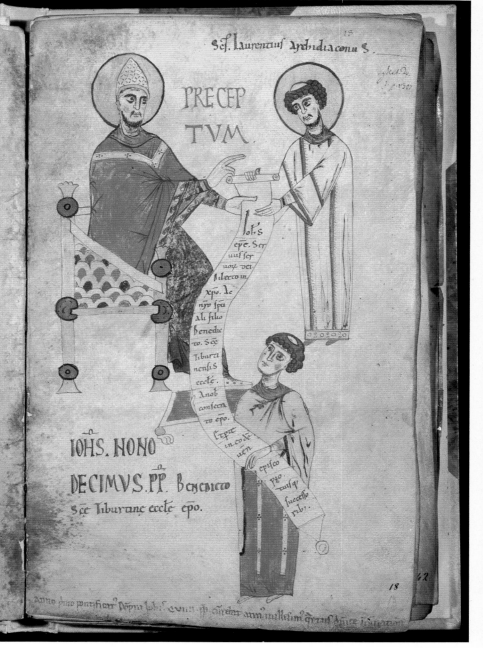

Scs. Laurentius Archidiaconuſ

PRECEP
TVM

IOHS. NONO
DECIMVS. PP. Benedicto
Sce Tiburtine eccle epo.

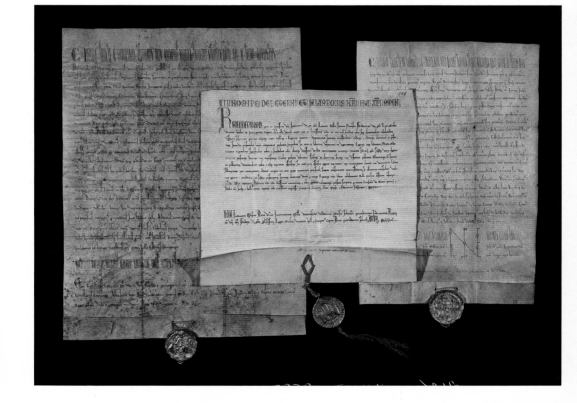

SILENTIVM

Oratio deuotissima edita a beato ysidoro yspalen ad impe-
trandum gratiam spiritus sancti pro directione iustitiae
dicenda per singulos dominos auditores in missa qui conue-
niunt collegialiter pro ministranda iustitia.

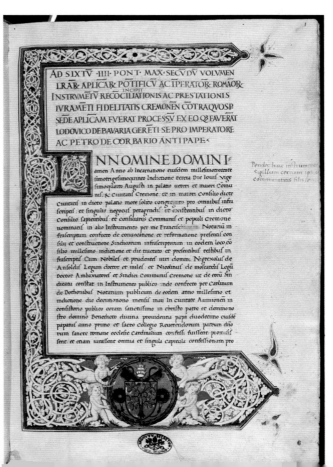

above: 148) The oldest depiction of a session of the "Sacra Romana Rota".

left: 149) A page from the *Collezione Platina*.

upper right: 150) A letter by King Henry VIII of England to Pope Clement VII.

lower right: 151) Italian cities surrender their keys to the vicar-general of Pope Innocent VI, whose residence was in Avignon.

below : 152) A letter of Spanish King Philip II and Mary Tudor, Queen of England, to Pope Paul IV.

lower left : 153) A letter from the Doge of Venice to Pope Sixtus V.

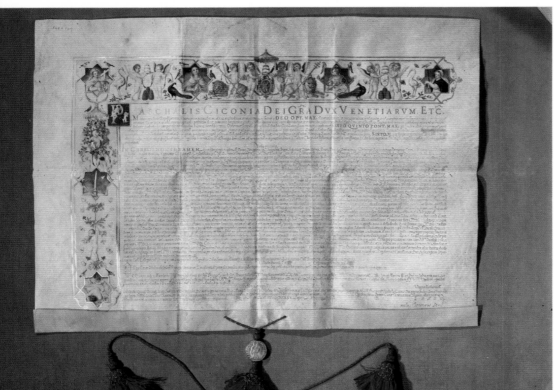

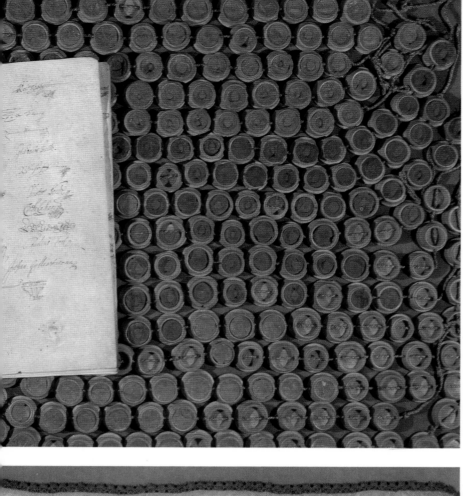

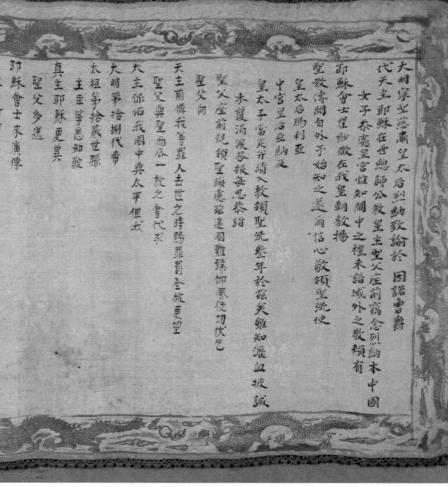

upper left: 154) The letter of abdication of Queen Christina of Sweden.

lower left: 155) A letter from the Chinese Empress Helena to Pope Innocent X.

above: 156) An illuminated page from the documentary collection of Cardinal d'Aragona.

above: 157) Documents from the Kings of Sicily.

below: 158) The concordat between the Holy See and the First French Republic, 1801.

THE SISTINE CHAPEL

The Sistine Chapel was named after Pope Sixtus IV della Rovere (1471–1484), who built it between 1475 and 1481 on the site of the former "Capella Magna" of Nicholas III. According to Vasari, the Sistine Chapel was designed by the Florentine, Baccio Pontelli, the favorite architect of the Pope. The documents in the archives mention only Giovanni dei Dolci, also from Florence; there he is not designated as an architect but as "superstans operibus," which indicates that he was a master-builder. To judge from the fresco which Perugino painted in this chapel, the *Donation of the Keys,* one would surmise that the chapel had been built by Dolci according to Pontelli's design. In fact, Steinmann has identified the man with the square triangle as Dolci. In the Vatican there is another example of this kind of collaboration. The Belvedere of Innocent VIII was built by Jacopo di Pietrasanta according to designs by Pollaiuolo for, as Vasari puts it, Pollaiuolo had absolutely no "building experience."

Although it is liturgically classified as a chapel, the Sistine Chapel has the dimensions of a church. The central nave is 40.23 meters long and 13.41 meters wide—the measurements which the Bible assigns to Solomon's temple—and the distance from the floor to the crown of the vault is 20.7 meters. The chapel originally had 14 windows with bull's-eye panes—six on each side wall and two above the altar. The latter were later walled up to provide room for Michelangelo's "Last Judgment." The area reserved for the clergy (presbytery) is separated from the area for the congregation by a beautiful marble choir screen. Like the decoration of the choir, this is attributed to Mino da Fiesole, who was assisted by Andrea Bregno and Giovanni Dalmata. The pavement consists of "opus Alexandrinum" (mosaic made of many-colored stone); parts of the floor are made up of material from the already razed chapel of Nicholas III.

The conspicuous simplicity of the building, the hardly noticeable intrusion of the few details, such as piers and cornices, and the preponderance of broad, smooth surface indicate the motive behind the design of this chapel. It was made to be decorated with frescoes, and is thus one of the typical examples of the affinity between architecture and painting so beloved by the theoreticians of the Renaissance. Giovanni dei Dolci, commissioned by the Pope to do the decoration, entrusted this task at first to four artists: Pietro Perugino, who assumed direction of the work; Sandro Botticelli; Domenico Ghirlandajo; and Cosimo Roselli. These artists were assisted by a number of others, many of them unknown at the time; others, like Pinturicchio, Piero di Cosimo and Bartolomeo della Gatta, were famous. Before the completion of the project, Luca Signorelli joined them. Two contracts were concluded with the painters: one on October 27, 1481, and the other on January 17, 1482. These contracts made it clear that each artist was to be responsible not only for the painting assigned to him, but also for the frame and Papal portrait pertinent to it in the area between the windows and the drapery below. The entire project was brought to completion with great speed, and on August 9, 1483, Sixtus IV was able to consecrate the new chapel with a High Mass. On August 15 it was dedicated to the Assumption of the Virgin Mary.

The fresco decoration indicates that the Pope undoubtedly intended to fall back on the iconographic scheme of the ancient Roman basilicas—like St. Peter's, S. Giovanni in Laterano, S. Paolo fuori le mura and others—although in the modern form of the 16th century. In these churches, too, episodes from the Old Testament are face to face with those from the New Testament, and there, too, we find beneath the frescoes drapery and the Papal portraits. In the Sistine Chapel, however, the Biblical portrayals are restricted to the life of Moses and Christ, whereby the former is represented as the forerunner of the latter. The Papal portraits here are not busts on a scutiform surface; they are instead figures in liturgical dress, placed in niches whose socle bears a short biographical note for each respective

Pope. These notes were probably composed by Bartolomeo Platina, prefect of the Vatican Library. As if in anticipation of Michelangelo's masterpiece, the decoration of the huge ceiling vault was limited to a simple blue-painted background, covered with golden stars; this was executed by the artisan, Pier Matteo d'Amelia, an assistant of Pinturicchio.

Before we begin with an account of the individual frescoes, it ought to be noted that their Latin "tituli"—which have been found during the many restorations—make possible a yet more exact interpretation. These inscriptions are not engraved, but were painted in Latin capital letters on the cornice above in each case; as a result, they are in a very poor state of preservation. Their text was renewed in accordance with existing outlines, with the aid of a brochure from 1513 that gives the arrangement of the cells set up for the cardinals in the Sistine Chapel during the conclave that elected Leo X. The names, with occasional errors in spelling, are listed beneath the "tituli" for each of the frescoes. Since no cells were set up along the narrow sides of the chapel, the inscriptions for the first two and the final pair of frescoes have been lost.

The cycles devoted to Moses and Christ began on the altar-wall with two frescoes by Perugino—to the left, *The Discovery of Moses in the Rushes* and, to the right, *The Birth of Christ*. Although at the same height as the others, they were smaller so as to allow room between them for a "wall tablet" (Vasari), i.e., for an altarpiece painted in fresco form, with frames painted by Perugino: *The Assumption of the Virgin Mary,* with Sixtus IV in adoration at her feet. These three works were later sacrificed for Michelangelo's *The Last Judgment;* thus each cycle now begins with the second episode.

The following list of the frescoes gives the name of the painter and the text of those "tituli" that have been found in recent times. Capital letters indicate those which have been found and restored; in small letters are those which are still hidden behind the whitewashing, their text having been revealed in the brochure. The frescoes are listed in pairs (Moses-Christ) in order to accentuate the typological similarity of the depicted scenes and their respective inscriptions.

Perugino: *Moses in Egypt* (OBSERVATIO ANTIQUE REGENERATIONIS A MOISE PER CIRCONCISIONEM).
Perugino: *Baptism of Christ* (INSTITUTIO NOVAE REGENERATIONIS IN BAPTISMO).
Botticelli: *The Temptation of Moses* (TEMPTATIO MOISE LEGIS SCRIPTAE LATORIS).
Botticelli: *Temptation of Christ and the Healing of the Leper* (Tentatio Jesu Christi latoris euangelice legis).
Roselli: *Crossing the Red Sea* (CONGREGATIO POPULI LEGEM SCRIPTAM ACCEPTURI).
Ghirlandajo: *Calling of the First Disciples* (Congregatio populi legem euangelicam recepturi).
Roselli: *Moses Proclaims the Law on Sinai* (PROMULGATIO LEGIS SCRIPTAE PER MOISEM).
Roselli: *Sermon on the Mount* (Promulgatio euangelice legis per Christum).
Botticelli: *The Punishment of Korah and his Rebels* (CONTURBATIO MOISE LEGIS SCRIPTAE LATORIS).
Perugino: *The Donation of the Keys* (Conturbatio Iesu Christi legislatoris).
Signorelli: *Moses' Final Worldly Deeds and his Death* (REPLICATIO LEGIS SCRIPTAE A MOISE).
Roselli: *The Last Supper* (Replicatio legis euangelice a Christo).

Another two frescoes were destroyed on Christmas Eve, 1522, when the architrave over the door collapsed while the Dutch Pope, Hadrian IV, was reading Mass in the chapel. These were *The Quarrel over Moses' Corpse* by Signorelli, and the *Resurrection of Christ* by Ghirlandajo. They were repainted by two mediocre 16th century artists (Matteo da Lecce and the Fleming, Arrigo Paludano). On the cornice over the Resurrection, one was able to make out the words RESURRECTIO ET ASCENSIO CHRISTI EVANGELICAE LEGIS LATORIS, which were then restored. On the other hand, not a trace of an inscription was found above the last fresco in the Moses cycle. To avoid any misunderstanding, it should be pointed out that these inscriptions, often extremely unclear, do not always refer to the main episode of each corresponding painting. For example, the inscriptions above *The Punishment of Korah and his Rebels* and above

The Donation of the Keys refer to two completely unimportant scenes—in the first case, the threatened stoning of Moses, on the far right side of the fresco (Ettlinger); in the other case, the reference is to the stoning of Jesus, depicted in one of the small groups in front of the temple. This explains the word "conturbatio," which, in the case of the second fresco, would be otherwise incomprehensible.

THE CEILING OF THE SISTINE CHAPEL

As early as 1506, Julius II contemplated completing the work of his uncle, Sixtus IV, by having the ceiling of the Sistine Chapel painted. In his view, only one man could be considered for this task—namely Michelangelo, a sculptor who had never before painted a fresco. He spoke with Michelangelo about this project in the early part of 1508, when the artist had just returned to Rome. The sculptor had hastily fled Rome two years before when the Pope decided not to have his tomb built, although Michelangelo had been working at it since 1505. Astonished, he now refused the commission, explaining that he was a sculptor and not a painter. However, Julius II, who recognized Michelangelo's genius and knew that he had the talent of a painter, was insistent, and the artist eventually accepted.

It was on May 10, 1508, that Michelangelo started to learn the difficult art of fresco painting, and he began painting the immense ceiling vault. The first design was relatively simple. He limited himself to the depiction of the twelve Apostles along the lateral spaces between the crown of the vault and the walls on either side (where today the prophets and sibyls sit). This theme, however, was too stiff and cold for Michelangelo's passionate genius, and he abandoned it with a humorous remark, contained in a letter that he wrote in 1524 to Fattucci: "The first design of the above-mentioned work consisted of the twelve Apostles in the lunettes and the usual decorative painting for the remaining area. However, after I had started working on it, the whole thing appeared so paltry, and I told the Pope that it was much too poor a thing to paint only the Apostles. He wanted to know why, and I said it was because the Apostles, too, were poor. Thus it was that the Pope bade me paint as I pleased." This is probably the only instance during the Renaissance of a principal granting the artist the freedom to choose the theme that appealed most to him. Each of these two men was worthy of the other. So it is that we have here what Michelangelo really wanted.

On the walls of the Sistine Chapel the painters of the 15th century related the story of two important historic epochs, "Sub lege" and "Sub gratia." On the ceiling Michelangelo wanted to portray those events that had preceded the first two epochs, namely the Creation of the Universe and the Creation of Man—an act of divine love—, the Temptation and Fall of Man, the Expulsion from Paradise, and the initial ordeal, the Flood. And, finally, the renewed development of mankind on the still sodden soil of earth through Noah's descendants; although condemned by the original sin, they were consoled by the promise of redemption—a promise that, having been nursed by Israel, was redeemed by the appearance of the Messiah. This allowed the frescoes on the ceiling vault to join with those on the walls in an historical and conceptual unity.

Although Michelangelo's thoughts had to take an abrupt leave of the tomb of Julius II, his artistic vision remained on the same plane and he designed the ceiling fresco in the expression of monumental sculpture. He gave the huge surface (520 square meters) a strict architectural structure, enriched with subdued contrasts. For a foundation, he painted a framework of gray stone and this is decorated between the segmental coping over the windows with protruding thrones. These thrones are joined together by perforated cornices; the problem of the spandrels he was able to solve by simply removing them from the play of light and shadow.

In the larger fields within this framework, and in the smaller ones contained in the large fields, he illustrated the story of Genesis—the "Separation of Light and Darkness" (above the altar), the "Intoxication of Noah" (above the entrance)—as if they were bound by no architectural framework, but were heavenly visions; and he did this without

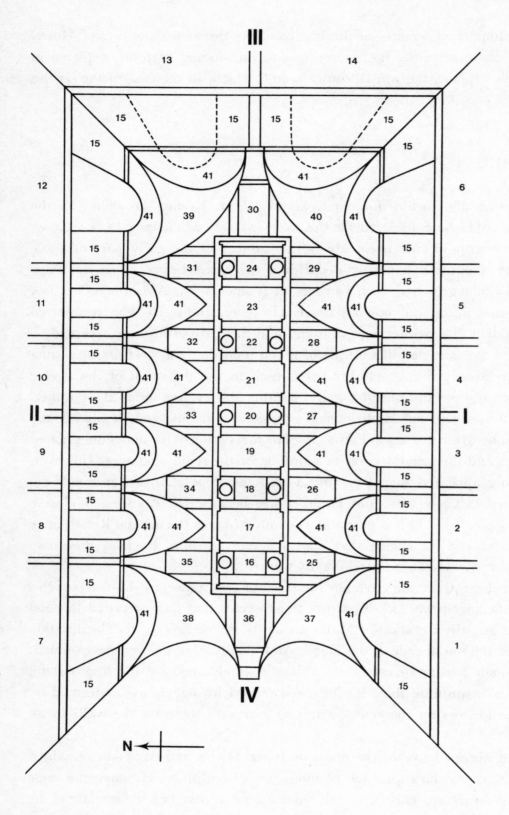

resorting to any perspective tricks. The episodes portrayed by Michelangelo from the Old Testament are in the following order, starting with the field above the altar and proceeding to the entrance (in other words, in a sequence the opposite of that in which it was painted): "Separation of Light from Darkness"; "the Creation of the Sun, Moon and the Stars"; "Creation of the Waters and the Creation of the Animals"; "Creation of Adam"; "Creation of Eve"; "Fall of Man and the Expulsion from Paradise"; "Sacrifice of Noah"; "Flood"; and "Intoxication of Noah."

This Biblical drama is re-enacted by the delightful "slaves" or "atlases," which are seated on socles on the corners of the smaller fields. These unusual figures of naked young men express primitive emotions, like joy, sadness and fear, and bear resemblance to the chorus in a Greek tragedy.

The Biblical drama of God and Man is also suggested by the Prophets and Sibyls, sunk in meditation over the primeval mystery and silently awaiting the promised Redeemer, as well as by the Ancestors of Christ (the medieval theme of root and branch of the tree of Jesse) in the lunettes above the windows. The four frescoes in the triangular ressaults, in the corners of the chapel, are also symbolic references to the coming of the Messiah. They are "David and Goliath," "Judith and Holofernes," "The Brazen Serpent," and "The Punishment of Haman."

The condensation of several days of creation in one field, the selection of episodes best conforming to his own ideas, as well as the arbitrary placing of the Creation of the Waters after the Creation of the Stars (the Biblical sequence is just the opposite, but this allowed him to put the scene with the most figures into the larger field)—all this serves to confirm what has already been suggested about Michelangelo's character: that this eager reader of the Bible really only carried out what he wanted to, without obeying the convention of conforming to a "program" drawn up by theologists and humanists.

On May 10, 1508, Michelangelo had begun painting the ceiling, and by the beginning of 1511 it was half finished. On August 14, 1511, Julius II insisted on having it uncovered and he went to look at it "without waiting for the dust, that had resulted from having had the scaffolding removed, to settle" (Vasari). It was on October 31, 1512, four months before his death, that Julius II was finally able to reveal to Rome and the world the second half of the work. The next morning, on All Saints' Day, Mass was celebrated beneath the greatest masterpiece of the Renaissance, whose existence we owe chiefly to the stubborn belief of Julius II in Michelangelo's genius.

THE LAST JUDGMENT

When Clement VII de'Medici (1523–1534) traveled to France for the wedding of Catherine de'Medici with Henry of Orléans, he met Michelangelo for the last time, on September 22, 1533, in San Miniato al Tedesco. There is reason to believe that on that occasion the Pope gave the artist the commission for painting *The Last Judgment* on the altar wall of the Sistine Chapel. At that time, the sculptor was working on the tomb of Julius II and on the Medici tombs in San Lorenzo in Florence; however, by the time the Pope died, on September 25, 1534, the project had not extended beyond the stage of initial sketches. The following October, Paul III Farnese (1534–1549) was elected. Shortly afterwards, and accompanied by ten or twelve cardinals, he visited Michelangelo in his house in Macel de'Corvi, where he looked at the cartoon for the fresco. He ordered that it be carried out "without any alteration of the present concept or form" (Vasari).

This decision raises three questions, which are usually overlooked by most experts. First of all, why did Clement VII want to seize once again upon a theme of medieval iconography, and one that had hardly been dealt with during the Renaissance?

Secondly, why did he suggest for it a location which was not in conformity with the liturgical customs—namely, the wall behind the altar instead of the wall at the entrance? And, thirdly, what was so extremely important that caused this son of Lorenzo the Magnificent to destroy—since there was no longer any room in the chapel for frescoes—not only the initial paintings of the Moses and Christ cycle, but also the "Ancestors of Christ," which Michelangelo himself had painted in the lunettes twenty years earlier?

The answer to these can possibly be found in the especially tragic event that took place during the reign of Clement VII: the sack of Rome in May, 1527, which, at the time, was seen by everyone as the wrath of God for the excesses of the Renaissance. From his place of refuge in the fortress Castel Sant'Angelo, to which he had fled, the Pope was forced to look on helplessly while the soldiers of Charles V overran Rome with fire and sword. For him, this "dies irae" had remained a strong recollection and a warning; it was a kind of artistic psalm of penitence and a personal "mea culpa" for his hesitant policies, which had been partly to blame for the catastrophe.

When he confirmed Michelangelo's commission, Paul III had been faced with the same problem; since, however, he had nothing to do with the sack of Rome, he could not solve it by relying on the argumentation of his predecessor. Did he not have a motive that was equally important? The answer to this question can possibly be found in the most significant event of his pontificate: the ecumenical council for the reform of the Church, and its defense against attacks by the Protestants. This council, so ardently desired by the Pope ever since his election, was finally convened in Trent, in December, 1545.

The Last Judgment was painted while the preparations for the council were going on. It thus contains many allusions to theological themes, such as, for example, the efficacy of good works in reliance on the promise of salvation, the preeminence of the Pope, Mariolatry and the cult of the saints, and the use of the rosary. On the other hand, the theme of the fresco represented a glorification of the value of deeds (although disputed by Luther), for there can be no judgment if there are neither sins to be punished nor good deeds to be rewarded. For Paul III, the painted psalm of penitence of Clement VII became a grandiose manifesto for the approaching council.

The preparation of the wall in the Sistine Chapel began in April, 1535. The already existing frescoes on that wall were removed and the wall was set with bricks in such a way that it had a forward incline of 28 centimeters; this was done to keep dust from settling on the surface. It was sometime between April 10 and May 18, 1536, that Michelangelo began painting *The Last Judgment*.

As in the case of the ceiling, he worked alone, and he completed the work in the autumn of 1541. On October 30 of each year, Paul III had the painting uncovered and, the next day, celebrated Vespers in front of Michelangelo's "dies irae," a work that inspired Rome with "astonishment and admiration," as Vasari put it.

Michelangelo, 61 years old when he began painting this work, was 66 when it was finished. In a period of five years he had covered a surface area of somewhat 200 square meters with 390 figures, many of which measured more than 2.5 meters in height. As with the ceiling vault, he did not attempt here to integrate the painting into the architecture. Instead, he overcame the structural limitations of the wall and disclosed in the darkening heavens behind it the second coming of Christ—now no longer Savior, but Judge. He is a Judge who causes time to stand still, calling together all to "give an accounting, and to justify all woeful and incumbent deeds," as Michelangelo put it in his sonnet. With the exception of the two lunettes in the upper section, in which angels carry the instruments of torture, the work is divided into three horizontal segments. Each segment contains three sections: one to the left, one in the center, and one on the right. High above in the center section are Christ the Judge, with the Virgin Mary and the Apostles and Martyrs (St. John the Baptist, St. Peter, St. Paul, St. Andrew, St. Lawrence and St. Bartholomew). The elect are also gathered about him, the women on the left, the men on the right side. The central segment contains, in its middle section, the angels of Resurrection—to the left are the resurrected souls, striving heaven-ward, while the souls of the damned, on the right, sink into the abyss. In the middle of the lowest segment one can see, in an open, cavernous sea of flames, a group of mocking demons—to the left of them are the souls rising from the dead; to the right is Charon's bark, in which the sinners are ferried across to the dreaded shore where Minos awaits them. This partitioning into several overlapping segments conforms with the old iconographic scheme of this theme. Michelangelo, however, overcame the bounds of this scheme by means of a whirl of movement that seems to originate from the glittering trumpets of the angels; it glides over past the horrible cavern, ascends on the right-hand side, resumes its turbulent motion in the hand of Christ, and then, abruptly sinking, it disappears with the damned souls into hell's desolation.

It is in this fresco that, for the first time, stylistic elements of Michelangelo's so-called "third style" are discernible. It was a break with the perfect classical harmony of form and content that distinguishes, on the other hand, the ceiling vault. Later on, in his frescoes in the Cappella Paolina—the Conversion of St. Paul and the Crucifixion of St. Peter—, this new style is depicted in an aesthetic expressiveness which is completely foreign to the art of the Renaissance.

D. REDIG DE CAMPOS

left: 160) *Donation of the Keys*. Fresco by Perugino, on the right wall.

above: 161) *The Punishment of Korah and his Rebels*. Fresco by Botticelli, on the left wall.

right: 163) *The Last Worldly Deeds of Moses*. Fresco by Signorelli on the left wall.

above: 164) "The Death of Moses." Section, upper left, of the adjacent composition.

MICHELANGELO'S FRESCOES ON THE CEILING OF THE SISTINE CHAPEL

right: 165) An overall view of the ceiling.

above: 166) "The Separation of Light from Darkness." First composition in the center of the ceiling-vault.

below: 167) "The Creation of the Sun and the Moon." Second composition in the center of the ceiling-vault.

right: 169) "The Creation of Adam." Fourth composition in the center of the ceiling-vault.

below: 170) "Adam." A section from the adjacent fresco.

above: 171) "The Creation of Eve." Fifth composition in the center of the ceiling-vault.

right: 172) "The Fall of Man and Expulsion from Paradise." Sixth composition in the center of the ceiling-vault.

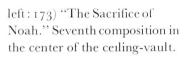

left: 173) "The Sacrifice of Noah." Seventh composition in the center of the ceiling-vault.

below: 174) "The Flood." Eighth composition in the center of the ceiling-vault.

above: 175) "Noah's Ark." A section from the previous fresco.

right: 176) "The Intoxication of Noah." Ninth composition in the center of the ceiling-vault.

below : 177) A portion of the ceiling frescoes, with the prophet Joel and the Eritrean Sibyl.

below: 178) The prophet Joel.

right: 179) The prophet Daniel.

lower right: 180) The prophet Jeremiah.

HIEREMIAS

left: 181) The Libyan Sibyl.

lower left: 182) The Persian Sibyl.

center: 183) The prophet Ezekiel.

right: 184) The Cumaean Sibyl.

lower right: 185) The prophet Isaiah.

CVMAEA

above: 186) The prophet Jonah.

left: 187) The prophet Zachariah.

right: 188) The Delphic Sibyl.

upper left: 189) *The Story of Haman.*
Fresco in the corner spandrel.

lower left: 190) *David and Goliath.*
Fresco in the corner spandrel.

right: 191) "Haman Crucified." A section
from illustration 189.

below: 192) *Judith Takes Leave of the Slain
Holofernes.* Fresco in the corner spandrel.

MICHELANGELO'S FRESCO OF
THE LAST JUDGMENT

right: 193) Overall view of the fresco along the frontal wall of the Sistine
Chapel.

next page: 194) Christ as judge. Center-piece of the *Last Judgment* fresco.

previous page : 195/196) Angels carry
the instruments of Christ's Passion.

left : 197) *The Last Judgment.*
Center and lower section.

lower left : 198) The angels of the
Resurrection sound their trumpets.

lower right : 199) The ferryman in
the Underworld, Charon.

right : 200) The Apostle
Bartholemew with the symbol of his
martyrdom, his skin.

HALLS AND CHAPELS

Since the time of Clement VII de'Medici (1523–1534), more renovation than restoration has been required as a result of the poor condition of the entire southwest section of the Papal palace—or, to be more exact, the rooms in which public ceremonies were held. A beginning was made in the Sala Ducale, which was partially finished when the Pope died. Paul III Farnese (1534–1549) commissioned Antonio da Sangallo the younger with the difficult task of completing a new building.

THE SALA REGIA

The greatest care was demanded by those rooms that belonged to the palace of Nicholas III, notably the Sala Regia, in which receptions for kings and their ambassadors were held, and the second section of the Sala Ducale. The Sala Regia was originally a gigantic hall with a raftered-ceiling that supported two floors. Following the razing of these two floors, Sangallo reinforced the outer walls, in order to erect upon them a vaulted ceiling resting upon a richly adorned cornice. With its new height of 18.9 meters (the other dimensions—33.6 meters by 11.8 meters—remained practically unaltered), the room was given a truly royal appearance, and this impression was reinforced by the generous use of gold for the friezes and the splendid stuccowork decoration of the barrel-vault. The architect himself designed the decoration—and this is documented by a sketch in the Gabinetto dei Disegni e delle Stampe in the Uffizi Gallery. It was executed by Perin del Vaga. He did the stuccowork, in which he inserted in the center-field the Pope's coat of arms, and the two ovals adorned with Greek crosses he decorated with the coats of arms of the Camera Apostolica.

According to Vasari, Perin del Vaga also had the walls prepared, "in order to design, with his own hands, stories in magnificent stuccowork, which were then carried on by the painter, Daniello Ricciarelli da Volterra." Nothing is left of the first work. The second work was destroyed by Francesco Salviati, who painted in its place a fresco—*Emperor Frederick Barbarossa Submits, in Venice, to Pope Alexander III* (illustration 212)—completed by Salviati's pupil, Giuseppe Porta, following Salviati's death. The historical event depicted by the painter is in conformity with the iconographic scheme for the room, which is supposed to represent "the dutiful subjugation and inferiority of earthly dignitaries to the priesthood" (Pastor).

Additional frescoes depict: *Otto I Gives the Church the Provinces that Belong to it*—attributed to Orazio Sammachini and Livio Agresti; *Peter of Aragon Takes his Realm as a Fief from the Pope*, by Livio Agresti; *Pippin III of France Donates Ravenna to the Church*, by Girolamo Siciolante da Sermoneta; *The Battle Near Tunis*, by Taddeo Zuccari (also responsible for the allegorical figures of Fame and Triumph above the door of the Cappella Paolina), although it was brought to completion by his brother, Federico. To celebrate his victory over the Turkish fleet, Pius V Ghisleri (1566–1572) had a fresco by Giuseppe Porta removed—*The Story of the Seven Kings*—to provide room for two large paintings recalling the Battle of Lepanto; carried out by Giorgio Vasari, it was later completed by Lorenzo Sabbatini. Also by Vasari and his assistants are *Gregory IX Excommunicates Emperor Frederick II; Gregory XI Returns to Rome from Avignon;* and the *St. Bartholomew's Night*. The decoration was interrupted time and again, and this also explains a number of additions and modifications. However, despite the heterogeneous nature of the artists and changing tastes, there is still a predominant style—that of mannerism—which endows the whole room with a unity of style, even in the face of the evident mediocrity of some of the artists. And even the pomposity has a certain elegance stemming from the strong white and gold of the decoration and from the architectural partitioning of the vault. It is only the architecture of Antonio da Sangallo that appears to be overwhelmed by the decoration, thus losing much of its simple geometric clarity.

THE SALA DUCALE

We have already mentioned that the Sala Ducale has a close relation to the Sala Regia. It consists of two sections—the aula secunda and the aula tertia. This second section is further to the east and had been used previously for Public Consistories. It belongs to the remains of a building by Innocent III, upon which the annexes of Nicholas III were erected. These two edifices originated at different times, and this fact explains the difference in the axes of the two sections. Bernini was able to correct this defect, or at least to extenuate it optically, by employing heavy opulent stucco drapery held by putti.

Unfortunately, this handsome and pleasant provisional solution was cancelled out by the renovation of the old terracotta floor covering. The new covering, set in a geometric pattern of many-colored marble, directs one's eye more than ever to the lack of uniformity of the axes and the irregularity of it all.

In this room, too, the decoration is mediocre, although it does contain some remarkable objects. On Sangallo's ceiling vault in the aula tertia is the coat of arms of Paul IV, who had it decorated by Pietro Venale with grotesques. Between them, according to a piece of false information from Baglione, Matteino da Siena is supposed to have painted landscapes depicting the Four Seasons. It is certain, though, that, during the reign of Pius IV de'Medici (1559–1565), Matteino did the grotesques on the south wall (those on the wall opposite did not originate until the pontificate of Benedict XV (1914–1922), shortly after the windows—furnished with Venetian blinds—had been walled up; it was through these windows that the women used to witness the ceremony of washing the feet of the poor: *"di dodici poveri, fatta del Papa il giovedi santo"*). On the other hand, the landscape on the frieze is attributed to a pupil of Giovanni da Udine—possibly to a certain Donato, who also assisted in the work on the third loggia. It is improbable that Jan Soens worked on the decoration, although he is given credit for the landscape in the fable by Phaedrus, *The Rooster and the Pearl*. Many critics also believe that Jan Soens collaborated with Mateo Bril on the landscape in the frieze of the aula secunda. Van Mander, however, is of the opinion that this is the work of Cesare Arbasia da Saluzzo, known as Cesare Piemontese. On the other hand, Lanciani reports that payments for the work in both these rooms went to Girolamo Gambatelli and Domenico Carnevali.

THE CHAPEL OF PIETRO DA CORTONA

The chapel is a small room, 4 meters by 4.4 meters; located at the southeast corner of the Torre Borgia, it is reached from the Stanza dell'Incendio. It is also known as the chapel of Urban VIII Barberini (1623–1644), at whose behest the Papal architects turned this room, in the year 1631, into a chapel. The work is documented by a series of payments (as listed by Pollak), and these were made to masons (December 19, 1631), to the painter, Simone Laghi, for "the gilding of the chapel in the old apartment" (September 1, 1631), and to Pietro da Cortona (September 12, 1634). *The Descent from the Cross, with the Evangelist, St. John, and Mary Magdalene,* in the fresco above the altar, is definitely the work of Pietro da Cortona. However, *Christ's Passion*—beneath the lunette—and the picture in the middle of the ceiling vault can be attributed to his pupils, who worked with sketches by their master. Richly gilded stucco ornaments enclose the various paintings and adorn the architectural forms. During the pontificate of Pius VI Braschi (1775–1799), passage through the chapel was permitted. This resulted in a connection between Raphael's Stanze and the Borgia Apartment beneath it, as well as between the Sistine Chapel and the Vatican Library.

THE GALLERIA DELLE CARTE GEOGRAFICHE

This Gallery of the Geographic Maps is 120 meters long and takes up most of the third floor in the long Secondo Braccio, which is in that wing of the palace that adjoins the west side of the Cortile del Belvedere. Bramante had already completed the east wing of the Cortile, but at his death only the foundation for the west wing had been laid. Until the accession of Pius IV de'Medici (1559–1565) this courtyard side remained closed off by a plain wall; this was then replaced by Pirro Ligorio (in conformity with the already completed wing) with a building consisting of a ground-floor and two storeys above it. It also had galleries which, though open toward the court, were later closed off. The third storey, already mentioned, was added on during the reign of Gregory XIII by the architect, Ottaviano Mascherino.

The gallery got its name from the topographic plans, or maps, of the various regions of Italy which embellish the corridor-like room. These include the islands of Sardinia, Sicily and Corsica, as well as the area around Avignon, at that time part of the Papal territories. The gallery also contains pictures of the most famous naval battles, as well as well-known ports and coastal cities.

The cartoons for the frescoes were done by Egnazio Danti. Pellegrino Danti, member of a noted family of mathematicians and cosmographers from Perugia, entered the Dominican Order in 1555, and assumed the name Egnazio. He soon excelled in the fields of mathematics and cosmography—there are a number of treatises by him—as well as in the field of art.

He had the professorship in mathematics, at first in Florence and later in Bologna, until Gregory XIII Boncampagni (1572–1585) appointed him in the year 1580 as Papal cosmographer and member of the commission for reforming the calendar. He was also commissioned with the decoration of this gallery. The work was not new to him. In Florence, Cosimo de'Medici had commissioned him with the painting of a number of maps on the cabinets of the so-called Guardaroba of the Palazzo Vecchio. The series in the Vatican consisted of 32 large frescoes, 16 on each wall, between the windows, "after I had carved Italy in half, with the help of the Apennines," as Danti himself wrote.

They are the perspective street-plans of the main cities, with depictions of the most important battles that had taken place in the area surrounding each respective city; the result was a successful synthesis of history and geography. In addition to these frescoes, mention should also be made of *The Siege of Malta* and *The Battle of Lepanto*, both on the narrower north wall, as well as the two frescoes located at the beginning of the long walls, *The Isle of Elba* and *The Tremiti Isles*. The harbors of Genoa and Venice are represented on the south wall, and, on the long walls adjoining it, are depictions of Ancona and Civitavecchia. Egnazio Danti has also told us that "the 80 scenes with figures on the ceiling vault above each fresco" depict traditional miracles from each province. These "scenes" are set into the rich and imaginative stucco and fresco ornaments with which the entire ceiling vault is embellished and which conform with the dominant note of this entire artistic creation: the mannerist style. Designed by Girolamo Muziano and Cesare Nebbia, the execution was entrusted to a group of artists that included Matteo da Siena, Antonio Tempesta, Paolo and Matteo Bril, and Marco da Faenza.

THE GALLERIA DEGLI ARAZZI

The tapestry gallery, originally an open loggia, is located between the Galleria delle Carte Geografiche and the Galleria dei Candelabri, all of which together form the floor of the "Secondo Braccio." Provided by Pius VI with a barrel-vault, it was selected by Gregory XVI (1831–1846) in 1838 to accommodate the famous tapestries which Pieter van Aelst had made, basing his work on designs prepared by Raphael and his pupils. Following many vicissitudes, the ten wall tapestries of the "scuola vecchia" (old school) finally found their place in the room in the Pinacoteca Vaticana devoted to Raphael.

Already known at that time as the Galleria degli Arazzi, the room continued to harbor another ten tapestries—those of the "new school," with depictions from the life of Jesus. Their artistic standard, somewhat inferior to the others, gives rise to the assumption that the designs are by Raphael's pupils, who may possibly have employed some of the master's sketches. The scenes represented are: *Slaughter of the Innocents* (three episodes); *Adoration of the Magi; Adoration of the Shepherds; Jesus in the Temple; Resurrection of Christ; the Banquet in Emmaus; The Ascension of Christ; Christ Resurrected before Maria Magdalena.* Mention ought also to made of the tapestry, *The Healing of the Centurion Cornelius,* woven in the first half of the 16th century in the studio of Vigevano.

Some years ago, another seven wall tapestries were hung here. They had been woven from 1663 to 1679 in the studio which Cardinal Francesco Barberini founded in 1627, which was directed by the Fleming, Giacomo van den Vliete. They had previously covered the walls of the main reception room in the Palazzo Barberini, the ceiling of which was decorated by Pietro da Cortona; the cartoons to these works are kept there today. After the tapestries had come into the possession of the Holy See, a thorough cleaning and restoration restored their former splendor, and they deserve to be hung alongside the tapestries of the school of Raphael.

Seven tapestries from the original series of ten from the Palazzo Barberini have been in the Vatican since April 17, 1937. They depict the following scenes from the life of Cardinal Maffeo Barberini, later Pope Urban VIII: 1. *Maffeo Barberini Receives the Doctoral Degree at the University of Pisa,* based on a design by Lazzaro Baldi. 2. *Monsignore Maffeo Barberini Regulating the Drainage of Lago di Trasimeno 1602,* based on a design by Urbano Ramanelli. 3. *Monsignore Maffeo Barberini is Appointed Cardinal.* 4. *Cardinal Maffeo Barberini is Elected Pope.* 5. *Contessa Matilde Bequeaths all Her Estates to the Holy See.* 6. *On November 18, 1626, Urban VIII Consecrates St. Peter's Basilica.* 7. *Urban VIII Annexes the State of Urbino,* based on a design by Domenico Cerrini. At this point we could mention another two tapestries which Angelo Roncalli, later Pope John XXIII, bought in 1947 from French antique dealers while he was Nuncio in Paris. These are: 8. *Urban VIII Approves of the Design for the Construction of Forte Urbana in Castelfranco Emilia* and 9. *Urban VIII Protects the City of Rome from the Plague and Famine.* In November, 1966, this series was completed through the permanent loan by the Musée Royale du Cinquantenaire in Brussels of a tenth tapestry: *Urban VIII Receives the Homage of the Nations.*

In 1956, some of the 19th century paintings which had been kept in the apartment of Pius V were placed in the rooms on the ground-floor of the Pinacoteca building. The thus vacated rooms, as well as the adjoining gallery, were restored and prepared to receive various tapestries from the 15th and 16th centuries. The extension and conclusion of the tapestry gallery can be found at the very end of the Galleria della Carte Geografiche—an intermezzo in keeping with the priceless collection. It is in this second section that two tapestries from Tournai (15th century)—*Passion and Faith*—and a 17th century series, made in Bruges according to designs by Cornelius Schut, a successor to Rubens—*The Fine Arts*—were fitting additions.

THE TORRE DEI VENTI

The architect Ottaviano Mascherino, already mentioned in connection with the construction of the third storey of the Secondo Braccio, was also responsible for building the Torre dei Venti. This tower, at the north end of the Galleria delle Geografiche, is 73 meters high and has three terraces whose size decreases in ascending order. It is in the tambour-like cupola of the second terrace that one finds the elegant heraldic symbol—the dragon—of the Boncompagni, family name of Pope Gregory XIII, who built this edifice. The lowest floor, planned as a celestial observatory, had originally an open loggia, whose arches were later closed by order of Urban VIII. Here, Nicholas Circignani, known as Il Pomarancio, painted *The Personification of the Winds*, which gave the tower its name. In addition, he painted *Apostle Paul's Shipwreck in Malta* on the south wall (the light coming through an aperture falls onto a meridian indicated on the floor), as well as *The Boat of the Apostle Peter* on the west wall. The decorative painting in the various rooms on the middle floor is, by unanimous agreement, the work of Matteo Bril, who put fantastic landscapes and lively little figures into the frieze that runs along the walls. Despite contrasting views, many experts today are of the opinion that the large panorama pictures in both rooms of the middle floor can be attributed to Paolo Bril (Hahn). Foggin believes that, following Matteo's death on June 8, 1583, they were completed by his brother, Paolo.

THE SALA DELLA CONTESSA MATILDE

This room, also known as "Galleriola del Romanelli," is the only remaining architectural monument in the Vatican dating back to the time of Urban VIII. Everything else was either re-done or restored—*"questo Papa essendo di restauro o di adattamento."* He had it built so as to create a passage between the "new" and the "old" sections, thus allowing one to avoid having to go through the loggie, which had provided the only connection. The Papal architects made use here of a free area between the apartment of Julius III and that of Gregory XIII. It measures 13 by 5 meters and was built by the "masons Scala and Ferrari," as a payment from August 18, 1631, indicates. Additional payments, from September 6 and December 15, 1637, suggest that the frescoes were executed by Giovanni Francesco Romanelli, who related in a clear style *The Most Important Scenes* from the Life of Contessa Matilde (after whom the gallery was named). These frescoes alternate with allegorical figures; in the middle of the two narrow sections above the door, supported by putti in stucco and flanked by allegorical figures in niches, is the coat of arms of Urban VIII. Additional scenes are on the ceiling, and these, too, alternate with allegorical figures.

MARIA DONATI BARCELLONA

THE CHAPEL OF NICHOLAS V

The chapel in the private rooms within the old Papal palace is known as the chapel of Nicholas V. It is on the second floor and can be reached from the "Stanza dei Chiaroscuri." Built by the humanist Pope Nicholas V Parentucelli (1447–1455), it was consecrated to the memory of the Deacons, St. Stephen and St. Lawrence. The chapel was painted by the Dominican, Fra Giovanni da Fiesole, known as Beato Angelico or Fra Angelico (1400–1455). He worked here from 1447 to 1451. According to accounts of that day, he created two other works in the Vatican—frescoes in a small work-room, and in the "Capella parva sancti Nicolai," which was destroyed by Paul III; these works, however, are not extant.

The chapel of Nicholas V has a cross vault that, in relation to the area—6.6 meters by 4 meters—is disproportionately high. This unusual ratio of size is explained by the fact that the chapel developed from two floors of a fortified tower. This was built by Innocent III (1198–1216) and incorporated by Nicholas III (1277–1280) into the initial Papal residence he built on the Vatican hill, today the center of the Renaissance palace. Inspired by the unusual height of the walls, Fra Angelico based his paintings on a medieval scheme. He told the story of the lives of the two saints in a series of large frescoes, the two equal in size and one above the other. By so doing, he followed the method Giotto had employed in Assisi and Parma. Unlike Giotto, he did not depict the scenes in chronological sequence, preferring to develop the story on the basis of analogous events against a uniform background. Between the arches on each side, the eight fathers of the Greek and Roman Churches are represented in Gothic niches, whereas the sections of the vault are used to depict the four Evangelists. The socle is decorated with painted drapery in various patterns and colors.

Nicholas V did not reside in this floor of the palace, but Julius II della Rovere (1503–1513) read Mass every day in this chapel, which was connected with his bedroom by a small door, now walled-up. There is reason to believe it was here, in this chapel, that Clement VII de'Medici (1523–1534) was at prayer when, on May 6, 1527, he heard the vanguard of the horde about to sack Rome; he was barely able to flee to the Castel Sant'Angelo.

The effects of the soldiers' destructive rage in this chapel were clearly seen during the renovation carried out from 1946 to 1951. On this occasion the socle, which Gregory XIII (1572–1585) had masked, was uncovered. It was also Gregory XIII who inserted a small window into the left wall, thus destroying a large section of the *Martyrdom of Saint Lawrence;* Papal artists managed no more than a poor job of repairing this damage. The altar, by then already lost—it was a *Descent From the Cross* by Fra Angelico—, was replaced by an ugly picture by Vasari. Since then, this picture has been superseded by a 15th century wooden cross against a crimson-red damask background. Every year on February 18th, the anniversary of Fra Angelico's death, a Mass is celebrated in the restored chapel.

The restorers' scaffolding has allowed the experts to make a thorough investigation of the frescoes. This has led to the discovery that all of the scenes in the chapel were painted by Fra Angelico himself, who permitted his assistants to lay hands only on unimportant parts of the room, as well as letting them do the decoration—especially in the upper part of the walls. On this project, Benozzo Gozzoli was one of his assistants. It is understandable that the work was carried out in this fashion, for Fra Angelico was a modest monk and he worked in the Vatican solely for Pope Nicholas V, to whom he was devoted.

An unusual problem was posed by another peculiarity that was discovered during the restoration. It is impossible to determine when each day's work was begun and ended on the various sections of the frescoes. There are absolutely no traces of powder or chalk, which are employed in transferring the cartoon on to the wall. On the first layer lies crude reddish Sinopia. The unusual fineness of the details is more appropriate to a miniature than to a painting, which has to be executed with the speed of a genuine fresco. Everything seems to indicate that the artist employed the fresco method only as a preparatory stage—that he actually carried out his designs in tempera, so resistant that it withstood the thorough cleaning. These artisan-like techniques, only just out of the 14th century, and the archaic partitioning of the walls are in keeping with the art of Fra Angelico, a pupil of Lorenzo Monaco. He strove toward certain stylistic values which would make clear his mystic vision of the universe; it was a vision he wished to transmit to the Renaissance without, however, completely ignoring the development in the field of painting.

THE CAPPELLA PAOLINA

The Cappella Paolina (like the Sistine Chapel, it is approached from the Sala Regia) was built in 1538 by Antonio da Sangallo the younger in commission from Paul III Farnese (1534–1549), whose name it bears. It was consecrated to St. Paul on January 25, 1540. As the Chapel of the Holy Sacrament, it replaced the 14th century chapel that had been consecrated to St. Nicholas. Although the latter had been painted completely in frescoes by Fra Angelico, in the process of extending the Scala del Maresciallo Sangallo had it torn down. It was the desire of the Pope that the new chapel be fitted out with frescoes to be painted by an artist who was no less important than Fra Angelico—by

Michelangelo Buonarroti. Here again we see the strange fate of this sculptor: he interrupted his work on his sculptures—the tomb of Julius II and the Medici tombs in San Lorenzo—to create the three great frescoes: the ceiling of the Sistine Chapel, *The Last Judgment* and the paintings in the Cappella Paolina. And in each case, the work was forced upon him by Popes and he accepted each commission with reluctance.

When the Pope asked Michelangelo to paint the new chapel, the altar wall of the Sistine Chapel had not even been unveiled. On two large surfaces (6.6 meters high and 6.25 meters long) along the side walls, two frescoes were to be painted: *The Conversion of St. Paul*, to the left of the entrance; and, to the right, *The Crucifixion of St. Peter*. Instead of the second theme, it seems that Michelangelo at first intended painting *Christ's Charge to St. Peter*, thus having the total effect of the decoration express the divine calling of the Apostle princes. The change in plan (if indeed there was one) must have been a very welcome one for Michelangelo, since the new theme contained much more "pathos." In any case, the main topic for theological discussions during the preparation for the Council of Trent was taken up in the Cappella Paolina: the glorification of Divine Grace by means of the clearest instance available—Saul, converted through repentance to Paul, a disciple of Christ, whose merciless persecutor he had been—, as well as the deeds of the true believer, Peter, whose voluntary martyrdom by crucifixion strengthened the faith of his brothers.

Although, starting with October, 1541, the execution of the frescoes was under discussion, the start of work on the project was postponed time and again; the reason for this was the still unconfirmed final contract with the Della Rovere heirs for the tomb of Julius II. In November, 1542, this contract finally arrived. As a notice dated November 16th indicates, a certain sum of money was paid "to Urbino, the servant of Master Michelangelo, painter, for the usual supply of paints for priming the chapel of St. Paul." This refers to the fresco that was the first to be completed, *The Conversion of St. Paul*. On the day it was finished, July 12, 1545, the Pope saw it, after having read Mass in the Sistine Chapel.

On August 10, 1545, Urbino was paid for the expenses incurred in preparing the other wall. It follows then that Michelangelo must have begun shortly after this date with the work on *The Crucifixion of St. Peter*. He completed the fresco in March, 1550, "after arduous exertion," as he told Vasari, "since painting, and especially fresco painting, is no art for an old man." A dispatch by the Florentine envoy to Cosimo I de'Medici notes that Paul III, at that time 82 years old, on October 13, 1549, "ascended ten or twelve rungs of a ladder to get a look at Buonarroti's painting in the chapel, which His Holiness had commissioned."

In his representation of Saul's miraculous conversion, Michelangelo conscientiously followed the New Testament text (Acts of the Apostles IX, 3–8). On his journey to Damascus, where he intended taking the small Christian community prisoner, Saul was struck down by a bright light, and the voice of God called out his name. The scene is depicted on two levels. High up on the wall and unusually shortened, Christ hurls the flash of lightning, surrounded by a group of angels without wings. In the lower section of the fresco, Saul has fallen off his horse, which rears up and gallops off. Slowly, and supported by the men journeying with him, he rises and tries to ward off the unearthly light with his hand, a light that penetrates his soul, exposing his hidden face. Around him is the confusion of his followers, struck with terror by the thunder and the invisible voice.

The ideal of the classical balance between form and content is completely missing here, in contrast to the ceiling of the Sistine Chapel, where it is supremely present. In *The Last Judgment*, this balance has been weakened somewhat by the marked emphasis placed on ethical considerations over those of an aesthetic nature. The sole significance of this picture lies in the passionate dialogue that takes place between Man and God, who, although he strikes Saul down, raises him up at the same time. This is (to use musical concepts) the expressive and melodic line of the composition. The rest is merely harmonic accompaniment. The fallen Apostle and the companions who support him are among the most marvelous figures ever created by Michelangelo—measured against even the aesthetic values embodied by the ceiling of the Sistine Chapel. If, however, one measures the angels and the scattering soldiers with the same standard, one must come to the conclusion that many of them are "incorrect," an opinion shared by his contemporaries. The total effect of the composition is anti-classical: the sky runs diagonally upward to the city of Damascus on the right-hand side of the picture; it is so much in contrast to the group of figures on the left-hand side that one gets the impression they are falling.

The Crucifixion of St. Peter on the opposite wall is completely different, as if Michelangelo wanted to gather his thoughts following the confusion of *The Conversion of St. Paul*. The scenery here is constructed with almost architectural stability; the groups are clearly delineated. They possess an inner coherence and are governed by varying sentiments, like those in *The Last Judgment*. In the center is St. Peter, nailed to the cross with his head downward; he attempts to stare into the eyes of those who are looking at him. Compared to the other figures, he is a giant. He is in a position to free himself from the cross and to put his persecutors to flight, but this he does not wish to do. A circular, rhythmical movement is formed by his arms and by those of his executioners, who are busily involved in setting up the cross. A second, heavier movement begins beyond the edge of the picture, ascends with the small group of legionaries at the edge of the lower left-hand corner, surrounds the cross, descends and declines with the youth carrying the beam on his shoulder, only to ascend finally in the figures of weeping women in the lower right-hand corner. This slow movement integrates and absorbs, on the left-hand side, the mounted soldiers and, on the right-hand side, a group of people who, though stiffened by sorrow, are too frightened to protest against what is happening. These are two symbolic groups. Like Savonarola, whom Michelangelo greatly admired, St. Peter was the victim of a disgraceful, although "legal" law, as well as of the cowardice of his followers. The law is represented here by he imperious bearing of the centurion; weakness is depicted by the other giant who, with crossed arms and lowered head, acquiesces like a Dacian prisoner to his fate. It is only the sole figure of a young man, in the upper portion of the middle group, who tries in vain to stem the inexorable course of fate; he urges the Righteous to remonstrate, but an allusion to the approaching soldiers silences even him, while an old man holds fast to his arm. Just as unimpressed by the danger of the situation are the women in the foreground, whose womanly sympathy is stronger than cowardly caution; and they are unable to hide their sorrow. The fateful current also fails to reach a blonde youth kneeling beneath the cross in the direction of the ditch. This figure illustrates a new concept of the *"cupio dissolvi"* (death wish), which the aging Michelangelo expresses in his later poetry and in his final *Pietà*. The young man has discarded both shovel and axe (painted in an eerie transparency) and plunges his naked arms deeply into the cold ground; it is almost as if he wanted to sink into the ground, drawn by the *"dolce calma"* of death.

D. REDIG DE CAMPOS

RIGHT: 205) *Descent from the Cross.* Painting by Pietro da Cortona in the chapel of Urban VIII.

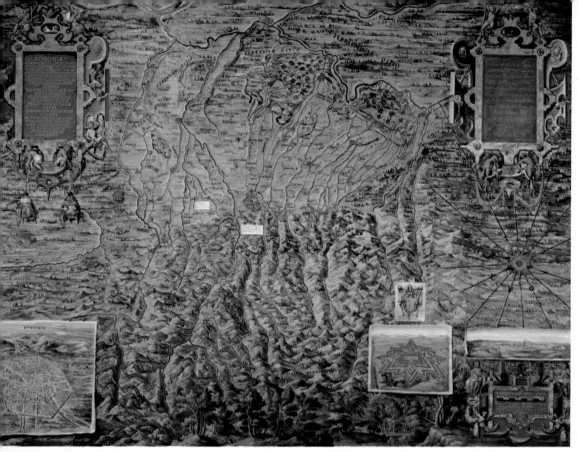

GALLERIA DELLE
CARTE GEOGRAFICHE

left: 206) The areas ruled by Bologna.

lower left: 207) Venice.

lower right: 208) Civitavecchia.

right: 209) A view of Malta.

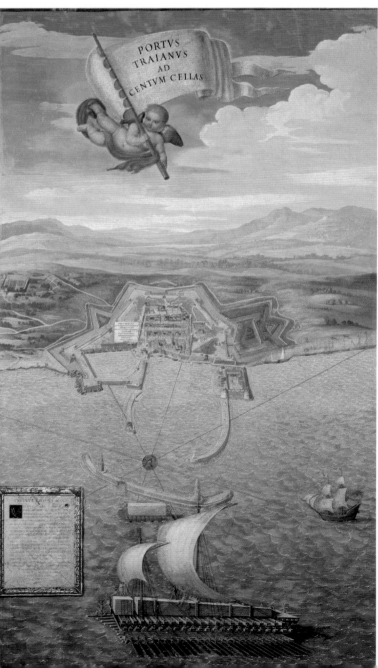

THE ANCIENT SCULPTURE COLLECTION

When Cardinal Giuliano della Rovere acceded to the Papal throne as Julius II in the year 1503, he had a statue of Apollo transferred from the garden of his titular church, S. Pietro in Vincoli, to the Vatican. He had it placed in the Belvedere court, thereby giving it its world-famous sobriquet of "Apollo of Belvedere." With the setting-up of this statue (illustration 237), the Papal collection of ancient sculpture in the Vatican began.

THE HISTORY OF THE COLLECTION

The *Laocoön* group soon joined it (illustration 256). Felix de Fredis, who discovered it, was amply rewarded by the Pope. His tombstone in the church of S. Maria in Aracoeli designates the re-discovery of *Laocoön* as his undying feat. It was January 14, 1506, that the statue was discovered, not far from the Sette Sale on the Esquiline. There, where Nero's Golden House had stood and where Emperor Trajan had had his thermal baths erected, Felix de Fredis had his vineyard. The discovery created a sensation. How strong the recollection of this event was in the memory of Francesco da Sangallo 61 years later is indicated by his letter from February 28, 1567: "I was still very young and for the first time in Rome when the Pope was brought the news that several very beautiful statues had been found in a vineyard next to S. Maria Maggiore. The Pope ordered a groom to go to Giuliano da Sangallo (my father) and to tell him to go there immediately. My father left right away. Michelangelo Buonarroti was at that time almost constantly a guest at our house, since his own house—which my father was building—was not yet completed. My father wanted him to accompany him. I went along without having been asked. We had hardly descended to the place where the statues were when my father said: 'That is the *Laocoön*, that Pliny mentions.'" The Pope acquired the *Laocoön* group by a breve on March 23, 1506, only a few weeks before the foundation stone was laid for the reconstruction of St. Peter's. Since that day, poets have written inspired verses in praise of the ancient masterpieces in the statuary court of Belvedere; artists imitate them, indeed they use them as standards of quality, and the approach art historians use today had its beginning here. "*Apollo* and *Laocoön* have become since then the most admired and most popular works of art" (Ferdinand Gregorovius).

The original garden in the Belvedere court, as it was designed by Julius II and Bramante, was a sweet-smelling orange grove embellished with ancient sculptures. This garden, *hortulus* or *viridarium* as it was called, was still without a colonnade; it was the inner court of the summer villa of Innocent VIII Cibo (1484–1492). The statue of Apollo was given the corner location it still has today. Next to it, and dominating the center of the wall, was the *Laocoön* group. The *Venus Felix* and an Anteus group were also here, as well as sarcophagi decorated with reliefs. Among the latter was the depiction of captured barbarians before the victorious general (illustration 300), and, above a bubbling fountain, the statue of the sleeping Ariadne, who was called Cleopatra in the Renaissance. So it was that the Pope created a secluded corner for himself; from the eastern vestibule, he sees the city at his feet and looks out onto the broad Tiber valley as far as the hills that enclose it.

In his *Privilegium* to the Tacitus edition by Filippo Bervaldo, Leo X Medici (1513–1521), son of Lorenzo Magnifico and the successor to Julius II, wrote: "Ever since the earliest days of youth, we have been accustomed to the thought that the Creator has given mankind nothing more important or more useful, aside from the awareness and adoration of His divinity itself, than those studies which not only serve to ennoble and beautify man's life, but which are also practicable and useful in every situation: consoling us in misfortune, and salutary and honorable in prosperity, the more so that we would have to renounce all the grace of life and all the obligations of the community if we were without them."

By these studies, the Pope was also referring to the involvement with ancient sculpture, thereby giving the collection its deeper purpose.

During the pontificate of Leo X, the river deities were set up in the Belvedere court. *The Nile* (illustration 260) was excavated in the year 1513 near the church of S. Maria sopra Minerva, on the site of a former ancient Serapis and Isis temple. The figure of the so-called *Tigris* has no distinguishing marks; its name goes back to the restorer, who installed a tiger mask in the urn. Around the opening of the vessel, he affixed a ring with the emblem of Pope Leo X.

The fame of the ancient, classical statues in the Belvedere court at that time was reflected in the desire of Francis I, the victor at Marignano (1515) to have the *Laocoön* group from the Pope. Leo X cleverly avoided the difficulty by commissioning Baccio Bandinelli to make a copy. It never got to France; it was instead placed in the court of the Medici palace in Florence. That was in 1531, during the reign of Clement VII. Following this unsuccessful attempt to carry off the *Laocoön* as a trophy of war (something that, almost 300 years later, Napoleon succeeded in doing), in 1540 Francis I ordered Primaticcio to get casting models of the renowned statues in the Belvedere for him. He had the classical statues re-cast in bronze and set up in his royal palace at Fontainebleau. This was done, according to Vasari, because it was the will of the king that a new Rome take shape. This example was emulated in 1560 by Philip IV of Spain, who had no less distinguished an artist than Velázquez make molds of the chief works of art in the Belvedere court, so as to have the bronze re-casts placed in his newly erected palace in Madrid. In the 18th and 19th centuries, casts were made with plaster, but no one knows how many of them were made. There is hardly a princely court or an academy of art which does not pride itself on having the *Apollo* or the *Laocoön*.

When the Dutchman, Hadrian VI, was Pope (1522–1523), he called the classical statues "heathen idols" and had the pleasure garden of the Belvedere closed, even though, under his predecessor, it was open to all. Only Venetian envoys managed to enter it, and their reports of the *Laocoön* are graphic and enthusiastic: "It is incomprehensible how human art can create anything so great and natural."

Giulio de'Medici, the cousin of Leo X and, as Pope, Clement VII (1523–1534), was, unlike Hadrian, fond of spending hours in the statuary garden of Belvedere. Benvenuto Cellini notes in his autobiography how he went into the Belvedere on the holy-day of the year 1524 to play the most beautiful motets at the table of the Pope. Despite the sack of Rome in May, 1527, which caused little real damage to the classical statues, Clement VII was able to acquire additional sculptures and to have them placed in the Belvedere court. Among them was the *Torso* (illustration 248), which, like the *Apollo*, got its name from this site, although it had spent hundreds of years at the Palazzo Colonna. Nothing is known of its origin, and it was Michelangelo's great admiration for it that secured the *Torso* its place of honor. The Genoese painter Giovanni Battista Paggi wrote that, as a student, he used to draw the *Torso del Belvedere*, and he confessed that later on he often studied it exhaustively. Bernini hands down this utterance of Michelangelo's: "Indeed, that was made by a human being who was wiser than nature itself! Too bad that it's a torso!" And as late as the year 1759, Johann Joachim Winckelmann's renowned description relies on Michelangelo's regard for it. The *Torso* is the only piece among the famous classical sculptures in the Belvedere that has not undergone alteration. When Pope Clement VII saw Baccio Bandinelli's restoration of the *Laocoön* group (completed in 1531), he decided henceforth to surround himself only with completely intact classical sculpture. In the early part of 1532, Michelangelo recommended his assistant, Giovanni Angelo Montorsoli, for such restoration work. He restored the *Laocoön*, basing his work on the design for the restored copy. *Apollo* followed, but his left hand and the fingers of the right hand are missing. Earlier visitors to the Belvedere court had already pointed out that *Apollo* had to be restored as an archer, like the late 15th century bronze statuette by Antico. In 1512 with express reference to Homer, Giovanni Francesco Pico della Mirandola declared the statue to be *Apollo Pharetratus,* Apollo with the quiver.

It was under Paul III Farnese (1534–1549) that the last of the renowned classical statues was placed in the Belvedere court: the so-called *Antinous*, a statue of Hermes (illustration 281). As a document from the Papal bursar notes, the Roman citizen Nicolaus de Palis was paid 1,000 gold ducats on February 27, 1543, "for a very beautiful marble statue which he presented to His Holiness and which the Pope had placed in the Belvedere garden." There is reason to believe that this statue was *Antinous,* for it had been found in the de Palis garden not far from Castel Sant'Angelo.

While Paul III Farnese and Julius III Ciocchi del Monte (1550–1555) were concerned with the classical collections of their families, with the accession of the Theatine monk, Gian Pietro Carafa, as Paul IV (1555–1559), the spirit of reform entered the Vatican. This spirit re-awakened the age-old hostility which the first Christians had felt toward the heathens of antiquity, and was responsible for Daniele da Volterra painting loin-cloths over the nude figures in Michelangelo's *Last Judgment*. Interesting in this respect is the remark made by Michelangelo, recorded by Vasari, that the Pope would do better to change the people than the paintings. The outlook that caused the naked statues of antiquity to be furnished with fig-leaves *"per decenza,"* elicted this comment from Winckelmann, in his letter to Bianconi on September 1, 1758: *"non è poco che non le abbia fatte castrare all'uso di serraglio del Gran Turco."*

The next Pope, Pius IV (1559–1565), from the Milanese family of the Medici, proved to be generous in the collection and donation of classical sculpture. Four boat-loads of classical sculpture were shipped to his name-sake in Florence, Duke Cosimo, as a sign of gratitude for the latter's aid and counsel, and he was just as unsparing in embellishing his own buildings with classical statues. The Casino, designed by Pirro Ligorio, was conceived largely in view of this form of adornment, and the inscription reads: *Pius IV pontifex maxiumus lymphaeum hoc condidit antiquisque statuis exornavit*. When the tournament grounds of the lower Belvedere court were dedicated, during carnival in the year 1565, they contained at least eighty statues and busts.

During the pontificate of Pius IV, the statues in the Belvedere court were dealt a bitter blow. The niches were enclosed in wooden boxes as a form of protection against ignorant and vandalous visitors. This must have taken place by at least 1565, since it is mentioned by Bernardo Gamucci in his book, *Antichità di Roma,* which appeared in that same year. The statues were to remain in this prison-like state for more than two hundred years. Thus it was that Raphael Mengs and Johann Joachim Winckelmann saw "the school of refinement, that shrine of the arts, the greatest accomplishment of sculpture" (Visconti), "the most unusual site for the arts in all Italy, indeed in the entire world" (Lalande). It was not until Clement XIV, and the founding of his museum in the year 1770, that the gods of antiquity in the Belvedere were liberated.

Not even a zealot like Pius V Ghislieri (1566–1572) dared touch the domain of the Belvedere court, although he gave away the statues on the tournament grounds and in the Casino of Pius IV, terming them "profane." Some of these sculptures were given to the people of Rome and placed on the Capitol, as an inscription there notes: *Senatus populusque Romanus statuas marmoreas PiiVpont. max. dono e Vaticano in Capitolium translatas... his posuit.* Pius V thus followed a precedent set by Sixtus IV one hundred years earlier when, in 1471, he transferred the classical bronze statues in and around the Lateran palace to the keeping of the Roman conservators.

If the 17th century brought the Vatican neither an increase nor decrease in its collection of classical sculpture, it did witness the development of some of the most glorious private collections, especially those in the hands of Papal relatives. Roman families in the 18th century viewed their inherited monuments from antiquity as a means to improve their finances. To prevent the conveyance of classical sculpture from Rome, the Popes, as sovereings of the Papal States, assumed responsibility for the arrangement and enlargement of the collections on the Capitol. Clement XII Corsini assigned to it, in 1733, the collection he had acquired from Cardinal Alessandro Albani; it was for the same cardinal that Winckelmann later on laid out the renowned collection in the Villa Albani. The next year, 1734, the Pope opened the Capitoline Museum, the first public museum. In 1750, Benedict XIV donated a famous statue of Aphrodite, the Capitoline Venus. By the second half of the 18th century there was no further exhibition space left in the crowded Capitoline collections, so Clement XIV Ganganelli (1769–1774), whose pontificate began one year after Winckelmann's death, found it necessary to create a new sculpture collection in the Vatican.

Two acquisitions in the year 1770 convinced Clement to make the Belvedere statuary court the focal point of a new museum: in August of that year he purchased for 4,000 scudi the Fusconi collection, to which the famous statue of *Meleager* by Scopas belonged (illustration 247); and one month later, he bought for 4,300 scudi the Mattei collection. There was no intention of installing the statues in the collections attached to the Library, the Museo Sacro, which Benedict XIV had founded in 1756; nor was any provision made for placing the classical works in the Museo Profano, which had been set up in 1767 by Clement XIII on the initiative of Cardinal Alessandro Albani. The requisite renovation in the summer villa of Innocent VIII began in 1771. Alessandro Dori was appointed architect and, after his death in January, 1772, he was succeeded by Michelangelo Simonetti. Toward the end of 1772, the first open loggia on the north side of the palazzetto was established as a sculpture gallery. In 1773, the old statuary court of Belvedere lost its orange trees, receiving instead an octagonal portico, based on a design by M. Simonetti (Cortile Ottagono).

The Pope collected the best that he could acquire in Rome and its vicinity by means of purchase, bequest and excavation: in May, 1771, the sedentary sculpture of *Jupiter Verospi;* in April, 1772, the statue of *Hera Barberini* (illustration 241); in August, 1772, the *Ara Casali;* and, in June, 1774, a section of the Museo Kirkeriano, following the disbanding of the Society of Jesus on July 21, 1773. The sculptures were installed under the supervision of Giambattista Visconti, successor to Winckelmann as the Commissario alle Antichità. The sculptor Gaspare Sibilla assisted him as restorer, but his actual advisor was his Minister of Finance, the Monsignore, and later Cardinal, Gian Angelo Braschi, who was wise enough to set up a lottery, the abundant revenue accruing therefrom making possible the acquisitions. In 1775, Braschi succeeded to the Papal throne as Pius VI. Pius VI (1775–1779) spared neither time nor money in his efforts to increase the collection initiated by his predecessor. He was assisted in this by his treasurer, Guglielmo Pallotta; his commissioner of antiquities, Giambattista Visconti; his sons, Ennio Quirino and Filippo Aurelio; and the sculptors Gaspare Sibilla, Giovanni Pierantoni and Francesco Antonio Franzoni. All available classical sculpture was assembled at the Vatican: from the Castel Sant'Angelo came the busts of Hadrian; from S. Constanza, the porphyry sarcophagus of the daughter of Constantine the Great (illustration 300); and, from the Lateran, the sarcophagus of St. Helena (illustration 299). By means of pre-emption, the Pope secured for himself the finds of the numerous excavations, including the *Zeus of Otricoli* (illustration 231) and the statue of *Apollo Citaredo* from the villa of the same name of M. Brutus, near Tivoli (illustration 239). Thanks to his endeavors, the Vatican was able to acquire the finds made in the Scipio grave, which was re-discovered in 1780 and caused a great sensation. He also purchased works of sculpture from sculptor-art dealers like Albacini, Cavaceppi and Pacetti, as well as from Hamilton and Jenkins. His zeal for collecting was not only focussed on statues, reliefs, sarcophagi, architectural ornaments and mosaics, for he loved miniature art, which he placed in the collections of the Library. He wished to create a new museum stretching from the Belvedere to the art collections of the Vatican Library and he succeeded in this endeavor in unparalleled fashion. It lives on today as the Museo Pio-Clementino.

In May, 1776, Pius VI entrusted his master-builder, Michelangelo Simonetti, with the new museum's plans. Mantegna's decorated chapel fell victim to the extension of the Galleria delle Statue. At this spot one can read today an inscription, whose letters have been set in bronze into the floor: *Pius sextus pontifex maximus museum ab hoc lapide ad bibliothecam a fundamentis erexit ornavitque.* In 1780 the Gabinetto delle Maschere, adjacent to the Galleria delle Statue, was completed; its name comes from a mask mosaic found in the floor of Hadrian's villa in Tivoli. The ceiling paintings by Domenico de Angelis refer to the statues of Venus displayed here. It was in the same year that the Sala a Croce Greca and the Sala Rotonda were completed. The first of these got its name from its ground plan, which is in the form of a Greek cross, and it was here that the two porphyry sarcophagi were placed. The Sala Rotonda, a masterpiece of Simonetti's, was inspired by the Pantheon. It is perfectly suitable for the exhibition of colossal works of sculpture, statues of gods and of heroic mortals. The gigantic, superb fountain was struck from one single piece of porphyry, and was set up in the center of the room in February, 1792; it originates from Nero's domus aurea and, under Clement XIV, had already graced the middle of the Belvedere statuary court. The two connecting rooms between the Sala Rotonda and the Belvedere court, the Sala delle Muse and the Sala degli Animali, were finished in 1782, in the seventh year of the Pope's pontificate. The first of these rooms is named after its chief attraction, a statuary group of the muses with Apollo as their leader, playing the cithara (illustration 239). The frescoes in the dome, painted by Tommaso Conca, also refer to these statues. The other room received its appelation from the animal sculptures therein, joined together to evoke the tranquillity of some unique zoo. The statue of *Meleager* (illustration 247) has also found its final site in this room. Thus Simonetti built his rooms, with decoration often having a thematic background. He avoided long galleries as well as small individual rooms all in a row. With great imagination, he brought cohesion to the buildings in the northern section of the Vatican.

The lay-out of the entrance to the museum was conceived in 1784, while the execution—with the Atrio dei Quattro Cancelli as ground-floor and the Sala della Biga as the upper floor—extended over a period of almost ten years. The collecting zeal of the Pope was still in no way exhausted. In 1788 the open loggia over the Museo Profano of the Library was closed and prepared for service as a museum. The suite of rooms is divided by six open arches with columns. On either side of these arches, ranged in pairs, are marble candelabra, which give this part of the museum the name Galleria dei Candelabri. To be found here is the statuette of the *Tyche of Antioch on the Orontes* (illustration 259), as well as the sarcophagi of Protesilaus and the children of Niobe (illustrations 295, 297). The Scala Simonetti joins this tract with the rest of the museum.

If the exterior appearance of the museum buildings is plain, one is indeed astonished by the festive splendor of the interior. The immense quantity of sculpture does not detract from the architecture; rather, sculpture and architecture form a harmonious blend. The master-builder of the Papal court, Simonetti—whose assistant, Giuseppe Camporese, succeeded to the post after his death—succeeded in creating an environment ideally suited to the importance of the art works. Truly a magnificent example of a museum in Roman style.

The Pope wanted very much to have his collection published, so the commissioner of antiquities, Giambattista Visconti, prepared a splendid work, with illustrations and explanatory text. The first volume appeared in 1782, and following his father's death in 1784, Ennio Quirino continued the publication. The sixth volume appeared in 1796, and the seventh and final volume in 1807. The fame of the Vatican collections was thus disseminated—a collection that contemporaries held to be the ideal form for a museum.

Pius VI died at the age of 82 on August 29, 1799, in Valence on the Rhône as a "prisoner in foreign land," and "the last and most venerable victim of the French Revolution." His successor, Pius VII Chiaramonti, was elected on March 14, 1800, in Venice. When he arrived in Rome, on July 3, 1800, the major works of his collection had been delivered to the French and brought to Paris, according to the terms of the treaty of Tolentino (February 19, 1797). Seeking to remedy the situation, he acquired sculptures by Canova, including the statue of *Perseus* (completed in April/May, 1801) and those of the boxers *Kreugas and Damoxenos* (1802). This latter work was set up, as a political document of the museum's fate, in the statuary court of Belvedere. It was placed opposite the *Apollo di Belvedere,* which had to be replaced by a plaster model until the original was returned in 1816.

With a letter from Cardinal Doria, and in the name of the Pope, on August 10, 1805, Antonio Canova was appointed to the post of Ispettore generale della Antichità e Arti in Roma ed in tutto lo Stato Pontificio. In the years 1807 to 1810, the Museo Chiaramonti—named after Pope Pius VII—was installed in the part of the corridor facing the

Palazzetto del Belvedere; this corridor connects the Papal palace with the former summer villa of Innocent VIII, and had already been built by Bramante under Julius II. An epigraphic collection, begun by Clement XIV, was considerably increased under Pius VI. Canova had it installed in the section facing the Papal palace, and it was classified and set up by Gaetano Marini. The Museo Chiaramonti, which is divided into 29 compartments by plain pilasters, contained classical sculpture of every kind and quality: originals and copies, statues of gods and portraits in stone and bronze, altars and architectural ornaments, urns and sarcophagi. In the fifteen lunettes, painters of the Accademia di S. Luca were commissioned by Canova to depict the Pope's activities as patron of the arts.

Napoleon's defeat in 1815 presented the possibility for returning the museum treasures. The Secretary of State, Cardinal Consalvi, represented Rome's interests and Wilhelm von Humboldt and the Duke of Wellington were successful in their efforts to break the understandable resistance of the French commissioners. In 1816, Canova was able to bring the classical sculpture back to the Vatican, with the exception of the deity of the River Tiber. It was an event which the picture by Francesco Hayez in a lunette of the Museo Chiaramonti has captured for posterity.

The return of the classical sculpture from Paris expedited the plans for extending the museum, a prime concern of Pius VII since 1805/6. The man chosen to carry out the project was Raffaele Stern, architect of the Apostolic See. The Braccio Nuovo runs between the two long, corridor-like arms of Bramante's court, above the library wing of Sixtus V (1585–1590) and parallel to it. Although intended to be no more than a connecting link, the Braccio Nuovo imparts the impression of an integral building, consisting of a large center-hall with dome and apse, as well as two similar barrel-vaulted side-wings. The antique-looking interior architecture appears to have been the optimum solution for a museum devoted to classical art; even the setting of the statues in niches harks back to antique decoration. *The Nile* (illustration 260) was given a new location under the dome, in the central hall; ever since the days of Leo X it had stood over a spring in the middle of the Belvedere court, together with *The Tiber* (which remained in the Louvre). This inscription can be read above the entrance to the Museo Chiaramonti: *Pius VII pont. max. novum claustrum signis ab se recuperatis comparatisque asservandis destinatum a fundamentis erexit anno sacri principatus XVIII.* Raffaele Stern died on December 30, 1820. The Braccio Nuovo was completed under the direction of Pasquale Belli and was opened on February 14, 1822. In that same year, a few months later, Canova died; in the year thereafter, Pius VII died. The Vatican sculpture collection was also considerably enlarged by individual finds: the *Atleta Apoxyomenos* by Lysippus (illustration 265) was found in 1849 in Trastevere; the *Augustus of Primaporta* (illustration 275) was found in 1863 in Livia's villa; the colossal bronze statue of *Hercules* was found in 1864 at Pompey's theater; and the Cancelleria reliefs (illustration 278) were uncovered in 1937/39 under the Palazzo della Cancelleria Apostolica. It was not until the 1960s, however, that a new museum for classical sculpture was built, when it became necessary to find a new home for the Lateran collections.

Pope Gregory XVI Cappellari (1831–1846), founder of the Etruscan and Egyptian Museum, had Giuseppe de Fabris, director-general of the museums, install a collection of classical sculpture in the ground-floor of the Lateran palace: the Museum Gregorianum Lateranense. The palace, which Pope Gregory XVI had first ordered renovated, was built between 1586 and 1589 by Domenico Fontana for Sixtus V. It housed, at first, casts of the Parthenon sculpture, royal gifts from Ludwig I of Bavaria and George IV of England. In 1839, the Antonelli family from Terracina bequeathed to the Pope the statue of *Sophocles* that had been found on their property (illustration 267). This was a worthy inducement to create a new, large museum of antiquity in the Lateran, and it was opened on May 14, 1844. Thus it was that, in addition, the statue of *Marsyas* (illustration 245), the Attic three-figure relief with Medea and the daughters of Pelias (illustration 252), and the front of the large philosopher's sarcophagus (illustration 298), all previously hidden away in the Vatican warehouses, were finally given a fitting exhibition area. In 1854, under Pius IX, and following the convening of the commission for Christian Archaeology, the Museo Cristiano Lateranense was founded. In contrast to it, since then the Museo Gregoriano in the Lateran palace has been called Museo Profano Lateranense. Pius IX occasionally participated personally, between 1855 and 1870, in the excavations in Ostia and transferred many of the finds to the Lateran Museum. The casts were eventually supplanted by additional numerous sculpture finds in Cerveteri, on the Via Latina, the Via Appia and the Via Labicana. Benedict XV Marchese della Chiesa (1914–1922) had the works re-classified. The final inscription in the Lateran palace notes that Pope John XXIII Roncalli (1958–1963) intended having this Apostolic palace restored and that Pope Paul VI Montini completed the project in 1967.

In 1963, the collections of the Lateran palace were transferred to the Vatican. A new building tract—*Romanoque ausu*, as the dedication text states—was built by a team of architects under direction of the Passarelli brothers; this was north of the Pinacoteca and parallel to it. Since June 15, 1970, the classical and early Christian antiquities have been displayed in their new quarters. A systematic re-arrangement of the antique sculpture was applied. Copies and re-castings of Greek prototypes from the classical era have been placed together, and the Roman sculpture from the late republic to the end of the empire has been chronologically and typologically arranged. The display of sculpture, minus its disfiguring traces of earlier restoration, was arranged for didactic coherence, and this called for a new kind of exhibition technique for which there was no precedent.

The systematically arranged display of classical sculpture in the Vatican museums was made public in 1960, with the opening of the Salette degli Originali Greci. The occasion was the re-discovery, by Hermine Speier, of a horse's head from Athena's brace of horses, formerly on the west pediment of he Parthenon (illustration 235). This horse's head is the focal point around which the Greek originals have been placed; difficult to locate, these pieces had previously been scattered through various sections of the museums.

SELECTION AND ARRANGEMENT OF THE ILLUSTRATIONS

The Popes collected classical sculpture out of love and admiration for art. Thus it was that, toward the beginning of the 16th century, the statuary court of the Belvedere, with its select works of art, developed. These works were held to be standards of excellence, models of perfection. When, in the 18th century, the export of classical works from Rome had run riot, the Popes stepped in as preservers and guardians of this heritage. Every fragment of an antique work of art was valuable enough to be kept as a document and expression of timeless humanity. This spirit of non-historic classicism and humanism is reflected in the abundant fullness of the Museo Pio-Clementino; its brilliant interpreter, Ennio Quirino Visconti, believed that classical art—from Pericles to Hadrian, from the 5th century B.C. to the 2nd century A.D.—must be maintained at the same high standard. Acting accordingly, he divided his catalogue into classes of monuments (statues, reliefs, and busts, including the hermae) and Appendix Miscellanea. These classes he subdivided into depictions of gods, heroes, mortals and animals from Greek and Roman history. That was the beginning of the Vatican sculpture collection and the concept on which the display is based.

The future of the museums, however, belonged to the illustrative display of the development of classical art, the guiding light of which was Johann Joachim Winckelmann. In brilliant fashion, using Roman copies in which he sought to find the Greek originals, he developed his History of Classical Art (1763). In this way he traced the origin, development, alteration and decline of that art, distinguishing between the "older style," the "high style" (the majestic grace), the "beautiful style" (the attractive grace), the "style of the imitators" and the "decline and fall."

In the 19th and 20th centuries, this approach was developed even further. In the morphological image of a finely ramified plant, scholars saw the metaphor of development, bloom and decay. To set up classical works of sculpture in the Vatican museums using these selection criteria would do justice neither to the illustration of a history of development nor to the basic nature of the collection; its earliest work of art dates from the 5th century B.C., a time when—to use Winckelmann's terminology—the high style was unfolding.

The following illustrations have been arranged according to thematic criteria. The first half comprise monuments from the realm of religion. At the outset is a small selection of renowned images of gods; this is followed by deified beings and mythological figures. The second half displays monuments in honor of mortals. These figures begin with honorary statues of victors in sporting events, of poets, thinkers, statesmen, generals and emperors. There follow, in conclusion, the tombs, Greek stelae and statues, Roman tomb reliefs, urns, altars and sarcophagi, as well as fragments of tomb decoration.

What makes looking at these works of art interesting is the special form of each monument—a form which mankind has set for itself, and which has been transmitted from generation to generation. We have attempted to indicate this in the short explanations to the illustrations in the appendix of the book.

GEORG DALTROP

RIGHT: 231) *Zeus of Otricoli*

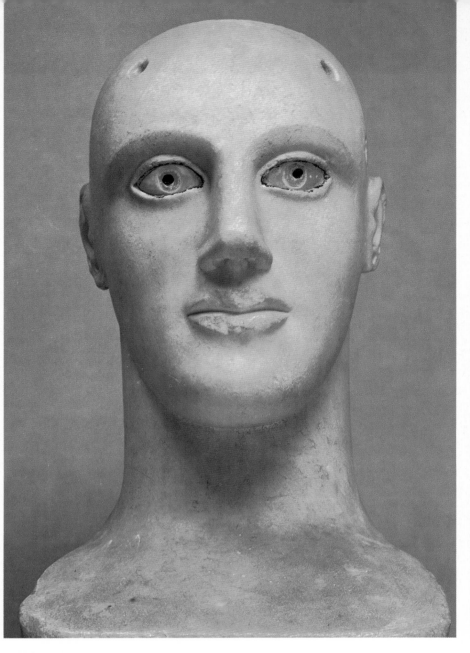

left-hand page
upper left: 232) *Athena Giustiniani*.

upper right: 233) A larger-than-life size head of Athena.

below: 234) A group of acolytes. Fragment of a shield from the *Athena Parthenos*.

above: 235) Fragment from the west pediment of the Parthenon of a larger-than-life size horse's head.

below: 236) The head of a young man. Fragment from the north frieze of the Parthenon.

left: 237) *Apollo Belvedere*.

below: 238) *Apollo Sauroctonus*.

below: 239) *Apollo Kitharodos*.

upper right: 240) *Demeter*.

lower right: 241) *Hera Barberini*.

left: 246) *Achilles as Doryphoros.*

below: 247) *Meleager.*

right: 248) *Belvedere torso.*

lower left: 249) Amazon, in the style of Kresilas.

lower right: 250) Amazon, in the style of Phidias.

right-hand page: 251) One of Niobe's daughters.

below : 252) *Medea and the Two Daughters of Pelias.*

right-hand page
left : 253) Relief with the Three Graces.

right : 254) Marble group with the Three Graces.

below : 255) *Triton with Nereids and Cupids.*

left-hand page : 256) *Laocoön with his Sons*.

right : 257) *Menelaus*.

below : 258) *Companion of Odysseus*.

left: 259) *The Tyche of Antioch*.

below: 260) Deity of the river Nile.

upper left : 261) Lares – relief from the period of the Vicomagistri.

upper right : 262) Scenes from the lives of Romulus and Remus.

left : 263) *Mithras*.

lower left: 264) *Discobolus*.

lower right: 265) *Apoxymenos* – Athlete, removing the dust after the match.

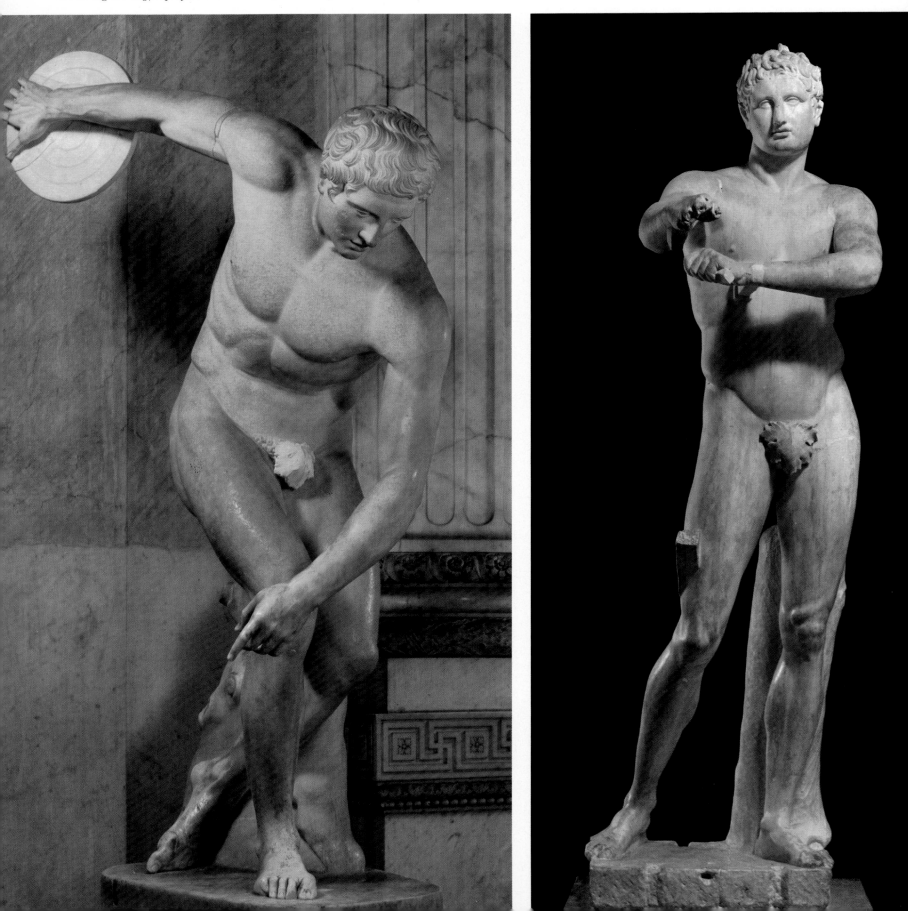

above: 266) *Demosthenes*.

right: 267) *Sophocles*.

left-hand page

upper left: 268) *Homer.*

upper right: 269) *Socrates.*

lower left: 270) *Plato.*

lower center: 271) *Pericles.*

lower right: 272) *Euripedes.*

above: 273) *Julius Caesar.*

left: 274) *A Roman general.*

left: 275) *Augustus.*

below: 276) *Claudius.*

right: 277) *Diocletian and Maximian.*

above: 278) A relief depicting the ceremonial exit of the troops of Emperor Domitian (Nerva).

lower left: *Sabina.*

lower right: 280) *Hadrian.*

right: 281) *Antinous.*

lower left: 282) *Caracalla.*

lower right: 283) *Phillipus Arabs.*

above: 284) Burial stele for a young man.

upper right: 285) Relief from the tomb of a horseman.

right: 286) Burial statue of a woman.

right: 287) Tomb relief of Lucius Vibius and his family.

below: 288) Marius Gratidus Libanus and his wife: an effigy group.

above: 289) The "Rose-Pillar" from the Haterii tomb.

upper right: 290/291) Life-size busts from the Haterii tomb.

right: 292) Roman burial altar.

above: 293) Tomb relief of a chariot race.

center: 294) Tomb of the miller P Nonius Zethus.

below: 295) Sarcophagus of a general.

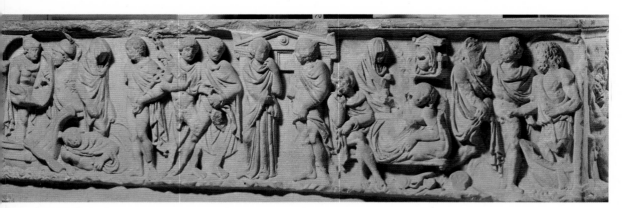

left: 302) Head of a bronze peacock.

THE ETRUSCAN MUSEUM

On February 2, 1837, Pope Gregory XVI Cappellari (1831–1846) dedicated his new Etruscan museum. It had been furnished in great haste, in only two months, undoubtedly to have the day of dedication coincide with the sixth anniversary of the Pope's election. The history of the collection, however, goes back much further.

The man responsible for housing Etruscan finds within the walls of the Vatican, alongside the more than 300-year-old collections of Greek and Roman objects, was ruler of a state extending over much of old Etruria (the region between the Arno and Tiber, the Apennines and the sea).

The abuses of the Napoleonic period were followed by resumption of a remarkably far-seeing series of laws in the edict of Cardinal Pacca in 1820, which were confirmed by the decrees ordered by Leo XII Della Genga (1823–1829). Among other things, the laws assured the public collections first refusal on all objects excavated in each region. This was effective, although only partial protection of the archaeological heritage was guaranteed. It also meant that the museums were able to announce the results of archaeological investigation without delay.

Looking back at the individual stages of the re-appearance of traces of Etruscan civilization, from the Renaissance to the present day, one can understand why the founding of the museum was of such signal importance, coming as it did mid-way between the initial, uncontrived excavation studies of the 17th and 18th centuries and the expert analyses of the 19th century. The latter, more and more definitive in their findings, were based on more exact study of the respective fields, fields which the continuing developments in the 20th century used as their point of departure.

The founding of the Etruscan Museum was the result of all these early endeavors; the museum remained at this stage of development because political upheavals between 1860 and 1870 severed those ties it had enjoyed with areas of excavation by assuring that any additional finds would benefit the collections of the new Italian state. If, in considering the Etruscan collection, several other works in the Vatican are included, works that harmonize astonishingly well with those in the museum, then the unique nature of the 17th and 18th century series of documents becomes clear. These objects permit one to reconstruct the "pre-history" of Etruscan science as well as the history of Etruria's rich past. Over the centuries, the conception of the latter has undergone gradual change.

Illustrated on page 262 is a larger-than-life marble statue of Emperor Claudius (41–54 A.D.). Together with other statues, it was found in the middle of the 19th century near the Etruscan capital city, Caere (Etruscan Kisria, known today as Cerveteri). A marble relief plate, held by most experts to be a side-section of the imperial throne, and considered in any case to be part of this group, was found with the statue and portrays three figures, representing the large Etruscan cities of Tarquinia, Vulci and Vetulonia. It is known that Claudius wrote an extensive history of the Etruscans in Greek, and that he was renowned for his knowledge of the Etruscan language. It therefore seems evident that the relief to which this plate belonged represented the Etruscan acknowledgement of these abilities. Such inordinate praise of the old emperor perhaps reveals an inferiority complex typical of "provinces" and minorities. Etruria was busy making its own monuments because it feared being forgotten. It flatteringly applauded someone like Claudius who had paid tribute to Etruria's former greatness, and by so doing bequeathed to us the astonishing diagnosis of its own downfall. It is unfortunate that the efforts of this early school of Etrurian scholars did not last; they failed to outlive the long period of neglect to which the overwhelmingly powerful Latin race had relegated the world of the Etruscans. Thus it is that none of these early scholars' writings has survived into our age.

It was not until the early Renaissance that a few individual Etruscan objects were re-discovered. Innocent VIII Cibo (1484–1492) was the first to take an interest in this field of study. He also built the Palazzetto del Belvedere, most of which is concerned with the Etruscan collection. In 1489, he sent an emissary to Corneto (formerly Tarquinii, known today as Tarquinia) to supervise the excavation of objects found in the so-called "Nicodemus tomb." A contemporary report on the considerable number of gold artifacts expresses surprise over this sensational discovery of a world that in the course of time had completely disappeared from the face of the earth. It is accepted that when Michelangelo began painting his *Last Judgment* in 1535, he expressed the entire richness of his own culture, including the various iconographic motifs of ancient monuments he had seen and studied. There is general agreement today over the classical origin of many of his figures. That the re-discovery of Etruscan art objects also influenced some of the demonic figures he placed in Hades is just as certain. The figure of Charon is almost identical to the Etruscan "Charun," to be seen on a famous amphora in the Bibliothèque Nationale in Paris. The face rising from the earth at the feet of Minos displays a more than coincidental resemblance to the "Charun" mask from Volsium (Bolsena/Orvieto), of which we have numerous examples. Everything is in accord: the frontal representation, the cynical smile, the nose, the eyebrows and the shock of hair reaching down to the sideburns. For an artist like Michelangelo, who was incapable of simply copying anything, this came as close as possible to the original. It is the presence of a world instinctively opposed to that of classicism that interests us here and that permits us to outline the initial archaeological concept of "Etruscan" (Claudius's concept can still be described as ethnological). From classical antiquity the painter daringly assumed the concepts of heavenly bliss and mortal perfection, whereas the Etruscan works helped him to create demonic visages. Here then, is the proof. A picturesque but poor country that in the course of centuries turned completely to agriculture and pasturage suddenly grants us a look into its past. Our imagination causes us to develop visions of mountains of gold and hellish tortures. Blurred conceptions of Greece and Rome may have allowed Michelangelo's contemporaries to picture a past peopled by beings of great vivacity, but Renaissance thought, by some retroactive process, endowed Etruria with a race of people somber and difficult to comprehend. It was a view precipitated by the sensational discoveries made beneath the mute surface of the earth.

It is certainly easy to grasp how romanticism was influenced by the initial reports on Etruscan civilization in the 18th century, as well as by the increasing number of discoveries. As far as the Etruscan Museum is concerned, twelve years of excavatory activity (1825–1837) sufficed to make a true museum—and today, one of the most copious collections in the world—of the original modest collection of small bronze figures, vases and several terra cottas which had been attached to the Vatican Library. The penultimate stage in the history of the Etruscan and old Italian artifacts in the Vatican museums has been captured for posterity in an 1818 painting in the exhibition room of the Vatican Library. It is a fresco from a series depicting the events during the pontificate of Pius VII Chiaramonti (1800–1823) and it shows the arrangement of several ancient vases and bronze figures (some of which are old Italian and others Etruscan) on the library's manuscript cabinets—and all this in the presence of the Pope. However, these objects did not remain long in this spot. In the same year, the Pope added to the sculpture collection the rooms on the first floor of the building that Pius IV de'Medici (1559–1565) had built on to the Belvedere villa of Innocent VIII. This is the Zelada apartment, thus termed because Cardinal Braschi—librarian and Secretary of State for Pius VI (1775–1799)—lived there from 1780 onward. Starting in 1831, the rooms were used to receive sealed baskets with objects that had been acquired, little by little, by the Papal treasury. They had previously been stored in the depot of Monte de Pietà. In 1836, it was finally ready. A letter from Cardinal Galleffi, chamberlain, to Monsignore Fieschi, administrator and prefect of the Palazzi Apostolici, convened a meeting of the advisory commission for antiquities and art on November 15 in the Zelada apartment. The purpose was to decide on details of the installation of the museum, which the commission had already resolved in principle. Especially significant on this occasion was the presence of the painter Vincenzo Camuccini, the sculptor Albert Thorvaldsen, the architect Giuseppe Valadier, and the archaeologist Pietro Ercole Visconti.

The meeting resulted in a classification of the objects based on each item's basic material (stone, terracotta, bronze, etc.). This classification is still maintained today. Gold objects and other small artifacts were placed in richly adorned small chests, and vases were put on stone consoles or tambours; various types of armory were reconstructed and other bronze objects hung on the walls. The brightly lit rooms facing the "Cortile della Pigna" had dark corners in which the preference for the "Etruscan secret" made a virtue of necessity. The effect of this arrangement, which one can still enjoy in engravings from that day and age, lies in the objective, uncritical interpretation of the objects. Not having yet been confined within a strict framework, they were able to unfold without hindrance to their elegance, richness, versatility and greatness. And even before a general criterion for exhibiting objects could be distilled from this experience, the collection had really been selected on the basis of its direct attractiveness. With the exception of several collective purchases, such as parts of the Candelori collection from Vulci, or objects acquired through government participation in the excavations, as, for example, in Campanari and again in Vulci, the treasury was offered for its collection mainly objects not only of historical value but also made with particularly beautiful artistry and priceless material, or in an outstanding state of preservation.

Shortly after its inauguration, the museum received its first extension, to accommodate the large quantity of newly acquired material, especially the finds from the Regolini-Galassi tomb in Caere, where excavations had taken place in the summer of 1837. The number of rooms in the museum, which until then consisted only of those which today bear the numbers I and XIV–XVII, was increased by adding rooms II and III–1. The museum remained unchanged until the beginning of the 20th century, though the collection was enriched by the addition of various individual acquisitions, including the magnificent sarcophagus from Caere (illustration 329), and the bronze objects from a grave in Bolsena, both found during the reign of Pius IX. Around the turn of the century, finds from a tomb in Castiglione on Lago di Trasimeno, and the Falcione collection in Viterbo were added to the museum which, by then, offered a comprehensive survey of objects from various periods and of varying origin. Further extensions and renovations were necessitated by the finds, which considerably improved archaeological techniques had made possible in the hundred years that had passed since initial investigations were made. Those were carried out, from 1920 to 1925, by noted Etruscologist Bartolomeo Nogara, director-general of the Vatican museums. He completely re-organized the display of the objects and added to the museum compartments 2 and 3 of rooms III and IV. Of decisive importance was the separation of the Regolini-Galassi finds from the other compartments, and the subsequent initial attempt to historically reconstruct them in room II, where they are today.

With some regret, however, it must be recorded that modern Etruscologists in this case behaved with a recklessness born of immaturity. As if to compensate for Etruscology's late entry into the Gregorian-Etruscan collection, their enthusiasm, born of an awareness of superior knowledge, knew no limits; neither respect for a traditional and clearly "19th century" form of classification, nor the wish to maintain the much more important "fidelity to the ancient object" (which had largely enlivened the old system of exhibition and classification, although, indeed, based on numerous errors) could bridle the Etruscologists' zeal. An example of this is the beautiful 18th century inlaid sundial of bronze or marble in the brick floor of the room named after it; today room XIV, it had previously been the observatory, installed by Cardinal Zelada. Although this sundial could not really have been a disturbing influence, it became a victim of the strictness of the new "scientific" point of view. The same fate befell the elegant marble consoles running along the walls and which had supported the Greek and Etruscan vases. It may be true that these objects were unprotected and within easy reach of the public, and they were in no exact chronological order; but the contemplator had direct and lively rapport with them.

In 1935, Marquis A. Benedetto Guglielmi, from Vulci, made a gift of his collection of Attic and Etruscan vases, buccheri (black pottery) and goldsmith's work from Vucli to Pius XI. The collection was housed in room V, added to the institution for this specific purpose, which meant that the museum had now been extended to include part of Innocent

VIII's Belvedere villa. The finds of the Regolini-Galassi tomb, the most impressive part of the Etruscan collection, were subjected once again to a critical examination which, conducted by L. Pareti, led to a re-organization of room II. All the Italic and Etruscan red-figured vases in the collection were analyzed between 1952 and 1954 by A. D. Trandall, who also installed them in room XVII according to a systematic arrangement of his own devising. Partitioned into three rooms, XVII had been the apartment of Antonio Canova, director of the sculpture collection, until his death in 1822.

In 1955 began the most recent thorough extension and renovation of the entire museum, which by then had expanded over the entire first floor of the Belvedere of Innocent VIII, as well as into the upper section of the "Nicchione" of Pius IV. The last bequest was made to Paul VI in 1968 by Mario Astarita, and consisted of a large number of Corinthian, Attic, Etruscan, Italic and Roman vases and fragments, and a small number of Italic bronzes and terracottas. The first group is situated in room XV, which contains the frescoes by Pomarancio (Biblical, mythological and allegorical scenes); the other objects have been added to the appropriate collections.

The last renovation was marked by a great deal of attention being paid to modern criteria of analysis and classification (smaller Roman finds were placed together; the very large collection of Greek pottery was classified by groups according to artist or school, based on research by Albizzati and Beazley). One could discern a respect for the ancient objects and their settings; the latter had to be worthy of the works being presented. That is the greatest service rendered the public by this unique museum.

At this point, a general explanation of the selection of works on display would lead to an unnecessary repetition of the history of Etruscan art, whose most important stages of development are represented in the museum. It is probably more appropriate to the character of the collection to spend a little time looking at some of its best presented "themes." Consider, first, a number of dark pottery vases (room VII, showcases A–B), somewhat conelike, with only one handle, affixed horizontally at the widest spot; they originally had a twisted vessel as a covering and were engraved with geometric patterns on the neck and bulge. The vases are called "Villanova" after the village of the same name near Bologna, where, in the middle of the 19th century, a burial site full of cinerary urns of the same type was found. These particular specimens emanate from southern Etruria; unfortunately, the exact place of origin isn't known, but it is probable they are from Tarquinia or Vulci (illustration 313). They come right at the beginning of the chronological arrangement of the museum objects and are typical of the style of urn in common use in Etruria during the Iron Age (9th–8th century B.C.). On the death of the owner, the jar was usually buried in the grave, either in a cylindrical hole, or in a pit dug out of the soft rock-strata of the region, and was often covered with an architecturally primitive roofing. Occasionally, the jar contained, in addition to the ashes, personal ornaments, like bronze clasps, parts of a necklace, arm-bands and rings. Around the jar were placed such modest articles as pottery vessels; later, these vessels were often brightly painted, or made of bronze. This significant separation of the various articles placed in the grave and, even more important, the constantly recurring anthropomorphic elements, such as helmets as covering, necklaces around the neck of the jar, etc., indicate that the jars themselves represented the body of the deceased. To bring about a more definite union between "spirit" and urn, the latter was fashioned in the form of a house, a form most popular, although not exclusively so, in the districts of Latium Rome and south Etruria.

A burial site of this type was found in 1816–1817 near Castelgandolfo and contained several interesting burial objects (showcase E). Mentioning it in 1817 for the first time in a public lecture at the Roman Academy for Archaeology, A. Visconti succeeded in attracting the attention of the still classically oriented archaeologists to the modest remains of the very old culture of Latium. These jars, also decorated with geometric patterns, are faithful copies of houses (of the 8th century B.C.), and traces of them have been found in Rome on the Palatine and Esquiline hills. They had also been placed in holes in the ground and protected by still larger vases, the latter containing the simple burial articles as well as the urn itself. Among these articles, human figures made of clay have been found—the earliest examples of Italian sculpture of this type. With respect to our subject matter, it should be noted that the burial house concept is missing completely here, although the impression still persists. The urn always represents the body of the deceased; it has the form of a house because it was held that the deceased's home had been just as much a part of him as his mortal remains and was thus just as effective an "aid" to him. This is confirmed by the presence of occasional combinations of both forms: for example, anthropomorphic urns of the Villanova type with helmet-coverings, the upper surface of which has the shape of a roof, or even (as in the case an urn from the same burial site, now at the Historical Museum in Berne) a Villanova urn with a door opening in the body and a roof-like covering. The urn displayed in showcase F is of the period 150 years later on. A comparison with other objects of similar rarity indicates that it is from Veii: of all Etruscan cities the one closest to Rome. The burial rites at this time permitted incarceration of the corpse in an intuitively "realistic" framework, the tombs having gigantic proportions and imitating human dwelling places, often to the very last detail. Since it no longer performed the function of the actual tomb, the urn did not have to bear the many symbols dealing with burial. Next to the famous "Canopi" type (anthropomorphic cinerary urns) from Chiusi, the type of urn under consideration, and of which this is the only known specimen, underwent the same change in concept. It is expressed in a combination of motifs (human figure and vessel, or buildings), which even the artist appears to have considered anomalous (illustration 314). On December 31, 1835, General Vincenzo Galassi and the archpriest of Cerveteri, Alessandro Regolini, asked the government of the Papal States for permission to dig for archaeological remains in the area known as "il sorbo"—southeast of the hill on which Cerveteri (the old Caere) lies. During the next two years, they discovered one of the largest Etruscan burial sites ever found. These tombs also conveyed the first complete picture of the period of "orientalization," which, around the 7th century B.C., saw Etruria's initially successful economic and cultural ties with the other Mediterannean lands. The burial site, which can be visited today, consists of a narrow, 18-meter-long corridor, running into a large round burial mound. An incomplete dividing wall of quadratic stone partitions the section in the back into a cell. Halfway down the corridor, two oval lateral chambers have been hewn out of solid rock. The corridor is covered entirely by a vault of stone blocks; these ascend in a slope toward the inside and are joined at the top by a row of horizontally arranged plates. The cell at the end of the tomb contained the corpse of a woman; a male corpse was in the corridor; the left-hand chamber, it appears, served merely as a repository for additional objects intended for the main tomb.

The unusual luxuriousness of the burial objects in both main tombs (the archaeologists found the tomb almost completely intact) points to the special significance of this discovery. The woman wore clothing interwoven with gold thread. The focal point of the luxurious decoration was a large ornamental plate adorned with concentric rows of constantly reiterated figures, which were stamped into the material. The clothing was covered with ornamental jewelry (gold and amber chains, gold and silver arm-bands, and the three large fibulae—illustration 312), made according to the varied techniques of the goldsmith's art: small repoussé or welded figures, finely engraved or molded. The motifs of the ornamentation were new and originated from the orient: friezes with exotic or fantastic animal figures, palmettes, divinities like the "Pater Theron," or the Master of the Wild Animals, etc. The old geometric ornamentation—"wolf's teeth" and ornamental ribbons, etc.—was pushed to the edge, or lower sections, of the frieze.

The warrior lay on a four-wheeled bronze carriage (illustration 304) which had brought him into the tomb. This can be deduced from the remains of the wheel-hubs, which were used to brake the carriage during the ceremonial procession. The "biga," re-constructed from the remaining parts of decorative and constructional material, had another function. This was the most important part of the warrior's martial equipment (it is not quite certain whether it was the man in the main corridor, or in the right-hand chamber), and the shields of hammered bronze, hanging on the walls, belonged to this warrior. These objects were supposed to fulfil a traditional magic function, as well as serving to recall the familiar environment of the deceased. We can thus assume that nothing was missing that had belonged to the deceased during his lifetime and which could serve to denote his social class. The woman's jewelry, with its

277

valuable material, large size and adornment, had no practical function and was intended, evidently, to impress others; the man's importance in public life, especially in the military sphere, was emphasized in the same way. Arranged around the well designated figures was evidence of the susceptibility for everything the culture of that time and place had to offer: objects from Greece (proto-Corinthian pottery-ware) and from the Aegean (silver cups, jugs, boxes from Cyprus) were found next to examples of the most beautiful artisan-work (both imitation foreign objects as well as original designs and highly developed works of local origin). Etruria's most important contribution (and thereby Italy's, too) to the development of European culture was the art of writing.

Visible at the bottom of the bucchero vase in showcase K (illustration 315) is a 25-letter Western Greek alphabet, while winding in a spiral around the walls of the vase is a table of syllables, indicating that the culture which made the vase knew how to use the alphabet and the syllables formed from it.

Another group of interesting objects is the "ex-voto," of which the museum owns a beautiful collection, thanks to the excavation which the archpriest of Cerveteri carried out in 1826 on his own land in the area of the old city. (A small number of objects are from Vulci.) These objects were brought into one of the temples of the city as "donations," either that one might ask the gods for special favors or to thank them for favors already granted, though they were probably also often merely symbols of submission. Many referred more or less directly to the boon desired (parts of the human anatomy, limbs, internal organs, figures of children in swaddling clothes, etc.) and others depicted the face of the donor, who was thus able to "remain" in the temple to assure for himself a preferred place in the thoughts of the tutelary divinity. Many of the heads were "mass produced," but cast without much exactness so that everyone could afford them. They were probably made in the studios responsible for the architectural adornment of the temples and sold in large quanitities inside the temples. Whenever bronze was employed for this purpose—not as unusual as the few finds of this nature would lead one to assume—a much more valuable version of the same artistic line was made for the rich. The current collection of votive figures attained completion by means of three of the largest bronze figures ever found in Etruscan-Italian soil: the Mars of Todi (illustrations 303, 327) and the two statuettes of boys, from Tarquinia and the Lago di Trasimeno (illustration 311). These two statuettes should be compared with similar figures of terracotta in the showcase in room VII.

We come now to the final "theme." Greek pottery is represented in all Etruscan museums, for the Etruscans liked to display it in their homes and included it among their burial objects. It should therefore be no surprise to come across it in the museum, particularly as, in the period prior to 1837, while the museum was being installed, its origins had not been finally determined. The famous "rapporto vulcente" of E. Gerhardt, which confirmed the Greek origin of the objects, was not published until 1831. It was not until the last thirty years of the 19th century, with the excavations in the potters' quarter and on the Acropolis in Athens, that the last doubts were allayed. Two of the largest importers of Greek pottery work in Etruria were, as the collection here indicates, Caere and Vulci—the former, a few kilometers from the sea and about 30 kilometers from Rome; the latter, further inland and about 100 kilometers north-east of Rome. In these cities the local pottery studios also flourished, including among their products large painted objects for mortals as well as the dead.

FRANCESCO RONCALLI

upper left: 304) Funeral carriage.

lower left: 305) Figures from a grave in Cerveteri.

upper right: 306) "Apollo Finds the Cattle which Hermes had Taken": A bowl by the "Brygos painter".

lower right: 307) Bowl by the "Jena painter", with a depiction of Triptolemos.

upper left: 308) Gold disks with metaphorical ornamentation.

lower left: 309) Cover of a bronze container for toilet articles.

above: 310) Golden diadem.

upper right: 311) Bronze statue of a boy.

right: 312) Large golden fibula.

left: 313) Urn of the "Villanova" type.

lower left: 314) Clay turn with a bust on the cover.

lower right: 315) "Bucchero" vase with written characters.

right-hand page

upper left: 316) Attic hydria by the "Berlin painter", with a depiction of Apollo on a tripod.

upper right: 317) Attic hydria by the "Mykale painter".

lower left: 318) Hydria from Caere: "Heracles Battling Alcyoneus".

lower right: 319) Polychromatic Attic Krater: "Hermes Entrusts Silenus to Dionysus".

upper left: 320) Back of a bronze mirror.

lower left: 321) Bronze disk with a mask of the deity of the river Achelous.

below: 322) Bronze statuette.

right: 323) A lion.

right: 324) Cylindrical krater with a depiction of legendary beasts.

below: 325) Terra cotta votive head.

lower right: 326) Head of a young woman.

right-hand page

upper left: 327) *The Mars of Todi*. Bronze figure (cf. 303).

upper right: 328) Winged horse made of clay.

below: 329) Limestone sarcophagus with the relief of a funeral procession and the prostrate figure of the deceased.

left: 330) Two drinking vessels.

center: 331) Terra cotta votive heads.

lower left: 332) Attic dish with a depiction of Heracles.

lower right: 333) Laconian dish with a depiction of Sisyphus and Tityos.

right: 334) Portrait head of a man.

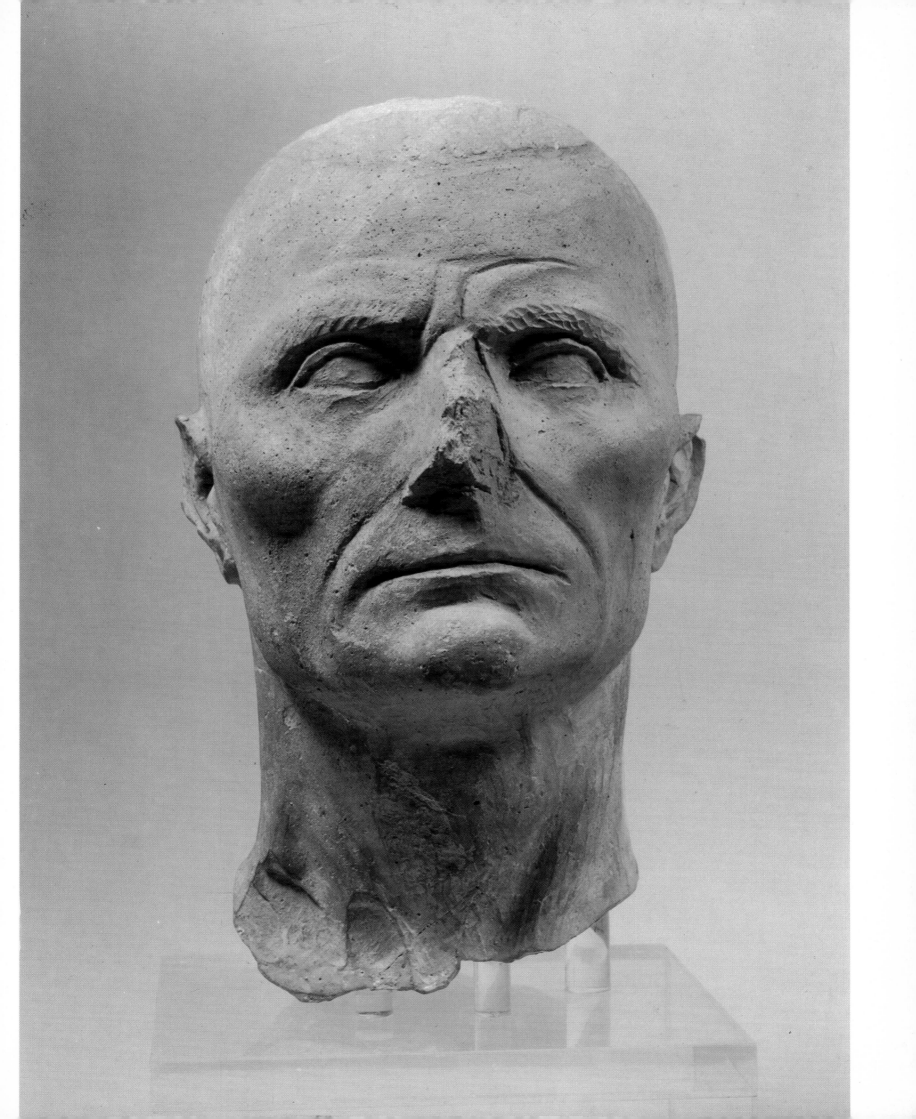

left-hand page:

left: 335) Attic amphora by Exekias, with a depiction rendered in the "black-figured" style: "Achilles and Ajax at Play".

right: 336) Attic oenochoe by Amasias.

below: 337) Proto-Corinthian wine jugs.

below: 338) A large late-Corinthian crater: "Menelaus and Odysseus Enquire in Troy about Helen's Return".

next page: 339) Krater by Asteas: "Zeus and Hermes at Alcmene's Window".

THE PICTURE GALLERY

Although the Vatican collection of classical sculpture was not brought within the walls of a museum until the 18th century, it sustained a long period of development. It began when Pope Julius II della Rovere (1503–1513) had the statue of Apollo conveyed to the Vatican; known as *Apollo di Belvedere*, it had been found toward the end of the 15th century on his property. But while one is certain of this chronology, it is no easy task to determine exactly when the collection of pictures began, and we are reduced to following the "Pinacoteca," or the picture gallery, of the Vatican through its various stages of development.

In the course of the centuries, the Popes, who were interested in expanding and decorating their residence, acquired paintings and wall tapestries from the most talented artists; and these works were hung in the various rooms of the Palazzi Apostolici, as a form of adornment.

Under Clement XI Albani (1700–1721) all the inscriptions of the sculpture collection were brought together and housed in the "Galleria Lapidara." This was followed by the decision under Clement XII Corsini (1730–1740) to found a museum of antiquities and to acquire valuable manuscripts for the library, as well as 200 ancient vases. There then ensued, under Benedict XIV Lambertini (1740–1758), the acquisition of Cardinal Albani's coin collection. It was in similar fashion that first Clement XIV, and then Pius VI Braschi (1775–1799) began to collect various paintings. During the organization of the museums, Pius VI wished, as Moroni notes, "that remarkable works of the art of painting should not be missing, and toward this end he transformed into a picture gallery the room with the open loggia above the Vatican Library and the connection between the Galleria delle Carte Geografiche and the Galleria dei Candelabri. He had a barrel-vault installed and commissioned able artists, like Bernardino Nocchi, Domenico del Frate and Antonio Marini, with the decoration…"

It is not known which works comprised the original collection at the end of the 18th century, but we do know that during the French occupation the paintings suffered the same fate as did the masterpieces of the museums, the library, various churches and collections in Rome and elsewhere in the Papal States. The Treaty of Tolentino, 1797, provided for the shipment of many works to France, where they embellished galleries and museums. Documents in the archives make it possible today to modify the number usually advanced when describing the total amount of works that were stolen. Although it was originally thought that 215 pictures had been removed from Rome and other places, it now appears more probable to place this number at 133, of which 53 were from the churches in Rome and other collections. Of these, only 26 were returned; of those that were expropriated elsewhere, the number of pictures returned varies from 55 to 58. Happily, among those pictures that were returned were the most important works; the others have disappeared without trace.

At the Congress of Vienna in 1815, it was decided to grant the plea of Pius VII and to have the stolen works of art returned to their rightful owners. In addition, the congress also recommended that the returned works be combined as much as possible and presented to the public at places accessible to it, so that everyone could view them and enjoy contemplating them. As we know, this recommendation by the congress was disregarded. The return of a large number of the art works was the result primarily of the wise diplomatic conduct of Cardinal Consalvi, who had been sent to Paris to negotiate the restitution. This was also facilitated by the skilfulness of the Papal mission; especially

Antonio Canova, who exploited his English and German friendships, with, for example, Lord Hamilton, Viscount Castlereagh and Metternich.

With the reorganization of the pictures, the Pope did indeed pay heed to the recommendation of the congress; and thus it was that several of the works, instead of being returned to their locations prior to having been stolen, were added to the collection in the Pinacoteca. In this connection, it is interesting to read the resolute reply which Cardinal Consalvi made in 1818 to the request by Signora Beliardi-Almerici of Ancona for the return of the painting, *The Blessed Michelina* by Barocci: "the abovementioned objects are not to be returned to private persons; they had been handed over to the government by our allies, who stipulated that they be assembled and made available to the public."

A new location was found for the pictures in the Borgia Apartment, which was ordered by the Pope to be restored so as to accommodate the paintings (altogether 44). The arrangement was supervised by Vincenzo Camuccini. This was certainly not an ideal solution; the room available was limited and the illumination was insufficient to allow the full effect of the paintings to be appreciated. Nevertheless, it was a further step in the history of the picture gallery, which used this occasion to expand by incorporating new and important works.

Because of the lack of space and light, in 1821, the pictures were transferred to the rooms of Gregory XIII on the third floor of the "Secondo Braccio" of the loggie. This was followed by a series of wanderings: after they were returned to the original location, the pictures were taken to the rooms of Pius V on the third floor of the "Torre Pia" (1836). At that time, the wall tapestries were placed in the gallery that had just been vacated and which was given the name "Galleria degli Arazzi." In 1857, the paintings were returned to the rooms of Gregory XIII. Taking everything into consideration, this seemed to be the best possible location, although it was not ideal; one had only to think of the difficulties facing visitors to the picture gallery, who not only had to traverse Raphael's stanze, but also the internal and private section of the palace. This site also offered neither enough room nor sufficient light nor the proper isolation for the works' exhibition. In 1908, during the pontificate of Pius X, it was believed that solution had been found to the essential problems, and the picture gallery moved once again. This time it was transferred to rooms under the lengthy library wing, in the west wing of the Belvedere court; the rooms had previously been used as a storehouse of the Floreria and as a coach-house. This location was most advantageous: since it was on the street leading to the museums, it offered the public direct access. There was more room and light, and this appeared at first to be a satisfactory solution to an old problem. After the rooms had been restored under the direction of the architect, Sneider, they were furnished and the collection moved in; it had been expanded by the addition of further works from the library, from various rooms and from the Lateran gallery. The collection, arranged by Seitz and D'Archiardi, was officially consecrated by the Pope on March 19, 1909.

During the years following its, selection as the site for the picture gallery, this location also turned out to have disadvantages; like uneven illumination, variations in temperature, and moisture. The large windows toward the east did not provide ideal illumination; and, in addition, they caused constant temperature variation, which was detrimental to the maintenance of the pictures. If the picture gallery was to fulfill its function properly, a solution had to be found not only to the problem of the location but also as far as optimal conditions for maintaining the paintings were concerned. With this in mind, the new Pope, Pius XI Ratti (1922–1939), reached a decision. His interest in art went back to the years of his youth and it had been strengthened during his membership in the "Collegio dei Dottori della Biblioteca Ambrosiana" in Milan. As soon as he had been elected Pope, he began attending to the problems of the museums and Papal galleries, and to the re-arrangement and safeguarding of the valuable works they contained. Of greatest urgency was the picture gallery. As prefect of the Vatican Library, he had recognized the serious disadvantages nf the picture gallery's site, and he now came to the conclusionn that the paintings had to be accommodated in a newly erected building of their own, where optimal conditions for a museum prevailed, according to the most modern research. In addition to exhibition rooms, the building would also have to contain a storage room for tapestries and smaller works, restoration studios, offices, libraries, etc. This new building, designed and constructed by the architect, Luca Beltrami, was located on a rectangular plot of land in the garden, between the Viale della Zitadella and the new street leading to the museums. The new site, situated between the new museum entrance in the Viale delle Mura and the old one, opposite the Atrio dei Quattro Cancelli, simplified the transition from the museums to the Picture Gallery. In addition, both entrances were joined to one another and to the Picture Gallery by an L-shaped colonnade. This project of the Pope's took ten years to complete; on October 27, 1932, however, the new and final building was ceremoniously opened by Pius XI.

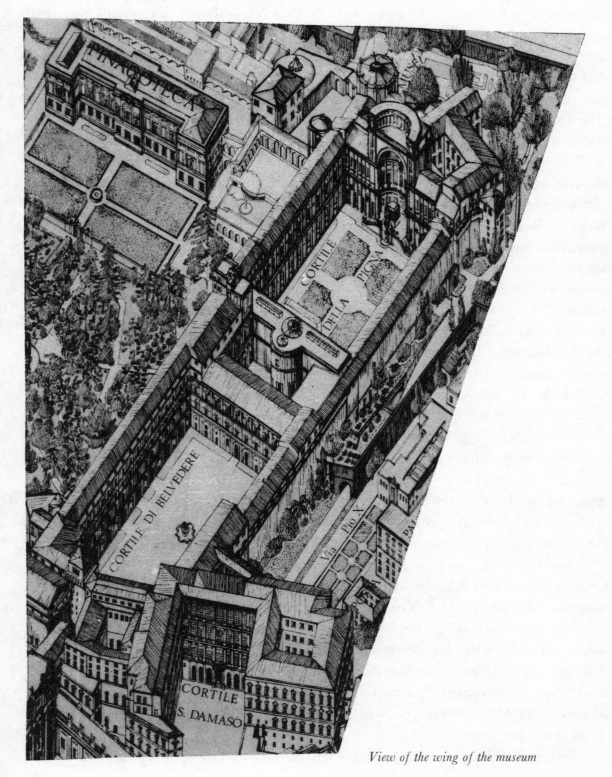

View of the wing of the museum

Even before the new building was completed, the director of the museums and galleries had acted upon an initiative of the Pope by setting up a laboratory for restoring the paintings. Another laboratory was established to allow experts to conduct the difficult work of repairing and cleaning the wall tapestries. For this latter task, the tapestry workshop of St. Michael, from the 18th century, was well suited, and Benedict XV wanted to re-establish it in the Vatican. Pius XI, however, remained true to the promise he had made when he was elected and decided that it was more important to save the existing tapestries than to create new ones. Thanks to his generosity the Picture Gallery was enlarged by the addition of new, important works.

The Picture Gallery continued its development even after the pontificate of Pius XI, although the accent was then more on the maintenance and restoration of the pictures and the enlargement of the collection. Finally, in 1960, under John XXIII, a section for modern art was opened. This happened at the behest of the Messa degli Artisti, whose representatives had been urging such a step since 1956.

As we have seen, many of the pictures returned from France were not given back to the owners but were incorporated into the treasury of paintings that the various Popes had collected; and, in 1816, they were exhibited in the Borgia Apartment. Among these 24 pictures were many significant works, including three by Raphael: *Transfiguration* (illustration 369), which had previously hung in San Pietro in Montorio in Rome; *Madonna of Foligno* (illustration 368), which had been painted for the church of Aracoeli and was brought to Foligno by the purchaser's niece; and *The Three Theological Virtues*, which originally formed the predella of *The Burial*, now in the Borghese gallery. Other works were: Fra Angelico's *The Miracles of S. Niccolò di Bari*, from the church of San Domenico in Perugia; Perugino's *Resurrection*, *eehe Madonna with the four Patron Saints*, that had been painteeed for the chapel of the Palazzo Comunale, and three Saints (illustration 366), which hung until 1797 in the sacristy of S. Pietro in Perugia. From Roman churches came, in addition to *Transfiguration*, *The Communion of St. Jerome* (illustration 377) by Domenichino (S. Girolamo degli Schiavoni) and Caravaggio's *Deposition* (illustration 384) from the Chiesa Nuova o dei Filippini. During the re-arrangement of the pictures following their transfer in 1836, several alterations were made. Many paintings were hung elsewhere, especially the classical ones, like the frescoes of the Aldobrandini Wedding Scene (illustration 136) and *The Six Nymphs*. Other important works were added to the collection, which thus increased from 35 to 42 paintings; among these additions was the fresco, *Installation of Platina by Sixtus IV* (illustration 359), by Melozzo da Forlì, which Domenico Succi had removed with great skill from the wall in the library and had put onto canvas, during the pontificate of Leo XII (1823–1829). During the collection's second transfer (1857), to the rooms of Gregory XIII, additional works were added, such as *The Coronation of the Virgin* (illustration 358) by Filippo Lippi, and Benozzo Gozzoli's *Donation of the Belt*.

Among the most important new acquisitions under Pius IX (1846–1878) was *St. Jerome* (illustration 373) by Leonardo da Vinci. In the 18th century, this painting had belonged to the painter, Angelica Kauffmann, and then disappeared. Cardinal Fesch found it at the beginning of the 19th century in badly damaged condition, but he was lucky enough to discover the missing head in a shoemaker's shop; since both parts of the painting could be put together, it was capable of restoration. When the Cardinal died, Pius XI bought the picture for the Picture Gallery. Other paintings were acquired—among them Fra Angelico's *Mother of God Between St. Dominic and Catherine* and *St. Margarete of Cortona* by Guercino—the number of paintings on display increasing to 50.

A further and considerable expansion resulted from the transfer of the Picture Gallery to the Floreria. This consisted of a group of 19 pictures which until then had belonged to the Palazzo Laterano, where they had been exhibited on the first floor. Added to this was another, more important group of 180 Byzantine paintings and primitives, which had been in the possession of the Museo Sacro of the library, as well as 21 from Papal rooms and store-rooms. The picture collection thus comprised a total of 277 paintings.

Most important of all, now that the collection had been arranged chronologically and according to the various schools of art, was that, for the first time, one was given a coherent impression of the development of painting styles. This was not restricted to Italian painting, but included other schools, especially the Byzantine.

The origin of most of the works in the so-called Byzantine collection is unknown. It is not even accurate to speak of a collection here, since this group of paintings was not put together according to any logical criteria; in fact, it developed almost by chance. In most cases, these are works which visiting priests and monks brought the Popes as presents; in the 19th century, they were then given to the Vatican Library, which already had a group of presumably similar origin. The paintings of the Italo-Greek school, however, stem presumably from churches and monasteries in the Adriatic region of the old Papal States. The varied quality of the pictures and their uneven artistic value could be confirmation of the theory that the collection came together by chance. As a matter of fact, one finds unimportant works next to others of great value. Nevertheless, they form the largest collection in Italy and give a clear conception of the variety of expression and development of the various schools of Byzantine art from the 5th to the 9th centuries. Especially remarkable are the Italo-Cretan works, the Greek works from monasteries—especially those from Mt. Athos—and the Dalmatian and Russian works.

In addition to the paintings of the Byzantine school, the Museo Sacro of the library also had a collection of early Italian painters. It consisted largely of pictures in small format by artists from the important Italian schools of the 15th and 16th centuries, like the Florentine, Venetian, Sienese and Umbrian schools. Situated as they were, between book cases and glass showcases in the southern section of the library, between the room with the *Aldobrandini Wedding Scene* and the chapel of Pius V, it was impossible to view them and to appreciate them. It was not until the expansion of the Picture Gallery in 1909 that it became possible to hang at least some of the representative pictures in that collection in a manner befitting them and to make them accessible to the public. The larger and decisive availability of space in the separate building made possible a further expansion of the collection, which now consisted of almost 500 pictures on exhibit, not counting those in storage.

Among the most important new acquisitions were Giotto's *Stefaneschi Triptych* and *The Angel and the Apostle* by Melozzo da Forlì (illustrations 357, 360) from the demolished apse of the church of the SS. Apostoli in Rome; until 1931 they had been stored in the sacristy of St. Peter's. There were, in addition, paintings by Spagna, Palmezzano, Girolamo Muziano, Scarsellino, Garofalo, Solimena and Cavalier d'Arpino; almost all of them were placed in the exhibition rooms. At the same time, ten tapestries of the "old school," by Raphael, were placed in the main gallery of the Picture Gallery.

During the following years, the treasury of art works was further enlarged by donations and purchases; among the new works, one of special significance was a round panel of *The Last Judgment*. It was at first held to be unimportant and was to be used for purposes of instruction. But subsequent careful cleaning revealed not only the original colors and inscriptions, but also the names of the painter and the purchaser. The significance of this painting for the development of art forms in Rome in the 12th and 13th centuries was now immediately grasped. (It is today No. 526 in the first room of the Picture Gallery.) Another valuable donation came from the former Bavarian royal family. It consisted of three panels from a predella by Guidoccio Gozzarelli, depicting the *Story of St. Barbara*. It had been bought from a dealer in antiques. The Picture Gallery was already in possession of another panel belonging to the predella.

Among the new acquisitions were also the Barberini tapestries, and the *Portrait of Pope Clement IX* (illustration 386), by Carlo Maratta; because of its high artistic quality, the latter work deserves special attention. Additional works were *Judith and Holofernes* by Orazio Gentileschi; *The Crucifixion of St. Peter* by Jacopo di Cione; *St. Francis Xavier* (illustration 380), by Van Dyck; and *The Apotheosis of a Warrior* by Rubens.

More recently, the collection has been enriched by the addition of a section for contemporary art, which consists almost entirely of works donated by the artists represented. This section comprises altogether about 30 works; and although it makes no claim to offer a complete survey of the current situation in the field of painting, it does contain works by such representative masters as Utrillo, Rouault, Fazzini, Mancini, de Chricio, Carrà, Soffici, Tosi, de Pisis, Morandi and Rosai, as well as from the sculptors Rodin, E. Greco, F. Messina and A. Martini.

On June 23, 1973, Pope Paul VI opened a collection of modern religious art, which is arranged in the rooms around the "Cortile del Pappagallo." It contains 600 works of contemporary artists from all fields and from all over the world, and all are presents to the Pope. The collection is strictly limited to religious themes and it is only works having something to do with this thematic concept that have been and will be accepted. The initiative for this collection stemmed from Paul VI and his address to the artists in 1964; and it is intended as a reply to the question of whether religious art is at all possible in our modern age. Toward this end, the Pope maintained in his speech in the Sistine Chapel opening the collection that "...even in our sober and secular world... there is enough almighty power, aside from the genuinely human power, to express that which is religious, divine, Christian."

It has already been mentioned that, beyond pictures, it was especially after the Renaissance that the Popes bought valuable tapestries; indeed, at that time, tapestries were among the most beloved decoration for the Papal rooms. Today, Flemish tapestries adorn the walls of the Papal rooms and the "Sala dei Santi" in the Borgia Apartment. The most valuable collection, however, is still the one which Leo X chose, in 1515, to decorate the walls beneath the 15th century frescoes in the Sistine Chapel. Of these, seven were hung there for the first time on St. Stephen's day in the year 1519. These tapestries depict scenes from the lives of Jesus and the Apostles and are divided into two groups. The first group, known as "old school" (Scuola Vecchia), was executed according to cartoons by Raphael and his pupils which had already been sketched and painted in December, 1516. The cartoons for the second group, the "new school" (Scuola Nuova), are by Raphael's pupils, who employed some of the sketches left behind by the master. The series of the "old school" includes the following: *The Blinding of Elymas, The Conversion of St. Paul, Stoning of St. Stephen, St. Peter Heals the Lame Man, Death of Ananias, Christ's Charge to St. Peter, Miraculous Draught of Fishes, St. Paul Preaching at Athens, St. Paul and Barnabus in Lystra*, and *St. Paul in Prison*. There is disagreement on the existence of an eleventh cartoon and the corresponding tapestry, *The Conversion of the Centurion Cornelius*. Reference is usually made to an order-to-pay made out to a certain "Raphael of Vitale for eleven pieces of material from Lyon"; then, too, there is the statement of the Count de Laborde, curator for antiquities in the Louvre, quoted by Muntz in his book on Raphael's tapestries. Most experts, however, believe that this was a replacement for one of the ten tapestries, *The Coronation of the Virgin*, which was later destroyed.

According to Cardinal Luigi d'Aragona, the tapestries were woven by Pieter van Aelst in Brussels in July, 1517, from Raphael's cartoons, which had been sent there. Following the transfer of the cartoon sketches to the material, which was completed shortly before the death of Leo X in December, 1521, the cartoons remained there. This explains the presence of many of the existing copies of the Vatican series not only in Italy (Loreto, Urbino, Mantua) but also in other countries (Dresden, Madrid, Berlin). Rubens found seven of the cartoons, damaged and worn after much use, in the house of the weaver's heirs, and he advised Charles I of England to buy them for a large sum of money. After the death of Charles I, they came into the possession of Cromwell, who bought them for £300. During the reign of William III, they came to Hampton Court palace and from there to the Victoria and Albert Museum, where they are exhibited today. The three other cartoons, *Conversion of St. Paul, St. Paul in Prison*, and *Stoning of St. Stephen*, are missing. The ten tapestries of the "new school," of much lower artistic standard, were also woven by Pieter van Aelst. The work went slowly, and it was not until 1530 that they were sent to Rome.

After they had been placed in the room devoted to Raphael during the re-organization of the Picture Gallery, these tapestries underwent stormy times. After the death of Leo X (1521), they were pawned for 5,000 ducats; and during the sack of Rome in 1527 they fell into the hands of the mercenaries, who sold them to a number of dealers. At first these dealers wanted to burn one of them, *The Blinding of Elymas*—the missing piece was replaced by tempera—in order to extract the gold which the material contained. They desisted from this, however, when they realized that they could make an even greater profit by selling the tapestries in Lyon. In 1545 the tapestries were once again in the Vatican, with the exception of two; these were found in Constantinople and bought back by a French diplomat, the Duke of Montmorency, who returned them to Julius III. During the French occupation, in 1798, the tapestries disappeared again from the Vatican, and this time they were auctioned off. A dealer in second-hand articles purchased them and took them to Genoa and, according to some versions, to Paris. It appears that they were offered for sale to the French Republic, but the financial difficulties of the times prevented their sale. They were instead bought, in 1808, by a Jew from Genoa, who later gave them to Pius VII.

Once the entire series was finally back in the Vatican, it was both used to decorate the Sistine Chapel and was hung in that part of the portico of St. Peter's between the bronze doors and the Sala Regia on high holidays. This custom was retained until Pius VII returned from imprisonment in France in 1814. He decreed that the tapestries were to be no longer used as decoration, but were to be preserved in the rooms of Pius V. By order of Gregory XVII in 1838, they were brought to the third floor in the east wing of the Belvedere court, in the room between the Galleria dei Candelabri and the Galleria delle Carte Geografiche, then known as "Galleria degli Arazzi." As already mentioned, the ten tapestries of the "old school" were finally accommodated in the Picture Gallery; in the Galleria degli Arazzi there remained only the ten tapestries of the "new school," which depicted scenes from the life of Jesus. In 1937/38, the collection was enriched by the addition of seven tapestries that had been made in the Barberini studio; they had scenes from the life of Urban VIII, whose family palace they had embellished. Other works were added to these, as for example, a reproduction of *The Last Supper* by Leonardo da Vinci.

To complete this list of the Vatican's valuable tapestry collection, mention must be made—in addition to those to which we have already referred in the Borgia Apartment—of those works now in the room in the Picture Gallery devoted to Melozzo da Forlì: the tapestry of the Credo, from Tournai (second half of the 16th century), a gift of the Queen of Spain for Leo XIII (1889); and the Flemish tapestry of Christ's Passion, which is among those kept in the rooms of Pius V. There is also an 18th century series from the Papal studio, St. Michael; part of it is in the Papal palace in the Lateran, and the other part is in the Sala del Consistorio in the Vatican. Finally, there are the tapestries which today adorn the Papal rooms in the Vatican and in Castelgandolfo; among them, the 17th and 18th century Gobelin series from the Tuileries, a present by Napoleon to Pius VII, is particularly noteworthy.

MARIA DONATI BARCELLONA

left: 341) A Russian icon: *Christ Enthroned Between the Virgin Mary and St. John the Baptist.*

above: 342) A Serbian icon: *A Holy Bishop.*

right: 343) A Greek icon: *Last Judgment.*

left: 344) St. Nicholas and St. John: "Last Judgment".

below: 345) The school of Rome: *Christ*.

right: 346) Margaritone d'Arezzo's rendition of St. Francis of Assisi.

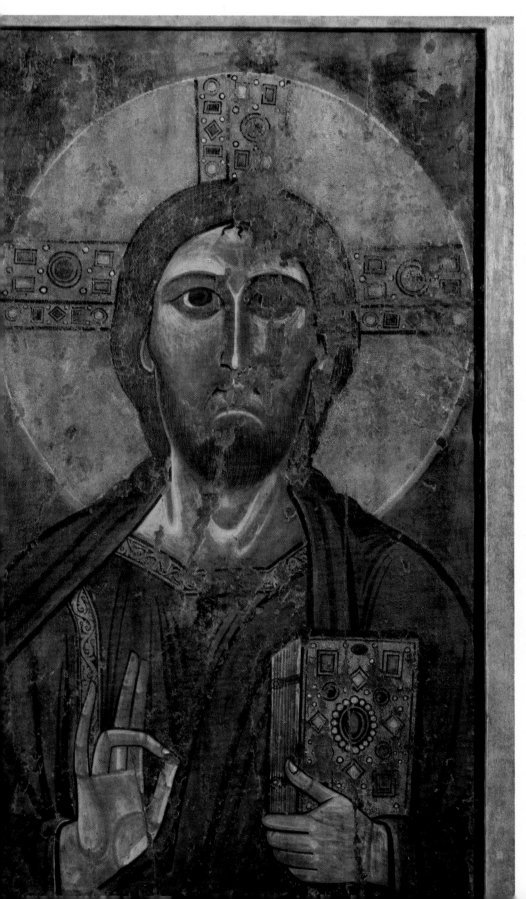

left : 347) A Tuscan
master : *Crucifixion*.

right : 348) Antonio
Veneziano : *St. James*.

.VITALIS .DE BONONIA .F.

left: 349) Vitale da Bologna: *Madonna*.

right: 350) The school of Giotto: *Crucifixion of St. Peter*.

below: 351) Francescuccio Ghissi: *Madonna del Latte*.

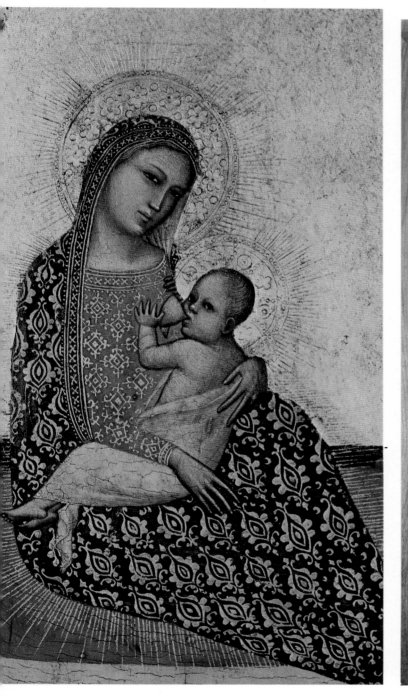

Questa e l'entrata e l'uscita della generale chabella del co
mune di siena. al tempo de laui buomini. pietro di giouani
batta chamarlengho. giouanni di simone di sere agniolo.
pietro di misere giouanni xpofani. antonio di guelfo piccicaiuo
lo. misere iacomo talomei. assegiutori. e giouanni di pietro pa
ni lini. Iscriptori. e ser giouanni di bartalomeo di pie
ro loro notaio per sei mesi i comiciati adi primo di
gennaio 1444 e finiti per tucto giugnio. 1445.

left: 352) Giovanni di Paolo: *Annunciation*.

right: 353) Masolino: *Crucifixion*.

below: 354) Lorenzo Monaco: *Nativity*.

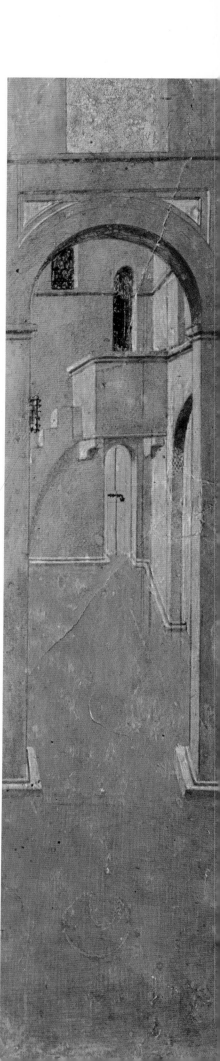

above: 355) Gentile da Fabriano: *Miracles of St. Nicholas.*

left: 357) Melozzo da Forli: *Angel with a Lute*.

below: 358) Filippo Lippi: *Coronation of the Virgin*.

right: 359) Melozzo da Forli: *Pope Sixtus VI Installes Bartolomeo Platina as Director of the Vatican Library*.

TEMPLA DOMVM EXPOSITIS:VICOS FORA MOENIA PONTES:
VIRGINEAM TRIVII QVOD REPARARIS AQVAM.
PRISCA LICET NAVTIS STATVAS DARE COMMODA PORTVS:
ET VATICANVM CINGERE SIXTE IVGVM:
PLVS TAMEN VRBS DEBET:NAM QVAE SQVALORE LATEBAT:
CERNITVR IN CELEBRI BIBLIOTHECA LOCO.

below : 360) Melozzo da Forli: *Head of an Apostle*.

right : 361) Francesco del Cossa: *Miracle of St. Vincent Ferrer*.

next pages.

above : 362) Carlo Crivelli: *Pietà*.

below : 363) Lucas Cranach: *Man of Sorrows*.

previous page: 364) Giovanni Bellini: *Pietà*.

upper left: 365) Pinturicchio: *Coronation of the Virgin*.

upper right: 366) Pietro Perugino: *St. Benedict*.

right: 367) Lo Spagna: *Adoration of the Magi*.

above: 368) Raphael: *Madonna of Foligno*.

left: 372) Sebastiano del Piombo: *St. Bernard.*

above: 373) Leonardo da Vinci: *St. Jerome.*

right: 374) Raphael: *Miracle of the Fishes.*

below: 375) Scarsellino: *Mary with Elizabeth.*

right: 376) Peter de Witt: *Holy Family with Anna and John.*

left-hand page

left: 377) Domenichino: *Communion of St. Jerome.*

above: 378) Pietro da Cortona: *Madonna Appearing Before St. Francis.*

below: 379) N. Poussin: *Gideon's Victory over the Midianites.*

lower left: 380) A van Dyck: *St. Francis Xavier.*

lower right: 381) Guido Reni: *Madonna with St. Thomas and St. Jerome.*

left: 382) Federico Barocci: *Head of the Virgin*.

below: 383) Guercino: *Doubting Thomas*.

above: 384) Caravaggio: *Deposition*.

right: 385) The school of Caravaggio: *St. Peter's Denial of Christ*.

left: 386) Carlo Maratta: *Pope Clement IX*.

below: 387) Baciccia: *Angels with Musical Instruments*.

right: 388) Daniel Seghers: *St. Gosvin, Wreathed with Flowers*.

left: 389) Francesco Solimena: *Archangel Michael Casting Satan from Heaven.*

below: 390) Georges Rouault: *Autumn.*

next page: 391) Maurice Utrillo: *The Church of St.-Auxonne.*

THE GREGORIAN-EGYPTIAN MUSEUM

The culture of ancient Egypt, at once magnificent and mysterious, has always exercised a strange attraction upon all those who have come into contact with it. Rome has been no exception, and the obelisk in the city, as well as the discoveries that have been made there during the past three centuries, bear testimony to this glowing admiration. It was thus unavoidable that this influence would also become noticeable during the excavations of classical monuments in the 18th and 19th centuries. The Popes found it necessary to make room in their collections of Greek and Roman sculpture for works from Egypt, or in Egyptian style. Under Clement XIV (1769–1774), Pius VI (1775–1799), Pius VII (1800–1823) and Leo XII (1823–1829), a supply of objects had been accumulated. These resulted from discoveries in Domitian's villa in Paola, in the villa in Tivoli, in the Horti Sallustiani (Villa Verospi), the Iseum of Campus Martius, and the Kanopos of Hadrian's villa, as well as from purchases made by Dr. De Assulle and Popes Pius VII and Leo XII. It was Gregory XVI (1831–1846) who decided to create the first Egyptian museum in the western world—an institution that was devoted exclusively to Egyptian culture, from its beginnings to the final stage of its decline. "He," as Ungarelli has written, in his somewhat ponderous style, "who saw that religion's point of departure did not lie beyond Egyptian architecture and that the latter was worthy of being united as subject and ally with the highest truth, he decreed that a wise selection should be made among the objects in Rome's possession, and that a considerable number of these objects should be set up in the Vatican" (*L'Album,* V, 394). That the Egyptian Museum was to be more than a mere repository or a collection of curiosities is proof of the "wise selection" among the finds now on display in Rome. Ungarelli concludes his minute description of the museum with the following commentary: "This is the sum total of scientific aids which have been brought together in the Egyptian Museum of the Vatican; and we have the wise endeavors and incomparable religious enthusiasm of the reigning Pope, Gregory XVI, to thank for it. For aside from the advantages which the arts will gain from this institution, theology is confronted here with the traces of the earliest traditions, pre-dating the revelations of Moses and the prophets. The inscriptions helped ecclesiastical philology to decipher the oriental Bible texts. What a great number of similarities there are in the customs of these two peoples, between God's chosen people and the Egyptians, whose histories are so closely interwoven! And thanks to the concordance of many of the scriptures with the Egyptian hieroglyphic inscriptions, a large number of Hebrew word forms and expressions appear in a new light!" (*L'Album,* V, 397). Strictly speaking, all this applies more to the study of Egyptology in general than to the Egyptian Museum in particular; nevertheless, Gregory XVI used these basic concepts as his point of departure. Following his death, very little was added to the museum, that which was added being more the result of the generosity of others (like the Khedive of Egypt) than of the interest of the subsequent Popes. The history of the museum can thus be easily summarized in three stages: finds from excavations and occasional purchases; acquisitions in large numbers, at the urgings of Gregory XVI; and later expansion, particularly under Leo XIII (1878–1903) and Pius XII (1939–1958) (Grassi room). It seems that the museum was consecrated without any special ceremonies in 1839, "on the sixth day of the month of the big flood" (February), as noted in the hieroglyphic inscription, designed by Ungarelli, which appears on the walls of the first two rooms.

Of greater interest, however, are the contents of the museum. Ungarelli expresses aptly the enthusiasm of the scholars in 1839 for the many objects that had been brought together in that one place: "The new Gregorian-Egyptian Museum offers an educated public an exact survey of the early history of the four most elegant arts, with which man expresses his intellectual abilities and with which he joins the pleasant with the practical. Referred to here are literature, painting, sculpture and architecture" (*L'Album*, V, 394). We must unfortunately note that the museum in no way offers an "exact survey of the early history" of the arts; in fact, it consists of chance finds and acquisitions. What has been particularly missing from the very beginning is an Egyptologist who could have tried to fill the gaps by attending to the historical structure of the institution and making eventual purchases. (After the founding of the museum, Ungarelli became director, without the funds for further important acquisitions.) Thus it is that the depiction of Egyptian history contains gaps too large to allow a comprehensive survey. On the other hand, the museum does possess individual pieces, or groups of objects, that are of great importance. The most significant and best known of these are: the head of a pharaoh (Mentuhotep), an example of the sculpture of the Middle Empire (2033–1980 B.C.); the colossal statue of Queen Tuya, the mother of Rameses II, from the 19th dynasty (1340–1172 B.C.); the "Temple Bearer," historically, the most significant work in the museum and the one that is studied the most; the Ptolemy group, a remarkable example of the Ptolemaic period in Egyptian art.

Perhaps of greater interest are the statues of the goddess Sekhmet, seven of which are sedentary and five erect. They are disfigured, and this was presumably intentionally done. It is probable that these statues were defaced by Egyptian Christians, who, thinking they were demons, wanted to render them harmless, thereby conforming to old Egyptian beliefs, whereby disfigured gods could no longer cause any harm. The statues which could be easily overturned, because they had no pedestals, were knocked down and severely damaged; those that either were too heavy or stood on pedestals, and thus could not be overturned, had hands and arms knocked off.

The wooden sarcophagi are another valuable collection. Many are painted and well preserved; others are undecorated. One old sarcophagus, later re-painted to correspond to the then prevailing taste, is of special significance. The six mummies also attract attention, since they contain objects that were discovered by the use of X-rays. The scarabaeuses are plain pieces, although some were conceived as commemoratives. Especially impressive is a scarabaeus commemorating the dedication of an artificial lake under Amenophis III (18th dynasty), in the eleventh year of his reign.

One of the most remarkable sections of the museum is the large collection of papyrus manuscripts from various epochs. Most of them originate from the necropolis in Thebes. During the past hundred years, they have been brought to Rome by Franciscan monks residing there. The most beautiful among them is the *Vatican Book of Death,* a 52-foot-long scroll which, although it is cut up into various parts, is very well preserved. This scroll contains most of the prayers that were added to the tombs to help the deceased deal with the monsters and dangers of the world beyond. Because of its clarity and the exactness of the writing, it is one of the outstanding examples among the well-preserved scrolls. The other scrolls are much shorter, and many of them are only in fragmentary condition. Nevertheless, they are of considerable scientific value, because of the scripts used (hieroglyphic and hieratic), the variety of the lettering and their contribution to the story of the origin (still very uncertain) of the *Book of Death.*

In conclusion, a few words about the rooms in which the museum is located today. They are the same rooms in the semi-circular corridor which Gregory XVI had made available for this purpose and which Fabris had decorated in somewhat clumsy "Egyptian" style. Following recent and thorough repairs to the "Nicchione" of Pirro Ligrio, the semi-circular corridor was given back its old splendor, with its plain, elegant lines. Only two rooms (rooms III and IV, based on the old enumeration) still contain the restored 19th century decoration. Rooms I and II, on the other hand, were transformed into the imitation of the main chamber of an Egyptian royal tomb (room II) with ante-chamber (room I). This reconstruction of the tomb serves as a fitting setting for mummies, sarcophagi, statues and smaller objects.

Thus we have, next to the fantastic and romantic 19th century conception of old Egypt, this new reconstruction, based on modern scientific knowledge. Like so much in the Vatican Museums, these two forms of exhibition are landmarks of the age in which they originated.

GIANFRANCO NOLLI

THE LATERAN MUSEUM FOR CHRISTIAN ART

After Pope Pius IX (1846–1878), in 1852, founded the commission for Christian archaeology "with the special mission of directing the excavations in the catacombs and arranging for their maintenance," he created, in 1854, the Lateran Museum. The latter was done to accommodate all those works which could not be kept in their original setting. The Pope commissioned Father Giuseppe Marchi S.J., secretary of the commission for Christian archaeology, and G. B. de Rossi with the collection of material from ancient tombs and basilicas, and with the establishment of the Lateran Museum.

The museum consists of two sections. The first is devoted to architectural fragments, sculpture and sarcophagi, whose iconographic variety is important both for the depiction of religious themes as well as for the development of early Christian art. The second section contains epigraphic material. The collection of sarcophagi, enriched for the sake of comparison by cast reproductions of originals from places beyond Rome, is really unique, both in quantity and quality. Some of the most significant specimens are illustrated in the second part of this chapter.

The second section has the largest collection of old Christian inscriptions, from the beginning of Christianity to the Middle Ages. G. B. de Rossi classified these as to content and origin. We can thus find here inscriptions from monuments of the Christian cult; epitaphs, inscriptions with chronological data, with indications of social class, hierarchy and native country; with symbols, emblems and rare forms.

Also worthy of mention is the special section devoted to Jewish inscriptions in Greek, Latin and Hebrew, most of which are from the Jewish cemetery on the Via Portuense near Monte Verde.

As a final item, one should note the unique Chinese stele, known as the stele of Sian-Fu (a place in northeast China, in the province of Shen-Si). Found in 1625, it was erected in 781 A.D. to commemorate the arrival of the missionaries in 653 A.D.

The inscription collection of the Lateran Museum is unique and its systematic arrangement is of great assistance to those studying the life and history of the early centuries of Christianity. Until 1963, the collections were maintained in the Lateran palace. They were then transferred to the area of the Vatican museums where previously only sculpture, mosaics and architectural fragments could be exhibited. The display of the large epigraphic collection is in preparation. One of the most interesting pieces in this collection, the inscription stone of Bishop Aberkios, can now be seen in the museum.

ENRICO IOSI

(RIGHT: 392) A FRAGMENT FROM A PAINTED RELIEF.

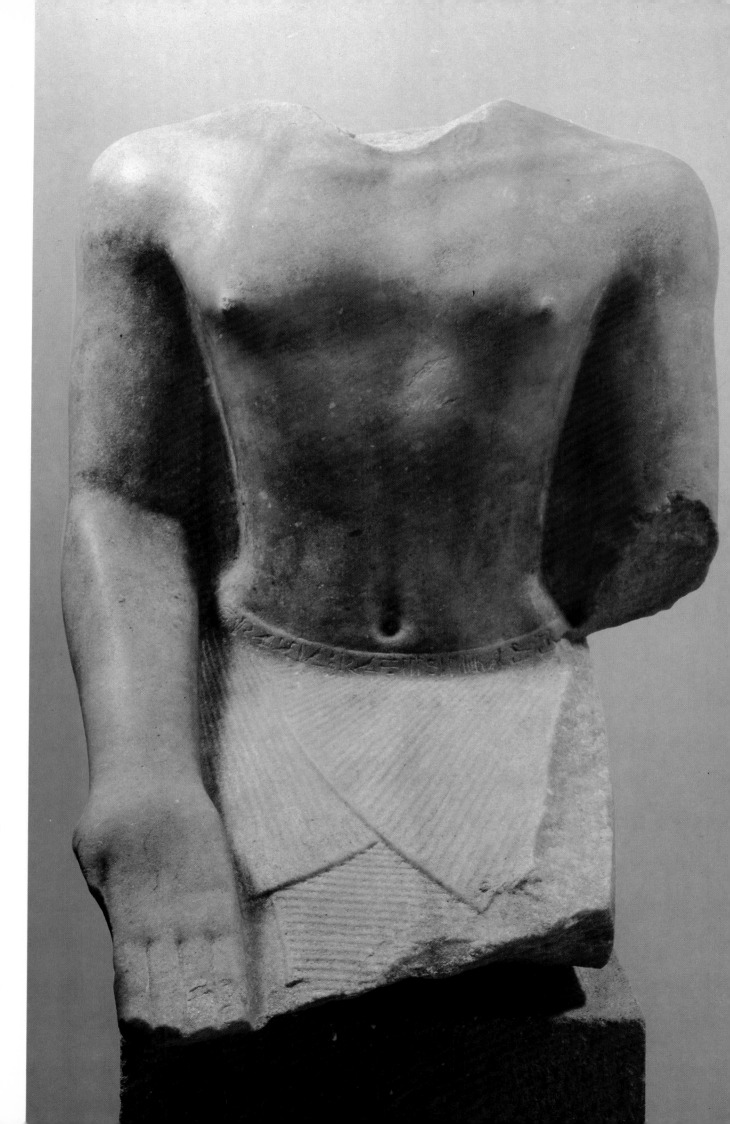

upper left: 393) Statue of Isis: *Beauty*.

upper center: 394) Temple Bearer – Naophoros.

upper right: 395) Queen Tuya.

below: 396) A papyrus burial scroll.

right: 397) Torso of a high priest.

left-hand page: 398, 399)
Sarcophagus with cover.

right: 400) Memorial stele.

left: 401)
Head of a princess
– from the cover of a
sarcophagus.

right: 402) Marble statue of
the Good Shepherd.

MVNIFICENTIA. LEONIS. XIII. P. M.

left: 403) The Good Shepherd.

below: 404) Sarcophagus with a ram at each corner.

right-hand page

above: 405) Theological Sarcophagus.

below: 406) Sarcophagus with the wine harvest and the Good Shepherd.

MVNIFICENTIA. LEONIS. XIII. P. M.

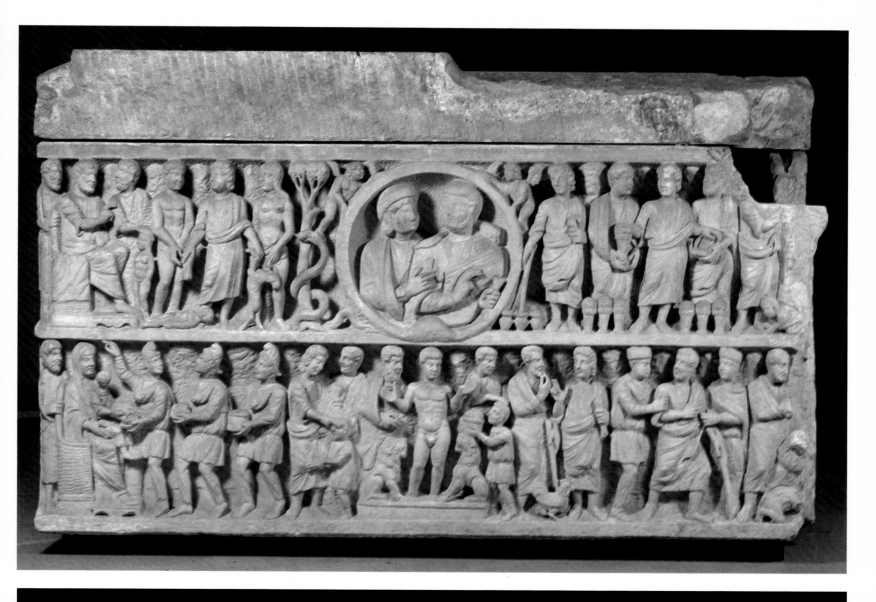

left: 407) Grave stone of Bishop Aberkios.

right-hand page

above: 408) Sarcophagus with olive trees.

below: 409) Sarcophagus of Junius Bassus.

next page: 410) The Cross of Justinian.

ST. PETER'S AND THE VATICAN BUILDINGS

1) A view of the dome of St. Peter's
The dome of St. Peter's is the culmination of Michelangelo's doubt-ridden artistic vision. The pairs of Corinthian columns encircling the drum form the beginning of the lines which continue upwards to become the ribs encircling the arc and finally end in the base of the lantern. The windows revealed in the drum are crowned alternately by triangular and arched tympana. This enormous project, on which Michelangelo worked until the end of his long life, was completed by Giacomo della Porta and Domenico Fontana, who modified his original plans by making the dome more pointed and less spherical. But despite this change, the dome embodies the synthesis both of the ideals of the great artist and of the Renaissance, and it points the way to artists of the Baroque. At Michelangelo's death, only the drum had been built. It was chiefly due to the relentless will of Pope Sixtus V that the dome was finally completed. In 1590, the dome was vaulted and crowned by the mighty lantern, surrounded by its pairs of columns. Despite the above mentioned alteration, the architects who completed the enormous undertaking proved themselves to be more than capable of building on the foundations laid down by Michelangelo, whose artistic genius is visible in every line of the finished work.

2) The fountain in St. Peter's Square
Bernini designed St. Peter's Square to give an impression of complete unity with the basilica itself, but at the same time revealing the latter in all its glory. The façade, often unjustly criticized, does indeed stand out. The fountain was remodelled from the one created by Maderna.

3) The façade of St. Peter's
Carlo Maderna, having won a contest arranged by Pope Paul V, found himself facing the difficult task of transforming the shape of the church into that of a Latin cross, and of building the façade. The latter extends on both sides beyond the walls of the church. It was planned to erect a bell-tower at each end of the façade to make the horizontal extension less apparent, but they were never built. The most impressive feature of the travetine façade is, apart from its sheer size, the mighty Corinthian columns which support the entablature and the roof on top of it. As Maderna had to take the already existing building into consideration, the façade does not bear the full stamp of the architect's personality. One individual feature, however, are the decorative Lombard carvings. The façade was completed in 1612, but work on the atrium continued until 1614.

4) A row of statues on the colonnades of St. Peter's Square
Bernini's majestic colonnades are crowned by a row of 140 statues of Popes, bishops and Apostles. This harmonious series of enormous statues reaching heavenwards adds the perfect finishing touch and gives a powerful chiaroscuro effect to Bernini's design, which was intended to highlight both Michelangelo's dome and Maderna's façade. Michelangelo had himself planned a similar decoration for the base of the dome, but Bernini was striving for a different effect—one which would represent the culmination of his striking architectural creation. The statues were carved by some of the leading sculptors of the day, including Francesco Mari, Michele Maglia, Lorenzo Ottoni, G. B. Theudon and Francesco Rondone.

5) The obelisk in the center of St. Peter's Square
The majestic complex of Vatican palaces rises above the colonnades of Gian Lorenzo Bernini. From left to right we see the following buildings: the triangular pediment of the Sistine Chapel, the courtyard of the "Maresciallo," the wing of Pope Paul V, the "loggie" of Bramante and Raphael and, finally, the great palace of Pope Sixtus V, built by Domenico Fontana. When confronted by a task as enormous as designing the square in front of the basilica, Bernini had to take many factors into consideration, including the size of the future square in relation to the great mass and proximity of St. Peter's. A plan to close off the square with a third arm was abandoned, as this would have blocked the view of the dome from the front. From the long and detailed

studies Bernini made in order to create his masterpiece, a drawing remains on which he has marked the exact point for observing both the dome and the square.
Bernini's colonnades are a glorious creation. Like a stage design, they provide an impression of complete unity. This theatrical effect encompasses both the basilica and its dome and the obelisk, which was raised on the square in 1586 by Domenico Fontana, and which had originally stood on the site of Nero's circus.

6) Columns at the base of St. Peter's dome
In the drum, the only section of the dome which had been completed by the time Michelangelo died, the arrangement of the paired columns standing out in bold relief to the retiring windows creates a strong impression of chiaroscuro in the massive stone. This pictorial effect is augmented by sculptural details such as the beautiful carved garlands and the decorative capitals of the columns. Sculptural details like these were an integral part of the grand architectural design. Michelangelo always emphasised that he was, after all, only a sculptor. Another great artist, Bernini, passed a different judgment: he admired Michelangelo both as a sculptor and as a painter, but as an architect, he considered him divine.

7) Looking beyond St. Peter's Square to St. Peter's and the Vatican Palace
Bernini chose the ellipse as the most dynamic form for St. Peter's Square and its surrounding complex of buildings. The square was not only thought of in terms of civic design but also planned as an atrium for the basilica. It was intended to highlight the impressive dome and to make Maderna's façade appear higher and more imposing. By combining the two sweeping arms of the semi-circle with the two straight sections which run up to the façade of the church, he created a synthesis among the arts of sculpture, painting and the theater. Work on the colonnades began in August 1656 during the pontificate of Alexander VII. Aesthetic reasons—for example, the desire to ennoble the shape of the square—and other, of a more practical nature such as the need to provide pilgrims with protection from the rain, influenced the Pope's plans. Bernini's combination of monumental classical forms with the Renaissance conception of space has been superbly realized. His sense of artistry can be seen in the enormous galleries which are to be found between the columns.

8) Gate in the courtyard of the Swiss Guard
This gate (architect possibly Giuliano da Sangallo, 1492) was modelled on the old St. Peter's gate in the walls of Pope Leo IV, dating from the 9th century. The present gate admitted pilgrims coming from the north into the square in front of the basilica. This is a view from the courtyard of the Swiss Guard.

9) View of the sacristy of St. Peter's
The sacristy, which lies on the south side of the church, is the work of C. Marchionni. It was not consecrated until 1784. This building, which is joined to St. Peter's by an archway, also contains the canons' sacristy and the treasure-vault, whose foundation dates back to the reign of Emperor Constantine.

10) The east apse of St. Peter's. To the right, the columns of the baldachin above the papal altar
For liturgical reasons, the proportions of the church had to be changed, and Maderna carried out the required extension. Although he accomplished his task sucessfully (especially the interior design), he was forced to sacrifice his own creative impulses. Following all this, Bernini found it extremely difficult to establish a harmony with the section dating back to the 16th century. The artist was aware of the need for establishing a focal point to attract the eye from the nave to the apse, so that both became a whole. To this end and out of the richness of his imagination—it was his intent to employ pictorial and lighting effects—came the magnificent design for St. Peter's chair.

11) Looking into the barrel-vault of the nave of St. Peter's
The nave was an architectural triumph for Maderna, who was commissioned to carry out alterations on the original plan. Faced with the task of continuing and completing work on a building which had been begun by another, he revealed his unusual talents—the main one being his exceptional sense of balance—in an original way. His work on the interior of the church had a considerable influence on the development of Baroque church architecture. Resting on huge piers is the entablature, above which rises the barrel-vault. The piers were decorated under Innocent X and the barrel-vault received its rich carvings during the pontificate of Pius VI.

12) The papal altar below the dome, with the baldachin
The baldachin, or canopy, is also the work of Bernini. It was carefully planned, partially to try and solve the problem of striking a note of unity between the section of the church designed by Michelangelo and that designed by Maderna. It finds its natural and harmonious continuation in the four piers of the dome. Bernini made niches in these piers and filled them with statues of the saints Longinus, Helena, Veronica and Andrew. Above them are the balconies, also created by Bernini, in which he installed the spiral columns taken from the "Pergula" of the old basilica.
Bernini's baldachin is a truly great work of art. The spiral columns which terminate in the beautiful volutes lend to it a sense of upward motion. The reflections of the gilded bronze have an intensely colorful effect which serves to accentuate the sculptural and architectural characteristics. The impressive result of all this not only bears witness to the richness of its creator's imagination, but also points forward to the characteristic elements of Baroque art. The columns, whose spirals are festooned with laurel branches in which putti play, are the work of Francesco Duquesnoy. The very beautiful decorative detailing on the column-bases and the entablature was carved in 1635.

13) Looking up into the dome of St. Peter's
Above the drum with its windows, crowned by triangular and arched "tympana," rises the mighty dome. The blue and gold mosaics on the dome are the work of highly skilled experts and were designed by Giuseppe Cesari, who was known as Cavaliere d'Arpino. Looking from the bottom upwards, they represent popes, Christ, the Virgin Mary, John the Baptist, the Apostles and, lastly, angels and seraphim. In the ring at the base of the lantern which shows the Eternal Father in the act of benediction, Pope Clement VIII ordered an inscription to be carved in honor of Pope Sixtus V, who was responsible for the vaulting of the dome. The mosaic figures of the Evangelists in the spandrels are the work of Giovanni De Vecchi, Cesare Nebbia and Marcello Provenzale.

14) "The Crucifixion of St. Peter." Bronze relief from the center door of the portico
In 1432, the Florentine Antonio Averulino, known as "Filarete," whose main claim to fame was his *Treatise on Architecture,* received a commission from Pope Eugene IV for the bronze doors of St. Peter's. He worked on them for more than twelve years, during the period when the Pope had been forced to leave Rome. The most interesting features of the work are the bas-reliefs on the borders framing the rectangular panels, as these depict events from the time of Eugene IV. They clearly reveal, as do the square panels below (the one in our picture shows the martyrdom of St. Peter), the influence of Donatello. This, however, has been tempered by the creative imagination of the artist himself, who looked back to the classical world, while at the same time giving free rein to his love of the pictorial and the fantastic.

15) Bronze statue of the Apostle Peter
On the right-hand side of the nave, in front of the transept, and on a Renaissance bronze chair, is the bronze statue of St. Peter, his right hand raised in benediction and his left hand holding the keys. The statue has been attributed to various artists. At first, it was thought to be the work of 3rd, 4th or 5th century artists; then, on account of the rigid posture, it was attributed to Arnolfo di Cambio (A. Venturi), and finally, mainly because of the curly beard framing the face, to a sculptor from the end of the 14th or beginning of the 15th century—for example, Nanni di Banco (Lavagnino). It can be reasonably assumed that the work was completed in the late Middle Ages. For the faithful, the statue has always been a special object of veneration.

16) "Triumph of the Cross." Fresco on the ceiling of the "Cappella della pietà"
The ceiling above the altar in what was formerly called the Chapel of the Crucifixion, but which is now known as the Chapel of the Pietà as it houses Michelangelo's famous work, was decorated by Giovanni Lanfranco (1582–1647) with a fresco known as *Triumph of the Cross.* This artist, trained in the school of Agostino Carraci, and, for a long time, a pupil of the Venetians and of Correggio, shows, in this work, the influence of these masters. In Rome, he was subject to the decisive influence of the "Luminismus Schedonis," and he also absorbed the pictorial characteristics of Annibale Carraci. The most impressive features of this fresco are its pulsating life, the bold movement of the masses and the brilliance of the colors.

17) Michelangelo's "Pietà"
The Pietà, Michelangelo's only signed work, was created between 1498 and 1499 during the artist's first stay in Rome as the guest of the merchant, Jacopo Galli. The statue was commissioned through Galli by the French Cardinal, Jean de Bilhères de Lagraulas, for a chapel in one of the buildings attached to the old basilica, the church of St. Petronilla, whose patrons were the French monarchs. *The Pietà* was placed in this chapel in 1499, but later was to be moved no less than 6 times. It was not until 1749 that was finally moved to the first chapel to the right of the new St. Peter's, where it was placed on a pedestal at such an angle that "it assumed a character far removed from Michelangelo's original intention" (De Campos). In this famous marble group, "the most moving work of the great master, who himself was deeply stirred by a suppressed, mute and yet passionate anguish," the influence of the Florentine tradition of the 15th century has been observed; likewise that of Ferrara in the pulsating rhythm of the drapery folds, and that of Leonardo in the statue's pictorial qualities. Critics have pointed out the iconographical origin of the grouping: the theme was born in Germany at the beginning of the 14th century and then spread right across Europe. The exquisitely beautiful face of Mary is possessed of a youthful and virginal purity. The pain it expresses is dramatic and yet subdued, a quality which is echoed in the submissive gesture of the left hand.

18) The tomb of Pope Alexander VII, by Bernini
As the documents in the Chigi archives prove, various artists worked on the tomb of Pope Alexander VII. The commission was accepted by the old Bernini "drained of all his strength" in order to show his gratitude to the Pope. The door underneath proved to be an obstacle, but at the same time inspired Bernini to create a work whose powerful and theatrical effect is highlighted by the rich decorations in colored marble. The statue of the Pope in prayer was executed between 1675 and 1676 by the French sculptor, Michele Maglia. Of the figures in the foreground, *Love* is the work of Giuseppe Mazzuoli, who also created the model for *Truth,* executed in marble by Lazarro Morelli and Giulio Catari. *Prudence* is the work of Catari together with Giuseppe Bararra, and it was also Catari who created *Justice.* The skeleton for *Death* was cast by Girolamo Lucenti.

19) "Love." A figure from the tomb of Pope Alexander VII
The Tuscan sculptor, Giuseppe Mazzuoli, who worked in Rome together with Ferrata, and therefore also with Bernini, created, between 1673 and 1675, the statue of *Love* in the left foreground of the tomb of Alexander VII. In the full female figure, holding a sleeping putto in her arms and looking down at the Pope in prayer, the influence of the statue *Love* on the tomb of Pope Urban VIII becomes clear. Despite the fairly harsh criticism to which Mazzuoli's statue has been subject and the inevitable comparisons with the Bernini figure, the smoothness of the modelling of the former and the loveliness of the facial expression are indeed remarkable. It is an interesting work from Mazzuoli's early period, "very 17th century and very Bernini" (De Logu). The artist later adopted a lighter and more elegant style which was typical of the 18th century.

20) An equestrian statue of the Emperor Constantine, by Bernini
The first Christian emperor is represented at the moment, when, on the eve of the decisive battle at the Milvian Bridge, he received a vision of the Cross together with a promise of victory. A cross of gilded wood has in fact been attached to the window which gives the statue light. In the background is

an enormous stucco curtain, whose folds emphasize the movement of the prancing horse and seem as if they are being blown by a whirl-wind coming from the Cross. The statue is, without doubt, one of the most brilliant theatrical works in the whole of Baroque art.

21) Façade in the San Damaso Court
The western arm of the loggie in the San Damaso Court was designed by Bramante as a new façade for the old papal palace. It was to replace the medieval façade which was likewise embellished with arches. Bramante left it unfinished but it was completed by his successor, Raphael; he added to the two galleries a third in the form of a colonnade, which corresponds to a third storey (also added) and which is now the office of the Vatican Secretary of State.

22) The arched gateway, by Bramante, in the San Damaso Court
For stylistic reasons, this beautifully executed gateway must be attributed to Bramante and not, as many critics maintain, to Antonio da Sangallo the younger, even though it was imitated by the latter in his re-modelling of the "Porta Julia" in the Belvedere Court, part of which had collapsed in 1531. Before he began the work, Sangallo drew up a precise plan on which this gateway with the six semi-circular steps in front of it can be seen.

23) In the Belvedere Court
The Belvedere Court was the architect Bramante's greatest dream, but it remained unfulfilled. His successors (Peruzzi and Santallo) continued the building in their own way. The construction of the massive buttresses against the inner wall for reasons of stability (this was begun under Pope Clement V) robbed the courtyard of its Bramantian character. It had in any case been destroyed beyond repair by the building of the Library of Pope Sixtus V, thus, virtually cutting it in two. Today, Bramante's original concept is very difficult to recognize. It is like trying to read the writing on a valuable but old and faded palimpsest.

24) A view from St. Peter's of the Vatican Museums
At the end of the street ("Stradone"), the entrance to the Museo Pio-Clementino can be seen (the Atrium of the Four Gates), the work of Giuseppe Camporeses (1793). The gate in the foreground on the right provided the entrance to the library of Pope Pius X. The ground-floor of this corridor (which, owing to the different levels, is the first floor if viewed from the Belvedere courtyard) is taken up by the Vatican archives, and the next two storeys by the Christian and Secular Museum, the Library and the Galleria delle Carte Geografiche. The last storey and the "Torre dei Venti" were added by Ottaviano Mascherino (the architect of Pope Gregory XIII) to the building erected by Pirro Ligorio under Pope Pius IV.

25) Portone di Bronzo, the entrance to the Vatican Palace
With great skill, Bernini fitted into the new entrance to the Vatican, which he himself had built, the main gate of the old papal residence of Paul II; this had been modernized under Pope Innocent VIII and then again by Carlo Maderna. The colorful uniforms of the Swiss Guard, who keep watch in front of it, are known throughout the world.

26) An exterior view of the west side of the Sistine Chapel
The contrast between the glowing colors of the exquisitely decorated interior of the Sistine Chapel and the war-like ruggedness of its exterior (architect, Baccio Pontelli; builder, Giovannino dei Dolci, 15th century) corresponds to the two-fold purpose which it served; firstly, as the palace chapel and, secondly, as a fortress which guarded the most accessible entrance to the Papal palace. In the foreground are the sacristy and the treasure-vault, both added by Popes Innocent VIII, Gregory XIII and Clement VIII.

27) The Scala Regia, by Bernini
This staircase is, as its name suggests, the courtly entrance to the Vatican Palace. False perspectives have the effect of making it seem longer than it really is. Bernini used to say that it was the most difficult to construct of all his buildings. In the carving over the entrance arch, two large angels blow long trumpets in honor of the founder, Pope Alexander VII, and they hold his coat of arms aloft.

28) The large niche in the Belvedere Court, with the pine-cone
The highest terrace of the Belvedere Court was closed off to the north by two-storey buildings which frame the famous exedra. This terrace was reached by the no less famous staircase of circular steps, the first half of which were convex, and the second half, up to the level of the exedra, concave. The exedra itself resembles a royal box in the theatre from which the Pope and his court were able to watch plays and other events taking place in the "curia superior." When this marvelous arrangement had to be destroyed for practical reasons and both wings and the exedra itself were raised a storey higher, the exedra looked like an apse without its arch. Pirro Ligorio, the architect of Pope Pius IV, took up, so to speak, the invitation offered by the building. He added the missing roof and transformed the ruined exedra into an enormous niche, which is in fact called the "nicchione." It is one of the boldest constructions of the whole Renaissance. Pirro Ligorio has sometimes been criticized for crowning his "nicchione" with a colonnade which was too small for its great mass. But this seeming disproportion can be generally observed in pictures of buildings painted by artists of the classical period, besides which it also has the effect of making the hemisphere of the "nicchione" appear higher and larger. Instead of the circular staircase—a product of Bramante's genius— we now find a staircase designed by Michelangelo, but even this has been ruined by alterations. In the middle stands the enormous bronze pine-cone (pigna) which was put up here by Pope Paul V. In the Middle Ages, it decorated a fountain in front of the old Vatican basilica. This is where it stood when Dante saw it and wrote of it in the *Divine Comedy* (*Inf.* 31, 58). Now it gives the "Cortile della Pigna" its name.

29) A view from the Vatican Gardens of St. Peter's dome
St. Peter's dome is the landmark of Rome. It can be seen by visitors to the Eternal City from a very great distance. The view of the dome from the Vatican Gardens is made especially beautiful by the contrast between nature and architecture.

30) The interior façade of the "Casino" of Pope Pius IV
Pirro Ligorio was very familiar with classical art. Known in his lifetime as an "antiquarian," we would describe him as an archaeologist. But here he has used his brilliant Neapolitan imagination to invigorate and enliven classical art. Without denying his roots in the glorious past, he has at the same time achieved unexpected results, which are unmistakably his own, and point the way to the creations of Borromini.

31) The lower façade of the "Casino"
The loggetta, which is decorated from top to bottom with frescoes and stucco, closes off the elliptic courtyard on the garden side. The building rises out of a fish-pond (the so-called "peschiera"). The lower section is decorated with niches containing classical statues. In the middle niche is a Cybele, under which the water of the fountain gushes forth. The four pilasters were decorated with enormous satyrs, but these were destroyed whilst reconstructions were taking place in 1824, under Pope Leo XII.

32) A view of the "Casino" of Pope Pius IV in the Vatican Gardens
Owing to the considerable slope of the ground, the loggia and the "palazzina" are built on an artificial terrace, on each side of which, two staircases lead from the villa down into the garden. The tower, looking as if it was only by chance part of the whole complex, does in fact provide the latter, as was intended, with the slightly carefree and rustic appearance that was thought fitting for a country residence.

33) The upper façade of the "Casino" of Pope Pius IV
In the center of the small court, which is covered by a simple mosaic in two colors, stands a charming little fountain with a putto spurting water at either end. It is the work of Jacopo da Casignola. The unique façade is completely covered by stucco work of a classical pattern. Its middle section, which has no windows, is not part of the first storey, but merely contains the arches of the rooms on the ground-floor.

34) The ceiling in the "Casino" of Pope Pius IV
The entrance-hall leads into the main reception room of the villa of Pope

Pius IV; it has a barrel-vault, decorated with frescoes and stucco. The stucco work was done by Tommaso Boscoli of Montepulciano, and the paintings are by Barocci, Federico, Zuccari and Santi di Tito.

35) The throne-room in the Papal apartments
The throne-room is known today as the Room of the Evangelists. The name comes from the statues of the Evangelists, works from the 15th century, which are arranged along the side-walls. The throne, which was inspired by classical models, contains several classical elements. Its arms are supported by two statues of St. Peter and St. Paul, attributed to the 15th century artist, Paolo Romano. They reveal "very evidently, the origin from which Papal power takes its authority" (R. Panciroli).

36) The library in the Papal apartments
The old red damask was recently replaced by materials of a lighter color, which set off the valuable old paintings. In the background one can see *The Resurrection of Christ* by Perugino, the teacher of Raphael.

37) The chapel of the Swiss Guard
This little 16th century church, now hidden behind Bernini's colonnades, is the chapel of the Swiss Guard. It is the only building which goes back to Pius V, the Pope of the victory of Lepanto. It was formerly decorated with frescoes by Giulio Mazzoni, but these were recently removed and taken to the store-rooms of the Vatican Pinacoteca.

38) Façade in the Library courtyard
Fontana was only responsible for the new architectural design for the wall of the western corridor of the Belvedere Court, that was built by Pirro Ligorio.

The façade here was decorated with black sgraffiti on a grey background, but today, most of these have disappeared.

39) The "Torre dei Venti"
The bold mass of the Tower of the Winds, which was built in the 16th century by Ottavio Mascherino, rises 239 feet, 6 inches above the Galleria delle Carte Geografiche. It was built for the purpose of astronomical observation and can be said to have been the first site of the famous Vatican Observatory (now housed in the Papal palace in Castelgandolfo). It was the meeting place of the commission set up by Pope Gregory XIII to carry out the calendar reform which bears his name. In the hall of the loggia, Circignani painted *The Four Winds*, the ship of St. Peter and the shipwreck off Malta. The other rooms contain 60 frescoes with landscapes and small figures by Matteo Bril.

40) A section of the mural decoration (architect Domenico Fontana)
The sgraffiti on the western wall of the Belvedere Court—built by Domenico Fontana and above which rises the "Tower of Winds"—are the work of an unknown artist. They represent allegorical figures and the heraldic emblems of Pope Sixtus V: the eight-pointed star and the pears (pere)—an allusion to the surname of the Pope (Peretti).

41) Bramante's spiral staircase
The bold construction of this staircase, which is to be found in the building housing the Museo Pio-Clementino, goes back to Bramante. It was built between 1512 and 1564. The columns become more tapered the higher up on the spiral they stand. According to the rules laid down by Vitruvius in his *De Architectura*, there are 16 Doric, 8 Ionic and 12 Corinthian columns.

THE BORGIA APARTMENTS AND RAPHAEL'S STANZE

42/43) The ceiling decoration in the Sala delle Arti Liberali
The splendid decorations of this beautiful ceiling, which were designed solely for the purpose of glorifying the Borgia Pope, are extremely effective. The Papal power of the Borgia coat of arms is shown in the golden rays surrounding the center of the ceiling, above which are the tiara and the keys. In the middle of the central arch, dividing the two cross-vaults, the golden bull—the heraldic animal of the Borgia family—is represented. A candelabra, with charming putti blowing fanfares on their trumpets—on the banners of which the Borgia bull appears again—is flanked by two animals in relief.

44) "Apostle and Prophet." Painting in a lunette of the "Sala del Credo"
Critics are of the opinion that Pinturicchio, both in the Sala del Credo and in the Sala delle Sibille, restricted himself to the design and direction of the work, without ever completing a painting himself. It is true that there is no trace of Pinturicchio's elegant style in the wooden and lifeless figures and in the chalky colors. Some critics attribute the work to Matteo d'Amelia, others to the even more indifferent artist, Tiberio d'Assisi. The Sala del Credo takes its name from the scrolls containing the articles of faith which each of the Apostles holds in his hand. At the side of each Apostle stands a prophet also holding a scroll with an inscription which refers to the same verse in the creed. This motif originates from medieval iconography.

45) A bust of Pius II
The most outstanding of all the objects to be found in the Sala delle Arti Liberali is probably the marble bust of Pope Pius II Piccolomini. It has been attributed to Paolo di Taccone, known as Paolo Romano. The subtle and lifelike manner in which the character of the Pope has been captured indicates that the artist was capable of compensating for the mediocre classicism of his other works by a true-to-life representation of his subject.

46) "Arithmetic." Painting in the "Sala delle Arti Liberali"
The Sala delle Arti Liberali is named after the liberal arts—the trivium (grammar, logic and rhetoric) and the quadrivium (geometry, astronomy, music and arithmetic). This theme, which often appears in medieval art, has been represented here in a Renaissance sense. The allegorical figures sit on thrones in a peaceful landscape against a richly gilded sky. They almost look like modern queens next to the people who have distinguished themselves in the arts that are represented. If the decoration of the room was designed by Pinturicchio—and the unity of ideas leads one to suppose that it was—the lunettes, on the other hand, show variations in the standards of execution, implying varying standards of ability on the part of different artists. Opinion among experts is still divided as to whom each individual painting can be attributed, but it is certain that Pastura and Tiberio d'Assisi played a not inconsiderable part. *Arithmetic* can probably be attributed to Tiberio d'Assisi. This is one of the better works, owing to a certain elegance of the figures and also to the smoothness and harmony of the colors—something which is otherwise absent.

47) "St. Catherine before Emperor Maximian." Painting by Pinturicchio in the "Sala dei Santi"
Most experts agree that the decoration of the Sala dei Santi was not only designed but also, for the most part, executed by Pinturicchio. The room is dominated by a huge fresco, occupying the whole of the wall opposite the window, which represents *The Disputation of St. Catherine* or *St. Catherine before Emperor Maximian*. The scene is set in one of those large, peaceful landscapes which seems as though it is merging into the distance, and it contains many naturalistic and imaginative features. The placing of the figures has been determined more by the need to fill the space with harmoniously balanced groups than by any strict adherence to the story, and they remain elegant

and indefinable—"pictures of a world of pure fantasy," resembling "beautiful animals of rare elegance" (Carli). St. Catherine, blonde, gentle and richly clothed, stands before the Emperor looking as though she were more inclined to indulge in some playful occupation rather than take part in a discussion demanding resolute concentration. This figure has been erroneously interpreted as a portrait of Lucrezia, the Pope's daughter. Equally mistaken is the idea that the Emperor is a portrait of her brother, Cesare. More probable, but also uncertain, is the interpretation that has been given to other figures: Andrew Paleologus as the man in the foreground to the left of the throne and, behind him, Antonio da Sangallo the elder and Pinturicchio himself.

48/49) "Barbara flees from her Father," "Susanna and the Elders." Painting in the Sala dei Santi
The two scenes on the left-hand wall, *St. Barbara*, and *Susanna and the Elders*, are considered to be almost entirely the work of Pinturicchio. The highly decorative character of the second composition is underlined by the shape of the fountain that follows the pointed curve of the lunette, and by the richness of the background, before which the somewhat unconvincing main figures have been placed. But the chief value of the painting lies in the beauty of the garden, filled with flowers and elegant little animals, and in the landscape, populated by small and lively figures.

50) "Madonna and Child, with Angels." Painting in the "Sala dei Santi"
The painted decoration of this room is completed by a gilded stucco roundel above the door leading to the Sala dei Misteri and it represents a *Madonna with Child*. Owing to a misinterpretation of the words of Vasari, this painting was for a long time considered to be a portrait of Julia Farnese. In fact it is, without doubt, one of the many Madonna paintings by Pinturicchio, as the high quality of the painting proves.

51) A marble frieze with a medallion portrait of Pope Alexander VI in the "Sala dei Santi"
The marble frieze which forms part of the border of the frescoes is decorated with allusions to the Borgia coat of arms. The carving of the bull appears repeatedly, as do other heraldic symbols and a shield depicting the sharply defined profile of Pope Alexander VI. The frieze is considered to be the work of a particularly capable successor to Mino da Fiesole.

52) "Isaiah." Painting in the "Sala dei Misteri"
The abundance of gold decorating the walls continues right up to the cross-vaulting, where the heraldic symbol of the Borgias appears once again. In the center of the eight corner spandrels there are medallions depicting figures of the prophets, including Isaiah, all holding scrolls with Biblical verses in their hands.

53) A mythological scene. Painting in the "Sala dei Santi"
In this room, the two vaults are divided by an arch which is decorated with octagonal panels depicting the story of Io and Argus. This is an allusion to the Pope's coat of arms. Io, who is loved by Jupiter, is changed by Juno's jealousy into a cow. The refined style of these paintings is characterized by a minutely observed exactness. The most remarkable among them is *Io, Argus and Mercury*. The god evokes a lyrical, almost musical atmosphere as he lulls Argus to sleep with his playing.

54) Pope Alexander VI. Painting (a section) in the "Sala dei Misteri"
There is one painting in this room which compensates for the shortcomings of the others. It is the remarkable portrait of Pope Alexander VI, contained in the somewhat indifferent *Resurrection of Christ*. Not only is it unquestionably the work of Pinturicchio, but, in this painting, the artist achieves previously unreached heights which place him on a level with the greatest portrait painters of the 15th century. Completely dominated by the powerful personality of Alexander VI, Pinturicchio at last allows something of his own nature to unfold; and he succeeds in revealing the striking contradictions in the complex character of this Pope. Capriciousness, intelligence, pride, sensuality and sensitivity—all these characteristics are revealed not only in the face with its well-defined features, but also in the fine, somewhat plump hands and in the whole impressive figure, swathed in the sumptuous choir-robe.

55) "Adoration of the Magi." Painting in the Sala dei Misteri
From an artistic point of view, the Sala dei Misteri ranks beneath the Sala dei Santi and is almost entirely the work of Pinturicchio's pupils. The master himself provided the plan for the painting and also possibly a few sketches, but he took little part in the execution of the work. Opinion among critics is divided as to whom the individual paintings can be attributed to, but they all agree that the excessive use of gold has reduced the quality of the paintings without concealing their fundamental weaknesses. *The Adoration of the Magi* is, however, one of the better works. Schmarsow has attributed it to a Florentine pupil of Pinturicchio, probably Bartolomeo di Giovanni, who, although no remarkable artist, did possess a sense of refinement and grace which is visible in this fresco.

56) "Saturn." Painting in the "Sala dei Pontefici"
Whereas the lunettes in the Sala delle Sibille, which depict alternately a Prophet and a Sybil, are the work of an indifferent successor to Pinturicchio, possibly Tiberio d'Assisi, the paintings on the ceilings and the octagonal spandrels are much more interesting. They were inspired by an astrological treatise entitled *De Sphaera*, and depict the planets and their influence on human behavior. The elegance of the figures and the type of landscape lead one to suppose that these frescoes—the one illustrated shows Saturn as an old man in a chariot drawn by a dragon—are the work of a Siennese pupil of Pinturicchio.

57) A ceiling painting in the "Sala dei Pontefici"
After the reconstruction work which took place in the 16th century, the only paintings which remain in the Sala dei Pontefici are those on the lunettes and the ceiling. The decoration of the central medallion in the vault is by Perin del Vaga. The medallion is placed in a square which was deliberately decorated with classical stucco figures by Giovanni da Udine, and also with strange emblems of the Evangelists; the latter seem to have lost their religious meaning in trying to meet the formal demands of a classical frieze. Perin del Vaga's elegant composition is made up of four angels. It is called *Dance*, and is one of his best-known and most successful works.

58) The "Baptism of Christ." Bronze-group, formerly in the "Sala dei Misteri"
In the show-cases in this room, one can see small statues from the 17th century that were erroneously considered to be models for larger ones. Of these small statues, *The Baptism of Christ*, by the Bolognese sculptor Alessandro Algardi, resembles almost exactly the bronze group by M. Caffa, from which many casts have been made. The most famous stands in the Museum of Pirano.

59) Raphael's Loggia
Exposure to air has had a pernicious effect on the frescoes and stuccowork of the loggia, especially on the pilasters, although less so on those in the vault. They were finally enclosed in glass by Pius IX, but the damage had already been done. Despite the lack of documentary evidence, the experts today are in agreement on attributing the various individual works to their respective artistic creators. The paintings in the first nine small vaults are by Penni, who worked in collaboration with Giulio Romano and Giovanni da Udine. One can safely attribute the following three to Perin del Vaga, and the last one to Tommaso Vincidor.
Perin del Vaga's name is also linked with that of Giovanni da Udine in the decorative grotesque paintings, which were clearly influenced by the Roman fragments of the "Domus Aurea." We know today how they must have looked because of two half-pilasters that were found under the 16th century wall, which closed off the final vault. The decoration it contains is very well preserved. Giovanni da Udine in particular was responsible for the stucco. After much experimenting, he discovered the formula for mixing material as used by the artists of the antique. However, he also employed objects from his own period, and one of his most charming compositions depicts Raphael's studio, in which five persons—including, perhaps, Raphael himself—are all busily going about their various activities, while (in a medallion) a boy is eagerly grinding colors.

60) "Disputa del Sacramento"—Triumph of the Christian Faith
Although the fresco in the Stanza della Segnatura is still given the traditional

name of *Disputa*, the unanimous opinion of the experts is that it is not a theological dispute that is depicted. What is represented in the painting is the "Glorification of the Holy Sacrament," or the "Triumph of the Christian Faith," in the form of the triumphant Church in Heaven and the militant Church on earth. The composition develops the theme on three different levels; and it has a broadness of vision and a largeness of conception that are new to the communicative facility of young Raphael, although they nevertheless belong to the 16th century. By carefully massing his figures along the curved lines, he was able to transform the large lunette into a concave, apse-like space. God the Father appears in the upper half in the brightest light, surrounded by a choir of angels. The Divine Son stands beneath this upon a semi-circle of clouds; to his right is the Madonna, while St. John stands on his left. On both sides are groups of figures that alternate between the Old and New Testaments. At Christ's feet, the Holy Ghost appears in the form of a white dove in the midst of four exquisite, small angels. They hold aloft the books of the Holy Scriptures and avert their heads slightly, as if they want to allude to a connection between heaven and earth. The bottom semi-circle depicts the militant Church, whose members are gathered on both sides of an altar; this latter is decorated with an ornamental pattern that was inspired by Leonardo da Vinci. The center of the composition is the monstrance on the altar. It is from this point that an imaginary line can be drawn, upon which are, in ascending order, the Holy Ghost, Christ and God the Father. This represents God's eucharistic corporeality, the subject of adoration by the Church on earth. All the perspective lines meet here; it is the point of departure for all the main sentiments expressed in the painting. The picture conveys an extraordinary impression of infinite space that appears to extend beyond the fresco's limits without detracting from the unity of the composition.

Sections from "The Disputa": 61) Group with Julius II.—62) God the Father.—63) St. Peter's, while under construction.—64) Group on the left side of the "Disputa."—65) Group on the right side of the "Disputa"

It has been said that this fresco was the first work in which the Renaissance attained full maturity. And it is indeed a classic example for the fusion, in line and color, of naturalistic observation with the imaginary—a fusion in which the insecurities and reminiscences of the painter, Raphael, are overcome and absorbed. Nevertheless, a careful examination reveals the sources of several influences. His early Umbrian training manifests itself in the large, still landscapes; in the rhythm of some of the figures; and in the almost wasteful use of gold in providing the figure of God the Father (62) with an aureole of light. The steady bearing and the clothing of various figures are reminiscent of the time he spent in Tuscany; while certain subtle color combinations, for example, in the portrait of Dante, are indicative of his growing interest in the Venetian palette. All in all, the dominant note of the entire composition is a clear and exemplary unity of style. Various personages of the heavenly and earthly Church have been identified. Often they are idealized images of famous historical figures; some of them can be made out by means of the name that, according to tradition, has been inscribed in each halo. There is no lack of successful portraits, like that of Julius II (61) to the left of the altar, where he is depicted, beardless, as Gregory the Great; or that of Sixtus IV (65) on the right side and, behind him, Dante; and, somewhat further back, Savonarola, the half-concealed monk with the black cowl. In the group behind Julius II (64) one can recognize, on the left, the Dominican monk, Fra Angelico, while the man leaning against the balustrade is Bramante. If the building taking shape in the background (63) is truly St. Peter's, this could be seen as Raphael's homage to Bramante, his fellow-citizen.

66) The "School of Athens," with the sections:—67) Center-group, with Plato and Aristotle.—68) Group of the geographers.—69) Group of the astronomers.—70) Group of the natural philosophers

In contrast to the glorification of the faith, we find on the wall opposite the glorification of rational knowledge, personified by man. In the first scene, the apotheosis of theology is completed by the vault of heaven. The apotheosis of philosophy, on the other hand, transfers the scene to the solid walls of a basilica, for which—according to Vasari—Bramante prepared the design. This is an acceptable theory, not only because the building resembles other works of Bramante's, but also because of the spaciousness and classical style,

both so typical of Bramante. Here, too, there is an allusion to the project of St. Peter's. One must give credit to Raphael for having understood how to create a composition that corresponds to the wide architectural space. Gathered around the central figures of Plato and Aristotle (67) are the old philosophers and sages, all grouped according to their respective schools. Seated on the steps is Diogenes (67), almost at the feet of the two representatives of the most important systems of classical thought, idealism and realism, and with his back to them. From the surrounding groups, we can recognize the following figures: to the left and further down, there is Socrates—next to a man with a turban (possibly Averroes); in addition, one can make out Epicurus, Pythagoras and, following an unidentifiable figure, Heraclitus, who is leaning on a stone block (70).

On the other side of the semi-circle, is Euclid, surrounded by pupils and leaning forward to describe a geometric figure (68). In the same section is Ptolemy—erroneously thought to be a member of the ruling dynasty in Egypt—depicted wearing a crown. Within the same group, Zoroaster can be identified by the globe he is holding in his hands (69). Further to the right and standing next to Sodoma is a young man wearing a black velvet cap: it is Raphael himself.

These are not the only portraits contained in the painting. As in the case of *The Disputa*, Raphael gave the faces of contemporary persons to figures of classical antiquity. This enabled him to draw a parallel between the past and the present. We can see Leonardo da Vinci as Plato, Bramante as Euclid, and Michelangelo—who was then working on the ceiling of the Sistine Chapel—as the pessimist, Heraclitus (70). This figure was added after the fresco had been completed, as indicated by the joints as well as by the fact that it is not among the cartoons in the Ambrosiana Library in Milan. What distinguishes it from the other figures is its undoubted resemblance to Michelangelo's Isaiah in the Sistine Chapel, as well as its plastic quality. All this is indicative of Raphael's return to the style of Michelangelo. This is perhaps a twofold tribute by the young painter to his mentor and rival. A lively interest in the classical world is revealed in the trompe l'oeil bas-reliefs, in the socle of the basilica and in the statues in the niches; of the latter, Apollo's rhythmic grace of movement harks back to some classical prototype that has yet to be pinned down by the experts. In this fresco, Raphael achieved greater maturity than in *The Disputa*. The change must have come about very quickly, for only a short span of time lies between the creation of the two works of art. Miraculously, all his insecurities seem to have disappeared. And even where certain eclectic elements remain, Raphael had a remarkable ability to assimilate them and make them part of his own style; at the same time, though, he acknowledged their origin. Note, for example, the influence of Leonardo da Vinci, whom Raphael met in Florence, in the soft chiaroscuro. Equally vivid is the influence of Sodoma (who may have worked with him) and that of the Venetian painters. Nevertheless, the expressiveness of his painting style is unmistakable and, although it has grown stronger, it has not lost any of its special harmony.

"Parnassus," with the sections: 71) Parnassus—Triumph of Poetry.—72) The poetess, Sappho.—73) The poet, Dante, from Parnassus.—74) Apollo, with the Muses, and the poets of antiquity.—75) The Muses, to Apollo's right

The ideal of beauty is expressed in the fresco, *Parnassus*, the mountain sacred to the art of poetry. Seated at its peak, next to the Castalian spring, is Apollo, who is depicted playing an instrument, the kithara. He is surrounded by the Muses, while classical and more modern poets are standing and sitting on the hillside (71). Like *The Disputa* and *The School of Athens*, the entire fresco is set in a semi-circle, in which the elegantly moving figures appear to be responding to the music issuing from Apollo's instrument rather than to the god himself. More than in the previous works, the figures—particularly those of Apollo and the Muses (74, 75)—assume the essence of classicism, in which idealism and naturalism coalesce in their joint quest for beauty. While they are indeed subject to mortal limitations, they attain the absolute by divesting themselves of everything that it not essential. We find portraits here too, and once again contemporaries have lent their features to the ancients, many of whose external appearance is unknown today. It is simple to identify Sappho, who holds in her left hand a scroll bearing her name (72). In the same group, somewhat more to the left, Petrarch stands next to a tree, with Aeneas at his side. Between Dante and Vergil (73) is Homer, whose face, turned skywards, mirrors the strong passions of the blind bard's poetry (74). Toward the end is a figure that is probably Statius. Next to the central group with Apollo (for whom Giacomo Sansecondo—a musician and improvisor at the Papal court—may well have been the model) and the Muses, we follow the descending line of the hillside and arrive at a bearded poet; there are those who are convinced this represents Ariosto, while others maintain it is Castiglione. Behind him, one can see the head of Boccaccio, as well as another young poet—perhaps Tibullus or Propertius. And, finally, one sees Tebaldes and Sannazaro. Hoogewerff claims that these last three figures represent the Greek tragic poets, Aeschylus, Sophocles and Euripides, while other experts (Passavant) see in them Horace, Ovid and Sannazaro.

"The Cardinal Virtues," with the sections: 76) Prudence, between Fortitude and Temperance.—77) Prudence.—78) Fortitude
The execution of the fresco post-dates that of *The School of Athens* but pre-dates the adding of the figure of Heraclitus; it was thus done prior to August 1511, before the paintings on the opposite wall, the wall of "Justice." The critics are not in agreement on its artistic value. According to some, Raphael's classicism had become academic and sterile. Other experts—indeed, most of them—believe that Raphael's depiction of beauty revealed, more than ever before, his inner world, thus enabling him at times to attain such a high degree of lyricism that the painting itself was transformed into poetry and music. On the wall devoted to "Justice," that greatest good, the artist had it appear as a "Virtue" in the lunette and as "Law" on both sides of the window. The three Cardinal Virtues, Prudence, Fortitude and Temperance, are arranged—like the three Theological Virtues—in the lunette in a balanced and clever interplay of forms and levels, all of which serves to solve the spatial problem. (The fourth Virtue, "Justice," appears in the vault.) In breast-armor and helmet is "Fortitude," which holds an oak-branch in allusion to the house of Julius II della Rovere (78). "Prudence" is represented with a double-face, while she looks into a mirror held aloft by a "puttino." The double-face, with a young girl on one side and an old man on the other, proclaims the value of experience; this prevents the repetition of past errors and sees into the future with the eyes of the past. Raphael devised the whole thing with extreme care and knew just how to harmonize both the traditional allegorical meanings and the aesthetic demands of the time by providing the bearded face of the old man with an elegant hair-style (77). Graceful and elegant, "Temperance" holds her symbolic emblem, reins and bridle. The three chief figures indicate a return to more solid forms, as previously seen in the figure of Heraclitus, in *The School of Athens*. It is, in subdued version, Michelangelo's style that has been completely absorbed into Raphael's personal artistic concept. Wind has identified the three Theological Virtues in three of the four putti, whose presence had previously been attributed to the requirements of the composition. The first one on the right, pointing heavenwards with a finger, could be "Faith"; the putto with the lit torch could be "Hope"; whereas the putto plucking acorns from the oak-branch could be "Charity,"

Ceiling frescoes in the Stanza della Segnatura: 79) "Astronomy."—80) "Adam and Eve"—The Fall of Man
In addition to the allegorical figures of Theology, Philosophy, Poetry and Justice in the roundels of the vault, rectangular medallions contain scenes which refer to the main frescoes. In *Study of the Globe* there is an allusion to "natural Truth" in *The School of Athens*; this is expressed either in the study of the vault of heaven by the science of astronomy (79), or in the initial gesture that set the world in motion. *Adam and Eve* (80) refer to the "felix culpa" that inspired the incarnation of the Savior and is thus a "miraculous Truth." Among the other scenes, *The Judgment of Solomon* refers to "Justice," while *Apollo and Marsyas* alludes to the "art of poetry." (The execution of this fresco is attributed to Peruzzi.)

81) "The Expulsion of Heliodorus from the Temple in Jerusalem."—82) The High Priest prays for succor. A section
The fresco, which has given the room the name of "Stanza dell' Eliodoro," depicts Heliodorus, treasurer to King Seleucus IV Philopator, as he is being driven out of the temple by angels of the Lord (81). This occurs in answer to the prayers of the high priest, Onias, who wishes to prevent Heliodorus

from stealing the temple treasury at the request of the temple governor, Simon. The composition—reminiscent of *The School of Athens*—gets its direct dramatic accent from the division of the foreground into two groups; and this division leads one's eye to the center of the painting, where the high priest is kneeling in prayer in front of the Ark of the Covenant and the seven-branched candelabrum. In contrast to the immobility of this figure (82), the rest of the scene is marked by a dynamic movement of the figures and the dramatic use of lighting. No other Raphael painting expresses such passionate feeling. The shimmer of light that illuminates the interior of the building also serves to underline the drama of the priest's prayer and the spiritual greatness of the Divine intervention. Outside the temple, the whirling motion of the figures attains a climax on the right side of the painting, where a white horse bearing one of the avenging angels rears up threateningly above Heliodorus, who has been thrown to the ground. The force of this attack has thrown the train of plunderers against the side-wall, crushing them. The left side of the picture is calmer. The relatively controlled gestures of the kneeling women and the men moving toward the column, turn into immobility as soon as we recognize the Pope with his bearers. His immobility is explained by his anachronistic presence in the painting. He takes no part in the action, and is a mere spectator. The employment of this figure has symbolic meaning. It alludes to the stubborn defense of the spiritual and temporal rights of the Church by Julius II.
Stylistically, this fresco is of great interest not only because of the use of lighting and the experiment with movement, but because of its color, which has a special meaning. As with the Venetians, the color has its own individual value, and is not used in Florentine manner as a mere addition to the composition. Raphael's artistic experience appears here to have been enriched by a deeper interest in the color-scale; and for this he is probably indebted to the influence of Sebastiano del Piombo.

83) "The Miraculous Mass of Bolsena."—84) Members of the Swiss Guard. Section
The deep interest in the possibilities of color—as previously indicated in *Heliodorus*—attained a climax in the *Miraculous Mass of Bolsena,* which illustrates an incident that took place in this city in the year 1263. The painting depicts the moment during Mass, celebrated by a Bohemian priest on his way to Rome, when, as in reply to his doubts over transubstantiation, he saw blood dripping from the Host (83). Here, Raphael was faced by a problem similar to that which he had more successfully solved in the case of "Parnassus." The irregularity of the wall, with a window that was not centered, he turned to his advantage. His solution—seen for centuries as a standard for optimal use of space—was to integrate the window into a series of steps and to assemble the architrave in one focus with the base of the podium, upon which the altar is placed, in the middle of the lunette. The work is brought to perfect completion by the balanced solution to the problem of the figures, the movement that pushes them left of center and their immobility on the right side. A remarkable choir pew in the center links up all the architectural details and transforms the entire scene into a relief; this makes the white altar cloths and choir shirts appear so white against the dark wood that the window seems to be darkened. The demands of the composition correspond exactly to its interpretation. The asymmetric arrangement of the steps and the restless motion of the figures behind the officiating priest express uncertainty and doubt; this is in contrast to the figures on the other side of the fresco, where solid, calmly kneeling figures allude to the certainty of faith. Even the flames of the candles have the same meaning: those on the one side are flickering, while those on the other side burn steadily. Certain moments of pure poetry stand out in the successful execution of this painting: the face of the officiating priest, enraptured and sunk in adoration; the portrait of the Pope, whose expressive strength is concentrated in his piercing gaze. There is, in addition, a deep painterly sensibility; this generates such varying shades of color as green, blue and yellow, to the pink and pale green of the female figures, to the red of the priest's chasuble. These are color combinations, such as in the case of the remarkable group of kneeling Swiss Guards (84), that had never before been attained. It has never been proved, but this particular color interpretation has led to the surmise that Lorenzo Lotti's contribution was not merely limited to his influence upon Raphael's artistic sensibilities. Some experts now think that he may well have participated directly in the painting of these figures (Longhi).

85) "Deliverance of St. Peter."—86) The Angel and the Apostle. A section
Once more Raphael was forced to work within a difficult space: a lunette interrupted by a large window in the center (85). The division of the space into three different phases of the miracle solved the composition problem. In this painting, the artist's expressive strength achieved great heights; the lighting burns so brightly—especially in the middle section (86)—that it almost extinguishes the light coming from the window. As in the case of *The Miraculous Mass of Bolsena,* Raphael viewed the difficulties here as a challenge and turned them to his own advantage; they thus appear to be an indispensable element of the painting's composition.

87) "The Great Fire in the Borgo"
The old basilica of St. Peter's forms the background here, enclosed by a colonnade on the left and by a covered fountain on the right. In front of these, the figures are carefully balanced and harmoniously posed; however,

the entire arrangement is so forced that no poetic feeling can break through. In addition, one notes here an abundance of scholarly allusions, relating to a study of classical prototypes; these, however, did not interest Raphael himself, but rather one of his chief assistants, Giulio Romano. It is to Giulio Romano, therefore, that we are indebted for a large part of this fresco, and he was aided in its painting by Francesco Penni. On the whole, the fresco is very academic, although several figures do possess elegance and even poetry.

88) "Moses and the Burning Bush." Ceiling fresco
Like the other scenes that decorate the imitation Gobelins of the vault, this fresco repeats the theme of the walls: the intervention of Divine Providence. The ideas certainly are Raphael's, as indicated by the designs, to which belongs a fragment of a cartoon showing Moses kneeling (now in the National Museum at Naples). The frescoes, however, were probably done by the same Guglielmo di Marcillat who had already assisted Raphael in the "Stanza della Segnatura."

THE STUFETTA OF CARDINAL BIBBIENA AND RAPHAEL'S LOGGETTA

89) Niche in the south wall; 90) A view of the Stufetta
Although numerous contemporary documents mention Raphael as the painter of the frescoes in the Stufetta, none of them attributes its construction to him—despite the fact that all are in agreement that it is indeed his work. This is so because, firstly, the style confirms his authorship and, secondly, he was at that time architect of the Papal palace. In addition, the apartment was intended for Cardinal Bibbiena, his patron and close friend. Despite its small size, the harmony of the proportions makes the Stufetta one of the most important monuments of Italian Renaissance architecture. We see here the south wall with the niche (90) in which Cardinal Bibbiena wanted to place the famous marble statue of Venus, and the niche in detail (89); it is a combination of classical reserve with grace.

91) "Venus Is Wounded by Amor." Fresco on the south wall
Venus, seated on a rock in a beautiful landscape, presses her left hand to her breast, which has been pierced by one of Amor's arrows; he is shown seated next to her right knee. The painting is in poor condition, the color cracked and peeling away from the wall, but it is nevertheless believed to have been painted by Raphael. This view seems to be confirmed by a sketch Raphael did of the figures of the goddess, which is today in the Albertina Collection in Vienna.

92) "Cupid in a Tub, Drawn by a Sea Serpent." Fresco on the pedestal of the east wall
A winged Cupid, armed with a quiver thrown over his shoulder, uses a reed to whip into action the two fantastic sea serpents that draw his vehicle, a tub on wheels, through the waves. The colors are in lively contrast to the dark background. This picture is better preserved than the previous one, and even the red frame is almost undamaged. The meandering ornamentation of the frame consists of tiny fish, the so-called lattarini of the Lake of Castelgandolfo; it was painted by the animal specialist in Raphael's studio, Giovanni da Udine.

93) "Birth of Venus." Fresco on the east wall
The rosy goddess, almost with her back to the contemplator, rises out of a green sea and places her left foot on a floating sea-shell, while the right foot is still immersed in the deep. The small dainty figure wrings its wet blonde hair with a gesture that recalls the Anadyomene of Apelles, although nowhere is there any reference to a particular antique prototype. Here, too, the condition of the painting is poor. However, what remains is of such high quality that we must list it among those Stufetta frescoes that were executed by Raphael himself.

94) "Venus and Cupid." Grotesque painting.—96) Grotesque painting, with a depiction of the river deity of the Nile.—97) Grotesque painting, with a depiction of a river deity
In the mythological paintings in the Stufetta, antique art is mirrored in that of the Renaissance, without any attempt to repress the particular hallmarks of the latter. In grotesque painting, on the other hand, it is antique art alone that dominates, and this without any alterations. The first case we can attribute to the realm of inspiration; in the second case, however, we are confronted by an extremely faithful imitation of both the form and the spirit of the painted decoration of Nero's "Domus Aurea." But it is an unusual kind of imitation and is probably unique in the history of art; for it does not merely enliven a lifeless facsimile, but is a work of art that, according to aesthetic criteria, possesses full validity. Indeed, Raphael's adherence to this style is so complete and deep that we get the impression he did not just imitate its external appearance. One feels that, through him, the art of the antique, after sixteen centuries, achieved a late flowering; it was thus able to fulfill the theoretical dream of the Humanists: namely Renaissance, or re-birth. That does not seem so unusual if one takes into account the basic component of his style: the brilliant eclecticism which Vasari had already noted enabled him to integrate apparently incompatible aesthetic concepts, like those of Michelangelo and Titian.

We show here three examples of the grotesque, in which Raphael's imitative abilities are clearly revealed. In illustrations 96 and 97 we see two small temples with extremely slender columns, similar to those in the underground colonnade of the "Domus Aurea." Between these columns, in each case a winged Cupid appears; one of them bears a silver vessel with ears of wheat, while the other carries a laurel wreath. In each of the works, we see further to the left a river deity. One of them leans against an amphora (97); the other (perhaps the Nile) leans against a lion (96), while a slave washes his hair. The "impressionistic" mastery of the brushwork in these paintings is so obvious that they cannot possibly be attributed to one of Raphael's pupils. They are, in fact, artistic standards that the master offers his pupils; based upon them, his pupils and assistants tried to emulate their master on the other walls of the Stufetta and later in the Loggia, but never did they attain Raphael's inspired lightness. The third picture belongs to this group and is perhaps the work of Giovanni da Udine. It depicts Venus and Cupid (94) in the middle of a picture in chiaroscuro on a black background, similar to a piece of Roman ornamentation. Seated on the sides—and painted almost in the style of 19th century realism—are two birds on vine sprigs that, against all physical laws, hang freely in space, winding their way upward.

95) "Pan and Nymph." Fresco on the west wall
In the shadow of a rock covered with bushes, Syrinx, the nymph whom

Pan desires, combs her long blonde hair, while the love-struck satyr stealthily approaches her from the right. In order to protect herself from him, the nymph was turned into a reed, from which Pan fashioned a musical instrument that is known as the Syrinx, or the Panpipe. The pose of the female figure recalls that of the *Aphrodite of Doidalsas*, or the kneeling Venus who, on antique ornaments, is depicted drying her hair in front of the Labrum (the Roman bathtub). This picture, too, is badly damaged; but what does remain of it allows one to assume that it was painted by one of Raphael's pupils—possibly Penni—on the basis of a sketch by the master. A reverse version of the composition was engraved by Marco Dante, a pupil of Raphael's favorite copper-plate engraver, Marcantonio Raimondi.

98) "Crane and Wild Boar." Fresco on the ceiling
The most severely damaged part of the Stufetta is on the ceiling of the ribbed vault; with its decorated panels, it too was inspired by the coffered ceiling of the "Domus Aurea." Following the restoration in the year 1954, the "legibility" increased considerably, although it is still inferior to that of the wall frescoes. The small picture depicts a crane that has shoved its bill between the jaws of a wild boar. Although one of the best preserved of the ceiling frescoes, it still allows one to draw no conclusions as to the painter. It is possibly by Giovanni da Udine.

99) A view of the Loggetta
Raphael's Loggetta, not listed by Vasari, was divided by walls into three rooms—most probably in the 16th century, at which time the paintings were covered over with plaster. This room had thus been completely forgotten until it was discovered during construction work in 1942. It was almost completely renovated during the careful art and architectural restorations that took place between 1943 and 1945, in the course of which difficult problems concerning the original condition had to be solved. The walls, with their musical alternation of niches with small statues and small paintings, have painfully large gaps; these were brought about by the removal of a number of doors. A decision was made to restore the former rhythm by repainting the missing sections wherever this was possible. It was also resolved that the new panels would be set apart from the others by enclosing each of them in a thinly drawn line; the repainted panels were also subjected to a more concise technique. This restoration has been generally acclaimed, because it satisfies the artist without deceiving the expert.

100) "Woman Spinning with a Cat." Fresco on the windowed wall.—102) "Woman Spinning with a Child." Windowed wall.—106) "Philosopher with a Lantern"
Among the most charming details of the painted decorations is a group with small figures, remarkable for their unmistakable style, which causes us to ascribe them to Perin del Vaga (1500–1547), another Florentine, who joined Raphael's group for the painting of the Loggia of San Damaso. Three of them have been selected in which Perin's character as an artist is clearly shown. Two women engaged in housework, and sitting on podiums, decorate the penultimate niche; and an old man in a toga strides in majestically, with a lantern in his hand, while winged genii bear compasses and other mysterious objects (106). Of the two women, one is working at a spinning wheel (102) and the other with a distaff (106). The first has her son, who is reading intently, on a chair next to her, and the other is smiling at her child, who is blowing a sphere-shaped instrument, while behind her a cat tries to catch the shuttle. Perin del Vaga repeated with minor alterations the motif of the woman with a spinning wheel on the left-hand edge of the tapestry of *The Miraculous Draught of Fishes*, and the same female type is to be found in the Venus from the *Banquet of the Gods*, which he painted in Castelgondolfo. His style, almost that of a miniaturist, stands out from that of his collaborators on the Loggetta. He takes less care than the others to imitate the impressionism of antique painting.

101) "Winged Genius Donning a Helmet."—103) The "Contest Between Apollo and Maryas." Painting along the niched wall.—108) Decorative grotesque figures between two niches.—109) The "Judgment in the Musical Contest on Olympus"
In the Loggetta, the parts which Raphael left to his collaborators—Giovanni

da Udine, Francesco Penni, Perin del Vaga and Giulio Romano—can be clearly distinguished from one another by their stylistic character. Giulio Romano (1499–1546) seems to be responsible for some peculiarities among the grotesque figures, such as the winged genius donning a large helmet (101): a playful motif which he later repeated in the portrait of Gradasso Berrettai da Norcia, the jester of Leo X, whom he portrayed in a fresco in the Sala di Costantino. With still greater certainty we can ascribe to him the three small paintings in light colors on a dark background that hang like votive pictures in the middle of the "grotesque figures" between the four niches (108). These show episodes from the fable of Apollo, the lyre-player, who was challenged by Marsyas, the flute-player. In the first (103), we see the famous contest; in the second (109), all Olympus pleads with the sun-god to spare the loser; while a third picture illustrates the agony of the impudent satyr, flayed alive by Apollo. These charming little pictures allow us to understand better the nature of Raphael's relationship to antique art, which he and his school strove to revive, for luckily we know the original classical model. Giulio Romano took it from the painted decorations of a Roman "columbarium" which has been destroyed but about the middle of the 16th century was copied by the Dutch humanist Stefano Wynants (also known by the name of Pighius). These drawings are today in the so-called "Codex Pighianus" of the Berlin Library.

104) Decorative grotesque painting on the ceiling.—107) Grotesque painting on the windowed wall.—111) Minerva. A section from the ceiling decoration
In the grotesque painting of the vault, Raphael's Loggetta shows particularly clearly its heavy dependence on the decoration of the "Domus Aurea". The same impossibly slender temples can be seen, peopled with small figures who stand absurdly balanced on delicate flower stems in a world of careless fantasy. Winged genii bear cornucopiae of ears of corn—an allusion to the name of Cardinal Dovizi (*dovizia*=abundance) da Bibbiena; while in the center of the vault, in two series of rows arranged rectangularly, eagles, lions, griffins and even an elephant and a giraffe are painted to satisfy Leo X's zoological tastes. Vasari said of him that he loved the company of "baboons, witches' cats, civets and other exotic beasts." Among the figures painted in the covered niches we can make out the Bacchus of Michelangelo and of Sansovino, and the famous Goddess of Victory of Brescia, which we meet again in stucco in the large Loggia. Here they appear in color as living beings, not as statues. No doubt arises in ascribing these grotesque paintings to Giovanni da Udine (1494–1561). The light brush, which could improvise with cheerful assurance, and the precise realism of the beasts portrayed, above all of the birds, provide a signature no less genuine than that which he scratched on the underground cloister (cryptoporticus) of the "Domus Aurea." With regard to the beasts, let us quote an important passage from Vasari's biography of Giovanni da Udine: "He particularly liked to paint birds of every kind, so much so, that in a short time he produced a book of them that was so colorful and beautiful, that it became the joy and plaything of Raphael."

105) "Cupids in Vulcan's Forge." Frontal wall.—110) An allegorical niche-figure
Of the four allegorical figures—probably the seasons—in the niches, painted in chiaroscuro on purple backgrounds with green frames, the first one to the left of the entrance was lost, and only the top has remained of the third. The fourth is reproduced here. The fairly sturdy build, the plump hands and the simplified and rounded forms seem to indicate the Florentine Giovan Francesco Penni (1488–1528), a devoted but mediocre pupil of Raphael. His style can again be recognized in the "Vulcan's forge." This scene, highly imaginative in its conception, now hangs over the southern door of the Loggetta. But despite its resemblance to Penni's other work, it was most probably executed by one of his unknown assistants.

112) Part of the Majolica floor tiles in the Loggetta
The beautiful floor of Spanish-Moorish ceramic tiles was in extremely bad condition, many of the tiles being broken or missing. The best preserved ones were re-arranged in various rectangles and fitted into a newly laid terra-cotta floor without decoration. Today the Loggetta is part of the office of the Secretary of State of the Vatican.

113) Bronze door to the Vatican Library

From the construction of the new papal residence under Sixtus V (1585–1590) and during the next three centuries, this harmoniously proportioned door of hewn travertine was the entrance to the Vatican Library. It opens into the middle of the Galleria Lapidaria (formerly called Galleria della Cleopatra on account of the statue housed there). Visitors had to go up from the Cortile di San Damaso, where a plaque pointed to the entrance to the Library and the museums. Above the cornice rises a large coat of arms of Sixtus V, and above the architrave is the inscription: Sixti PP.V. Biblioth. Vatic. The bronze doors bear two coats of arms and the name of Pope Urban VIII (1623–1644). The bees in the coats of arms, and the letters, are gilded.

114) The Salone Sistino in the Library

This impressive hall (23 feet long, 49 feet wide and 30 feet high) is divided into two naves by six pillars. It has a rib vault, decorated with two cycles of frescoes whose common theme is the glorification of Writing and the Book as a means of communication and of protecting Truth, and the representation of the annals and work of Sixtus V. On the pillars runs a sequence depicting the inventors of the alphabet, and on the walls, one depicting the ancient libraries and the Ecumenical Council. In the back and in the lunettes there are painted scenes and episodes from the pontificate. The design of the objects, ascribed to the curator of the Vatican Library, Federico Ramaldi, and to scholars of the Papal court, belongs to the time of the Counter-Reformation. According to tradition the work was carried out by a hundred painters led by Cesare Nebbia and Giovanni Guerra; the frescoes, referring to Sixtus V, originate from Brill and Antonio Tempesta. The closed wooden cabinets along the walls and around the pillars were installed in 1614 to keep manuscripts. The Salone represents the historical site of the Vatican Library and today shelters a constant exhibition of its treasures.

115) The inaugural inscription by Pope Sixtus V

In the vestibule, the walls on both sides of the door leading to the Salone Sistino bear large marble plaques with Latin inscriptions. On the left-hand one, illustrated here, the severe Pope ceremonially forbids under pain of excommunication the removal of books or parts of books: "*a fidelium communione ejectus | maledictus | anathematis vinculo | colligatus esto*" (the same measure also applied in other libraries founded by the Church). The other plaque contains a survey of the Library from its beginnings onwards, and a description of the new Vatican Library, founded by Sixtus V and consecrated in 1588.

116) The Second Council of Constantinople. Fresco in the Salone Sistino

One of the frescoes of the Salone Sistino, on which the Ecumenical Councils from Nicaea through Trent are depicted, portrays the Second Council of Constantinople, the fifth in the sequence. It was convened by Emperor Justinian, although Pope Vigilius was absent and sent no representative. It was opened on May 5, 553, in the assembly hall joining Hagia Sophia, and closed on June 2 of the same year with the condemnation of the so-called *Three Chapters* (the work of three writers infected with Nestorian principles: Theodore of Mopsuestia, Theodoret and Ibas, Bishop of Edessa) and of the writings of Origenes, who had been dead for three hundred years. In the picture, the Emperor sits to the left of the altar, and to the right is a deacon, who is reading out the condemnation from behind a lectern. The fresco is considered the best of the cycle. It was not possible to make out the painter.

117) A Vergil manuscript

This codex, written in rough majuscules in the 6th century, seems to have originated from a less cultivated province. In fact, its miniatures (twelve full-page and seven smaller) are all inferior to those of the Vatican Library and show a certain naivety in their execution. In the Middle Ages, perhaps as early as the 8th century, it appeared in France in the Abbey of St. Denis. In 1475 it was in the Vatican Library, where Poliziano, Michel de Montaigne, Mabillon, Montfaucon and others saw it. It is almost square in shape, and contains 309 parchment pages, with a large part of the Eclogues, the Georgics

and the Aeneid. The codex contains three similar portraits of the same size showing Vergil sitting in an arm-chair between a reading-desk and a basket of books. The miniature shown here and the others of the codex are interesting for their details.

118) A Greek Bible

This codex, containing the Old and New Testaments, is slightly damaged at the beginning and end; it begins with Genesis XLVI, 28 and ends with the Epistle to the Hebrews IX, 14. Together with the Codex Sinaiticus in the British Museum, it is reputed to be the oldest complete manuscript of the Greek Bible extant. It did not appear much later than the 4th century. The characteristics of the text and the inclusion and order of the books corresponding to the canon of Athanasius, support the theory that it is of Egyptian origin. Its external appearance, the lack of decoration, the simplicity of the title page and the inscription testify to its age. The text, normally in three columns on each page, is in straight regular uncials. The codex is almost square (10.1 inches by 10.5 inches). Marginal notes and corrections show that it was frequently used for several centuries. Its history before its appearance in 1475, or 1481 at the latest, in the Vatican Library is unknown.

119) Cicero: De re publica

In December 1819 the Prefect of the Vatican Library, Angelo Mai, announced the discovery of this lost work by Cicero, and shortly afterwards made it accessible to the public, to the great delight of scholars. The palimpsest codex from which it was extracted was probably written in uncials in Italy in the 4th century and rewritten with a commentary on the Psalms by St. Augustine in the monastery of Bobbio, which he had entered towards the end of the 7th century. In 1618 it was presented to Paul V and placed in the Vatican Library. The text of the work *De re publica* remained hidden behind later ones for more than a thousand years. In 1934 Giovanni Mercati published a photocopied edition.

120) Terence: Codex Bembinus

This codex, which was written between the 4th and 5th centuries, is one of the smallest of that time. It contains the most reliable text of a large part of Terence's comedies. The first two of the fourteen quires of which it originally consisted are lost, and the third and last are partly mutilated. The hands of three commentators who worked on it at different times have left their traces on the text. Of the history of the codex in the first thousand years nothing is known, but in 1457 it was bought by the Venetian Bernardo Bembo, probably from the humanist, Giovanni Porcelli. It then came into the possession of Pietro Bembo, the famous learned Cardinal, and then into that of Fulvio Orsini. Shortly after 1602, the codex entered the Vatican Library as a bequest of the last owner.

121) Frederick II, Holy Roman Emperor: De arte venandi cum avibus

This is a parchment codex from the second half of the 13th century, with two columns of Italian Gothic script. It contains the first two volumes of a treatise on falconry by Emperor Frederick II with supplements by his son Manfred (the title of King bestowed on the son dates the text between 1258 and 1266). More than 900 drawings, almost all in color, decorate the pages of the codex. They portray not only falcons, falconry and its equipment, and scenes from this sport, but also a large number of other birds. The illustrations are faithful and exact; in the direct naturalistic observation and skilled execution we see the full Arabic influence. In 1596, the manuscript belonged to Joachim Camaerarius, a doctor from Nuremberg; not long afterwards it reached the Palatinate Library in Heidelberg, and from there, it went to the Vatican Library.

122) A Livy manuscript

A page from *The History of Rome*. *The History* was a multi-volume work arranged in groups of ten. There were a total of 142 volumes. They comprise a most significant contribution to our understanding of Augustinian culture.

123) A parchment scroll of The Book of Joshua
This relict is one of the most famous and most discussed works of Byzantine art. The scroll, which is damaged at its beginning and end, consists of fifteen pieces of parchment of different size, which once (until 1902) formed a strip 34.5 feet long. The scenes were all taken from *The Book of Joshua,* and followed one another as if they were sections of a continuous frieze. According to Kurt Weitzmann, the leading expert in this field, the scroll dates from the 12th century. The individual illustrations have been taken from an older codex, and in order to link the individual scenes, the artist used a considerable number of classical elements, landscapes and figures, which are typical for miniatures in mythological or bucolic manuscripts. The early history of the scroll is not known in detail. In the 13th century it was still in a Greek-speaking country. In the middle of the 16th century it became a part of Ulrich Fugger's collection and from there entered the Palatinate Library in Heidelberg. The fourth section, shown here, portrays the raising of the twelve stones from the bed of the Jordan (Joshua IV, 8).

124) The Library vestibule—Sala degli Scrittori
The bronze door leads into a rectangular room with a vaulted ceiling, on which grotesques are painted. Between the coat of arms of Sixtus V and the putti appear the eight Sibyls (the Cumaean, the Delphic, the Tiburtine, the Eritrean, the Phrygian, the Samian, the Libyan and the Persian) and six landscapes portraying men producing paper and printing books. These scenes allude to the establishment of the Tipografia Vaticana, which the founder wanted to create together with the Library. The grotesques are ascribed to Cherubino Alberti, the Sibyls to Marco da Faenza and the landscapes, which artistically are more significant, to Paul Brill. Over the chairs and benches hang the portraits of the Cardinals who served as Librarian, an office created in the 16th century, and one which continues today. The remainder of the iconographical series is in other rooms. This room, illuminated by a large window onto the Cortile del Belvedere, was used until the end of the 19th century as a work room for the Librarians (scrittori) and scholars.

125) An illustration from the "Vatican Vergil'
This codex can be dated between the end of the 4th and beginning of the 5th centuries; an excellent example of Roman calligraphy, it is especially famous on account of its 50 miniatures, all of which have been preserved. The text is heavily mutilated. Only ten pages of *The Georgics* and 65 with parts of *The Aeneid* have survived. The manuscript contains several addenda by ancient and later commentators. Its origins are unknown, as are the names of its owners for nearly a thousand years. In the 15th century, it appears in the possession of the humanist Giovanni Gioviano Pontano, from whom it passes to Pietro Bembo and then to his heir Torquato, who sold it in 1579 to Fulvio Orsini; Orsini finally presented it, in 1600, to the Vatican. It is called *The Vatican Vergil* to distinguish it from other ancient Vergil codices in the same library (the Roman, Palatine, Augustan). The miniature illustrated here belongs to page 36 and shows Dido in conversation with Aeneas (*Aeneid* V, verse 305 ff.).

126) A Dante manuscript, from Urbino
On a commission of Federico, Duke of Urbino, the copying of the codex onto almost 300 sheets of first-class parchment was concluded in October 1478 by the secretary of Volterra, Matteo de' Contugi. The sheets were then brought to Ferrara, a renowned artistic center, for the execution of the miniatures. The chief artists were Guglielmo Giraldi and Franco de' Russi, with their associates and assistants.
The former was responsible for almost the whole of *The Inferno* (with a few miniatures) and the superb title picture of *The Purgatorio.* The latter executed almost the whole of *Purgatorio.* Although de' Russi had an artistic personality of his own, he tried to produce a work similar to that of his predecessor. The Duke of Urbino died in 1482 and the illustration of the codex was interrupted until the beginning of the 17th century, when it was resumed on a commission from Francesco Maria II della Rovere with the third part of the Cantos. But this last work proved to be very mediocre. Of the 120 miniatures in the form of little pictures, 58 are of the 15th century and, with their high level of decoration, are of extraordinary artistic merit. Page

99, illustrated here, contains the miniature portraying Vergil as he girds Dante with rushes (*Purgatorio* I, 133).

127) Illustration by Botticelli for Dante's "Divina Commedia"
This great painter of the Renaissance, famous for his works of the highest spirituality and beauty, illustrated an edition of Dante for Lorenzo di Pietro Francesco de' Medici, a cousin of Lorenzo the Magnificent. The work, begun after 1482, was never completed; moreover, not everything the artist drew has been preserved. Twenty pages have survived, divided up today among the collections of the Vatican, East Berlin and Berlin-Dahlem. The large sheets of parchment on which Botticelli worked never formed part of a codex, but were to have been an illustrated commentary, revealing the artist's detailed knowledge of the poetry and its meaning. The illustrations were silverpoint drawings, strengthened by pen; only a few were treated with tempera colors. On the reverse, the pertinent Canto is written in four columns. Apart from the general drawing for *The Inferno,* the sheets of the Vatican contain the illustrations to Cantos 1, 9, 10, 12, 13, 15 and 16. Of these, five only are drawn. One has only the preliminary coloring and one is completely colored.

128) A Bible from Urbino
This great Latin Bible in two volumes, consisting in all of 312 pages of parchment, was ordered by Federico of Urbino from the Florentine bookseller Vespasiano da Bisticci, who had it finished very quickly in his workshop. The first volume was completed in 1476, the second in 1478. The writing was carried out by the French secretary, Hugue de Comminelles de Mézières. As with most larger books the miniatures were executed by several excellent artists of various schools, under the direction of Bisticci himself. There are no records or signatures extant that could tell us anything about the artists. It is nevertheless possible to recognize the style of the master, Vante di Gabriello di Vanti di Francesco, known as l'Attavante, and his pupils. The main scenes are illustrated by large miniatures with great artistic and pictorial effect. The decoration is opulent, with varied friezes, medallions and gilded capitals. The work counts as one of the highest achievements of Italian miniature painting of the Renaissance.

129) A letter from King Henry VIII of England
The love letters of Henry VIII and Anne Boleyn are a surprising possession of the Vatican Library. There are seventeen manuscript letters, which are certainly genuine; nine are in French, the courtly language, and the rest in English. They are undated, but seem to have been written between 1527 and 1529, the first years of the King's passion. He married Anne Boleyn early in 1533. The letters were stolen; how they were brought to Rome is unknown.

130) A manuscript by St. Thomas Aquinas
This manuscript codex on parchment contains fragments of three works: *Summa contra gentiles, Commentarium super Isaiam* and *Commentarium super Boetium De Trinitate.* At first sight, the handwriting of the great philosopher and theologian seems illegible. The words are abbreviated in the way customary in old handwriting, and the resulting form is characteristic. In the first treatise, St. Thomas writes clearly in two columns with wide margins; the letters are hastily formed but not obscure. However the original script has been altered by repeated and persistent corrections, effected at various times by obliterations, alterations and additions. The margins are filled with occasional writing in different hands, squeezed into the confined space. In this way the pages lose so much of their original clarity that even the author himself took the trouble to guide the copyists by special signs. The codex came into the possession of the Vatican Library in 1876.

131) A letter by Martin Luther
The codex is composed of 21 manuscript pages of varying content: a paraphrasing of *Aesop's Fables* in German, two letters of 1515 in Latin and three others in German. The letter reproduced here is addressed to Elector Johann of Saxony, and is dated July 6, 1531.

132) A manuscript by Michelangelo
The codex is a valuable collection of manuscript writings, letters and prose

fragments. The last three pages contain prescriptions and formulae against eye complaints (at his death, the great artist was nearly blind). The verses, sonnets, madrigals and various stanzas have religion and love for their subject matter. Many of them are addressed to Vittoria Colonna.

133) A sketch by Raphael
This sheet unites various studies in movement, probably intended for a picture of the Madonna.

134) Petrarch's Cantos
In this codex, one of the treasures of Italian poetry, Petrarch collected and arranged in his declining years *The Rerum Vulgarium Fragmenta*. It was partly written under the watchful eye of Petrarch by the young secretary Giovanni Malpaghini in the years 1366–1367, and the poet himself continued it until his death in 1374. On the leaves of parchment we see the regular half-Gothic script of the secretary alternating with the hand of the poet, himself a calligrapher; in later years, his writing grew quite varied. The artist waited with great patience to give the masterpiece its final shape. The manuscript, which Cardinal Bembo bought in 1544, later passed into the hands of the Roman collector, Fulvio Orsini, who in 1620 bequeathed it, together with the rest of his collection, to the Vatican Library. In 1965 it was stolen, but, after a few days, it mysteriously reappeared.

135) A page from Giuliano da Sangallo's sketch-book
Giuliano da Sangallo (circa 1452–1515), a celebrated architect and military technician, collected in a large parchment codex some of the most wonderful things he had seen in the field of architecture, especially ancient architecture. Although the drawings look as if they are sketches done while he contemplated the monuments, they are in reality remarkably precise, carefully executed with ruler and compasses. Many Italian towns are portrayed, among them Florence, the native town of the artist. The most important series is the one of the monuments of Rome and Latium, almost all from antiquity: arches, gates, amphitheaters, theaters, temples, forums, colonnades, basilicas and obelisks. They testify to the passion for antiquity which Sangallo shared with all artists of his day. They are also a documentary testimonial to the state of the classical ruins of Rome. The "book" was probably sold towards 1655 by Sangallo's heirs to Cardinal Giulio Sacchetti, and apparently it passed from him to the Barberini Library. In 1902 The Barberini collection was incorporated in the Vatican Library.

136) The "Aldobrandini Wedding Scene." Left half of the fresco
This fresco from Augustan times was found in 1604/5 on the Esquiline hill behind the Church of San Girolamo and was set up in the villa of Cardinal Pietro Aldobrandini. In 1818, Pope Pius VII acquired this significant work for the Vatican. The fresco, part of a frieze running round a room of a Roman villa, portrays scenes from a wedding ceremony. On the right of our picture (in the complete fresco it is in the middle of the scene), the veiled bride is sitting next to a naked woman: Venus, the Goddess of Love. Next to her is another female figure, probably an attendant of Venus. On the left of the picture the bride's mother is preparing the bridal bath. In the picture, forms of Roman wedding usage are mixed with mythical figures, making the meaning of the picture controversial.

137) "The Laestrygonians Prepare for Battle." Scene from a frieze of eleven pictures with scenes from "The Odyssey"
This unique frieze dates from the middle of the 1st century A.D. and was probably based on a Greek model for the decoration of a Roman patrician house; it was discovered in 1848 during excavations in Rome, and was presented in 1851 to Pope Pius IX by the City of Rome. The preserved scenes show: *The Arrival of Odysseus in the Land of the Laestrygonians—The Laestrygonians Prepare for Battle—Destruction of the Ships of the Companions of Odysseus—The Flight of Odysseus—Odysseus in Circe's Palace—Odysseus in the Underworld—Penitential Figures in the Underworld*

138) "Madonna Enthroned." From the Rambona Diptychon. On ivory. Circa 900.
In this diptychon, in which Langobardic, Moslem and Byzantine influences are mixed with the style of the Italian carver, the left section shows the crucifixion of Christ, with a representation of the Roman she-wolf below. The right section shows in the upper half the enthroned Madonna between Cherubim, with three figures of Bishops among them. The inscription identifies an Abbot Odelricus as commissioner of the diptychon for the monastery of Rambona. It is probably the Abbot who is portrayed as the concluding figure of the right section, in a half lying position.

139) "The Annunciation." Syrian (?) silk embroidery. 7th to 8th centuries. From the treasure of the Sancta Sanctorum
Perhaps this embroidery is the material which Leo III donated for the altar of St. Peter's.

140) Golden reliquary cross with enamel depictions. Executed under Paschal I 817–824). From the treasure of the Sancta Sanctorum.
Scenes from the life of Jesus are portrayed in cloisonné probably by a Greek artist working in Rome. In the center: the Nativity. Above: Annunciation and Visitation. Left: Flight to Egypt. Right: Adoratión of the Magi. Below: Presentation in the Temple and Baptism. The cross is considered the most valuable possession of the treasure of the Sancta Sanctorum.

THE SECRET ARCHIVES OF THE VATICAN

141) A portrait of Paul V, the founder of the Secret Archives, above a door to one of the rooms of the Secret Archives
Earlier, the rooms on the first floor were reached through what is now the Salone Sistino of the Vatican Library. High above, one can see the portrait of Pope Paul V (Camillo Borghese), the founder of the Secret Archives. The well-preserved, decorative cabinets of poplar wood still contain, as they always have, the *Registri Vaticani:* numerous lists of briefs and volumes of minutes. However there are also other books and documents, especially those dealing with the activities of the Camera Apostolica.

142) A frescoed room in the Secret Archives
The rooms which Paul V chose for the new archives were furnished with frescoes and copious cabinets, on which are depicted in relief eagles and dragons—the armorial beasts of the Borghese family. During the pontificates of Popes Innocence X, Alexander VII and Innocence XII, smaller cabinets were added to these original ones. On the walls there is a series of magnificent paintings, portraying royal and imperial gifts to the Church in the course of the centuries, from Constantine through Charles VI of Luxemburg.

143) In the Archives—a room for diplomatic correspondence
Urban VIII and Alexander VII chose the rooms of the second floor of the Archives for the lists, volumes and books of the State Secretariat's correspondence with Princes, Cardinals and Bishops, and especially that with the Papal Nuncios at the courts of the various states of Europe, and with the Governors of the Papal States.

144) A letter by the Eastern Roman Emperor (Byzantium)
This is the letter of the Emperor of Byzantium, John II Comnenus, to Pope

Callistus II on the unification of the Churches (June, 1124). A magnificent scroll of purple parchment (14½ inches wide and 13 feet long), contains the text of the document in Greek; its Latin version and the Imperial signature are in red ink. The golden script is framed by an ornamental border of oriental style.

145) A document confirming the privileges of the Bishopric of Tivoli
This is an illustrated page from the *Regesto Tiburtino*, a rare and valuable codex from the 12th century. Pope John XIX is portrayed sitting on the throne; supported by St. Lawrence, the Archdeacon, he is dispensing a privilege to Benedotto, Bishop of Tivoli. Granted in 1029, this confirms once again the places and rights in the possession of the Tiburtine Church.

146) Two letters from the Khan of Persia in the Mongolian language, addressed to the Holy See
Both letters are written on paper and bear the square red imprint of the royal seal. On the left is a letter of safe-conduct, drawn up by Abaka for the Bishops delegated by the Pope (1267 or 1279). On the right, a letter from Gazan to Boniface VIII (1302), in reply to a message of the Pope.

147) Three documents from Holy Roman Emperors
These are three of the oldest documents in the Archives, each one possessing a golden seal: in the foreground, the document by Frederick II of Hohenstaufen (King of Sicily, and Emperor) on the occupation of vacant churches in Sicily (February, 1211); half concealed is the promise of Otto IV, King of Rome and Emperor, to Innocent III (1209), and a document from the same monarch on behalf of Count Hildebrand (1210).

148) The oldest depiction of a session of the "Sacra Romana Rota" (1468)
The members of the tribunal are sitting at the characteristically round table. On the right is the text of the prayer "Adsumus," which is still spoken today at the beginning of every session of the Sacra Rota.

149) A page from the "Collezione del Platina"
This is the first page of the second of three volumes of the so-called *Collezione del Platina*, produced between 1476 and 1480 on the orders of Bartolomeo Platina, the Librarian, of Sixtus IV, to whom it is dedicated. The volumes contain the most valuable papers of the Church, in beautiful Humanistic calligraphy: imperial, Papal and royal documents, and those of the ecclesiastical and temporal authorities of the Middle Ages; on the orders of the Pope, these papers were kept in the treasury of Castel Sant'Angelo.

150) A letter by King Henry VIII of England to Pope Clement VII
The letter was addressed on July 13, 1530, to Pope Clement VII, to secure the King's divorce; the peers of the realm request the Pope to annul the first marriage of their king to Catherine of Aragón. This ceremonious document bears the personal signatures of the petitioners and 85 red wax seals.

151) Italian cities surrender their keys to the Vicar-General of Pope Innocent VI, whose residence was in Avignon
Cardinal Egidio Albornoz, Papal Legate in Italy and Vicar-General of Pope Innocent VI, receives the keys of the frontier cities, which, during the years 1355–1356, were once again subjected to the rule of the Church. The miniature is a ceremonious beginning for the *Regestrum recognitionum et iuramentorum fidelitatis civitatum sub Innocentio VI*.

152) A letter from the Spanish King, Philip II, and Mary Tudor, Queen of England, to Pope Paul IV
Philip II and Mary Tudor, the rulers of England, appoint the three ambassadors who are to go to Rome to swear ceremonially to Pope Paul IV obedience in the name of the whole English nation (June 6, 1555). In the large oval of the initial letter, the king and queen are portrayed sitting on the throne beneath a canopy; elegant patterns decorate the upper edge of the document.

153) A letter from the Doge of Venice to Pope Sixtus V
Doge Pasquale Cicogna presents Pope Sixtus V in the name of the Venetian Republic with the palace chosen as the residence of the Papal Nuncio (August 3, 1586). The letter, written in golden characters, is richly decorated and has a golden seal.

154) The letter of abdication of Queen Christina of Sweden
The abdication followed on the Queen's conversion to Catholicism in June, 1654. It is a ceremonial document in the form of a dossier containing the signatures of members of parliament and 306 red wax seals.

155) A letter from the Chinese Empress, Helena, to Pope Innocent X
The Empress and her son, Constantine, had coverted to Catholicism. The letter (November 4, 1650) is written on silk in Chinese characters and bears the impression of the imperial seal. The symbolic figure of the dragon is repeated several times at the edge of the costly material.

156) An illuminated page from the documentary collection of Cardinal d'Aragona
The collection of Cardinal Niccolò Roselli d'Aragona (1356–1362) contains the copies of various documents, descriptive texts and lives of the Popes. The volume opens with an illuminated page. The arms of Cardinal Rodrigo Borgia (later Pope Alexander VI) on the lower edge are, however, a later addition.

157) Documents from the Kings of Sicily
These are documents from Charles VI, King and Emperor of Sicily (1723), Charles VII, King of Sicily (1739) and Ferdinand IV, King of the Two Sicilies (1760). Valuable cases are suspended from the document on thick gold cords ending in knots; beautifully worked in silver or gold, they contain the red wax seal of the three Kings.

158) The Concordat between the Holy See and the French Republic, 1801
This is the document of ratification on the French side (Paris, September 8, 1801). The exchange of documents of ratification followed two days later. The document, kept in the Vatican Secret Archives, bears the personal signatures of Napoleon Bonaparte; the Foreign Minister, Charles Maurice Perigord (Prince Talleyrand); and the Secretary of State, Hugues-Bernard Maret. The silver gilt bull bears the seal stamped in the red wax of the Republic. Next to it, in a closed dossier, lies the document of ratification of the Concordat between the Holy See and the Italian Republic (November 2, 1803).

THE SISTINE CHAPEL

159) An interior view of the Sistine Chapel
The Sistine Chapel is without doubt the world's largest chapel. It has very few architectural projections on the walls and none in the vault. This is a clear indication that it was intended from the very beginning to be decorated with frescoes. The decoration occurred on three different occasions, so that one is justified in talking of a Sistine Chapel of Sixtus IV (1471–1484), of Julius II (1503–1513) and of Paul III (1534–1549). In their entirety, the frescoes offer an excellent anthology of Italian Renaissance painting—in its youthfulness, its maturity and its decline. At the same time, the paintings form a powerful synthesis of the history of the universe and of mankind,

from the very first day to the end of time—and all seen in the light of Divine Revelation.

160) "Donation of the Keys." Fresco by Perugino, on the wall to the right
In the midst of an expansive site stands Solomon's temple: a fantastic octagonal structure, situated between two triumphal arches that were inspired by Constantine's triumphal arch. Christ gives the keys of the twofold power to St. Peter, who, unassuming and majestic, kneels at the Lord's feet. There are many portraits to be found in the two lateral groups. Some of them are of particular interest, like these of Giovanni de' Dolci and Baccio Pontelli,—the former, master-builder, and the latter, architect of the Sistine Chapel (second and third figures from the right); and of Perugino himself (the fifth figure in the same row). The youthful Raphael is said to have found in this fresco the inspiration for his *Wedding of the Virgin* in the Brera Gallery in Milan. Among the lively small groups in the background is one depicting the attempted stoning of Christ; it forms a pair with the stoning of Moses in Botticelli's painting (cf. 164). The inscription, "*Conturbatio Jesu Christi Legislatoris,*" can only be in reference to this secondary episode and not to the central motif of the work.

161) "The Punishment of Korah and his Rebels." Fresco by Botticelli, on the wall to the left
The rebels, who denied the civil and religious authority of Aaron and Moses over the Jewish people, are punished by the Lord—as related in the Book of Numbers. On the left, Dathan and Abiram are being swallowed up by the earth; in the middle, one sees Korah and his followers, who were consumed by a mysterious inner fire after having come to light their censers at the flame of the altar. To the right, we see the attempted stoning of Moses, a very unusual theme in the history of art (Ettlinger). The background is dominated by Constantine's arch; on the right is the building of Septimius Severus, with its columns still intact. On the left there is in profile, the bust of the young Alessandro Farnese—later Pope Paul III—next to his teacher, the humanist Pomponio Leto. The only recently discovered inscription above the fresco reads: "*Conturbatio Moisi legis scriptas latoris.*"

162) "The Holy Calling of the Apostles Peter and Andrew." Fresco by Ghirlandajo, on the wall to the right
Like almost all the frescoes from the cycles from the Old and New Testaments, this one is divided into three sections with various secondary scenes depicted in the background. To the left, Christ appoints Peter and Andrew, and the two Apostles kneel down in the middle foreground to receive His blessing. On the right, Christ repeats the ceremony, appointing this time James and John. Among the figures to both sides of the central group are many portraits; their large number, the uniformity of their bearing, and even the care taken in painting each individual face, endow them with a sense of foreignness in this scene—and this, despite the fact that each one of them has been painted with standards of high quality. The inscription on the frame reads: "*Congregatio populi evangelium accepturi.*"

163) "Moses" Final Worldly Deeds. Fresco by Signorelli, on the wall to the left.—164) "Death of Moses." Section from the adjacent fresco
Moses, seated on a high podium, proclaims the Law once again to the tribes of Israel, while on the left we see him giving the rod of authority to Joshua, his successor. Above it all, an angel leads him up to Mount Nebo, where he is shown the Promised Land in the distance. In the upper left corner of the fresco, he dies (163), is laid out on the ground, and is mourned by those who were close to him. Although Signorelli was late in joining the team of painters working in the Sistine Chapel, his work there was of such quality that he aroused the admiration of Michelangelo. The latter probably conceived the idea for his "ignudi" from the figure of the young man, who is seated naked in the group attending to Moses' words—naked, because he symbolizes the tribe of Levi, from whom the priests are drawn, thus elminating them from participating in the apportionment of the Promised Land. The inscription reads: "*Replicatio legis scriptae a Moise.*"

165) Michelangelo's frescoes on the ceiling of the Sistine Chapel
It was from the year 1508 to October 1512 that Michelangelo painted the fres-

coes on the world's largest ceiling vault (it measures approximately 5,600 square feet). He thus created in the Sistine Chapel the greatest work of art of the Italian Renaissance, then at the culmination of its power; at the same time he created the most sublime religious expression of his or any other time.

When he reluctantly accepted the commission from Julius II, he was forced to terminate work prematurely on a project that appealed to him even more: Julius's tomb. This monument was to have been set up in the middle of the new basilica and, according to Vasari, was supposed to have surpassed "every old and imperial tomb in beauty, size, beautiful ornamention and abundance of statues." When he tackled the new project, Michelangelo's imaginative power continued working along the lines of architecture and sculpture, and he transformed their forms into painting with the self-same unity of style that one finds later in the Medici Chapel in Florence. Indeed, it is impossible not to see the affinity between the *Moses* of San Pietro in Vincoli, the *Prisoners* of the Louvre, and the prophets and "ignudi" of the Sistine ceiling.

166) "God Separates Light and Darkness." First picture in the center of the ceiling vault
In painting the Sistine ceiling, Michelangelo proceeded chronologically in a sequence whose order was inverse to the scenes represented—in other words he painted from the entrance wall to the altar. Still unaccustomed to fresco painting, he perhaps wished at first to get some intitial experience before starting on the first scenes, which were to be dominated by the figure of the Creator; as it turned out, these scenes were the last to be painted. What we see here is the very beginning of the Creation. Against the heavenly skies, on the other side of the vault, is the Lord, arms raised, as He separates light and darkness. His circular motion is accentuated by the folds of His loose wrap, and His head is shortened. The picture appears somewhat blurred, with the details restricted to only the most essential. In no other work of art is the theme so transformed in an effort to allude to the "spirit."

167) "God Creates the Sun and the Moon." Second picture in the center of the ceiling vault
We have already seen how all the frescoes in the nave represent not only the main theme but also numerous secondary themes; thus it is that the figures of Moses and Christ appear more than once in the same fresco. In the second picture of the story of Genesis, Michelangelo reverts to this medieval technique, although in another spirit. On the right, God the Father storms onto the scene, His hand extended in a commanding gesture that creates the sun on one side, and the moon on the other. On the left, the same figure continues to hover in space, causing the first plants to sprout green on earth. Michelangelo is not afraid to reverse the Biblical order of things; for aesthetic reasons (e.g., the necessity to place the sun in the center of the vault) he has put the creation of the plants into the third day and the creation of the stars into the fourth.

168) "God Divides the Water from the Land." Third picture in the center of the ceiling vault
When Michelangelo painted this fresco, he must have thought of the Biblical verse (Genesis I, 2) which reads, in the Latin text of the Vulgate: "... the Spirit of God was carried (ferebatur) over the face of the waters." Astonished angels, wrapped in the folds of his garment (the old symbol for the universe), arrest the flight of the majestic fatherly figure, whose hands are extended in the act of creation and benediction. This event, too, is in the wrong chronological order, since, in Genesis, it precedes the aforegoing acts of Creation Since no theologian developing an iconographical theme would have taken such liberties, it may be presumed that Michelangelo worked without clerical aid.

169) "God Creates Adam." Fourth picture in the center of the ceiling vault.—170) "Adam." A section from the adjacent fresco
Like in the previous painting, God's motion is arrested by angels enveloped in his garment. He extends His index finger toward Adam's and lets life flow into the already existing body. The two hands do not touch one another, in keeping with the immaterial nature of the soul that has been given man, who was created in God's image. Like no other figure, Adam's nude body

illustrates the Renaissance ideal of male beauty. The figure of God the Father is odd in that it unites the head of an old man with the body of a vital youth. This may have been Michelangelo's way of putting the difficult theological concept of eternity into visible and symbolic form. Most usually, though not theologically, eternity is seen either as a moment beyond time (thus the youthful body), or as time without end (which would explain the head with the shock of white hair).

171) "God Creates Eve." Fifth picture in the center of the ceiling vault

The creation of Eve is depicted in similar fashion. The woman rises from her position next to the slumbering figure of Adam. Slowly she achieves an erect stance by obeying the command of God's hand with her own prayer-like gesture. In the figures of Adam and Eve, one can see the influence of Jacopo della Quercia and of Masaccio. The disproportion between the size of the fresco and the figure of God the Father, which is able to fit into the space allotted it only because the head is bowed, is certainly intended; it alludes simultaneously to God's infinity, as well as to His love, which causes Him to bow His head to His creatures.

172) "Fall of Man and Expulsion from Paradise." Sixth picture in the center of the ceiling vault

The form the composition takes in this fresco has particular importance. On the left, as if they were following a curvature, Adam and Eve stretch out their arms to the tree of knowledge of good and evil. On the right, they submit to their burden of guilt and begin their way into the desert of the world. In the center is the fateful tree, out of whose trunk two figures emerge: the snake of temptation with the face of a woman, and an angel, seemingly emanating from the background, that hovers above the ground and extends its sword menacingly toward Adam. The entire painting is an interplay of strongly significant contrasts, which are in the form of a triptych: Paradise, shaded by a solitary branch of the tree, and the dry sun-burnt earth; the still innocent pair, young and brilliantly beautiful, and the now wise pair, suddenly heavier and older; and, finally, tempters and avengers, who remind one of a verse by Michelangelo himself: "Great sin goes hand-in-hand with horrid vengeance."

173) "Sacrifice of Noah." Seventh picture in the center of the ceiling vault

Noah and his family make God a sacrificial offering. The composition, inspired by Roman bas-reliefs, is full of movement and yet it does not seem to have been painted by Michelangelo with the same spirit he employed on the other frescoes. This is perhaps because of the non-dramatic subject, a usual everyday scene depicting a religious ritual. In the depiction of the animals, however, the painting has an aspect otherwise unknown in his art. The Bible (Genesis VIII, 20) speaks of a sacrificial offering made by Noah after the flood, and several experts have interpreted this fresco as describing this sacrifice; reasons of space caused Michelangelo to set this incident before the flood. However, this break with the chronological sequence of the Bible would have been only too evident in this case. It is more probable that he describes a scene in which Noah, the believer living in a faithless world, makes God a sacrificial offering prior to the flood—a ritual act that justifies the salvation of the ark, along with himself and his family, as represented in the next fresco.

174) "The Flood." Eighth picture in the center of the ceiling vault.—175) "Noah's Ark." A section from the previous fresco

The Flood is Michelangelo's very first fresco, his apprenticeship piece in the difficult art of fresco painting. He had called together a group of painters from Florence, from whom he had hoped to learn how to make frescoes. However, after a short trial he sacked them all and, as Vasari notes, he started on his task alone. One can see the result of his lack of expert knowledge in the figures here; they are too small to be seen from below. This error he corrected in The Intoxication of Noah, which he painted next. According to Biagetti, one can see the hand of the assistants in parts of the composition that are technically perfect, although done with exaggerated conscientiousness, something to be expected from an artist who is merely following another's design. As Biagetti notes, other sections of the fresco, technically less perfect but marked by the freedom of genius, are by Michelangelo himself. The Flood is a poem of despair and arduous salvation and is thus a forerunner to The

Last Judgment; the style, on the other hand, resembles that of the youthful "Doni-Madonna," with the figures designed in 15th century style.

176) "The Intoxication of Noah." Final picture in the center of the ceiling vault

The drunken naked figure of Noah lies in a low-roofed shed; he has been overpowered by sleep. From the right comes Ham, who shows his brothers, Shem and Japheth, their father's nakedness. Shem and Japeth cover their father, averting their faces. Outside, a man is shown digging a hole; it is an improvised figure, painted onto the fresh plaster without the help of a sketch (Biagetti). The scene is composed like a bas-relief of Ghiberti's, and it indeed recalls (as many maintain) the Noah on the doors of Paradise in the Baptistery in Florence. A comparison with the previous fresco indicates how quickly Michelangelo mastered the art of fresco painting. It may seem strange that the solemn Biblical symphony concludes with an almost burlesque "scherzo," but the story of the intoxication of Noah is the indispensable link between the fresco cycle on the ceiling and the cycle on the walls. For Noah's family, life begins anew on the ravaged earth, now linked for better or for worse to the evil of original sin. Here are depicted both moral evil and physical illness; the former is personified by the action of Ham, and the latter in the intoxication of the aged patriarch. A Redeemer was promised to this unregenerate nature. For centuries this pledge was kept by the Chosen People, and it was redeemed by Christ's death on the cross and by his Resurrection. Thus, the ceiling cycle is linked to the wall cycle both historically and conceptually, symbolized by the frescoes which mankind—"sub lege" and "sub gratia"—has dedicated to Moses and the Messiah. In addition, Noah is the first of the patriarchs—that is, of the religious and political leaders, of whom Moses is the greatest.

177) A portion of the ceiling frescoes, with the prophet Joel and the Eritrean Sibyl.—178) The Prophet Joel. 179) The Prophet Daniel.—180) The Prophet Jeremiah.—181) The Libyan Sibyl—182) The Persian Sibyl.—183) The Prophet Ezekiel.—184) The Cumaean Sibyl.—185) The Prophet Isaiah.—186) The Prophet Jonah.—187) The Prophet Zechariah.—188) The Delphic Sibyl

Seated on consoles between the vault spandrels are, alternately, seven prophets and five sibyls, all of whom ponder the drama of Man and the promised Redeemer. An old Christian legend endowed the visionaries of the heathen world with a dark fore-knowledge of the coming Messiah. The motif of pairs of prophets and sibyls (also employed by Pinturicchio in the Borgia apartments) was a common one in the Middle Ages. Here, as later in The Last Judgment, Michelangelo did not disregard iconographic tradition but integrated it into his own imaginative vision, bringing it to the highest fulfillment. This series of frescoes also began at the entrance wall and continued to the altar wall, and, like the frescoes of the Biblical cycle, they increase in size. Whereas "Zechariah" (187) the first to be painted, sits comfortably on his majestic throne, "Jonah" (186)—the last one painted, over the altar—would not even fit into his seat if he did not lean back in it. If one contemplates these figures one-by-one, one realizes that Michelangelo used each of them to represent the various ways of seeking truth, i.e., they are various types of savants, who differ psychologically very much from one another. Let us begin with the first figure to the left of The Last Judgment, with "Jeremiah," the prophet of the lamentations (180). He is marked by the sadness born of knowledge and, seated next to the painting showing the beginning of Creation, he sheds tears over the imminent coming of evil and the destruction of the Holy City. A piece of paper with the word aleph has fallen to his feet; corresponding to the Greek alpha, aleph is the first letter of the Hebrew alphabet and is also a symbol for a beginning. This alludes to the beginning of his Biblical book, where, horror-stricken at having been ordained a prophet by God, Jeremiah replies: "Ah, Lord God! behold, I cannot speak: for I am a child" (Jeremiah I, 6). Seated next to him is the "Persian Sibyl" (182), a short-sighted and humpbacked giantess; she holds a written sheet close to her face, that is shrouded in shadows—a symbol of imperfect revelation. "Ezekiel" (183), the quarrelsome prophet, is shown arguing with a nonvisible partner; he underlines his words with the typical Neapolitan gesture of the right hand, while next to his head an angel smiles with Leonardo-like irony and points his finger toward heaven, as if he wanted to say that not all wisdom can be found in books. (A similar figure can be seen in the group at the far left in Raphael's Disputa.) The "Eritrean Sibyl" (177) symbolizes the beginning of learning and study; she touches the pages of a large book on the lectern, while a small "genius" holds the light for her. "Joel" (178) seems to be engrossed in a manuscript that he studies with great attentiveness. His face recalls Bramante's (Euclid in Raphael's *School of Athens*). "Zechariah" (187) seems to personify the typical absent-minded scholar, who is looking for a page he has already read before, but has forgotten where. The "Delphic Sibyl" (188) is one of Michelangelo's most beautiful female figures; looking out into a distant, visionary future, she neglects the scroll she has just read. The virginal purity of her face stamps her as a relative of the Madonnas: the *Pietà* in St. Peter's, and that in Bruges. "Isaiah" (185), whose meditations have been interrupted by an angel, turns his head, closes his book—somewhat impatiently, it would appear—and keeps his finger in it so as to mark his place. When, in August, 1511, Julius II had the scaffolding taken down to take a look at half of the Sistine's ceiling vault, Raphael saw this figure, and it caused him to change his style. He copied it freehand in Michelangelo's style and used it for the figure of the meditative Heraclitus which he inserted in the already finished *School of Athens*. The "Cumaean Sibyl" (184) is depicted as a very old woman with a small head on a gigantic frame; she is intently trying to comprehend a difficult text—an activity that causes her two accompanying angels to break out in smiles of compassion. The abnormality of this figure is dominated and made acceptable by the harmony of the composition. "Daniel" (179), young and impetuous, takes note of something that has attracted his attention in the large volume supported between his knees by an angel. The very graceful "Libyan Sibyl" (181) is closing her book and is getting ready to leave her seat; symbolizing the end of learning and study, she corresponds to the "Eritrean Sibyl" (177), who personifies the commencement of this activity. Her elegantly turning movement and the elaborate hairdo place this "Libyca" on the border of mannerism. And, finally, there is "Jonah" (186), the symbol of resurrection, who is shown sitting on the console above the fresco of *The Last Judgment*, although this work had not yet been conceived when the Sistine ceiling was painted. A masterpiece of perspective, this figure turns to the back in a direction directly opposed to that in which the surface was painted. It reveals the heights Michelangelo's art was capable of reaching. The coloring—here more important than in most of the Sistine frescoes—anticipates the painting of Pietro da Cortona. And it was undoubtedly in Bernini's mind when he created the Fountain of the Four Rivers in Piazza Navona.

189) "The Punishment of Haman." Fresco in the corner spandrel.—191) Haman Crucified. A section from 189
In the corner spandrels of the ceiling vault Michelangelo illustrated the stories of Esther, David, Judith and Moses, all of whom were seen by theologians as prophetic forerunners of the Messiah. These four frescoes have a great dramatic intensity that ensues from their common theme: the exuberance of the victory of Biblical heroes and heroines over opponents stronger than they,—victories won through God's intervention. In the first spandrel, to the left of the alter, we find the three main incidents from the book of Esther. Ahasuerus sends Haman to fetch Mordechai, who sits at the entrance to the palace: at the opposite end of the painting is the banquet, at which Esther unmasks Haman as a persecutor of the Jews. In the middle, Haman is shown dying on the cross, which he had ordered built for the innocent Mordechai.

190) "David and Goliath." Fresco in the corner spandrel
David has discarded his sling; standing now, legs apart, above Goliath, he presses the giant's head down with his left hand and, with his right hand, he holds aloft the sword of his enemy. The composition is rich with balanced contrasts; these are strong and yet, at the same time; simple in magnificent though inconspicuous manner. The surfaces that were available to the artist in this corner spandrel are triangles with the apex facing downward. The two warriors are also constructed in the form of a triangle, with, however, the apex facing upward. This form is repeated in the white tent in the background, whose circular base mirrors the swinging motion of David's arm as he is about to come down with the sword.

192) "Judith Takes Leave of the Slain Holofernes." Fresco in the corner spandrel
In this Judith-spandrel, too, great psychological tension dominates. In contrast to the David-spandrel, the development of the theme is cautious and tranquil. As in the scene with Esther, we are able to see through the missing wall into the pavillion; in this fresco, one sees the bed, with the beheaded figure of Holofernes. Judith, who has left the room, has covered with a cloth the head of her enemy, which her maid is carrying. The maid bends her knee to make it easier for Judith to reach the tray she is carrying; Judith turns her head toward the dead man. It almost seems as if she still feared him. In the shadows, we can make out huge armed guards, who have been overcome by sleep.

193) "The Last Judgment." Fresco on the altar wall.—197) "The Last Judgment," lower segment
In reality, it is a strict orderliness that dominates the only apparently confused structure of *The Last Judgment*. It abides by the basic concepts of the iconographic design, which has been handed down from the Middle Ages. The artist, however, has enlivened it with new spirit and has filled it with a new kind of movement, permitting the old theme to have the greatest possible expression. In order to understand the innovative genius which the artist brought to his work, we need only recall the audacity with which Michelangelo solved the difficult artistic problem, ignoring all the aesthetic norms of his age: he had to make the new painting fit into the fresco scheme already prevailing in the chapel, as well as making it conform with the room's architectural character. His solution consisted of refusing to look for one. He abandoned his quest for artistic and structural links in his new work and he painted the entire huge wall right to the very edges; one thus gets the impression of a sudden "*fortissimo*," that stifles every other sound. The Lord... shall come in a day when he looketh not for him and in an hour that he is not aware of... (St. Matthew XXIV, 50).

194) Christ and the Virgin Mary. Center-piece of "The Last Judgment"
In the middle of the upper segment, the Son of Man appears in a blazing aureole; He has come to judge according to pure justice and without mercy. He calls the elect to His side and resigns the damned, in a whirlwind, to the shadows of hell. His body is that of a Hercules, and His head reminds one of the *Apollo di Belvedere*. When it was painted, and even later, it became the subject of reproaches made against Michelangelo. He was accused of having turned a Christian ideal into one that was heathen. It was actually the exact opposite of this that he had intended: namely the Christianization of universal values that the art of the antique had expressed in forms he felt were worthy of being transferred to holy works of art. The unknown sculptor of the catacombs had intended just that when he turned the "Hermes Kriophoros" into an allegory of the Good Shepherd. Michelangelo had to paint the body of the gloriously resurrected Son of God, and he had to do this with beauty and strength. His imagination, that of a Renaissance man, turned as a matter of course to the ideal of beauty found in the image of Apollo, and to the strength of a Hercules. Seated within the same blazing aureole as her son is the Mother of God; although a completely perfect creature, she still appears human and is thus not capable of Christ's divine dispassionateness. Instead she turns her head to the saved souls, who strive heavenward, preferring to look at them rather than at the destruction of the damned. But she does not beg for mercy (as in some designs for this fresco), for at this moment there is no longer any mercy. Most of the figures in *The Last Judgment* are anonymous; some of them can be identified on the basis of the attributes of their holiness, while others, like the giant to the right of Christ, are of uncertain identity. Vasari, and many modern authors, call him Adam; but Condivi believes he is St. John the Baptist, an opinion that, for many reasons, is more acceptable: Condivi is a more reliable historical source than Vasari and his biography was written almost under Michelangelo's supervision. In the traditional iconography, Adam always appears on judgment-day in the company of Eve, but the person represented here has only a young man with him. In addition, the figure of the fore-runner is an important part of this tradition, in which St. John the Baptist, together with the Virgin Mary and Christ, form the so-called "Deesis." Finally, Adam is always depicted as being girded with foliage; the figure here, however, is clothed in a girdle of skin about his loins, which corresponds to St. Mark's description of St. John the Baptist (St. Mark I,6). The characteristic cross held by the other figure allows one to identify him as St. Andrew.

195/196) Angels carry the instruments of Christ's Passion
The merciless justice of Christ the Judge has its moral and theological explanation in the two lunettes along the upper edge of the fresco, where closed groups of powerful angels do not merely carry the instruments of the Passion to judgment; it is more fitting to describe them as being dragged by the instruments as in a whirlwind. As is well known, several years previously these lunettes had been painted with frescoes based on the cycle of the Ancestors of Christ, and the artist was Michelangelo himself. As the cartoons in the Casa Buonarroti indicate, he had tried to salvage these frescoes at first (Wilde). He decided later to have them removed and to paint in their stead the symbols of the Lord's Passion, to the glory of mercy; it was a mercy that was available as long as there was time, but which was now denied and for which one begged in vain. Michelangelo painted these groups without paying much consideration to the rest of the composition, and they give the appearance of intruding upon it. The effect is thus partially coincidental, although it was certainly intended by the artist. Another reason for adding these angels was probably Michelangelo's desire to devote the entire wall to *The Last Judgment*.

198) The angels of the Resurrection sound their trumpets
In the center of the middle segment, a group of angels sounds their trumpets to call those risen from the dead to the day of judgment, and the angels show them the book of life and death. Like all the angels Michelangelo ever painted, these have no wings. He felt that such accessories would not be compatible with the beauty of the human body and that they would interfere with the essence of his style: the idealization of realism. Michelangelo's faith, as expressed in his art and poetry, is replete with the belief in divine mercy. One of his verses reads: "He opened his arms to receive us on the cross." However, he did not forget the "harsh" words in the Bible, as indicated by the difference in size of the two books: the small one is opened to the rising flock of the Redeemed, whereas the other volume—large and heavy enough to be carried by two angels—is full of the names of the damned.

199) The ferryman in the Underworld, Charon
Dante took the episode of Charon's bark from the Aeneid; and Michelangelo got it from *The Divine Comedy*, as Vasari (and many others after him) noted, without bothering to subject the relationship between poem and picture to a close examination. In fact, when we get behind the superficialities we see that the Charon of the Sistine Chapel is somewhat unlike Dante's Charon. True, we also have here "Charon, the demon with eyes of fire, with wheels of flame around his eyes." But in *The Divine Comedy*, "the ferryman of the living swamp" fells "with his oar all those who hesitate" to enter the boat; and when they reach the other shore, they run toward their punishment, "because divine justice so incites them, that fear becomes desire." Michelangelo's Charon does not hit the damned with his oar until they have reached the other shore, the "Shore of No Return," thus causing them to jump from the boat. This is less correct theologically, but it makes rather more sense.

200) The Apostle Bartholomew with the symbol of his martyrdom, his skin
St. Bartholomew leans forward (like St. Lawrence seated next to him) to avoid the rays of divine damnation. He shows the judge the knife with which he had been skinned, while he holds his own skin in his left hand. In his

gesture one can easily see an echo of *"Dies Irae"*: "Which teacher shall I call when not even the just feel safe?" In the folds of the martyr's skin La Cava discovered Michelangelo's self-portrait. distorted to a tragic caricature. In this figure's mighty body one finds clear allusions to the *Torso di Belvedere*, a classical sculpture which Michelangelo boundlessly admired.

201) Ascent of the redeemed
The redeemed souls ascend in various poses heaven-ward, each according to his spiritual quality. Some of them manage this on their own, while others require the aid of their brothers, or of the angels. Of particular significance for grasping Michelangelo's religious attitude are the two Africans, both of whom are drawn up on a rosary upon which they hang as if on chains.

202) Descent into Hell of the Damned
From Vasari, we know that when Clement VII commissioned Michelangelo with *The Last Judgment* the Pope also wanted the artist to paint the entrance wall with the fall of the rebellious angels. This project never got past the planning stage, but there are some experts who see in this furious battle of the angels to protect the entrance to paradise the result of Michelangelo's meditation on the scheme.

203) Resurrection of the dead
Upon hearing the trumpets' blast, the dead souls rise from earth and assume once again the human forms they had had while alive; it is a kind of reverse decomposition, a gradual "composition," inspired by Ezekiel's prophecy: "And I will lay sinews upon you, and will bring up flesh upon you, and cover you with skin, and put breath in you, and ye shall live; and ye shall know that I am the Lord" (Ezekiel XXXVII, 6). Two figures have been taken directly from the *"Dies Irae"*: the meditative skull which, in a gesture of astonishment, places its hand on its chin—next to it, the heavy body that has come crawling out of the earth: *"Mors stupebit et natura, Cum resurget creatura, Iudicanti responsura."* And in reality this skull is not that of a dead person but of death itself, who is astonished at the end of its dominion; its empty eye sockets are illuminated by the power of thought—power that the other resurrected souls will not find until the end of their ascent. The battle between devils and angels for the souls of the just—a traditional iconographic motif in the old depictions of the Last Judgment—assumes here a new form, one of an intensity never before seen: two angels are battling to pull out two giants, while the demons within the cavern are doing all they can to prevent this—they hold fast to one of the giants' hair, and to the other's feet.

204) One of the damned, in despair
In the figure of this damned soul, Michelangelo created an unforgettable picture of utter and final despair. Cowering and bent over, he is being slowly and powerfully pulled downward by a tangle of ponderous demons. One of his eyes he has covered with his hand, while the other eye glances panic-stricken into the abyss of hell. In the Sistine Chapel, the bodies seem to have an inverse gravitational pull; rather than falling downward, their motion is more of a slow ascent—both the saved and the damned. The manner in which the "Disperato" tries to resist this tendency endows him with an unrivalled expression of fear.

VATICAN ROOMS AND CHAPELS

205) The Chapel of Pope Urban VIII: "The Descent From the Cross"—a painting by Pietro da Cortona
Here we are exposed to one of the painter's most genuine creations. Its best qualities are expressed principally in the colors, which, in this instance and more than in most other examples, retains the "harmony" of light tones

dominating the subtle transitions to half tones with the use of a few dark strokes. Also worth mentioning, in addition to the painting's pulsating colors, are a clever composition and a genuine concern for the subject matter which even the rather synthetically dramatic pose of the Holy Virgin does not seem able to impair.

206) *The areas ruled by Bologna. By Egnazio Danti*
The city of Bologna lies in the center of an area under its rule and at the edges of a zone between mountains and flatland. A map of the city is inserted. The artist prepared this as a separate sheet which could be pinned to a wall if the occasion arose. Of the two artistically framed panels above, the one refers to the historical origins of the city and the other describes the area and its boundaries. The corresponding information appears on a smaller panel below at the right. These same components are repeated on the remaining 31 maps.

207) *Venice. By Egnazio Danti*
The artist-cosmographer elaborates on his depiction of the city and surrounding area by including numerous arriving and departing ships, thus pointing up Venice's significance as a trading center. The usual historical reference to the city's origin is also found—condensed into a few words—appearing on the open pages of a book carried by a winged lion, the city's emblem.

208) *Civitavecchia. By Egnazio Danti*
The fresco shows the walled city and the surrounding area. Also clearly discernible are the famous fortifications, whose construction was begun by Antonio Sangallo the Younger on behalf of Julius II. They are reported to have been completed under Michelangelo's supervision. The depiction of the city and the harbor, probably as they looked in the 16th century, is accompanied by a cherub carrying a scroll containing a reference to the city's Roman origins and its name in classical antiquity, *Centum Cellae*.

209) *A view of Malta. By Egnazio Danti*
This is perhaps the most successful example of the artist's talent at synthesizing history and geography. In this case he links a meticulous reproduction of the city with an historical event. The Siege of Malta by the Turks under Sultan Solyman II began at the end of May 1656 and lasted until September 7 of the same year. Displaying enormous courage, the Knights of Malta survived the siege with the aid of relief expeditions from Spain, Genoa, Naples, Sicily and Tuscany. The siege ended with the defeat and the withdrawal of the Turkish armada.

210) *"The Last Supper." Tapestry from a Tournai workshop*
The scene of *The Last Supper,* here set under the arcade of a gothic building, occupies the center of the tapestry. There is a distinct kinship between the tapestry and miniature painting of the time that can be seen in the treatment of the figures and the folds in the robes. Equally noticeable in this tapestry is the persistence of Gothic taste then still popular in Flanders. In Italy, on the other hand, the Renaissance had already reached its highpoint. The colors reveal a subtle play of contrasts based on the artistically related tints alongside bright colors—predominantly red and green.

211) *"Cardinal Maffeo Barberini Regulating the Drainage of Lago di Trasimeno"*
Even though this tapestry originated in a workshop headed by a Fleming, Giacomo van den Vliete, it is nonetheless dominated by Italian taste. The setting, as well as the figures, repeat typical elements of 17th century Italian painting. The tapestry's true value lies in its colors, whose original intensity has been recovered through cleaning and restoration, thus facilitating a proper appreciation of the work.

212) *"The Submission, in Venice, of Emperor Frederick Barbarossa to Pope Alexander III". A fresco by Francesco Salviati and Guiseppe Porta in the Sala Regia*
The scene shown here alludes to the peace agreement made between the Pope and the Emperor on July 2, 1177, in Venice. The agreement concluded a long struggle by Frederick for the privileges of imperial sovereignty, at the end of which he was forced to recognize the Pope's prerogatives. Keeping in mind the purpose of the painting, the artist interpreted the event as a genuine act of submission by the Emperor to the Pope. Between the background, which consists of St. Mark's Cathedral, and the foreground, an unordered and anonymous mass of people have been assembled. The group at the left, however, is remarkable for its rhythmical, animated composition achieved through a play of contrasts among the individual figures. In evidence in the painting is a style derived from Michelangelo and the Venetians.

213) *Decorative painting by Giovanni Pietro Venale on the ceiling in the Sala Ducala*
The artist was apparently determined to follow the predominant taste of his time. In so doing he was intelligent enough to lend the decorative motif, which ran the danger of becoming monotonous and banal if exploited too unscrupulously, an elegant, yes, an even original turn. Even though Venale may not have achieved the artistic level of the most celebrated examples of decorative painting, he did avoid the pitfall just mentioned.

214) *Drapery by Bernini*
The simulated stucco drapery, held up by numerous lively, graceful cherubs, once again bears witness to the artist's inexhaustible imagination and inventiveness. The drapery was meant to correct optically the difference in the axes of the two sections of the Sala Ducale. The verisimilitude is so persuasive and the drapery is so imaginatively natural in its arrangement that what might otherwise be regarded as virtuosity turns out in reality to be genuine art.

215) *"Apostle Paul's Shipwreck in Malta." By Niccolò Circignani*
The event described here has a connection with the general concept of the loggia, insofar as its theme is closely tied to the problem of the "winds." The painter shows less artistic skill in this painting than where he is occupied with the personification of the individual winds. The overly stylized poses of the figures are partially counteracted only through a clever selection and harmony of the colors. Above the picture is an aperture through which a ray of light falls onto a meridian indicated on the floor.

216) *Matteo Bril: "Abraham and the Three Angels"*
The Biblical episode illustrated here is less important than the landscape, which is the true "hero" of this story. The tree in the foreground dominating the composition makes the space disappear into the distance even more impressively. The entire frieze is enlivened through the rhythmical alternation of landscape with elegant women.

217) *"The North Wind." By Niccolò Circignani*
The artist painted the personification of the North Wind on the surface between the two original arches, later closed at the behest of Urban VIII. Even if the composition's rhythm reveals what one might regard as the authentic influence of the mannerists, it is without doubt to the artist's credit that he exploited the mannerist style so that the scene could be designed to fit the limited painting surface available.

218) *Decorative painting along a window*
Rectangular windows were placed in the openings of the vaults closed by Urban VIII. Over each of these is a lunette bearing the coat of arms of the Pope, over which is the Papal emblem. The side parts of the enclosing wall are decorated with grotesques. It is easy to sense the difference between this type of decoration and that of the preceding 16th century. In keeping with the taste of the time, the decorative elements have become heavier and more opulent.

219) *Paul Bril: a landscape with bridges and ruins*
This is one of the most eloquent landscapes in the entire series. Here the tendency towards naturalism has been subordinated to an imaginative romanticism, disclosed in the ancient ruins towering over the cliffs and commanding the center of the viewer's interest. The ruins suggest an island joined to the remaining landscape through small bridges, almost like ships' gangways, upon which figures are seen moving animatedly. The short bridge in the foreground at right is especially effective.

220) *Paul Bril: a view of Rome with Castel S. Angelo*
This attempt to copy reality faithfully—even though the composition is still romantic in nature—plus the broader expanse of the composition, as well as the lighter tones, force the observer to the conclusion that this fresco was painted by Paul Bril and not by his brother, Matthijs.

221) *Matthijs Bril: landscape with obelisk*
The subject matter offers the artist an excuse to create a traditional landscape,

in which the observation of nature and imaginatively realistic details—not without their romantic accents—are mixed. The interest in the small pictures is heightened through the elegant frames and the graceful cherubs, probably created by an associate, that alternate with the landscapes.

222) Giovanni Fransesco Romanelli: "Visitation." Part of the ceiling in the Sala della Contessa Matilde
The scene of the Visitation is one of the small pictures which decorate the barrel-vault in this room. The characteristics of Romanelli's particular style are revealed here in the determination to convey graceful movement, in the almost dancing rhythm of the two women encountering each other, and in the colors. Also very effective are the two flanking, allegorical figures.

223) Giovanni Fransesco Romanelli: "The Meeting Between Duchess Mathilde and Pope Gregory VII"
The artist's compositional skills, his palette of exquisitely subtle colors, and the elegance of his figures, justify the renown which he enjoyed during his time, even if the origins of his artistic education are all too evident. In this painting, the influence of Pietro da Cortona is transparent in the figure of the Virgin Mary, a fact that does not lessen the merits of the painting.

224) "St. Jerome." A fresco by Fra Angelico
The great church educator is portrayed here in unusual attire: the cowl and leather belt worn by Augustinian monks. A cardinal's hat lies at his feet. The inscription on the pedestal, *"Sanctus Bonaventura,"* suggested the theory that the painted figure was the Augustinian cardinal, Bonaventura Paraga, a friend of Petrarch, who was canonized by his order for being killed while defending the rights of the Church. A recent restoration, however, has revealed that the inscription on the pedestal was added later and was accidental. On the other hand, it was possible to make out weak but very real traces on the halo of the proper name, that is, St. Jerome.

225) Fra Angelico: "The Apostle Peter Ordains St. Stephen as a Deacon"
St. Peter stands on the steps of an altar with a tabernacle in a 15th century church in order to give the kneeling Stephen the communion chalice and plate. At the center in the rear, six of the twelve apostles are aligned like monks in two rows to witness the ceremony. The lines of perspective vanish next to the head of the last figure at the right. This fresco is straightforward and not one of the loveliest in this chapel, but it does contain one of Beato Angelico's masterpieces: the face of St. Peter, which radiates goodness and reveals him as both modest and aware of his calling.

226) Fra Angelico: "The Pope Gives St. Lawrence, as Deacon, the Church Treasure"
Two soldiers, in peculiar dress suggesting something halfway between antiquity and the Middle Ages, attempt to break open the entrance to the bishop's palace in order to take Sixtus II (who can be seen at the right, handing the Church treasure to the deacon) prisoner. In the course of the painting's restoration, it was discovered that the Pope shown in the painting was Nicholas II. The nose, damaged by a halberd during the sack of Rome in 1527 and then reduced in size by Gregory's restorers, has now been restored to the original size; this was indicated by traces discovered during the last restoration. The façade of the Tuscan building is remarkable for its elegance.

227) Fra Angelico: "St. Stephen Preaching"
Like the other two lunettes (the one over the altar is filled by a window),

this one shows two events. The first of these is St. Stephen preaching in a Tuscan city that is protected by battlements and towers. Women and children are sitting in the foreground, and at the rear there are standing men. The painting is reminiscent of the artist's version of St. Bernard of Siena preaching. The second event, the dispute or the exchange of words between the first martyr ever, St. Stephen, and the Council of Elders, takes place, oddly enough, in a prayer house open on one side and located on the square. This pictorial arrangement recalls 14th century painting.

228) Fra Angelico: "The Stoning of St. Stephen"
The saint, who has been led to the city wall as if it were an altar, is shown kneeling in a landscape, whose tranquility is only interrupted by charming white and rose-colored country villages, and hills similar to those near Fiesole. While being stoned, Stephen prays for his tormentors, among them, Saul, who, after his conversion confessed he had worn the enemy's frock. It is possible to recognize the difficulty with which Beato Angelico was faced as he tried to express such powerful emotions as hate and malice. The faces of St. Stephen's executioners, however, reveal only indifference. The artist neither wanted to, nor could he, go any further than that.

229) Michelangelo: "Conversion of Saul"
To Vasari, as to every 16th century critic, everything in this fresco must have appeared alien, considering to what extent it violates the accepted aesthetic principles of the Renaissance. He praises it, in fact, only in general terms, without noting—or wanting to note—the unbalanced composition, the treatment of the figures according to ethical, not aesthetic, considerations, and other special characteristics. These mirror the steadily growing mystical fervor in Michelangelo, which was sparked by Vittoria Colonna, and his gradual disavowal of the things of this world, even of the painting and sculpture of his later years. During this period, he expressed himself principally in his magnificent *"rime spirituali"* and in the musical power of his architecture, the dome of St. Peter's, on which he worked without remuneration, until his death, as pure service to God.

230) Michelangelo: "Crucifixion of St. Peter"
In this fresco Michelangelo, appears to want to recuperate from the confusion reflected in the "Saul" fresco, which is in complete *contrapunto*. Contrasting with the passion and the outbursts of emotion in the former "theophany" is his balanced treatment of the masses, who are arranged in a circle around the cross; the movement of the groups is slow; and if the Christian hero dominates the scene, at least the other figures each have individual traits and are not peripheral or lost in anonymity, as in the previous fresco. This is Michelangelo's last work of figurative art for the general public; thereafter he devoted himself entirely to architecture and refused to show anyone the sculptures he was creating privately. These were the two *Pietà* groups recalling his youth: the one in the cathedral and the almost other-worldly *Rondanini Pietà*, alongside which he died.
As a man of the Renaissance, Michelangelo envisioned St. Peter as a Christian Prometheus nailed to the instrument of his martyrdom but who is not subjugated, and who accepts as the greatest consecration of all, the fate predicted by his master. In this fresco St. Peter is, as in *The Last Judgment*, a giant, a symbol of the divine power of the Church—especially of its ordeals. The doubting Apostle who denied Christ three times is shown here as a symbol of absolute faith, strengthened through the Lord's prayer:
"Ut non deficiat."

231) "Zeus of Orticoli." Colossal marble head. Found during excavations at Ortoli in 1782. Sala Rotundi

"And the ruler's Ambrosian locks of hair flowed down from his immortal head." This is the way Homer (*Iliad* I 529ff.) describes Zeus, the "father of the gods and mortal men" who embodies the greatest physical and spiritual powers in his nature (*Iliad* XV 106ff.), and this is the way we imagine Zeus to be represented in this sculpture. His head encircled with locks of hair conveys nobility and dignity. The bearded head was sculptured at the beginning of the Roman Empire (1 B.C.–1 A.D.). A Greek prototype associated with Bryaxis, a great sculptor of the 4th century B.C., is regarded as the basis for this facial type. It must be imagined that Bryaxis visualized Apollo as a regal figure. Restored by G. Pierantoni in 1783: a wide, outer band of the hair of the head, part of the left cheek with a piece of hair from the beard, tip of the nose, back of the head, neck and bust.

232) "Athena Guistiniani." A larger-than-life-size marble statue. Probably found at the church S. Maria sopra Minerva. Braccio Nuovo

The helmet pushed back, the aegis, a kind of breastplate decorated with the Gorgon Medusa, the spear and the sacred Acropolis snake coiled at her feet—all this characterizes the virgin goddess Athena, who sprang from the head of Zeus. Since a number of copies of this sculpture are known to exist, we may conclude that the original sculpture was created in Greece around 400 B.C. and was probably made of bronze. "If I am not mistaken," Goethe observed on January 13, 1787, during a visit to Italy, "it represents a style in transition from the austere and sublime to the beautiful, a bud that blossoms, a Minerva whose character so well reflects this transition." At first owned by the Giustinianis, from whom the statue received its sobriquet, it was subsequently acquired by Lucien Bonaparte in 1805, from whom Pope Pius VII bought it in 1817 for the Vatican. Parts of the statue have been restored slightly, such as the right hand holding the spear and the snakehead. The sculpture was cleaned thoroughly after its discovery, at which time it was also refinished.

233) Larger-than-life head of Athena

According to its shape and finish, it was part of a garbed statue, a cult idol. Eyeballs of gray, semi-precious stone (chalcedony), iris and pupils of glass flux (lost in the meantime), eyelids cut out of thin bronze plate, earlobes punctured to accommodate ornaments for the ears. Holes over the forehead and sideburns, as well as in the neck, for the securing of a helmet with crest. Only Athena, the clear-sighted, ingenious daughter of Zeus, wears a helmet on her head in keeping with her role as champion female warrior. The piercing stare emanating from her stern but beautiful countenance produces a fascinating effect. From a stylistic point of view, this fragment recalls an original greater Greek cult idol dating back to around 460 B.C. This work has been associated with the sculptor Pythagoras of Rhegion.

234) Fragment of a shield from the Athena Parthenos. Relief section showing a group of rescuers. From the Palazzo Rondanini. Base of the relief in large part restored, figures only slightly

The cult idol in gold and ivory in Athena Parthenos's temple was created by Phidias between 447 B.C. and 438 B.C. Its dimensions were enormous: it was some 39 feet, 5 inches high. The powerful effect which must have emanated from this work is testified to not only by its many imitations but equally by numerous literary allusions. The goddess appeared in her complete armor and carried a Nike in her outstretched right hand. In her left hand she held her spear, and her shield was at her feet. The battles between the Athenians and the Amazons were portrayed on the shield's exterior, encircling the head of the Gorgon in the center, who was surrounded by snake coils. A few remnants of the shield can be seen on the fragment of a copy (Inv. 1738). Individual groups represented on this shield relief were also copied during the Roman Empire and transferred onto a rectangular plate, as Inv. 10461 reveals, on which a wounded Athenian is shown being pulled out of the thick of a battle by his comrades.

235/236) Fragments from the sculptural ornaments of the Parthenon. Fragment from the west pediment of the Parthenon of a larger-than-life horse's head.—The head of a young man from the north frieze of the Parthenon

Athena, as able-bodied protectress of the city which carried her name, had an ancient shrine on the Acropolis. In 480 B.C. the Persians laid in ruins all the structures on the Acropolis. Under the aegis of Pericles, the Acropolis was rebuilt more magnificent than ever before. From 447 B.C. to 432 B.C., the architectural masterpiece, the new Parthenon, the temple dedicated to the honor of the virgin Athena, was erected under the supervision of Phidias. The unique sculptural ornaments embrace 92 metopes, 555 feet, of frieze, and the two giant pediments. Battles of remote antiquity are portrayed on the metopes, thus illustrating the securing of an orderly world: battles against giants, centaurs, Amazons and Trojans. The head reproduced here shows the victor of a battle with a centaur. On this frieze, the inhabitants of Attica appear in the sacred procession of the Panathenian festival. The pictured youth carries a bowl containing a cake offering. Athena is the center of focus among the Twelve Olympians in the pediments: The east pediment shows her birth, the west pediment her contest with Poseidon for possession of Attica. The fragment of the horse's head belongs to the brace of horses with which she rode to the citadel for the contest to prove herself protectress and ruler of Attica.

237) "Apollo di Belvedere." Larger-than-life-size marble statue

Pope Julius II placed the statue in its present position in 1503; it is suspected that the statue was originally found in the vicinity of S. Pietro in Vincoli, Cardinal Giuliano della Rovere's titular church, where it previously stood in a garden. Restored by G. A. Montorsoli after 1532: left hand and right arm. The restorations were partly removed in 1925. Apollo appears inaccessible with his light, gliding step. Self assured, he pauses and looks to the side in the direction of his outstretched left arm, whose hand holds the bow: the long-distance archer, the revengeful, human hybris and the god who punishes wanton presumptuousness. The right hand carried a laurel branch with bandages attached to it as a sign of his purgative and healing powers: the god who wards off evil. The figure's beaming, youthful appearance became the epitomy of the sublimity and purity of the Apollonian character for all those ensuing epochs turning to classical antiquity. Judging from its artistic form, the statue is a Roman reconstruction dating back to around 130 A.D. that used a bronze statue as a model; this has been linked with the Attic artist Leochares, who was active in the second half of the 4th century B.C. His statue of Apollo, the basis for *The Apollo di Belvedere*, stood in front of the Apollon Patrous temple in the Athens marketplace.

238) "Apollo Sauroctonus." Marble statue. Found on the Palatine in 1777. Numerous minor restorations and improvements.

This bronze statue of Apollo as a boy, known as "Apollo Sauroctonus," was created by no less a sculptor than Praxiteles, according to Pliny (*Naturalis historia* 34, 70) and Martial (XIV 172). It shows him, with his arrow, waylaying a lizard creeping towards him. Graceful and lissome, the boy, concentrating on his easy quarry, leans against a tree and waits for the most propitious moment to impale the lizard inching up the tree stump. The image of the god Apollo, who purges humans of their impurity and guilt, has been captured and fashioned by Praxiteles in this instance by conveying the playful, carefree character of Apollo's existence as a young god.

239) "Apollo Citaredo." Marble statue. Found during excavations by Domenico de Angelis in 1773–1774 south of Tivoli, in the so-called villa of M. Brutus. Much minor restoration

Apollo, feet wide apart, has his hand on the strings of a kithara. He wears the long robe with the high belt of a kithara player, and a cloak falls over his shoulder. His head is decorated with a laurel wreath. He holds his head high while singing. This is the way he leads the chorus of the Muses, with whom this statue was found in the villa of a wealthy Roman. The statue was executed during the Roman Empire in the 2nd century A.D. and patterned after Greek models from the Late Classical and Hellenistic times. Presumably it was sculptured at first as a separate work and then positioned as Musagetes with the Muses.

240) "Demeter." Larger-than-life-size statue. Once stood in the Cancelleria Palace courtyard; brought to the Vatican in 1784 under Pope Pius VI. Its presumable origin: the theater in Pompeii. Both arms restored
Demeter was visualized in the form of a majestic statue and for this reason ears of grain were placed in her right hand. This representation certainly brings a goddess to mind; the outstretched left hand no doubt held a scepter. The severe flow of the vertical folds of her shawl, a peplos with belt, underscores the towering aspect of the figure and emphasizes the sculpture's simple, unified, elementary form. Nevertheless, the statue adheres in its composition to the principle of movement and counter movement, common in classical antiquity. The Greek model for this copy dating back to the Roman Empire originated around 420 B.C. among the circle of sculptors working with Phidias.

241) "Hera Barberini." Larger-than-life marble statue. Found on the Viminal in the first half of the 17th century; acquired by Pope Clement XIV in 1772 from the Palazzo Barberini
The identification of the august and majestic figure as Hera cannot admittedly be completely certain, but the statue's conception and individual details can be best explained through this identification. The appurtenances of scepter and phial have no doubt been restored. The statue was modelled in the 2nd century after a no longer extant Greek original. Even if this Greek model appears to have suffered alterations and coarsening in the copies made during the Roman Empire, the rhythmical construction and the reproduction of the classical Greek robe of around 420 B.C. comes to the fore so persuasively that it might be possible to ascribe the original sculpture to Agorakritos, a pupil of Phidias. The figure is well preserved; only the two arms, which were specially fashioned, and parts of the feet have been restored. The head and the bare part of the bust have been fashioned from a special piece of marble and then mounted, a technique which was carried out with a great deal of skill in classical antiquity.

242) "Venus of Cnidos." Somewhat larger-than-life marble statue. Place of discovery unknown. Head does not belong to the statue, but comes rather from another copy of the Cnidian Aphrodite. Much minor restoration
Homer described in *The Iliad* (III 396ff.), how Aphrodite appeared to Helen: "When she recognized the goddess's lovely back, her charming bosom and the gracefully radiant eyes, she was very much surprised." And, on another occasion (XIV 198ff.) Hera asks of Aphrodite: "Give me the powers of desire and love with which you are able to force your will on everyone, the immortal gods as well as the mortal humans." Praxiteles created a sculpture for Cnidos of the goddess Aphrodite in the middle of the 4th century B.C. This work is one of the most frequently mentioned and celebrated sculptures in the literature handed down to us from classical antiquity; furthermore, Cnidos imprinted this image of Aphrodite on its coins. This marble copy corresponds exactly, as far as type is concerned, to the reproduction appearing on the Cnidian coins. Thus, we have here a copy modelled after the very masterpiece by Praxiteles which prompted people to travel from remote parts of the world to Cnidos to view this work of art, as Pliny the Elder reports (*Naturalis historia* 36, 20). The goddess of love appears disrobed and ready to take a bath. She lays her robe over the jug already containing water. It is as if no one sees her, just as she, tranquil and undistracted, is unaware that she is seen.

243) Venus kneeling. Larger-than-life-size marble statue. Found around 1760 in the Tenuta Salone at the Anio ("Prato bagnato") and acquired under Pope Pius VI
Aphrodite is kneeling to bathe. The water is supposed to gush down on her from above. She wants to try to catch the rush of water with her raised left hand. She turns her face away. There are numerous copies of this statue. The one reproduced here from the Roman Empire once decorated the bath of a wealthy Roman, as the place where the statue was discovered testifies. The motif's composition is characteristic of the early Hellenistic style in the 3rd century B.C. This kneeling Aphroditian type also appears on coins from Bithynia. If this fact is linked to a citation by Pliny (*Naturalis historia* 36, 35), it is possible to identify the sculptor as the Bithynian, Diodalsas.

244/245) Myronian Athena-Marsyas group. Fragment of a slightly smaller-than-life marble head. Helmet, with a large part of the forehead, as well as the neck and bust, restored with plaster.—Slightly smaller-than-life marble statue of Marsyas. Found in 1883 in Via Quattro Cantoni on the Esquiline in the vicinity of what was a sculptor's workshop in classical antiquity; the workshop's stone seal dates back to 134 A.D.
"There, too (on the Acropolis overlooking Athens), stands Athena beating the silenus, Marsyas, because he picked up the wind instrument which the goddess had thrown away and no longer wanted," records the travel writer Pausanias (I 24, 1) around 160 A.D.; and Pliny reports hearing that Myron had created not only a satyr fond of playing aulois, but also a sculpture of Athena. The Myronian masterpiece has been reconstructed with the aid of the descriptions offered by these writers and that of images on coins. The head fragment of Athena and the statue of Marsyas are copies from the Roman Empire and are modelled after a Greek sculpture made of bronze. Myron of Eleutherai created this offering around 450–440 B.C., and it could be seen on the Acropolis overlooking Athens during Pausanias's time: Athena, the originator of flute playing, observes in reflecting water how the playing of the double auloi distorts her image. She throws the instrument away. The silenus Marsyas, seduced by Athena's playing, leaps to her side to pick it up. The goddess's gesture, however, checks him from doing so.

246) "Achilles as Doryphoros." Larger-than-life marble statue. Origin unknown. At its present location since 1822. Broken many times; repaired and restored on numerous occasions, including the right arm, and the left hand holding the spear
"Effigies Achilleae," representations of Achilles, is what Pliny the Elder calls the statues of naked spearsmen which often adorned the schools of classical antiquity. The memory lives on in this sobriquet for the original sculpture, the bronze statue of Achilles created by Polycletus of Sicyon around 440 B.C. It reveals the hero in the form of a Doryphoros, with a long spear used in battle. This work is handed down to us in numerous copies. The copy shown here comes from the Early Roman Empire. The Doryphoros Polycletus is marveled more as a work of art than as a representation of the mythical hero Achilles, the strongest, youngest and most handsome Greek hero to take part in the Trojan War. Simple and clear as the pose and bearing may appear, the arrangement of the parts are equally artistically thought out. The standing leg and the arm supporting the spear, the non-supporting leg and the arm hanging down loosely are all equivalents in terms of opposing function: the principle of repose and that of movement are united and carried out in detail in this statue so that it conveys a sense of animation. Each limb is related to the total conception in its proportion and rhythmical movement. Unfortunately the theoretical writings of Polycletus, his canon on the principle of porportion in the human body in the representational arts, have not been handed down to us. The classical pattern of Polycletian art has been preserved, however, in the copy of the Achilles sculpture.

247) "Meleager." Larger-than-life-size marble statue. From Rome; probably found on the Janiculum at the Porta Portese; known of since the 16th century; acquired by Pope Clement XIV for the Vatican
Meleager stands lingering, his right hand resting behind his back; and in his left hand, the hunting spear that has been laid down has yet to be restored. His watchful hunting dog has crouched beside him. The quarry, a boar's head, is represented on the other side. Meleager slew this monster while on the great Calydonian Hunt, in which Greece's most famous heroes took part. Artemis, the mistress of wild animals, had sent this terrible beast because Meleager's father, Oeneus, the king of Aetolia, had neglected to give thanks to Artemis for a prosperous year. A fateful argument over the head and hide of this boar led to Meleager's death. The version shown here of Meleager, with his accoutrements of boar's head, dog and hide, was created in the Antonian period in the 2nd century A.D.; it is based on a great statue of Meleager by Scopas from the late classical phase of Greek art, around 340–330 B.C.

248) "Torso del Belvedere." Larger-than-life-size marble statue. From the possessions of the Colonna "in monte cavallo" under Pope Clement VII. Placed in the Belvedere in 1523–24
The torso is that of a powerful man sitting on a boulder over which an animal hide has been spread out. The upper part of the body is bent forward

and turned towards the left side. The right arm hung down; the left arm was raised to the side. The right foot is placed forwards and the left to the rear. On the front of the boulder is the artist's inscription: "The Athenian, Apollonius, son of Nestor, is the creator (of this work)." This sculpture, admired and celebrated since the early Renaissance, was regarded as representing Hercules until about the end of the 19th century. Once the hide was no longer held to be a lion's but a panther's, the tendency was to view the statue as representing either Marsyas, Sciron, Polyphemus, or Philoctetes. Nevertheless, these interpretations were no more definitive than the old supposition. The torso, of course, conveys less to the historian than to someone who understands the language of form, as J. J. Winckelmann has taught us in his masterful description of the subject. The Athenian Apollonius created this work around the middle of the last century B.C.

249/250) Amazons. Larger-than-life marble statue. At one time part of the Mattei Collection; thus labelled "Amazone Mattei"; acquired under Pope Clement XIV for the Vatican. The head belongs to another Amazon. Restored: neck, both arms, both lower legs.—Life-size marble statue. From the Villa Aldobrandini in Franscati; known as early as the 17th century. Restored: both arms, the right leg, the lower left leg, quiver, support and base

The two Amazons are easily recognized as members of the mythical race of female warriors: firstly through their garments—the short belted horseman's chiton that is tied on one shoulder—and secondly, through their weapons—the quiver and the spear, which, in these two instances, have been preserved only in part. The two women lean on these for support, since both of them are wounded: the one, on the upper left leg, the other under the right armpit next to the breast. The Amazons were proteges of Artemis, in whose temple in Ephesus they sought sanctuary after being defeated and wounded in battle. Pliny the Elder records (*Naturalis historia* 34, 53) that a shrine was erected for them in Ephesus. The great sculptors of the Periclean Age around 430 B.C. competed with one another to create the best statue for this shrine. Two of the Amazon statues erected in the temple of Artemis in Ephesus have been preserved for us here in the form of copies of average quality dating from the Roman Empire: the one by Phidias and the other by Kresilas.

251) One of Niobe's daughters. Somewhat larger-than-life-size marble statue. Presumably found in Hadrian's villa at Tivoli; later in the garden of the Quirinal; then, until 1907, in the Museo Chiaramonti; since then called Niobide Chiaramonti. Unrestored

Niobe, the daughter of Tantalus, was the wife of Amphion, the king of Thebes. She had seven sons and seven daughters, a fact she boasted about in the presence of Leto, who gave birth only to Apollo and Artemis. Both gods took terrible revenge for the offense against their mother: Apollo killed the sons and Artemis the daughters. One of the daughters is represented here. She is identifiable since the main characteristics of the statue correspond to a statue in the Uffizi Gallery, Florence, which has been identified as a daughter of Niobe through various related findings. Pliny the Elder (*Naturalis historia* 36, 28) describes a sculptural group of dying daughters of Niobe (*Niobe liberos morientes*) in the Apollo Sosianus temple in Rome, which was created by the Greek sculptor Scopas or by Praxiteles. In all probability, the *Niobide Chiaramonti* preserves the characteristics of this sculptural group from the 4th century B.C. Because of its outstanding quality, the statue is occasionally regarded as a Greek original. But evidence against this theory is the clearly defined base which was popular with the neo-Attic artists of the 1st century B.C. The frantic figure, in a high-belted chiton and fluttering cloak, fleeing from the arrows of the revenging gods was presumably copied – minus sisters and mother – as a separate work.

252) "Medea and the two daughters of Pelias." Marble relief. Found in the courtyard of the Palazzo Simonetti at the Corso in 1814. Unrestored

The relief shows the preparations being made for the murder of aged King Pelias. At the left stands Medea, daughter of Aeëtes, king of Colchis. With Medea's help, Jason had come into possession of the Golden Fleece, which he then gave to his uncle, Pelias. Pelias, however, failed to make Jason king of Ioclos in return, as he had promised. This was the motive for the murder. Medea, dressed in a long robe and a kind of Phrygian hat with a wide hanging veil, holds a pyxis containing magic herbs in her hands. She is about to drop the herbs into the cauldron as soon as Pelias, the father of the girls,

who are also shown in this relief, has been slaughtered, cut into pieces and thrown into the Vessel. Pelias, or so Medea promised his daughters, would rise rejuvenated out of the boiling cauldron. While one of the daughters hangs the pot on its three-legged support, the other stands, vaguely suspicious, alongside with the butcher's knife in her right hand. This particular relief, of which other replicas are known, is a neo-Attic copy from the 1st century B.C. It is believed that three other three-figure reliefs, also extant only in the form of copies—Orpheus with Eurydice and Hermes, Heracles with Theseus and Peirithous, and Heracles with the Hesperides—belong as a single group to this Pelias relief. The mythological themes of this three figure relief were the subject of famous Greek dramas in the 5th century B.C. This has led to the supposition that this relief once decorated Sophocles's tomb. It will, however, probably never be possible to substantiate this.

253/254) The Three Graces. Marble relief. Found at the hospice of S. Giovanni in Laterno in 1769.—Smaller-than-life three-figure group made of marble. From the Palazzo Ruspoli. Numerous restorations

The Three Graces of the Romans, called Charities by the Greeks, were the daughters of Zeus and Euryome. "Mortals owe their grace and nobility," proclaims Pindar in his 14th Olympian Ode, "entirely to them... Even the gods cannot reign without the magnificent Charities of Dance and Festivity." Their names are Aglaia (Radiance), Euphrosyne (Joy), and Thalia (Festivity). They appear as personal attendants of the gods and bestow upon mortals and immortals alike, grace, beauty, and the pleasures associated with festivities. The Three Graces are shown moving slowly hand in hand on this relief. Since Pausanias mentions the sculptures and the cult of the Graces at the entrance to the Acropolis overlooking Athens, it is believed possible that the Acropolis may have provided the prototype for this relief. The relief was created around 470 B.C. during the austere phase of classical Greek art, and appears here in a neo-Attic version from the 1st century B.C. The Three Graces are also revealed in a lovely pose in the statuary group. The composition, attuned to the single perspective, has an appeal owing to an artistic play of alternation and repetition, in keeping with the vogue present in the last phase of Greek art, in the Hellenism of the 1st century B.C. The statuary group is a Roman copy dating from the 2nd century A.D.

255) Triton with Nereids and Cupids. Marble statuary group. Found in front of the Porta Latina in 1778 and presented to Pope Pius VI. Greatly restored

During Hellenistic times, the tritons and nereids were attendant upon the god of the sea, Poseidon, and were equivalent to the satyrs and maenads, Dionysos's swarming retinue of landlubbers. The artists of ancient Greece represented the appearance and behavior of these colorful sea folk with imagination and enormous virtuosity. Holding the resisting nereid under his arm, the triton, accompanied by figures of Eros, skips over the waves. A conduit indicates that a stream of water once spurted forth between the triton's legs, this making for a charming fountain. The theme, composition and workmanship point to the late phase of Hellenistic art in the 1st century B.C., which can be labelled as classical rococo.

256) "Laocoön." Life-size statuary group made of marble. Found on the Esquiline at the Sette Sale on January 14, 1506, in the vicinity of the domus aurea and the Titus hermae; the group was re-assembled in 1957–58, and the original right arm, discovered by L. Pollak around 1904–05, was added

Laocoön and his two sons, entangled in the coils of two powerful serpents, stand on the steps of an altar. One of the serpents prepares to sink its fangs into the left thigh of Laocoön, who rears up and attempts vainly to hold the serpent's head away from him. The other serpent has already bitten the side of the smaller of the two boys, and writhing with pain, he collapses. The remnants of the symbol for a priest of Apollo, a laurel wreath, can be discerned in Laocoön's hair. Pliny the Elder is one of the earliest to mention the statuary group (*Naturalis historia* 36, 37), and he prefers it over all other works of art; it was erected in the home of Emperor Titus (79–81 A.D.) and was created by Hagesander, Polydoros and Athenodoros—all of Rhodes. The most exhaustive description of the fate of the Trojan priest of Apollo is given by Vergil (*Aeneid* II 40ff. and 199ff.): Laocoön warns the Trojans of the Wooden Horse, which the besiegers have left behind as a propitiary offering to Athena, and he throws a spear at it. He thus arouses the wrath of the goddess, who then sends the sea-serpents. Neither Laocoön's, nor Troy's fate can be averted. Only Aeneas recognizes the true meaning of the Wooden Horse and rescues himself and his family, a fact that was of importance for the Romans insofar as the Julio-Claudian imperial family cites him, the Trojan forbearer, in support of its claims.

257) "Menelaus." Larger-than-life marble head atop a bust created at a later date. Found during excavations undertaken by Gavin Hamilton in 1772 in Hadrian's villa at Tivoli. Considerably restored

Menelaus, the son of Atreus and the brother of Agamemnon, was Helen's consort and had assumed the reign of the Spartan kingdom from his father-in-law, Tyndareus. After Helen was abducted by Paris, he united all her previous suitors in a military expedition against Troy. In particular, he acquired renown by protecting and recovering the corpse of Patroclus during the ensuing battle, which Homer describes exhaustively in the 17th book of *The Iliad*. Towards the end of the 3rd century B.C. a Greek sculptor created a statuary group portraying Menelaus with the corpse of Patroclus. It must have been extremely famous, since a number of copies are known to exist, among them, this head in the Vatican, with its splendid Pergamenian helmet and those bearing Pasquino's name. The crest of the helmet is decorated with scenes in relief from the battles of the centaurs.

258) A companion of Odysseus. Somewhat larger-than-life marble head on a modern bust. Probably found in 1771 in Hadrian's villa at Tivoli. Heavily restored

On his journey home, Odysseus came to the land of the Cyclops. With his companions, he was penned up in the cave of the one eyed giant, Polyphemus, the son of Poseidon. The Greek hero got the Cyclops drunk on wine and heated a sharpened pole of green olive wood—"and his companions gathered round him, and a daimon instilled us with great daring. They (the companions) seized the pole of olive wood, that had been sharpened to a point at the end, and plunged it into his eye, but I plunged it in from above and twisted it" (Homer, *Odyssey* IX, 380–384). This scene was depicted in a sculpture group in the Tiberius grotto by Sperlonga. The prototype to the Polyphemus group can be found in Pergamum toward the beginning of the 2nd century B.C. The head of Odysseus's companion, illustrated here, was presumably created for Hadrian's villa in ca. 130 to 140 A.D.

259) "The Tyche of Antioch." Larger-than-life-size seated marble figure. Found in 1780 in the Tenuta Barberini on the Via Latina. The head of the goddess, though antique (the tower-crown was added later), is from another statuette

In Greek, "Tyche" means that which happens—according to Thucydides, Fortuna or chance. Such a power, immanent in fate, was considered to be divine, and it was revered and personified. The goddess of chance and fortune was thought to be linked not only to the fate of individual humans, but also to that of cities. It was particularly in the period following Alexander the Great that she was popular as the locative deity for newly founded cities. When, in the year 300 B.C., Antioch was founded by Seleucus Nicator, Eutychides, a pupil of Lysippus, was commissioned to do a statue of the city deity, Tyche. On the basis of descriptions in antique literature and coin likenesses, the type of the Tyche of Antioch has been identified. The one illustrated here was identified through a copy from Rome's imperial period. The goddess sits cross-legged, her left arm extended, on a rock—Mount Silpion—under which the river god Orontes swims. Both outcropping and river allude to the location of the city, above which the goddess sits, enthroned.

260) River deity. Colossal marble statue of a reclining figure. Found during the reign of Leo X in 1513 near the Church of S. Maria sopra Minerva (the area of the Serapis and Isis temple in antiquity). Restored under Clement XIV by Gaspare Sibilla

River divinities are common in Greek and Roman mythology. The cult of the rivers was already fully developed at the time of Homer (*Iliad*, XXI, 130 f.). "Not even the silvery billows of the glorious stream will protect you—the stream, to which you have sacrificed so many steers." In early times, the river deities were thought of as having animal form (particularly that of a steer); in later periods, they appeared as reclining male figures, with long hair and beard. Here the sphinx and the crocodile characterize the figure as being the river Nile. In his arm he holds a cornucopia with flowers and fruit as a benediction. The sixteen boys, at various levels on the monument,

represent the number of yards by which the Nile rises whenever it floods the land, making it fertile. It was executed according to a Hellenistic prototype in the Roman imperial period—probably in the 2nd century A.D.

261) Lares. Section from the marble relief from the "Period of the Vicomagistri." Found in 1937/39 in the vicinity of the tomb of the consul Aulus Hirtius on the Campus Martius, under the western section of today's Palazzo della Cancelleria Apostolica

Lares were the household gods; they were also the tutelary gods of the crossroads (lares compitales) and of the fields. Their cult was in the care of the Vicomagistri; each section of the city (vicus) had four magistrates (magistri). Augustus revived this old Roman cult when he reorganized the city of Rome, from 14 to 7 B.C. It is from this period that the altar stems. As the inscription notes, it was dedicated by the Senate and the people of Rome to Emperor Augustus, the son of the deified Caesar, as Pontifex Maximus. Augustus appears on the relief as Pontifex Maximus with the Vicomagistri; he gives the acolytes the two Lares statuettes and those of the Genius Augusti.

262) Romulus and Remus. Reverse side of the so-called Ara Casali. Found in the 2nd half of the 17th century on the Caelian hill. It was the possession of the Casali family, which donated this Ara to Pius VI

The beginning of the Romulus and Remus saga is depicted in four pictures. Above, Mars hurries tiptoe to the Vestal Virgin, Rhea Silvia, who is asleep under a fig tree. Behind her is the divinity of the river Tiber, depicted with a bundle of reeds in his arm. Beneath this, one can see Rhea Silvia with her two children, Romulus and Remus, on her lap. Seated alone on the banks of the Tiber and admired by its divinity, she glances upward with a supplicant look. She turns away from the two servants of her uncle, Amulius, who have come to take the twins away from her. In the next scene, the two lads, having been placed at the edge of the river, raise their arms in a supplicant gesture. They are surrounded by their step-father-to-be, the Tiber; by the mountain divinity, Palatinus; and by their father, Mars, who stands in panoply in a protective attitude at the left edge of the scene, while the servants do their duty. In the lower frieze, two shepherds stand in wonderment before the miracle of the she-wolf suckling the twins. The scene takes place on the banks of the Tiber.

263) "Mithras." Marble group, somewhat less-than-life-size. Acquired by Franzoni, under Pius VI, for the Vatican from the estate of the sculptor, Vincenzo Pacetti. Greatly restored

On order of the sun, the Persian god, Mithras, slays the primeval bull. The adherents to the Mithras religion believe that the sacrifice of a bull is the beginning of creation. All fauna and flora develop from the animal's body and sperm—despite all the efforts of the scorpion, which grasps the genitals, to poison the source of life, and despite the snake, the impure creature that is an ally of the evil spirit. A dog, the faithful companion of Mithras, licks the blood that flows out of the wound and which contains the animal's soul. Thus the steer-killing hero was the creator of all creatures, and a new and fruitful life resulted from the act of slaying the steer. The Mithras mysteries became popular throughout Italy during the 1st century A.D.

264) "Discobolus." Marble statue, somewhat less-than-life-size. Found in Hadrian's villa near Tivoli in 1791. Restored by Albacini: head and neck, left arm, right lower leg with foot. The inscription on the tree trunk is modern

The statue of a victor during the climax of his sporting competition is represented here: "You speak of the discus thrower, who is bent over, ready for the throw. His face is turned away from the hand that holds the disk; and with his foot he bends somewhat, as if he wished to raise himself with the throw." That is Lucian's description of the discus thrower (*Philopeudes* 18). There is no doubt that he was referring to the bronze work by Myron of Eleutherai, the great sculptor of the middle of the 5th century B.C. It is a copy of this work that is illustrated here. In it, the artist has caught the decisive moment of the discus throw. All the athlete's limbs are concentrated on the throw, which is portrayed with liveliness and audacity.

265) "Apoxyomenos." Marble statue, somewhat larger-than-life-size. Found in Trastevere in 1849. Restored by Tenerani

Depicted here is the victor of a sporting event, after the match. He is cleaning off the dust of the palestra. He holds his right arm stretched out fully, with the strigil—the scraping iron—in his left hand. Exhausted by the match, he looks apathetically into the distance. It is not the image of a happy victor, but rather the moment immediately following a completed effort. Literary evidence concerning the proportions preferred by Lysippus could make the original work his; this is a copy from a bronze from around 320 B.C.

266) "Demosthenes." Marble statue, somewhat larger-than-life. Probably found in the area of Tusculum and acquired from a villa near Frascati. Many small restorations
The identification of the statue was made from a small inscribed bronze bust that was found in the villa of the Piso family in Herculaneum on November 3, 1753, and which is today in the museum in Naples. The almost 50 known repetitions of this likeness of Demosthenes are proof of its popularity. They all go back to a bronze statue by Polyeuctos. On the initiative of Demochares's nephew, in 280 B.C., it was displayed in the marketplace in Athens, 42 years after the death of Demosthenes. On its base stood these words: "If you had had as much power as insight, Demosthenes, the Macedonian war-god would never have subjugated the Greeks." Fearlessly, Demosthenes spoke out for the freedom and independence of the Greeks from the Macedonians. This caused him, in 322 B.C., to be condemned to death. Sixty-two years old, he fled to the temple of Poseidon in Calauria. To avoid imprisonment, he took poison.

267) "Sophocles." Marble statue, somewhat larger-than-life. Found in 1839 in Terracina, and donated by the Antonelli family to Pope Gregory XVI. Restored by Tenerani: improvements to the face (in plaster); right hand and base with feet and scroll-receptacle
Positive identification of the statue was made from the inscribed herma-portrait in the Sala della Muse in the Vatican. Both likenesses were copied from a Greek prototype in bronze from the Roman imperial period. Literary sources record two likenesses of Sophocles: one was erected by his son, Iophon, following the poet's death (406 B.C.), in the form of a statue (*Vita Sophoclis* 11); another notation mentions an application by the orator, Lycurgus, in the 110th Olympiad (340–336 B.C.), to erect bronze statues of Aeschylus, Sophocles and Euripides—probably the same statues mentioned by Pausanias (I 21, 1) as being in the Dionysus theater in Athens. Reasons of style cause us today to believe that the marble statue in Terracina was copied from the prototype in the Dionysus theater. The poet is depicted as a vigorous man, in the prime of life, standing freely and self-assured, his robe wound about his frame and his eyes looking out into the distance. The fillet in his hair alludes to his priestly rank; he took the god of the physicians, Aesculapius, into his home when that cult began in Athens. Following his death, the Athenians glorified him. "Darling of the gods" (theophilés) and "Fortunate One" (eudaimon) is what his contemporaries called him; and yet he knew the depths of human sorrow, as proved by his tragedies, seven of which—of a total of 123—have survived to our day and age.

268) "Homer." Somewhat larger-than-life-size, marble head on a modern herma pillar. Acquired during the pontificate of Clement XIV
Homer, the first epic poet of the western world, and the author of *The Iliad* and *The Odyssey*, is believed to have lived in the 8th century B.C. It is known that there are many copies of this type of portrait bust, all dating back to the same bronze prototype, now lost. The original has been dated to the middle of the 5th century B.C., almost 300 years after the poet's death. This likeness had been previously identified, on the basis of the closed eyes, as that of the Cretan poet, Epimenides. The unopened eyes were taken to be a symbol for sleep, and Epimenides is said to have slept for 40 or 57 years. In memory of this earlier identification, one often sees this image of Homer described as the Epimenides type.

269) "Socrates." Somewhat larger-than-life marble head on a non-matching herma. Found and acquired during the pontificate of Pius VI in the Via Appia in the villa of the Quinctilii. Upper portion of the herma pillar bears an antique inscription, which does not pertain to the head
The likeness of Socrates can be recognized from the descriptions of his contemporaries: Alcibiades says, in Plato's *Symposium*, that Socrates was most similar to one of the sileni, Marsyas. Hence the wilful head-form, the high arched forehead, the small eyes with the arched eyebrows, the thick stub nose and

the powerful beard. Even in this copy of Socrates' face from the Roman imperial period one can still see something of the immediacy of expression, so characteristic of the wise man. The original was presumably cast in bronze not long after Socrates' death. An Athenian court sentenced him to drink of the poison hemlock in the year 399 B.C., when he was 70 years old. The main points of the accusation against him read: "He did not acknowledge the gods of the state cult; he introduced new divinities; and he corrupted the youth."

270) "Plato." Somewhat larger-than-life portrait–herma in marble. Acquired during the pontificate of Clement XIV at Naples. The inscription "Zenon" on the herma is said to be modern. Only slightly restored
The identification was made possible by an inscribed herma in Berlin, identical to this Vatican likeness. Another source of identification of this work as Plato is the presence of another replica of this head in the Vatican, in which it is joined to a likeness of Socrates as a double herma. Written records indicate that Plato had a broad forehead, a somewhat peevish countenance, and arched eyebrows. It may be that the original has been copied here, but it nevertheless appears lack-luster. The prototype of all the copies is presumably a statue of Plato in the academy in Athens. Commissioned by the Persian, Mithridates, it was made by Silanion. The academy was founded between 387 and 367 B.C., i.e., between Plato's 40th and 60th birthdays. The scion of an old, rich and renowned Athenian family, he died in 348/47 B.C. in Athens at the age of 80. He was buried in the academy.

271) "Pericles." Somewhat larger-than-life marble head on a herma pillar. Found in the so-called Brutus villa near Tivoli in 1774. Minor restorations and additions
The inscription on the herma identifies the figure as Pericles, son of the Athenian, Xanthippos. He is wearing a Corinthian helmet, the insignia of the office of strategist, his official rank. According to Thucydides Pericles, in his famous funeral oration in honor of the fallen soldiers, given in the winter of 431/430 B.C., said: "As far as official standing and individual reputation are concerned, preference within the community does not depend upon membership in the ruling classes but rather upon personal ability." Among the surviving copies of the likeness of Pericles, it is the one in the Vatican that best preserves the stern character of the prototype. It is probable that the original was a bronze statue. Pausanias saw it on the Acropolis in Athens in the 2nd century A.D. Experts believe this statue was made by Cresilas, and as evidence for this conjecture they point to a notation by Pliny the Elder (*Naturalis historia* 34, 74), who also wrote of Cresilas: *"nobiles viros nobiliores fecit."* This statue of Pericles was erected shortly after the death of the statesman, who was almost 70 years old when he died, a victim of the plague, in 429 B.C.

272) "Euripides." Somewhat larger-than-life bearded marble head on a modern herma pillar. Acquired during the reign of Pius VI in 1792 from the sculptor, Carlo Albacini. Greatly restored
It was easy to identify this portrait of Euripides, since the herma pillar with his likeness—now in the museum in Naples—contains the poet's name in an inscription that was made in antiquity. Almost 80 years old, the great Athenian tragedian died in the year 406 B.C. Of the 75 dramas, which the Alexandrian scholars accepted as genuinely his, only 18 have survived to our times. His popularity is indicated by the many copies that were made of his likeness. All of them go back to the original, made in the period from 340/330 B.C., or 70 years after his death. Accordingly, this likeness is less a portrait of the great poet than an idealized memorial erected by his admirers. The fine features, with the high curved forehead, the narrow beautifully formed nose, and the critical gleam of his eyes combine to reveal the nobility of the tragedian who sought in his dramas to unmask the mysteries of human existence.

273) "C. Julius Caesar." Life-size portrait head in Marble. Origin unknown. Additions: neck and nose
Caesar's likeness is known to us from coins. It was at the beginning of the year 44 B.C., only a few weeks prior to his assassination, that the 56-year-old statesman was granted permission by the Senate to strike coins with his likeness, something never before permitted a living person in Rome. All traditional

reports have it that Caesar, handsome and distinguished, took great pains with his personal appearance. The well-groomed hair of this portrait head seems to bear this out. His face has character. The forehead is hard and smooth. The small, lively eyes have a sharp and critical look, perhaps reflecting an awareness of his own superiority. The small-lipped mouth is compressed, forming a slightly ironic smile. The striking facial features are marked by self-control. Here is the man who prepared the way for the Roman imperial era, his name becoming the title for emperors.

274) "Roman general." The upper section of a somewhat larger-than-life bronze statue. Origin unknown. Came into the Etruscan museum during the pontificate of Gregory XVI in 1842. The clothing has been largely restored in modern times. The eyes are missing
The general appears in heroic pose. He has thrown his toga over his left shoulder. He holds his right arm extended, and it is probable that he is leaning on a long lance. Despite the idealized rendering of the body, the portrait head is strongly realistic, resembling other statuary heads during Rome's late republican era in the 1st century B.C. Striking are the long neck, the relatively small head with close-cropped, straightly cut hair above the forehead, as well as the characteristic spiral hook above the left ear. This type of statue and the material used in making it are indicative of a renowned personality and an official statuary tribute. Since traditional reports of Sulla conform with this description, this has been thought to be his likeness. He was appointed dictator from 92 to 79 B.C. "to restore the state." He resigned this office voluntarily and died a year later, at the age of 60.

275) "Augustus." Somewhat larger-than-life marble statue in armor. Found in Livia's villa near the Prima Porta on the Via Flaminia on April 20, 1863. When found, traces of color were still recognizable. Restored under the supervision of Tenerani
Augustus can be easily identified by his characteristic portrait head. He appears here in the armored dress of a field general; his left hand holds a scepter, and his right hand is raised in an oratory gesture. The relief on the armor breast-plate depicts an incident that took place in the year 20 A.D., a Parthian submitting his field-standard to a Roman legionary. In the sober language of the *Res gestae*, Augustus' factual report, the emperor said (29): "I have forced the Parthians to return to me the booty and the insignia of three Roman armies and to get down upon their knees to beg for the friendship of the Roman people." In the breast-plate relief the entire cosmos takes part in this act of pacification: on top is the god of heaven, Caelus, with billowing cloak, as well as the sun god, Sol, atop the quadriga with Aurora in front of him; the lower section depicts Tellus, the earth's fertility; to either side are Apollo and Diana; the middle scene features flanking images of the personifications of pacified provinces. Next to the leg bearing Augustus' main weight is a dolphin, ridden by Cupid. This is an allusion to the Julian clan, which claimed descent from Venus. The naked feet are characteristic of the heroic style. It is probable that this statue was made for Livia following the death of Augustus (14 A.D.). It was based on the bronze memorial statue that was officially erected in 20 B.C. in honor of the diplomatic peacemaker.

276) "Claudius." Larger-than-life marble statue. Found in Lanuvium in 1865. Completely restored were both arms, and the upper section of the eagle
Emperor Claudius died at the age of 64, in the 14th year of his reign (41 to 54 A.D.). He was the victim of his wife's (Agrippina) attempt to poison him. Suetonius reports that he was buried with all imperial pomp and was included among the ranks of the gods. He is depicted in this statue as a god, his pose being that of Jupiter: His toga is slung about the lower part of his body, he holds with his left hand his scepter, and the eagle at his right foot is the symbol of Jupiter. His head is crowned with a wreath of oak leaves, the corona civica (citizen's crown), which was granted by the Senate *"ob cives servatos."* In contrast to the idealized type of statue, the face seems very realistic. A point of reference for judging the character of this emperor has been handed down from his step-grandfather, Augustus, who is supposed to have said of him when Claudius was a young man (according to Suetonius): When he is unhappy, the nobility of his soul appears, in its basic components, clearly for all to see.

277) "Diocletian and Maximian." Porphyry column with relief. According to F. Alber-

tini, *"Opusculum de mirabilibus Romae" (1510), it is from the area of the Aurelian sun temple. Initially installed in the chapel of Sixtus IV in Old St. Peter, consecrated in 1479. It was brought to the Vatican Library during the pontificate of Pius VI*
Diocletian was an Illyrian soldier of humble origin. At the age of 44, as commander of Numerian's praetorian guard, and following the latter's murder, he was acclaimed emperor by the army in 284. In the year 285, he appointed as Caesar a Pannonian officer, Maximian, Diocletian's friend in the field and his equal in age. On April 1, 286, Maximian received the rank of Augustus. In 293 Galerius and Constantius Chlorus were appointed Caesars. This new system of government, the tetrarchy, allowed the supreme power of Rome to be simultaneously present in all parts of the empire. The porphyry relief depicts two of the rulers in brotherly embrace: Diocletian and Maximian. Dress and accessories are the same for each: armor with toga; laurel wreath on the head, with a jewel in the middle; and, in the left hand of each, a globe. This representation demonstrates the peaceful harmony (concordia) of the wide-flung power of Rome. Diocletian and Maximian abdicated on May 1, 305. The former died ten years later at his palace in Salona; the atter committed suicide in the year 310.

278) Domitian/Nerva. Frieze A of the Cancelleria reliefs, a marble relief with almost life-size figures. Found, 1937/39, on the Campus Martius in Rome under the western section of today's Palazzo della Cancelleria Apostolica. Missing is a plate on the left edge of the frieze
Clothed in a tunic and travelling cloak (paludamentum), the emperor is surrounded by gods and genii, lictors and soldiers. The direction of movement shows this to be his ceremonial exit (profectio). At the front are Minerva, Mars, the lictors and Victoria, whose wings can still be seen. Virtus leads him, his hand on the emperor's arm. The two genii, Senatus and Populus, stand behind and lift their right hands in a farewell gesture. To the rear are soldiers with their commanding officers. All the figures are in reference to the emperor. He lifts his right arm in a commanding gesture. In his left hand, he holds a scroll. His face has been reworked so that the original likeness of Domitian (81–96 A.D.), still identifiable by means of his hair-style, is now that of his successor, Nerva (96–98 A.D.). Thus Domitian fell victim to the *damnatio memoriae,* the attempt to remove him from the record of history.

279) "Sabina." Life-size portrait bust in marble. From the villa of Antoninus Pius in Lanuvium. No restorations, but the surface has been noticeably reworked
Sabina, Hadrian's wife and Trajan's grand-niece, died at about the age of 50 in 136 A.D. She used to accompany Hadrian on his journeys. In the year 128, she was granted the title of Augusta and was given the honor of having her likeness appear on coins. It is believed that this date coincides with the making of this type of portrait bust. The bust is completely preserved, with a high base and a profiled index tablet. Characteristically, her hairdo is parted in the middle, the hair combed back, fastened above the neck in a loosely twisted bundle and tied in a knot at the crown. The hair is adorned with a thick circlet. Her eyes comprise an iris ring and sickel-shaped pupils, one of the earliest forms by which sculptors created the illusion of life in the eyes of marble statues and busts.

280) "Hadrian." Colossal portrait head in marble. From Castel Sant'Angelo. The breast-piece has been added on
Hadrian was a native of Italica, in Spain, near Seville. He was Roman emperor from 117 to 138 A.D., from the age of 41 to 62. He sought to use peaceful policies to secure the borders of the Roman empire, which his predecessor, Trajan, had greatly extended. Six years before his death, he began the construction of a tomb for himself and his family on the right bank of the Tiber, the Castel Sant'Angelo of today. It was brought to completion by his successor in 139 A.D. The likeness illustrated was set up in this mausoleum. Both the site and the size of the portrait head allow one to conclude that this was an important official honor bestowed posthumously upon Hadrian. It was intended less as a realistic image of the emperor than as an idealized portrait of this self-willed ruler. Literary narratives from that era indicate that Hadrian had a large and stately appearance, that he took great care of his personal appearance and his well-groomed hair, and that he had a beard. This latter fact is remarkable, since all the Roman emperors who had preceded him had been clean-shaven.

281) "Antinous." Colossal portrait bust in marble. Found in 1790 in Hadrian's villa near Tivoli. The nose, several locks of hair, parts of the left shoulder, the stump of the right arm and the round base are restored

Antinous, a young man from Bithynia, used to accompany Emperor Hadrian on his travels. He drowned before the emperor's eyes in the Nile on October 30, 130 A.D.; he was only 20 years old. In honor of his favorite, Hadrian founded a city on the banks of the Nile: Antinoöpolis. The inscriptions on the memorial coins with his likeness call him Heros and Theos, indicating that he had been deified. The bust depicts him in "heroic nudity" above an acanthus-leaf chalice. The corkscrew locks at the back of his head remind one of Apollo. Among the many likenesses of Antinous, this portrait bust is unique in form, and both the site and the work's size permit the assumption that the emperor may have had a personal interest in the creation of this particular work of sculpture.

282) "Caracalla." Life-size portrait bust in marble. Found in the vicinity of the Constantine basilica around the year 1780. Additions: most of the bust, the socle and the nose

Emperor Caracalla, eldest son of the North African, Septimius Severus, and the Syrian, Julia Domna, was a 23-year-old when, in the year 211 A.D., his father died and he took power. This he did in conjunction with his brother, Geta, whom he soon had murdered. Six years later, on April 4, 217, he was himself murdered near Carrhae in Mesopotamia, at the behest of his praetorian prefect and successor. His likeness shows him turning his head to the side, his brows arched, his eyes glancing about suspiciously. His hair appears coarse and short, and a short beard covers his cheeks and chin. As a soldier-emperor, Caracalla tried, by conquering the Parthian empire, to emulate Alexander the Great's claim to rule the world. As this portrait bust indicates, he also tried to imitate Alexander the Great in his appearance, pose and countenance.

283) "Philippus Arabs." Life-size portrait bust in marble. Found in Porcigliano in 1778. Non-matching bust-base and index tablet. Intact, except for the tip of the nose

Philippus Arabs was a native of the Trachonitis, the area of the Hauran Mountains south of Damascus. When, in February 244 A.D., Gordian III died in battle against the Persians on the banks of the Euphrates, the 36-year-old praetorian prefect became emperor. In September 249, near Verona, he lost both the battle and his life to his successor, Decius. He had felt himself to be a Roman. This is indicated not only by his spectacular celebration of Rome's thousandth anniversary, on April 21, 248, but also by his likeness. He wears both tunic and toga. The latter raiment is folded in such a manner that the broad, even strips of cloth lie across his breast almost like a board. In similar manner, his toga is draped vertically about his body—a fashion (contabulatio) that was characteristic of the 3rd century A.D. The realistic rendering of the head recalls, in its severity, the Romans of the Republic.

284) Burial stele for a young man. Marble relief. In the 16th century, it was in the Villa Cesi. The upper section was donated to Leo XIII in 1902, after its rediscovery in the church of S. Lorenzo in foro piscium; the lower section was found in the same church in 1950. No additions

A youth is depicted, his head somewhat inclined. He has raised his left forearm, with the flat, extended hand, in a gesture of greeting. In front of him, in a leaning pose, stands his small servant, only half as large as he is. In the servant's left hand can be seen the handle of a strigil—an instrument with which athletes used to scrape their skin of dust and dirt following a match. In his right hand he is holding a round aryballos with oil. This slender relief, probably crowned with a palmetto fan and with an inscription carved into the base, was erected above a grave-mound as a memorial monument. It is representative of early classic-Greek art of the period around the year 450 A.D.

285) Relief from the tomb of a horseman. Fragment of a relief in Boeotian limestone. Removed from Greece as war booty by the Venetians under Morosini in the year 1687. Acquired for the Vatican during the pontificate of Pius VII. Minor restorations

A bearded, middle-aged man rides his spirited horse without a saddle. He is clothed in a short chiton and the chlamys, the riding cloak. His hands hold the reins, which were of bronze and have, unfortunately, been lost.

The interplay of forces of stress between the impetuous steed and the calm horseman are the source of the work's unique charm. One thinks immediately of the Parthenon, from whose horseman's frieze this relief may well have originated. In any case, it was made at about the same time: ca. 440/430 B.C.

286) Burial statue of a woman. Smaller-than-life sedentary figure of a woman, in marble. The head was added, although it appears to be of classical origin. Restored: right hand, right leg, lower section of the stone seat

Represented here is a woman in a chiton with long sleeves and a cloak drawn over her head. She is in a sitting position, with her right leg crossed over the left and her head inclined forward, supported by her right hand. Sunk in meditation, she seems to be recalling the life she has departed. This form became standard toward the end of the 5th century B.C. It originated in Greek Ionia. This imitation from the early Roman imperial era has sometimes been interpreted as a representation of Penelope.

287/288/293) Roman tomb reliefs.—Tomb relief of L. Vibius and his family. Only minor damage.—Effigy group of M. Gratidius and his wife, Gratidia M. L. C(a)rite. In marble. The base plate has been added.—Tomb relief of a chariot race in the Circus Maximus. Originates perhaps from Ostia. Well preserved

"The tombs are charming and moving, and they always depict life. There is a man sitting next to his wife in a niche, and they appear to be looking out of a window. Here are father and mother, with the son in the middle. And here, a couple extends its hands to one another." Thus did Goethe see the kind of tombs illustrated here on his journey to Italy (the excerpt above is from a notation he made in Verona, on September 16, 1786). Indeed, the deceased do have the appearance of life. The inscriptions provide their names; they are Romans from the period of transition from republic to empire, at the end of the 1st century B.C. On the tomb, or gravestone, the married couple and their child are depicted next to one another, in a frontal attitude. On the other monument, the husband and wife extend their right hands to one another in a gesture that serves to encompass all those human relationships in which fidelity plays a role and is expected; it is a documentation of fides and concordia, especially significant during marriage (dextrarum iunctio). In the third relief (293), the deceased appears in full-form, and larger-than-life. His wife is sitting next to him; much smaller than he, she offers him her right hand. He had probably held the office of director of games, the dominus factionis. The chariot race takes place in the Circus Maximus. Judging from the style, this relief belongs to the period of Trajan, around 100 A.D.

289/290/291) "Rose-Pillar." Marble.—Life-size busts of a man and woman, in marble, in an "aedicula"

The portrait busts and the pillar are from the mausoleum of the Haterii on the Via Casilina (in ancient times, Via Labicana), in front of the Porta Maggiore, and not far from Centocelle; they were discovered on that site in 1848. Together with an additional 36 fragments—inscriptions, reliefs and decorative architectural sections—they came into the former Lateran Museum. The gravesite was rediscovered in the early part of the year 1970. The depicted persons were members of the family of the Haterii, as indicated by inscription fragments that were found with the main objects. The aedicula, the enclosure for the busts, had been presumably recessed into the wall. The turn of the head of the two portraits links them together. The man has arched his eyebrows and his eyes peer into the distance with interest. A cloak is thrown over his left shoulder and, instead of the usual base, the bust has the figure of an entwined snake—a heroic reference to the deceased. The woman is completely clothed. Wearing a buttoned stola and a palla (cloak), she contemplates the world with a somewhat detached look. Her enclosure is adorned with rose blossoms. The motif of the budding and blooming rosebush is fully developed on the pillar-relief from the same tomb. Roses twine about a candelabrum, which, on the bottom, is surrounded by olive branches. On the sides, and atop the candelabrum, pairs of roosting parrots pick at the roses. The busts and the rose-pillar belong to the early Hadrian period, ca. 120 A.D.

292) Roman burial altar. Four-cornered marble block, festooned with lunettes; relief representation and inscription. Site of discovery unknown. No restorations

The inscription held by two figures of Eros says that Vitellia Cleopatra has dedicated this altar to the good gods *(dis manibus)* of her husband, Publius Vitellius Sucessis. The married couple appears in the relief scene above the inscription, depicted at the funeral meal. He is reclining on a cushioned dining sofa *(lectus)*. A table laden with food stands in front of him. At the foot of the sofa sits his wife, holding her husband's right hand. At the head of the sofa is a date tree, beneath which an unbridled horse impatiently paws the ground. The inscription and the relief scene are uniformly enclosed by a leaf-molding. In the lunette between the cushion volutes, there is a depiction of the busts of the man and woman; they are the same portrait heads as at the funeral meal. Griffins crouch along the narrow borders. The manner in which the representation was done, as well as the woman's hair style, date the altar at the beginning of the 2nd century A.D.

294) Tomb of the miller, P. Nonius Zethus. Marble block in relief, with recesses for installing cinerary urns. From Ostia
The tomb resembles a sarcophagus in form. The eight conical recesses were for urns. Only the front of the tomb is in relief. The inscription tablet contains the names of the maker: P. Nonius Zethus Augustalis, and of those who are buried with him: the freedwoman, Nonia Hilaria; his wife, Nonia Pelagia; and one P. Nonius Heraclio. The two flanking reliefs—enclosed on the sides by pilasters—relate the deceased's past: He was a mill-owner and a flour merchant. To the left, a donkey pulls the millstone, while, to the right, there is a depiction of a collection of flour vessels.

295) Sarcophagus of a general. Sarcophagus case in marble. It has been in the Belvedere since the 16th century. Its origin is unknown
The main figure on the front of the sarcophagus is a bearded general in armor and traveling cloak, with a sword in his left hand. He is enthroned as imperator. Behind him stands Victoria with a palm branch, suspending a wreath above his head. Prisoners are being shown to him. One of them, with a Phrygian cap, kneels before him. On the other side of the sarcophagus front, an old woman with child begs a young, clean-shaven Roman officer to spare her. The forefront of the sarcophagus relief is framed by trophies, with prisoners in bondage on the ground. Judging from their dress, the prisoners are Sarmatians, against whom Marcus Aurelius did battle after the year 167 A.D. One of the emperor's generals most probably commissioned this sarcophagus.

296) Protesilaos sarcophagus. Sarcophagus case in marble. Found at the second milestone on the Via Appia Nuova. No additions
The sarcophagus, which retells the tale of Protesilaos and Laodamia, glorifies the power of love over death. From left to right: Protesilaos leaves the ship and touches Asian soil, as the first of the Greeks who sailed off to make war on Troy. Disembarking, he is killed at the landfall, as the oracle had predicted. He lies on the ground. His shade follows Hermes. His young wife, Laodamia, is so beside herself with grief that Hermes brings Protesilaos back to earth from the Underworld for one day. In the center, one sees Laodamia and Protesilaus standing in front of the palace gate. Their uncarved heads were intended to be fashioned into portraits of the potential owner of the sarcophagus. In the next scene, one sees the married couple intimately united. Hermes then accompanies Protesilaos to Charon, the ferryman in the Underworld. The sarcophagus was fashioned in ca. 170 A.D.

297) Orestes sarcophagus. Marble sarcophagus, with cover and consoles. Found in 1839 near the Porta Viminalis; bricks of the mausoleum bore markings from the years 132 and 134 A.D. Excellent state of preservation
The vengeance and expiation of Orestes are related in four scenes on the front of the sarcophagus. From left to right: (1) The shadow of Agamemnon appears as a veiled shadow in the burial vault to his son, Orestes, and his friend, Pylades. (2) Aegisthus, who has murdered Agamemnon, is attacked from behind, thrown from his throne, and lies dead on the ground. Orestes tears the king's cloak from the body of his step-father, who had arrogated it to himself. The nurse turns away, horrified. (3) Orestes murders his mother, Clytemnestra. Two furies, spirits of vengeance, with snake and torch, pounce upon him. (4) With the bared sword that he has received from Apollo to complete his acts of vengeance, Orestes passes over one of the mollified furies (Eumenides). The expiation takes place at Delphi, as indicated by the tripod,

the laurel tree and the omphalos. The relief on the cover depicts an incident with Orestes and his sister, Iphigenia, in Tauris. The sarcophagus can be dated to the period around 135 A.D.

298) Sarcophagus showing Niobe's children. Marble, with cover. Found in 1776 in the Vigna Casali on the Via Appia. Numerous minor additions in marble and plaster
Depicted on the front of the sarcophagus case is the slaying of Niobe's children. Apollo and Artemis appear from the right and the left. They avenge their mother, Leto, whom Niobe had insulted. Niobe's children are thus slain by the infallible arrows of the divine twins. There is no escape for them. Niobe herself, shown next to Artemis, holds in her arms one of her daughters who has been fatally stricken. The nurse holds the head of another of the mortally wounded children. A lad seeks refuge with his bearded mentor. In front of Apollo, to the right, one of Niobe's sons lies on the ground; another collapses; and a third, holding several hunting spears aloft, tries to flee. The sarcophagus reliefs were made during the Antoninian period, around the middle of the 2nd century A.D.

299) Sarcophagus for a philosopher. Fragment from the front of a marble sarcophagus. Presumably from the Vatican necropolis. No additions. Ancient color traces
The front of the sarcophagus depicts a bearded philosopher. He is sitting in his chair *(cathedra)*, dressed in tunic and toga. He has spread out a scroll, and his eyes are raised in meditation. Listening to him, as in a "*sacra conversazione*," are a bearded man and two fully clothed women. The woman to his left is in a pose that imitates one of the nine Muses, Polyhymnia. This depiction contains an allusion to the never-ending joy of life after death, for his association with one of the Muses marks the philosopher as immortal. To either side of this central group are two further bearded men; each has his head turned, so that their eyes are fixed on something outside the relief scene. To the right is part of a sundial. Plotinus has been suggested as the scholar for whom the sarcophagus was made. He came to Rome in 244, remained there, and died in Minturnae in 270 A.D. This interesting hypothesis has yet to be confirmed. It is certain, however, that the sarcophagus was fashioned around the year 270 A.D.

300) Sarcophagus of Constantia. Sarcophagus in dark red Egyptian porphyry, with reliefs on four sides. From the rotunda, Santa Constanza, on the Via Nomentana, near S. Agnese fuori le Mura; in the Renaissance, it was called "Sepolcro di Bacco"
Constantia, also known as Constantina, was the eldest daughter of Constantine the Great. She died in the year 354 A.D. During the lifetime of her father, who died in 337, she was given the diadem and the title, "Augusta." Construction on her mausoleum was begun before her death. The sarcophagus stood in the nave, opposite the entrance. Its reliefs display winged figures of Eros (genii) during the vintage and the pressing of the grapes; they are surrounded by vine-branches and acanthus-like vine-shoots. The theme has an ancient appearance, and can be easily associated with Dionysian concepts. Seen from a Christian point of view, the Bacchic motif could also be a symbol of the joys of Paradise. The transubstantiation of the wine into the blood of God is part of both the Dionysian mysteries and the Christian religion.

301) Sarcophagus of St. Helena. Sarcophagus in dark red Egyptian porphyry, with reliefs on four sides. From the mausoleum of Empress Helena on the Via Casilina (Porta Pignattara). Numerous restorations
Dark red porphyry stone could only be used by the imperial family. St. Helena, mother of Constantine the Great (she died in 336 A.D.), is traditionally associated with this sarcophagus. Depicted in bas-relief are triumphant Romans on horseback and captured barbarians. This representation does not immediately call the pious imperial mother to mind; a more relevant connection would be with a field general, proud of his martial exploits. Emperor Constantine himself could well have commissioned the sarcophagus prior to his conversion.

302) Head of a peacock. One of several peacocks cast in bronze. At one time they were gilded. Presumably from Hadrian's mausoleum (Castel Sant'Angelo). In the portico (Paradise) of Old St. Peter's, they adorned the columned structure that housed the pigna fountain. Partial additions have been made: both legs and feet, and the lower section of the neck
Native to India, the peacock was known to the ancient world chiefly through

Alexander the Great's India campaign (327–324 B.C.). Because of the star-like gleam of its feathers, it was sacred to the goddess Hera (Juno). As Pausanias reported in about 150 A.D. (II 17,6), Emperor Hadrian (117–138 A.D.) dedicated a peacock made of gold and sparkling stones to Hera of Argos. As the bird of apotheosis, it appeared on the coins of consecration of empresses.

The first recording of this was for Faustina the Elder, the wife of Antoninus Pius (who died in 141 A.D.). The peacock's connection with death and the deceased became especially noticeable in the period after the 2nd century A.D. For early Christians, this bird symbolized the splendor of Paradise, and thus resurrection and eternal life.

THE ETRUSCAN MUSEUM

303) Head of Mars from Todi. Bronze. Beginning of 5th century A.D.
See note 327.

304) Funeral carriage. Cerveteri. Regolini-Galassi Tomb. Second half of the 7th century A.D.
Both the architecture and furnishing of the tombs of Cerveteri demonstrate to a pronounced degree the theme of imitating houses, common from the end of the 7th century onwards. The Regolini-Galassi Tomb consists of a room provided with "real" furnishing (even though merely for display): signs on the walls, chairs, a throne (for the woman in the end chamber) and this bed with cylindrical feet, which terminate in severed cones similar to capitals. This type of bed is found in every Etruscan necropolis. It was reserved for men, whereas women were provided with a type of coffin. The illustrious owner of this most beautiful burial-place was laid on the bed and then transported in ceremony on this carriage, the wheels of which were braked by distinctive knobs.

305) Figures from a grave in Cerveteri. Regolini-Galassi Tomb. Second half of the 7th century A.D.
Discovered in the chamber to the right of the main burial-place were 33 statuettes, representing men and women. They all wear long tunics supported by belts and their hair has been tied into pigtails, which reach down to the seam of their tunics. The workmanship is very simple, but the expression in their faces and the position of their arms are clearly important and emphasized. Although the exact meaning of the gestures made by the individual figures is unknown (the eight here are holding their hands under their chins), it is doubtless connected with their presence in the tomb as they perform a number of ritual acts for the deceased.

306) Bowl by the Brygos painter: Apollo finds the cattle stolen by Hermes. Around 490 B.C.
In the Homeric Hymn to Hermes it is recounted that the newly born God of Olympus stole Apollo's cattle and hid them in a cave. Here, Apollo finds them after a long search. Apollo wanders among the animals he has just found, while Maia, mother of Hermes, goes to the cradle where the precocious little thief has curled himself up again as if nothing had happened. In reproducing this episode, the painter has tried to cover as much of the surface of the bowl as possible and has exploited to the full the humorous potential of the story, subordinating his design only to the function of the vessel. Tucked away under the handle is the young boy, the small, partly hidden instigator of the upheaval, while other parts of the painting are devoted to dovetailing various effects such as the excited coming and going and the agitation of the lowing herd.

307) Bowl by the Jena painter with a depiction of Triptolemos. Vulci. Beginning of the 4th century B.C.
The outside of the vessel (not shown here), which is ascribed to a different painter than the one who did the inside, demonstrates all too clearly with its jaded banality the slow death that was overtaking Athenian vase painting (cf. the introductory explanation under 319). The inside, however, manages to avoid this banality by using an object which the elegant draftsman obviously borrowed from the motifs of general painting: Triptolemos, hero of the Eleusis cult, whom Demeter presented with ears of corn so that he could teach men the art of sowing, is riding on a winged carriage drawn by two snakes.

308) Gold disks with figurative ornamentation. Vulci. 4th century B.C.
These ornaments were hung on leather straps round the neck or arm as pendants and contained amulets. The three illustrated here are among the most richly decorated and best preserved. They are framed by stylized wave motifs. The middle pendant depicts Venus between Adonis and a winged Eros against a background of very fine points, while the two outer disks show Jupiter and Athene on a wagon drawn by winged horses.

309) Lid of a bronze cist. Vulci. 3rd century B.C.
A boy and girl are sitting on the backs of two swans, whose tails join to form the grip of a cist (vessel for women's toilet articles: mirror, combs, cosmetic containers, etc.). The presence of swans, which are dedicated to Venus, has prompted many specialists to interpret the two figures as Venus and Adonis; thus the group would accord perfectly with the frivolous purpose of the vessel. This lively scene demonstrates the unrestrained imagination of Etruscan craftsmen, who were always prepared to break away from customary art forms for the sake of inspiration.

310) Golden diadem. Vulci. 4th century B.C.
A broad diadem of oak leaves has been cut out of fine sheet-gold and veined by punching from behind. Both of its semi-circular ends are affixed to a ribbon adorned with small palms. The suppleness of the garland, caused by a hinge which can be opened in the middle, testifies that such diadems, which are often reproduced in Etruscan painting, metalwork and sculpture, were not only used for burials, but worn by the women during their lifetime.

311) Bronze statuette of a boy. Tarquinia. 2nd century B.C.
The inscription engraved on the left arm indicates that the statuette was a votive offering to Silvanus. The disk with an amulet hung round the neck denotes high rank or possibly only a non-slave. Portraits of boys, especially in terracotta and modelled according to Hellenistic principles, were frequently found in temples. Therefore it is unlikely that the statue represents Tages, the legendary boy with the wisdom of an old man; brought forth out of a lump of clay, he supposedly taught the Etruscans in Tarquinia the art of Haruspex (ascertaining of the divine will by examination of the entrails of sacrificial animals). Nevertheless, this boy is not playing any child's game; he is speaking and looking steadfastly at something higher than himself. His face, although not a portrait, does not belong to his body, which is that of a typical Hellenistic putto. All this leads one to suppose that this statuette combines two traditional themes: the playing child and the "wise child," Tages.

312) Large golden fibula. Cerveteri. Regolini-Galassi Tomb. Second half of the 7th century B.C.
This piece of jewelry clearly indicates the high rank of the woman buried in the end compartment of the tomb. Seen from above, as it would have appeared on wearing, it resembles a type of fibula well known during the orientalized period of Etruscan art—a disk-shaped fastener and a violin type bow. The bow is of thin sheet-gold and lacks elasticity; and the disk does

not act as a fastener because, for decorative reasons, the pin is hidden below it instead of resting on it. Moreover, the two horizontal bars on the underside, which are provided with hinges, serve to reduce the rigidity of this heavy ornament. In short, this fibula is an ostentatious adornment for a person of princely rank. On the disk are two garlands of palmettes framing five lions, which are cut from sheet-gold, embossed and welded onto the base. The edges and details on the body are marked with the finest granulation. The bow is covered with sculpted ducks and an occasional repoussé lion.

313) Urn of the Villanova type. Origin unknown (Tarquinian?). 9th–8th century B.C.
This cinerary urn is typical of Etruria's Iron Age culture known as Villanova). Note the biconical shape, the distinct dividing line between the two parts and the single horizontal handle. Sometimes these urns had a second handle which was ritually broken off. The missing lid was usually an upturned bowl, less frequently a pottery helmet, and, in exceptional cases, a helmet of hammered bronze. Even though it was modelled without a potter's wheel, the shape is very fine and artistic. The slightly curved profile of the lower section, the dilated rim, the incised decoration of large concentric squares with swastikas below and bands of repeated meanders around the neck are reminiscent of similar vessels from Tarquinia and Vulci.

314) Pottery urn with a bust on the lid. Origin: Veii? Beginning of the 6th century B.C.
Emerging from the semi-cylindrical lid is a small head on barely suggested shoulders. This urn formed a pair with another one, of which only the head remains. Both stood along the wall of a burial chamber. The liveliness of the head, which reveals little sense of plasticity, stems from the simple yet effective surface lines which model the head.

315) Bucchero vase with written characters. Cerveteri. Regolini-Galassi Tomb. Second half of the 7th century B.C.
Incised around the foot of this vase from left to right is an alphabet of 25 letters. It is of the Western Greek type and includes letters which Etruscan phonetics were unable to use—the voiced explosive consonants of b, d, g and the vowel o. A table of syllables (incomplete) forms a spiral around the wall of the vase, from the top downwards, in which the four vowels i, a, u, and e are combined in this sequence with the consonants known in Etruscan. The flask probably had something to do with the art of writing—an inkpot or a vessel for quill-pens. It is a fascinating testimony to the first moment when the language, recently introduced into the Italic world by Greek colonists of Magna Graecia and spoken by only a few privileged persons, was suddenly regarded as worthy of use for ornamentation.

316) Attic hydria with a depiction of Apollo on the Tripod. By the Berlin painter: Vulci. Around 480 B.C..
Seated on the Tripod at Delphi, Apollo flies from the northern land of the Hyperboreans back to the land of the Greeks. He is carrying a quiver over his shoulder and playing a lyre. This vase is the work of one of the most brilliant and elegant painters of the red-figure technique during the first quarter of the 5th century. Despite the awkward shape of the vessel, which was used for drawing water, the painter has nevertheless continued his design over the sharp edge of the hydria's shoulder. He has thus succeeded in separating the cheerful image of the God from the mundane lake, teeming with aquatic creatures and hardly touching the slender feet of the tripod. He has achieved this by placing them in different perspectives so that the two can never be seen completely at one glance.

317) Hydria from Caere: Heracles fighting Alcyoneus. Vulci. 540–530 B.C.
Among the large centers of southern, maritime Etruria, Cerveteri was notable for its wealth and "international" outlook during the 7th century. Moreover, an important type of vase, almost certainly of Caere origin, confirms that the town retained its position in the 6th century too. They are large hydrias which, due to the similarity of their structure, technique, ornamental motif and artistic style, can be attributed to the same artist, a genius of vase painting. He had an Ionic training and perhaps came from a Greek colony in Asia Minor, but he had a deep and productive relationship with Etrurian and particularly Caere culture. In a free, somewhat nervous style, and using an intensive yet controlled polychromy, he took pleasure in depicting mythological events, always with a lively sense of humor. Here we see Heracles, armed with a club and a bow, attacking Alcyoneus, the giant shepherd from the island of Pallene. We are unmoved by the cruelty shown in the scenes, because emphasis is placed on Hercules' imperturbable leap and on the embarrassed fear expressed by the black howling monster.

318) Attic hydria of the Mycale painter. Vulci. End of the 6th century B.C.
This hydria is attributed to one of the most outstanding artists in the field of Etrurian black-figured pottery. A comparison with the preceding vessel reveals similarities in the composition and draftsmanship, but marked differences in sensitivity. The loose drawing is pleasing, but the lively style of this master of hydria contrasts with the meaningless activity of this procession of purely ornamental female figures. Humorously, he has made their limbs look like long octopus tentacles. The painter has obeyed the demands made by a surface in need of decoration, and he has not been deterred by the risk of jeopardizing the credibility of his chosen objects. There is, for example, a conflict between the rotary movement caused by the running figures and their necessary reduction in size when they run under the handle. The hare depicted in the frieze on the shoulder of the vase is disturbingly large compared with the dog and hunter.

319) Polychromatic Attic crater: Hermes entrusts Silenus with the young Dionysus. Vulci. 440–430 B.C.
The development of the so-called minor arts, such as pottery, often led to a breaking through of the barriers of its particular idioms, and, increasingly, to an imitation of the techniques and fashions of the "major" figurative arts. This fact frequently produced creations of great subtlety, and yet the freedom of technique and expression attained also represented a destructive element. Between the two extremely elegant ornamental bands with their well-balanced, sloping palmettes, between the firm, gleaming handles and the foot—subtle vestiges of an idiom peculiar to pottery—the body of the vase disappears, heightened only by the glistening, ivory colored ground. On this ground one of the best painters of Phidias's generation has depicted Hermes handing the young Dionysus to aging Silenus with the help of the nymph Nysa. It has been suggested that, besides its affinity with general painting of the age, one can perhaps detect the influence of theatrical performances on the crater. In this context, it is interesting to note that old Silenus's custody of young Dionysus is mentioned by Sophocles in a fragment of *Dionysiskos*.

320) Back of a bronze mirror. Vulci. 475–450 B.C.
The oldest examples of Etruscan bronze mirrors date back to the end of the 6th century, and they were produced in large quantities during the 5th and 4th centuries. The mirror side was carefully polished and the back usually bore an engraved decoration whose figuration was sometimes extremely involved. Mirrors with a relief decoration, such as this one, are rare. Eos, goddess of the dawn, abducts Cephalos, the young hunter, and flies off with him. The subject, which had previously been used in Etruscan art, fits particularly well onto the surface. The artist undoubtedly had an opportunity of observing the same subject on red-figure Attic vases. He added a touch of color to the inlaid, silvery ivy garland embellishing the edge.

321) Bronze disk with a mask of the river god Achelous. Tarquinia, necropolis of Monte Quaglieri. End of 6th century B.C.
The mask of the Greek river-god Achelous, bearded and with the horns and ears of a bull, was a symbol to ward off misfortune and was frequently used in Etruscan religious art. Such disks were hung on the walls of burial chambers and perhaps even on the sides of death beds to protect the local inhabitants from a hostile presence or malevolent influences. This splendid head was intended to evoke the theme of magical fear. One must imagine the transparent glass eyes standing out against the uniformly gleaming gilded bronze surface. All the details (both the genuine fringe of hair and the fanciful pointed horns, the real mustache and the animal ears) have become abstract symbols; the sculptor's intention was not to create an organic effect but to engender fear.

322) Bronze statue. Origin unknown. Around 520 B.C.
The rectangular hole in their backs shows that the two figures, the best pre-

served of which is shown here, were probably decorative symmetrical elements in front of a piece of furniture: for example, the front supports of armchair rests. They are wearing diadems on their conical-shaped coiffures, flimsy chitons with short sleeves lifted slightly with the left hands, cloths draped over one shoulder and large pointed shoes. Not only the garments and bearing, but also the compact form and still fluid outline, shows that these small statues belong to the tradition of Greek-Ionic sculpture. In Etruria, they can best be compared with the female figures on the Caere sarcophagus of the "married couple" in the Villa Giulia museum and the Louvre.

323) Lion. Vulci. End of the 6th century B.C.
In order to protect the deceased in his grave, the concrete abode of his life after death, the Etruscans (like other Mediterranean peoples) set up pairs of lions, or sometimes sphinxes, hewn from local volcanic rock, on either side of the entrance. The shape of this lion is simplified in the extreme, but the details are dramatized, thus making it typical of Etruscan art. The characteristic feeling for plasticity found its most mature expression at the end of the 6th century B.C. in the School of Veii. The distinctive features of the lion—the muzzle with wide open jaws, wrinkled skin and enormous paws—were modelled by an artist who had never seen the deceptively sluggish manner with which a lion lies in wait; he replaced it by the nervous apprehension of a watch dog.

324) Cylindrical crater with a depiction of mythological creatures. Cerveteri. Regolini-Galassi Tomb. Second half of the 7th century B.C.
Very few examples of Etruscan painting from the period prior to the middle of the 6th century B.C. have been preserved. Consequently, this vase is particularly interesting. It is made of red clay typical for Cerveteri. Painted on it is a frieze whose technique and style resemble those of the few painted objects dating back to this period. Between two ornamental bands, whose contours were etched and then painted white, are eight figures of the oriental type. Four of these can be seen in our illustration: from the left, a winged lion looking to the left, a male sphinx, a lion, a centaur with club and wild animals.

325) Terracotta votive head. Vulci. First half of the 5th century B.C.
From the end of the 6th century B.C., and most noticeably during the 5th century B.C., Attic art began to exert a dominant influence on Etrurian artefacts. The solid terracotta was coated with a reddish, ivory colored film which emphasizes the extreme delicacy of this Ephebic head. The only archaic feature is its complete frontality. The eyes and mouth, with a faint yet radiant smile, are horizontally placed. The rounded chin, levelled cheek-bones, and the thick frame of hair divided into small locks remind one immediately of Attic art during the years between the battles of Marathon and Salamis (490/480 B.C.).

326) Head of a young woman. Origin unknown. End of 4th to beginning of 5th century B.C.
The slightly asymmetrical features and the turned head in relation to the chest allow us to reconstruct a figure just over 3 feet in height, bent forward slightly, walking from left to right and with the head facing in the opposite direction. Is it Aphrodite? Or perhaps Artemis? At any rate, we can well imagine that this charming figure was part of a frieze on a pediment of medium size (the rest was certainly half-relief). The shape of the face, the hair-style and, most of all, the tranquil thoughtful expression, devoid of exaggerated pathos, remind one of the portraits of deities in 4th century Greek art. The lively and distinctive treatment of the hair and subtle modelling of the beautiful face render this figure one of the most superb examples of Etruscan pottery sculpture during the late 4th or early 5th century B.C.

327) "The Mars from Todi." Bronze. Beginning of 5th century B.C.
The craving for valuable metals during the late antiquity resulted in the destruction of most antique bronze statues; this was saved only because it was hidden, presumably during a ritual burial. It portrays a warrior, with his raised left hand resting on an iron spear, protected by a helmet (lost) and a cuirass. He is carrying a cup (recently discovered) containing a drink-offering in his right hand. There is an Umbrian inscription on the strap

hanging from the middle of the cuirass: "*Ahal Trutitis dunum dede*" (Ahal Trutitis made the offering). The work was cast in seven separate sections with the help of various types of cire perdue process (head, arms, legs and the torso in two parts). But the artist failed to fuse the sections into one stylistic entity. In fact, one is left with the impression that the head and limbs were joined, somewhat unconvincingly, to an empty cuirass, under which no signs of a body are evident. The Attic model, which the Etrurian craftsman in an Etruscan center near Umbrian Todi probably copied with mechanical faithfulness but with limited success, can be dated safely to around 450–425 B.C. We can certainly trace the bearing, the type of face, the stylized locks of hair, etc., back to the Attic model, but the only unity our artist strove to attain was that of investing the splendid offering, which was probably meant for a shrine dedicated to Mars, with its religious function. The lively eyes of white stone, the painstaking reproduction of all the details on the cuirass's leather and metal, and the presistent accuracy of the anatomy all reveal the fear that the work, even in its smallest details, might fail to satisfy its main purpose as an "image."

328) Winged horse made of clay. Cerveteri. First half of the 5th century B.C.
This Pegasus, which embellished the corner of a temple, has the same artistic background as the votive head (325). When facing the building, the animal would have stood out against the sky in the lower left corner of the pediment, with its front legs projecting freely. Etruscan temples often had roofs adorned with winged figures. The large weathered beam on the right of the figure was decorated with a row of frontal tiles, on which the motifs visible behind the horse's wing continued: a simple string-course with meanders between a molded cornice, bearing a wave-like decoration and with a thick protrusion painted with a shell pattern.

329) Limestone sarcophagus with a relief of the funeral procession and the prostrate figure of the deceased. Cerveteri, necropolis of Banditaccia. Beginning of the 4th century B.C.
The deceased is reclining on the lid, whose ends are shaped like gable roofs. In his right hand he is holding a drink-offering cup and in his left a garland, which he is wearing round his neck. His neck and left arm are adorned with *bullae* (golden pendants with amulets), while his head bears an olive crown. The funeral procession with music and dancing is depicted on the two visible sides (the sarcophagus stood in the left hand corner close to the entrance of the burial chamber). It is a work of most exacting craftsmanship; the features of the face and the position of some of the figures demonstrate the indiscriminate use of elements of Attic art, widespread throughout the entire second half of the 5th century B.C.

330) Two drinking vessels. Vulci.
Particularly common during the first half of the 5th century B.C. was a type of vessel shaped like a human or animal's head and composed of two halves shaped in molds. The example on the left, with two female faces, can be dated back to around the beginning of the century; while that on the right, with the head of Heracles back to back with a Negro, was produced during the second quarter. These shapes were particularly popular in Etruria during the following centuries. It is believed they may have been inspired by bronze sculptures of the period.

331) Votive heads made of terracotta. Cerveteri. 3rd–2nd century B.C
Most of the offerings brought to temples by the faithful consisted of terracotta heads. The lack of vitality in the shapes reflects often centuries-old ideal types, introduced into Etruria from Attica between the end of the 5th and the 4th century B.C. In view of the aesthetic meaninglessness of the end product, more or less pronounced elements of portraiture were haphazardly added to the mechanically produced casts. Examples are the two on the right, with beards indicated by small holes punctured on the cheek and chin of a still undefined Polyclitus-like mask; and, as required, blond or dark hair was added to the feminine face, which still reminds one of a watered-down Skopas original.

332) Attic dish with a depiction of Heracles. Vulci. Around 500 B.C.
This dish, with only the medallion on the inside painted, is the work of

the painter Oltos, who worked for many potters during the last 25 years of the 6th century. He was one of the first to use the red-figure technique and to paint details on the figures instead of only incising them. The art of vase painting thus began to reflect the contemporary problems and techniques of general painting. It is already apparent from this dish that Oltos preferred to paint crowded and lively narrative scenes: the Heracles depicted here was obviously removed from a far more complex scene and, gesticulating, has been enclosed in the small tondo-style composition like a shrivelled giant in a bottle.

333) Laconian dish with a depiction of Sisyphus and Tityus. Cerveteri. Around 550 B.C.
A local pottery school in Sparta flourished during the middle of the 6th century and was represented primarily by dishes of this kind. The man on the left is carrying a heavy block on his shoulders, while a snake rises up behind him. Another man on the right has his hands and feet tied to a Doric column, while a bird of prey is pecking at his chest from which blood is flowing. If one attributes the usual interpretation to the snake, this scene takes place in Hades, and the two men are Sisyphus and Tityus.

334) Portrait head of a man. Cerveteri. 1st century B.C.
The statue to which this head probably belonged was looking slightly to the left, with the eyes staring upwards into the distance. This proud posture leads one to suppose that it represented a man of some importance. A great deal has been written about the famous Etruscan-Italic portraits (the Capitoline Brutus, the L'Arringatore in Florence's Archaeological Museum, etc.), to which this belongs. The successful attempt to create individual features has enveloped the entire head, and the stylized details which Greek art continued to supply the minor arts have been discarded.

335) Black-figure Attic amphora by Exekias: Achilles and Ajax at play. Vulci. Around 520 B.C.
The man who perfected the technique of painting black figures on the natural ground of vases was undoubtedly Exekias, whose signature appears on this vase as the potter and painter. The subject, Achilles and Ajax at play, was by no means an innovation in Attic pottery, but precisely for this reason, we are able to assess the vitality which inspired Exekias here. The rhythmic composition generates an atmosphere of complete serenity, as if time had stood still. Even the smallest detail deserves and receives the same loving attention, while the purity of the empty background gains in value and depth by way of contrast. The crystal clear area of the room and the serenity enveloping the figures are the brilliant reply of a convinced advocate of the two-dimensional technique to the growing number of experimenters in the revolutionary red-figure technique.

336) Attic oinochoe by Amasias. Vulci. 530–520 B.C.
The workshop of Amasias, to whom this jug is unanimously attributed, pro-

duced very few objects during the last third of the 6th century. Amasias's works are counted among the most beautiful examples of Attic vases. Below the handle and around the thick smooth neck, the clay is swollen like blown glass, forming a roomy and very light vase body. Well-balanced zones of thick gleaming black paint make the figurative bands, which stretch as far as the eye can see, appear reflected rather than painted on the body of the vase. It is a domestic scene; a young boy, who has perhaps won a prize in a music contest, is being congratulated by his parents and brother. The manner in which the figures stand out against the warm orange-colored ground, the rich colors applied in wholly overlapping and superimposed zones, and the original treatment of the garments, all these reveal the painter's penetrating mind and his consciousness of the same problem which the highly gifted Exekias solved on a more profound level: volume and space for the figures (cf. 335). The black-figure technique was unable to evolve beyond the boundaries fixed by the efforts of this artist.

337) Proto-Corinthian wine jugs. Origin unknown. 650–640 B.C.
Both jugs belong to the period when Corinthian pottery, which had reached its highest degree of artistic and technical perfection and had captured the Etruscan market. The olpe on the left, with its purely ornamental decoration, exhibits a keen sense for very delicate engraving and highly artistic polychromy. On the right-hand oinochoe we find the typical oriental animal frieze, whose figures are arranged harmoniously on the light-colored clay. Noticeable on both jugs are the characteristic dotted rosettes.

338) Large late-Corinthian crater: Menelaus and Odysseus Enquire in Troy about Helen's Return. From the Astarita collection. Origin unknown. 575–550 B.C.
The last flowering of Corinthian pottery at a time when Attic art was beginning to prevail is characterized by large vases on which animal friezes are subordinated to large figurative scenes; these illustrate mythological themes which are generally explained with written names. One can regard these portrayals as a faithful reflection of the various genres of Corinthian painting. This crater, whose designer is unknown to us, depicts Menelaus and Odysseus in Troy asking about Helen's home-coming.

339) Crater by Asteas: Zeus and Hermes at Alkmene's Window. 350–325 B.C.
At about the beginning of the 4th century, a kind of theatrical farce, a phlyax comedy, was flourishing in southern Italy *(Magna Graecia)*. The male characters always wore a mask which faked a grotesque, accentuated nakedness, perhaps derived from an antique plant demon. A considerable number of vases produced in Magna Graecia illustrate these popular comedies, which parodied every aspect of daily life and of myths. On this particularly famous crater, attributed to Asteas, one of the principle potters working in Paestum, Zeus himself is held up to ridicule. Here he is represented as an old man with a hunchback, a bald head and a long white beard. With the connivance of Hermes, he is in the process of placing a ladder against a window at which we can see Alkmene, Amphitryon's wife, whom Zeus desires.

THE VATICAN PICTURE, GALLERY

340) "Death of the Virgin Mary." Greek icon
The colors and composition of this picture tend toward stasis rather than drama. It is derivative of a Byzantine movement which flourished in particular in Crete. This painting can be dated back to the 16th century.

341) "Christ enthroned between the Virgin Mary and St. John the Baptist." Russian icon
The richness of the composition is enhanced by the addition of silver and enamel. The wealth of ornamentation and the refined elegance of execution have caused experts to ascribe this work to the "School of Moscow" at around 1620. But the style of the picture is still Byzantine combined with Slavic elements, as can be seen from the inscriptions.

342) "A Holy Bishop."
Serbian icon
The name of this saint, which is written at the bottom of the picture in barely discernible red letters, is today illegible. The painting belongs to the Byzantine school, but has certain characteristics appertaining to 14th century Serbian art. Evident in the severe modelling and the tendency toward compactness and bulk, which accord with the general concepts of Byzantine art, is a propensity to unite elements of different cultures.

343) "The Last Judgment." Greek icon
Together with two other panels, this formed part of a triptych attributed

to a late period of Byzantine art. (The left-hand panel depicts "Paradise" and the right-hand one "Christ in Purgatory" and "Scenes of Hell"). This icon stems from an artistic movement which developed on Greek soil about the 18th century. One can detect different and sometimes opposing influences in this overcrowded composition of figures. The unknown artist seems to have obtained his inspiration from a wide variety of sources. The result is somewhat confusing, but the work is interesting because it testifies to the survival of old forms in Byzantine art of a later period.

344) "The Last Judgment." Painted on wood. Round wooden panel with a kind of predella

This painting was commissioned by two Benedictine nuns, Domna Benedicta Dei and Constantia Abatissa, and bears the signatures of Nicolaus et Johannes pictores. The picture remained in the Benedictine cloister of St. Maria in Campo Marzio until at least the end of the 17th century. Some art historians have dated it to the 12th or 13th century, but it belongs to the Benedictine school at the end of the 11th century or—the latest theory is that it was painted between 1061 and 1071. Two factors lend weight to this assumption: the name of both artists and the stylistic features were associated with the Benedictine church in Castel St. Elia near Nepi; and the punctuation and abbreviations of the inscription can be linked with the Benedictine school. This painting is in fact the most important evidence of an extremely active group of stylistic innovators whose influence would be felt for at least two more centuries.

345) "Christ." School of Rome. Canvas on wood

This painting, which can be dated back to about the end of the 12th century, has been compared by scholars with The Saviour of Tivoli, a masterpiece of Roman art of that period. Even though the two works are of different artistic quality, one can recognize in both how the Byzantine style of depicting Christ was being gradually transformed under the new influence of typically Roman elements.

346) "St. Francis of Assisi." Painting by Margaritone d'Arezzo. Wooden panel

This signed work is of special interest, mainly due to the iconography of the saint, to whom Margaritone devoted other works which are today in the Pinacoteca of Arezzo, the Museo Civico of Montepulciano, the church of S. Francesco a Castiglione Fiorentino and the church of S. Francesco a Ripa in Rome. The saint is here shown without a halo. The inspiration behind the stylized treatment of the figure and the obvious mannerism of the drawing and light effect are clearly Byzantine, but the influences of Florence and Lucca are also evident.

347) "Crucifixion." A Tuscan master. Wooden panel

This picture of Christ on the cross, painted on a cross-shaped panel, is representative of a genre of 13th century art which continued into the next century. It consists of two iconographical types. One is of Christus triumphans, depicted alive on the cross and triumphant in his divine majesty, which was preferred by the various western trends in Roman art. The other is of Christus patiens, which glorifies the sufferings of God incarnate and inspired the Byzantine artists. This work, which can be dated to the first half of the 14th century, exhibits iconographic features peculiar to the Byzantine style in the elongated figures and pronounced outlines, although there are signs of an attempt to give the figures body. The painting is attributed to an anonymous Tuscan master, although some specialists believe that it is a product of the Pisa school, while others suspect that it is a work of the "Maestro di S. Francesco."

348) "St. James." Painting by Antonio Veneziano. Wooden panel

The artist's earlier Venetian training is evident in his exquisite use of color. Other influences are also apparent: Gothic—perhaps due to Orcagna—and Sienese. In his highly personal style, light is used to accentuate both the heavy shadows and the colors.

349) "Madonna." Painting by Vitale da Bologna. Wooden panel

Vitale degli Equi, known as Vitale da Bologna, was one of the leading representatives of Bolognese painting in the 14th century. His somewhat complex training began with his experience in local miniature painting and it was supplemented by contact with various Tuscan genres of painting, especially the Sienese and associated French influences. This panel, which bears his signature, has an obvious affinity with the Sienese school, particularly as regards the colors, which have lost their Bolognese vitality and become more controlled, and in the smooth linear movement and unusually soft chiaroscuro with which the face is modelled. The result is a work of great delicacy and charm.

350) "Madonna del Latte." Painting by Francescuccio Ghissi. Detail from a lancet-shaped panel

This artist from Fabriano, a pupil of his fellow countryman Allegretto Nuzi, often repeated the subject of this panel, dated 1374. Yet the other versions never achieved the astonishing charm of the figure of the Virgin Mary, here swathed in costly material and contained by a line both strong and supple.

351) "The Crucifixion of St. Peter." Painting of the Giotto School. Detail of the Stefaneschi triptych. Wooden panel

This picture comes from the Confessio Altar of the old basilica of St. Peter's and is painted on both sides. The front depicts Christ Enthroned in the middle, with The Crucifixion of St. Peter and The Beheading of St. Paul on either side. Painted on the back of the center section is Peter Enthroned, and the reverse of the two side panels depicts The Apostles St. James and St. Paul and St. Mark and St. John the Evangelists. Giotto was probably commissioned with the altar in the year 1300 during his stay in Rome. It is assumed that the work was completed between 1320 and 1330. Generally speaking, art historians think the altar was not painted by Giotto alone. However, there are also those who admit the large role played by the Giotto school and especially the "Maestro delle vele" (Salmi)—recognizable in the Sienese elongation of the figures and the colors—but who insist that Giotto directly intervened in the painting of The Crucifixion of St. Peter. They attributed to him those areas where the shapes are less distinct and the chiaroscuro merges with the colors somewhat.

352) Annunciation. Giovanni di Paolo. Panel

This small panel, bearing the date 1444, was the cover of a book in Siena's Ufficio di Biccherna (public treasury). The series of so-called biccherna covers is a valuable documentation of the development of 14th century Sienese painting. The oldest displays the figure of the "camerlingo" (treasurer) in office or his coat of arms. Later, the subjects become more varied, deriving from the iconography of the saints, from allegory or from local history. The painter of this Annunciation has provided an excellent example of an extroverted and highly personal artistic idiom which incorporates different and often contradictory influences. The rather harsh colors contained by sharp lines, the elongated figures and the folds with an almost metallic gleam create refined and imaginative images.

353) Masolino: "Crucifixion." Panel

Together with the predella, illustrating The Death of the Virgin Mary, in the Pinacoteca Vaticana, this forms part of the Polittico della Néve (Polyptych of Snow), commissioned for the basilica of S. Maria Maggiore in Rome in 1425 and painted on front and back. Today, the altar is no longer intact. Two of the center panels, The Miracle of Snow and The Assumption of the Blessed Virgin Mary, are in Naples' Museo di Capodimonte, and two side panels with St. John and St. Martin and St. Peter and St. Paul are in the Johnson Collection in Philadelphia. Two further panels, with St. Liberius and St. Matthew and St. Hieronymus and St. John the Baptist, which are recognized as the work of Masaccio, are in the National Gallery in London. The remaining sections of the altarpiece have been lost. The influence of Masolino's young assistant, Masaccio, is clear from the painter's tendency to adopt a monumental style, which finds expression in large, simple shapes reminiscent of the "Collegiati di Empoli," even though the general arrangement still retains a Gothic sense of form.

354) Lorenzo Monaco: "The Nativity." Panel

This small panel is part of a predella, of which a similar section is preserved in Copenhagen's Fine Arts Museum. This artist, who was probably born in Siena, went to Florence at a very early age. He succeeded in synthesizing the impressive compactness of form characteristic of the followers of Giotto with the Sienese fluidity of line and subtle choice of colors. On this section of the predella we find both perspective and a suggestion of bodily substance uniting to impart a feeling of lyrical tranquillity.

355) Gentile da Fabriano: "Miracle of St. Nicolaus"
This is one of the lateral scenes on the predella of an altarpiece which Gentile painted for the Quaratesi family. It was completed in 1425 and was meant for the church of S. Niccolò Oltrarno in Florence. It was taken apart during the last century, the most important panels being in the National Gallery of London and the Galleria degli Uffizi in Florence. Four scenes from the predella are in the Pinacoteca Vaticana and a fifth is preserved in Washington's National Gallery. Visible on the larger panels are the effects of new discoveries in Florentine art, especially those of Masolino. On the predella, however, whose high artistic merit has been underscored repeatedly by experts since the days of Vasari, one can again detect elements from Gentile's early training with Lombardic miniaturists. This is revealed in this scene by the use of pointillism, the stylized elegance of the figures and the glowing, refined colors.

356) Sassetta: "Vision of St. Thomas Aquinas." Panel
This is part of a predella of an altarpiece, painted between 1423 and 1426 for the Arte della Lana (Guild of Wool Merchants). It has been possible to trace only very few of the panels. We know from historic documents, however, that the central panel depicted The Eucharist and the two side panels bore portraits of Abbot St. Antonius and St. Thomas Aquinas, whereby the illustrations on the sections of the predella are related to the theme of the large panels. Here we have one of the two sections of the altar's socle related to St. Thomas. The painter demonstrates his affinity to the Florentine style of international Gothic, whose main protagonists were Masolino and Giovanni da Milano. Typical of this period is the architectural framework in which St. Thomas is shown praying in front of a crucifix, while a voice says the words "Bene scripsisti de me, Thomas." It is a successful study making assiduous use of the new laws of perspective originated by Masolino. But, as with Masolino, the outstanding feature is the departure from the new naturalistic approach. The artist attempts to create an ideal setting for the mystical encounter between St. Thomas and Christ by means of a series of empty, tranquil rooms.

357) Melozzo da Forlì: "Angel with a Lute." Fresco. Melozzo da Forlì: "Apostle." Fresco
These are two of fourteen fragments depicting angels and apostles. They were saved for posterity by Padre Sebastian Resta in 1702, when the Roman Church of the Holy Apostle was in danger of collapsing and had to be demolished. In the apse of this church Melozzo painted The Ascension, the middle section of which, "Christ enthroned," is preserved in the Quirinal. Melozzo fell back on the experiments of Mantegna in the field of perspective, and succeeded in creating a bold composition in which the viewer sees from below Christ ascending into Heaven, with the eyes of the apostle following his movements. Hovering above are angels, with which the painter replaced the purely static forms of his teacher Piero della Francesca, by a joyous liveliness. Unfortunately, today we can imagine what suggestive power this painting may have had.

358) Filippo Lippi: "Coronation of the Virgin Mary." Panel
Carlo Marsuppini von Arezzo, Secretary of the Republic of Florence, commissioned this painting for the chapel of S. Bernardo in Arezzo. The sponsor can be seen kneeling in the right-hand corner. This work is evidence of this painter's significance. Even though he seldom achieved any real depth of feeling, he was searching persistently for essentially human touches which found expression in the charming liveliness of his pictures and in a pleasing color combination, e.g., the various shades of blue in this picture.

359) Melozzo da Forlì: Pope Sixtus IV Installs Bartolomeo Platina as Director of the Vatican Library. Fresco transposed on canvas
Deep psychological insight enabled the artist to depict the two main characters in such a way that their different personalities are evident. Equally accomplished are the portraits of the Pope's two nephews, Giovanni and Giuliano della Rovere (later Pope Julius II), and of Girolamo and Raffaello Riario. Piero della Francesca's influence is revealed in the crystal light and in the

formal groupings of the various persons, although the figures are less rigid and lacking in expression than those of Piero. As regards perspective, the interest lies in a problem already familiar to Mantegna, namely, that of looking upwards from below. The intensity and depth of color, rare in frescoes, can be traced to the methods employed by Flemish painters working in Italy at that time.

361) Francesco del Cossa: "Miracle of St. Vincent Ferrer." Detail
The panel constituted the predella of an altarpiece known as the Grifoni Triptych, which was painted between 1470 and 1475 for a chapel of the same name in San Petronio in Bologna. The center panel of this altarpiece is today in London's National Gallery, while the side panels are in the Milan Brera. It is obvious that this painter belonged to the Ferrara school, for this work contains all the characteristics of this school: an eccentric imagination which placed architectural and natural features side by side in the landscape, glowing colors which glitter like enamel or precious stones, and a linear rhythm which alternates between severe restlessness and idyllic calm. The figures are modelled almost like sculpture, with clear outlines and a convulsive energy that is evident both in their gestures and in their metal-hard clothing. A bright light, reminiscent of the work of Piero della Francesca, floods the scene and makes it appear even more other-worldly.

362) Carlo Crivelli: "Pietà." Panel in the shape of a lunette
This lunette is signed "Opus Caroli Cribelli Veneti" and can be dated to the year 1490. It must have formed part of a lost altarpiece. The picture's value is contested; it seems to have been painted at a time when the artist was under the influence of the Umbrian school, and especially of Niccolò Alunno. Most art historians count it among the artist's less important works, perhaps even painted during a period of decline (L. Venturi). The scene, certain features of which recall north European painting, lacks any real pathos. Admittedly it engenders admiration due to its masterly technique (with the all-pervasive gleam of gold, metal and colored marble, the panel looks like an enamel work from the glassworks of Murano), but it fails to convince or move us.

363) Lucas Cranach: "Man of Sorrows"
In this painting, not considered one of the artist's most important works, hardness and roughness are not mitigated by the elegant stylized outlines or the expressiveness of some of his other paintings. Nevertheless, he demonstrates his considerable skill with colors. Also visible is the influence of Altdorfer and Dürer, who were responsible for an essential part of his artistic education.

364) Giovanni Bellini: "Pietà." Panel
This panel belongs to an altarpiece with the "Coronation of the Virgin," which was originally in the church of San Francesco in Pesaro and is today in this town's Museo Civico. It was painted in 1478 and marks the turning point in this painter's career. Due to his personal sensitivity and awareness of the possibilities of color, his acquaintance with the works of Piero della Francesca opened his eyes to a new interpretation of light and color through the creation of perspective variations. The modelling of figures in this Pietà is strong and precise, and the arrangement of folds has a sculptured hardness reminiscent of Mantegna. The warm, full blooded colors blend smoothly into a chromatic harmony which is already tonal. The composition along the diagonal axes also accords with the new idea of distances which extend beyond the framework of the painting.

365) Pinturicchio: "Coronation of the Virgin." Painted on wood and transposed onto canvas
This altarpiece was commissioned for the High Altar of the church of S. Maria della Pietà in Castel della Fratta (today Umbertide). Even though there are three documents testifying that payments were made to Pinturicchio and his assistant, G. B. Caporali between June 27, 1503, and October 30, 1505, Carli asserts that this painting can be attributed to Caporali alone, whereas Pinturicchio's contribution was restricted to a somewhat meager sketch. He maintains: "Nowhere in the painting is it possible to detect or even infer the direct intervention of the maestro." This theory is refuted by more modern historians, who almost unanimously allege that the painting

bears certain characteristics peculiar to Pinturicchio. Others, perhaps erroneously, go so far as to ascribe some of the figures to young Raphael.

366) Pietro Perugino: "St. Benedict." Panel
Together with another panel representing St. Flavia, this formed part of the socle of *The Ascension of our Lord,* which is now in the Louvre and was painted by Perugino around 1495. Despite a tendency toward sentimentality in the face, there are indications that this was completed at a high point in the career of this great artist. Most remarkable are the color harmony and the painterly treatment of form.

367) Lo Spagna: "Adoration of the Child Jesus." Panel
This scene of the Epiphany is also known as the *"Madonna della Spineta,"* for it originally came from the monastery of the "Riformati della Spineta" near Todi. The painting was completed around 1507 and is remarkable for the prevailing sense of dignity and for the atmosphere of spellbound tranquillity essentially due to the spacious arrangement of figures. Lo Spagna, a pupil of Perugino, reveals the influence of his teacher, even though certain elements of Perugino's artistic idiom have been changed. This is particularly visible in the sumptuousness of the garments and in the emphasis on the changing interplay of light. Even though the result as a whole is pleasing, this artist's style is lacking in strength and depth of feeling.

368) Raphael: "Madonna of Foligno." Painted on a wooden panel and transposed on canvas
This painting, which was completed around 1511–1512 as an altarpiece for the Aracoeli church in Rome, was commissioned by Sigismondo de' Conti, monsignor of Pope Julius II. De' Conti, who can be seen on the right of the picture, meant the painting to be a votive picture for a grace received from God. His house in Foligno, which was struck by lightning, miraculously suffered no damage. The event is illustrated here by means of light rays against the back-cloth of a beautiful landscape. Some scholars have detected the influence of the Venice and Ferrara schools in the painting. Others put forward the theory that Raphael was assisted by the Ferrarese painter, Dosso Dossi. The problem has still to be solved, for during its restoration several layers of varnish were removed, which were added in Paris when the painting was transferred from wood to canvas. This produced some surprising changes. The warm, almost amber-colored tones were replaced by cold silver ones, resulting in an alteration to the picture's color relationships. A completely new critical evaluation of the painting is now necessary.

369) Raphael: "Transfiguration of Christ." Section
This painting, which was commissioned by Cardinal Giulio de' Medici for the cathedral in Narbonne, was Raphael's last work, unfinished at his death. Vasari reported that he was painting Christ's countenance, and, "just as he was putting the finishing touches to it, death overtook him and the brush fell from his hand." The painting was hung over Raphael's deathbed and later presented to the church of S. Pietro in Montorio by the donor. This work differs greatly from the previous one. The painter's style embraces forms of even more spacious concept and sublime inspiration, and he abandons previously achieved color harmonies, approaching the Venetian type of coloration. The figure of Christ is remarkable for the spirituality of the face, and the landscape and sky are noteworthy for colors of an intensity reminiscent of Titian. The lower section of the painting was sketched by Raphael and executed by his pupils, Giulio Romano and Gianfrancesco Penni. Typically, these two artists contrived to exaggerate their master's style in a theatrical, academic and manneristic fashion.

370) Titian: "Madonna of San Niccolò dei Frari. Painted on wood and transposed onto canvas
This altarpiece was painted for the church of S. Niccolò dei Frari in Venice, whence it was transferred to Rome in 1770 (Vasari). The upper section was originally curved, but it was cut straight to match Raphael's *Transfiguration.* Apart from this mutilation, the painting was in such a bad condition that it had to be transposed recently from wood to canvas. During this process, it was possible to observe and photograph the composition of the undercoat below the painted surface. It was executed in three shades and was probably

the first draft of the painting. The restoration work also confirmed that the picture was painted when Titian had already left behind him the world of Giorgione and was aiming for a greater monumentality of vision, although he still continued to model his figures with color. Indeed, he retained this mode of expression even when he adapted his style to that of Raphael's and, more important, to that of Michelangelo's, despite the fact that his palette still had subdued tones, dominated by a dull gold. Various scholars have dated this work between 1523 and 1542.

371) Paolo Veronese: "Allegorical Scene." Ocatagonal canvas
This painting on canvas, typical of the Venetian style, formed part of a ceiling and originally belonged to the Sacchetti family. Two other panels from this ceiling are in the Galleria Capitolina in Rome. Also in the possession of the Sacchetti family was Veronese's *St. Helen.* In this picture Veronese achieved a chromatic tonality derived from the overriding importance he attached to light and which is characteristic of his more mature works. It had momentous repercussions on the future of Venetian painting, especially of the 18th century. In technical terms, he achieved this brilliant effect by placing pure colors side by side in such a way as to create light vibrations, thus unwittingly observing the law of complementary colors.

372) Sebastiano del Piombo: "St. Bernard." Panel
This is a work of suggestive force and almost monochromatic tonality. In an ash-colored robe, the saint is standing unsteadily over the Evil One. Bernard's face is turned timidly toward the cloister, which almost disappears into the grey depths of the sky. The painting reveals features and characteristics peculiar both to Venetian painting and the works of Michelangelo. It has a very carefully constructed composition, which has induced some scholars to maintain that it could be ascribed to one of Sebastiano del Piombo's successors, a painter by the name of Marcello Venusti. However, this artist never achieved such a high degree of expression in any other works.

373) Leonardo da Vinci: "St. Jerome." Panel
The picture is a monochromatic, unfinished sketch, probably belonging to the period after the painter had left the court of Ludovico il Moro in Milan. It is precisely this incompleteness which makes the work so impressive, for it is an outstanding technical accomplishment. The largely olive-brown color of the background underscores the strict and bitter spirituality of the hermit saint, with his ascetic and tormented face. His ghost-like presence is brought into relief by the light from a dark rocky outcrop in the center of the picture. The painstaking attention to physical shapes in the other imaginary fragments of rock which emerge from the greenish distance and the analytical composition of the naked saint reveal the "desire to fathom the secrets of nature," which was so typical of Leonardo. Despite its restoration, one can still see the traces left by vandals who removed the head.

374) Raphael: "Miracle of the Fishes." Tapestry
This is one of the most valuable tapestries of the "Scuola Vecchia," woven in the Brussels workshop of Pieter van Aelst. In this more than any other we can detect the hand of Raphael. This argument is based primarily on the cartoon. The setting, inspired by the Gospel according to St. Luke (Ch. 5, verses 1–10), is the Sea of Galilee, whose clear waters mirror a tranquil landscape. After a drawing by Giovanni da Udine, the lower edge depicts a simulated bas-relief of Cardinal Giovanni de' Medici's procession to Rome for the conclave, from which he emerged as Pope. He appears again in the right-hand scene wearing papal vestments, and his coat of arms is woven into the edges of this tapestry and of the others in this series, designed by Perin del Vaga.

375) Scarsellino: "Mary with Elizabeth." Canvas
Scarsellino was educated in Ferrara, which already tended toward the Venetian style of painting. He then spent four years in Venice and deepened his knowledge of the Venetian painters, especially of Veronese. It is clear from this painting how much importance the artist attached to color harmonies, for color has even been added to the shadows in this beautiful landscape. Scarsellino must have executed this painting at a time when he was closely following the Venetian genre.

376) Peter de Wit: "The Holy Family with Ann and John." Panel
This artist, who was also known under the name of Pietro d'Elia Candido, was probably born in Bruges. In 1570, he and his father moved to Florence, where he remained in the service of the Grand Duke until 1586 and was strongly influenced by Tuscan and Venetian artists. In his works, and especially in this *Holy Family,* one can detect faint traces of Michelangelo's style in the solid, sculptural characteristics of the figures and in the composition. On the other hand, there is no sign here of the tendency toward mannerism apparent in his other works.

377) Domenichino: "Communion of St. Jerome." Canvas
The artist shows his best characteristics in this work, painted for the Roman church of S. Maria in Aracoeli. Even though he was directly inspired by one of Agostino Carracci's paintings in the Pinacotèca of Bologna, he developed the idea in a completely different manner. Venetian influences are evident in the importance he attached to the fluffy, almost Tintoretto-like colors which coat the molded shadows, and in the beautiful landscape visible in the background. Yet despite these reminders of his early training, the simplicity and grandeur of his personal style, based on a synthesis of all the genuine elements of antiquity, has produced some remarkable original effects. Also noteworthy is his interest in the psychological interaction among the different characters.

378) Pietro da Cortona: "The Madonna Appears to St. Francis." Canvas
This painting, copies of which are in the Hermitage and in Arezzo, belongs to the artist's period of maturity. Although all the elements match each other perfectly, we can still trace the results of a complex artistic culture, in which the concepts of Rubens, Caravaggio, Bernini and the Venetian painters have been grafted onto an original Tuscan stem. The balanced composition, the harmony of colors and the elegance of the figures render this picture one of the best works of this painter from Cortona.

379) N. Poussin: "Gideon's Victory over the Midianites."
Poussin's early training in France was enriched by his contact with Florentine and Roman art circles, when the painter visited Italy in 1642. He settled in Rome where he remained until shortly before his death. Even though he was mainly influenced by Raphael, he was not completely indifferent to impulses from the Venetians, Titian, Veronese and the Carracci brothers, and he showed interest occasionally in Caravaggio's style. This painting can be dated to the period when he was influenced by Caravaggio; this is revealed in the glimmers of light which illuminate and accentuate the forms. This canvas, which was recognized only recently as a work of Poussin, forms part of a series called *Biblical Victories,* whose two other pictures are now in the Hermitage.

380) A. van Dyck: "St. Francis Xavier." Canvas
This picture was painted between 1622 and 1623 for the Rome church of Al Gesù during van Dyck's stay in the city, and was added to the Vatican Collection in 1938. It was identified as a work of van Dyck by De Campos, who was later able to substantiate this with documentary evidence. It is a painting of his youth in which the influence of Rubens is still visible in the charming little angels. The sensitive and "spiritual" hands of the saint are characteristic of van Dyck.

381) Guido Reni: "Madonna with St. Thomas and St. Jerome." Canvas
Here we have one of the artist's most highly acclaimed works. Malvasia called it a "wonderful painting." It was painted between 1625 and 1630 and thus belongs to Reni's mature period. He had abandoned any influence from Caravaggio, which is discernible in the "Crucifixion of St. Peter" (Inv. 387), and used charm and harmony to acquire a classical yardstick reminiscent of Raphael, combined with a color scheme defined in cool, silver tones. The result is an elegant and unusual style, a perfect expression of "his ideal of an abstract and elevated art."

382) Federico Barocci: "Head of the Virgin Mary." Paper
This is a study for *The Annunciation,* painted in oils on paper. In a study of this type one can see the typical suggestive poetry and refined elegance of Barocci's style, especially the wealth of colors with their pastel effect. This represents a characteristic feature of his painting and it anticipated the style

of the 18th century. His paintings were executed in a very personal technique, but they still manage to create an impression of spontaneity. Perhaps this may be attributed to the artist's innate sense of proportion, preventing him from lapsing into mawkishness, combined with an incessant striving after charm and a perceptive subtlety in the choice of colors.

383) Guercino: "Doubting Thomas." Canvas
This picture stems from the painter's best period, which ended with *The Martyrdom of St. Petronilla* in 1623 (now in the Pinacoteca Capitolina). Besides elements from his early artistic training, which began among Ferrarese painters and was perfected by a visit to Venice, one can discern traces of Caravaggio's art, which Guercino adapted in a very personal manner. The fluid light contains amber-colored reflections, and the depths of the shadows are filled with soft, glowing colors. Even though the result is lacking in drama, the work possesses descriptive and narrative qualities of a high degree.

384) Caravaggio: "Descent from the Cross." Canvas
This picture, which was painted between 1603 and 1604 for the chapel of the Pietro Vittrice family in S. Maria in Vallicella or the Chiesa Nuova in Rome, belongs to Caravaggio's second or "black style." From his youth onwards the painter had used light as a means of emphasizing and distinguishing forms, and colors to underscore the molding of forms. In this particular period, his efforts were concentrated on achieving brilliant effects in a vision devoid of all superfluous and unnecessary elements. Aesthetically speaking, this signalled the artist's spiritual return to nature, to the world round about him, and very often to the world of the people. In this picture he has abandoned the clear, luminous idiom of his youthful works; the drama of the descent from the cross is depicted violently by the light tearing the scene's shadows apart. At the same time, the solid modelling of the figures in the composition creates an impression of depth, whereby the perspective study in the form of the tomb's marble slab is balanced by the diagonal created by Christ's body. Moreover, the almost Baroque striving for effect in the emphatic gesture of Mary Kleophas (considered a later addition by Argan), does not detract from the picture. Indeed, its strong dramatic impact is underlined by the convincing characters. They are portraits of the man in the street, and, in the case of Nicodemus, of the artist himself.

385) Caravaggio School: "Peter's Denial of Christ." Canvas
There is a tendency to regard this still anonymous painter as someone who was associated with Carlo Saraceni. In fact, the delicate tones and the use of shafts of light are typical of Caravaggio's school. In this powerful painting, which is dominated by the sudden vehemence of light threatened by shade, there is a clear link with the characteristic elements of Caravaggio's art when he was changing from his first to his second phase, a period in which considerable emphasis was placed on light effects. Nevertheless, the name of this talented painter must remain a matter of conjecture, for some scholars have detected French, and others, Dutch elements in his artistic education.

386) Carlo Maratta: "Pope Clement IX." Canvas
Maratta overcame his leaning toward the academic in this portrait, and his keen psychological insight enabled him to reveal the Pope's character in his beautiful, sensitive hands and finely chiselled face. The high painterly quality has made the work a masterpiece. Color is treated in the style of the great masters, from the Venetians to Velazquez and Baciccia, the author of another famous portrait of the same Pope in the Galleria dell'Academia di S. Luca, outstanding for its light and color harmonies. Every brush-stroke seems to be saturated with light, so that the color disperses and vibrates.

387) Baciccia: "Angels with Musical Instruments." Canvas
This painting, originally attributed to Lanfranco, was finally recognized as the work of Baciccia after it had been thoroughly cleaned and the colors were restored to their initial brilliance. It can be regarded as a sketch for one section of the frescoes in the dome of S. Ignazio in Rome. Its date can be fixed between 1672 and 1673, and it comes from the Castellano Collection. There is an obvious tendency in this painting to avoid closed forms and break out of static frames, which are typical of the artist's main works—as are the charm and lightness of his shapes and the animation of his figures.

The swift, almost summary brush strokes, which are sometimes missing in his completed work, are particularly attractive to the 20th century viewer.

388) Daniel Seghers: "St. Gosvin Wreathed in Flowers." Canvas
This painting forms part of a series of four pictures, *Madonna with Child, St. Ignatius Enthroned,* and *Ecce Homo,* in which the central figure is surrounded and almost overwhelmed by a frame of elegantly stylized flowers in flowing colors.

389) Francesco Solimena: "Archangel Michael Casting Satan from Heaven." Canvas
The painter, one of the leading representatives of Neapolitan art in the 18th century, reveals the distinctive features of his personal style in this picture: an elegant, well balanced composition and a choice of harmonious colors. Even though his training was based on a study of the works of L. Giordano,

M. Preti and Pietro da Cortona, his boundless inventiveness and lively imagination enabled him to introduce a personal touch into his paintings.

390) Georges Rouault: "Autumn." Panel
In this expansive composition are all the most distinctive elements of this French painter's artistic idiom: the strong, thick impasto of color which resembles enamel, and the firm, decisive lines reminiscent of his studies of Gothic stained-glass windows in France. The result is a highly impressive work of art.

391) Maurice Utrillo: "The Church of St. Auxonne." Panel
This small painting, which was presented to the new department of the picture gallery by the artist's widow, is perhaps one of the artist's most poetic concepts. It is expressed in a dazzling, though melancholy, harmony of white and gray.

THE EGYPTIAN MUSEUM

392) Fragment of a painted relief. Bright sandstone
This fragment was part of the wall decoration in a tomb. In deep-set bas-relief, it depicts the figure of a man. The wonderful harmony of the entire work allows one to surmise that it originated in the period of the Old Empire (2585–2235 B.C.).

393) "Beauty." Black basalt
This is a statue of Isis, or of a woman who resembled Isis. Because of its conspicuous elegance and harmony of form, it has been called "Beauty." Although it is from a later period, it has the rigid bearing, the frontal representation of the face, and the large modelling surface so typical of ancient Egyptian art. However, the exact folds of the robe and its harmonic drapery, the slender body—which accentuates the full breasts and the round abdomen— and the long legs are characteristic of the classically regarded forms of the New Empire. Such forms were popular during the Ptolemaic period (332–30 B.C.). Since these characteristics remained valid for a number of centuries, it is difficult to date this statue exactly.

394) Temple Bearer—Naophoros. Green basalt
This statuette depicts a man holding a small temple (naós) in his hands. The head is a reconstruction; the rest of the body, including the bare portions of his breast and arms, display, however, no additions. This is a beautiful piece of sculpture, and it is based on the stylistic rules of the late period from which it originates. The long inscription that adorns the small temple and the figure's dress has great significance. It refers to the first invasion of Egypt by the Persians in 525 B.C., and refers especially to the kings, Cambyses and Darius I. In autobiographical form, the dignitary reports that he had been commandant of the warships of the Pharaohs Amasis and Psammetich III. When the Persians arrived, he was ordered to the royal court and was appointed director of the scholars. He advocated the liberation of the temple of goddess Neith by the military. He also made it clear that he was once again available for ritual ceremonies, and that, as in former times, he had his own financial resources. The good deeds that this personality accomplished for his countrymen, and particularly for the gods, assured him well-being and the perpetuation of his memory. This inscription provides us with exact historical facts; it is the only source of information for a period of Egyptian history that is still masked in darkness.

395) Queen Tuya. Dark, speckled granite
Tuya was the wife of Sethos I and the mother of Ramses II (19th dynasty, 1340–1172 B.C.). On the basis of the work's stylistic and artistic qualities—the youthful face and majestic bearing—this statue is rightly considered to be a masterpiece. The dimensions are cleverly distributed, thus avoiding any

hint of heaviness. The almost mature face emerges directly from the compact shock of hair. The heaviness of breasts and arms is offset by the elegant line of the scepter, while the slim hips are accentuated, almost corrected, by the outstretched right arm, which, although somewhat plump, is geometrically satisfactory. Finally, the legs, with their classic forward gait, endow the entire work with a lightness that has its counterweight in the exactly detailed form of the feet.

396) Burial scroll. Papyrus
This is one of the many papyrus manuscripts in the museum, and one of the best preserved. It contains three magic prayers from the so-called *Book of the Dead:* number 26 (the first one on the right side), which was used "to give a man in the necropolis his heart"; number 30 (center) "so that the heart will not be taken from the person in the necropolis"; and number 100 (left), "to bring the departed to perfection and to lead him to the sun-boat." The script is hieratic, almost cursive, because of the slightly shortened hieroglyphics from the Saitic period (720–332 B.C.). Represented here is the famous courtroom scene, the "weighing of the heart," by which it was determined whether or not the deceased was worthy of immortality.

397) Torso of a high priest. Alabaster
From several of the surviving sections, it is possible to conclude that the statue depicted the high priest in a kneeling position, during the acceptance of a sacrifice. Judging from the arm stump, the left hand must have had a posture similar to that of the right hand. The anatomical characteristics are depicted in a manner that conforms with the strict rules of Egyptian art: angular collar-bone; outstanding breast; curved sides; recessed midriff, ending at the navel. The entire work expresses both elegance and power. It originates presumably from the era of Psammetich I (26th dynasty, 663–609 B.C.).

398/399) Sarcophagus. Sycamore wood
This sarcophagus, embellished with graceful painting, was done with extraordinary exactness of detail and remarkable skill. Intended for the mummy of a woman (the poetess of Amon, Get-mut), it is particularly noticeable because of the inside decoration. The painter depicted two mummies—one of a man, and the other of a woman; the difference between the sexes is expressed in the hair color. Each of them receives the water of life from a priest, while a female mourner embraces the woman's feet. The section above the head is painted as one would paint the ceiling of a room. All this indicates that the artist had not thought of the sarcophagus as a burial receptacle for one person, but for a married couple. The exterior, to the right, contains a scene that is seldom seen on sarcophagi: the burial procession taking the mummy

from its home to the tomb. It was made presumably in the 22nd dynasty (935–759 B.C.).

400) Memorial stele. Bright yellow sandstone
The five-line inscription on the bottom indicates that this stele is intended to recall the restoration of the walls around the necropolis of Thebes, carried out by Queen Hatshepsut (18th dynasty; 1555–1340 B.C.). The four figures represent, from left to right: Amon-Ra, the greatest of the gods and ruler of Karnak, whose temple lay on the east bank of the Nile; Queen Hatshepsut, who, as seen here, liked to be depicted in male clothing; the young Tutmosis III, who ruled with Hatshepsut for some time; a woman who symbolizes the necropolis of Thebes located on the west bank of the Nile—she is thus called "she, who faces the god (Amon-Ra)." The workmanship is somewhat sketchy, and the space between the figures is not uniform (particularly between the last two). On the whole, however, this is a beautiful example of a memorial stele.

401) Cover of a sarcophagus (mummy casket). Composed of stucco, plaster and clay from the Nile valley
The exterior decoration of this mummy casket was of gold and painted stucco. Depicted here is a princess, as indicated by the holy snakes adorning her forehead and the winged disc. Numerous divinities are represented on the two bands suspended over her breasts and ending in two crouching sphinxes with crowned hawks' heads. It is not known for certain when this work originated, although we can say with approximate surety that it is of the late period.

MUSEO PIO-CRISTIANO

402) Marble statue of the Good Shepherd. 3rd–4th century. Restored portions: legs and bottom section of the tunic, arms, parts of the face and the sheep's legs. In the 18th century, it belonged to the Mariotti collection. At first in the Vatican Museum, it was transferred to the Lateran Museum
The shepherd is young and clean-shaven. Over the ears he has long, curly hair. His head is turned to the left (in contrast, his weight is on the right leg); he wears a sleeveless tunic and carries a shoulder-bag. Very little remains of early-Christian detached sculpture, and perhaps very little was made; this may have been because of the ideological desire to avoid the creation of graven images. This extraordinary statuette's bearing was clearly influenced by ancient classical models, and from the iconographic point of view, it was less an invention of Christianity than a rediscovery. The representation of a shepherd with a calf, sheep or ram on his shoulders had been used in the Mediterranean area (Greece, Cyprus, later in Attica, Arcadia and Campania) since the 7th century B.C. A well-known example of this is the Moscophoros in the Acropolis Museum in Athens. Here, however, we have the ancient theme in a completely new context. Previously, it was the believer who brought his sacrificial animal to the altar. Here it is shepherd and lamb together: the Good Shepherd of St. Luke (XV, 4-5—"And when he hath found it [the lost sheep], he layeth it on his shoulders, rejoicing") and of St. John (X, 10-18—"I am the good shepherd...", "...I am come that they might have life, and that they might have it more abundantly.").

403/404) The Good Shepherd. Marble sarcophagus with the narrow sides rounded. About the middle of the 3rd century. Found on the Via Salaria, near the mausoleum of Licinius Petrus, in 1881; bought in 1891 by Pope Leo XIII
In the center, between two trees, is the Good Shepherd: bearded, with a ram on his shoulders and two others (or perhaps they are sheep; the heads were restored) at his feet. Sitting on the left is a bearded man, clothed as a philosopher, instructing two attentively listening figures. On the right are three women; one is standing, and the others are sitting. The composition is bordered on both ends by two large rams. The frieze obeys the rule that says the heads of all the figures depicted in a frieze must be at the same level, whatever their true proportions and bearing. The two sitting figures are emphasized by their size; they represent the couple to whom the tomb belongs.

405) Large marble sarcophagus, known as the Theological Sarcophagus. Second half of the 4th century. From the foundations of the baldachin in S. Paolo fuori le mura
The front is divided into two rows. In the middle are two winged figures of Eros; they hold a medallion, in which are the busts of the deceased couple in the form of incomplete portraits. In the first section to the left is the Holy Trinity during the creation of man; then Christ, between Adam and Eve; behind Eve is the tree of the knowledge of good and evil, and wound around it is the snake, with the forbidden fruit in its mouth. Christ shows Adam ears of grain and Eve a sheep, symbols of the work to which God has condemned them as a result of the expulsion from Paradise—they must now work to get food and clothing. To the right of the medallion is the transformation of water into wine, the multiplication of bread and fish, and the raising of Lazarus. In the bottom row: to the left, the Adoration of the Magi; the healing of the blind; in the center, Daniel in the lions' den; to the right, Christ tells St. Peter that he will deny him thrice (the cock at their feet proclaims the fulfillment of this prophecy); St. Peter being taken prisoner; and Moses and the miracle of the well.

406) Marble sarcophagus, embellished on all sides. Found near the Praetextatus cemetery)
The scene on the front takes place around the figures of standing shepherds, on three adorned socles. The figure in the center has a beard and carries a ram on his shoulders. The two on the sides are clean-shaven and carry sheep. Their short tunics, breeches and boots, the stick and shoulder-bag, all combine to complete the "official" picture of the shepherd; it is a picture that we have already seen on one previous sarcophagus (403, 404) and in the famous statue of the Good Shepherd (402). Within the framework of this motif, and in avoidance of monotonous repetitions of the same theme, every possible variation has been employed here, in the manner in which the animal is held on the shoulders and in the shepherd's turn of head. The entire surface is covered with the crowded scene of a wine harvest; small winged figures of Eros climb upon the vine shoots, pluck the grapes and pour them into a tub (bottom right) to be pressed. A figure of Eros stands approximately center-right; a Psyche, with basket and grapes, turns toward him. To the left, a figure of Eros is shown milking a goat.

407) Fragments of the original tombstone of Aberkios
The text on the original fragment contains several Greek half-lines. They are the same as those that had been fully known as the result of an anonymous legend from the end of the 4th century; it had been written in the form of a biography of a bishop of Hieropolis in Asia Minor. In this vita, or biography, Aberkios is depicted as a renowned worker of miracles. In order to accentuate the bishop's fame, an episode is inserted that links Aberkios with the imperial court in Rome. According to this tale, the daughter of Emperor Marcus Aurelius and Empress Faustina is possessed of the devil. All attempts to cure her fail. The demon within the girl calls out: "I shall not depart from this creature until Aberkios, the Bishop of Hieropolis, comes." The emperor sends for Aberkios. At the time of his arrival in Rome, the emperor is at the Rhine with his troops, trying to stem an invasion by the barbarians; only the empress is in Rome. Aberkios exorcises the devil, expelling the evil spirit from the Princess's body; Aberkios commands it to carry an altar from Rome to Hieropolis, and this it does, to the accompaniment of much moaning and groaning. After a long journey, Aberkios returns to Hieropolis and begins

to think about erecting his tomb. At this point, the biography notes: "He had a square tomb erected, upon which he placed the altar that the demon had brought all the way from Rome at his command; but first he had the altar inscribed. It was an inscription that, although understandable and useful to Christians, was incomprehensible to non-believers." So much for the biographical notes, whose legendary form caused people to doubt the authenticity, and even the existence, of this inscription. Surprisingly enough, while engaging in excavations near the ancient city of Hieropolis, in Glaucos (in Asia Minor), in the year 1883, William Ramsay found the two fragments with Aberkios's inscription, as illustrated here. They confirmed both the existence of Aberkios and his assertions of the legend. An important 2nd century church leader come within our historic ken; he was an ecclesiastic who resided in the time of Emperor Marcus Aurelius, as the tomb's inscription expressly notes— and he thus visited the successor to St. Peter. One thousand and seven hundred years after Aberkios's tomb had been erected, both Sultan Abdul-Hamid and William Ramsay presented the two preserved fragments of the tombstone to Pope Leo XIII in 1892, the occasion of the Holy Father's 50th anniversary of his ordination as priest. Thus it was that the tombstone, which—as legend has it—originated in Rome, finally returned to the vicinity of the *"tropae Petri,"* the vicinity of St. Peter's.

408) Marble sarcophagus. Second half of the 4th century. The front, divided into five sections, is decorated with olive trees, in the branches of which doves roost. From the sepulchre of the Confessio of S. Paolo fuori le mura

In the first section, we see God the Father, sitting on a block of stone and receiving the sacrificial offering of Abel (in the foreground) and Cain (partly hidden). In the second section, St. Peter is taken prisoner. In the center, between two soldiers—one of them asleep, and the other looking up at him—is the symbol of Christ's victory over death: a cross. Two doves sit on its arms, and at the top is a laurel wreath with Christ's monogram in the middle. To the right is St. Paul being led to his martyrdom. In the last section is Job; he is seated and is being tempted by Satan (holding a potsherd in his right hand). Because of his great patience, Job is being scolded by his wife, while his three friends comfort him (only one of them can be seen in the background).

409) Sarcophagus of Junius Bassus, in Pentelicus marble. Found in front of the altar of the crypt of St. Peter's in 1597, during work enlarging the Confessio of Gregory the Great, by Giacomo della Porta. In the course of this work, the cover was destroyed. Parts of the inscription in the middle were found during the excavations that Pope Pius XII initiated (1939–1945)

The inscription on the upper border of the front says that the sarcophagus belongs to the senator, Junius Bassus, the prefect of the city, who, as a late convert, died at the age of 42 years and two months on the 25th of July in the year in which Eusebius and Hypatius were consuls—i.e., in 359. Another metrical inscription, in eight distichs, on the center panel of the cover, describes the grief of the populace and its participation in the funeral, as well as the honor granted his memory. The sarcophagus is divided into two horizontal rows, each of which contains five panels, set off from its neighbors by columns. The upper row contains, from left to right: Abraham's sacrifice; the imprisonment of St. Peter; Christ enthroned between two Apostles, his feet resting on the head of a bearded male figure, Heaven, which holds its cloak over its head like an arch; Christ with Pilatus; Pilatus, whose confusion is indicated by his left hand being held to his chin before he washes his hands (St. Matthew XXVII, 24). The lower row, from left to right: the scene with Job (see number 408 above); Adam and Eve; from the right, the imprisonment of St. Paul; and Daniel (the figure has been completely restored) in the lions' den. In the middle can be seen the entry of Jesus into Jerusalem; he is sitting on a donkey, and several in the multitude spread out their clothes on the ground as he passes by, while others cut branches from the trees and strew them in the streets.

410) Cross of Justinian. Treasury of St. Peter's

This priceless cross is made of gold and chased silver, with inlaid jewels, semi-precious stones dangling from the arms. It was given to the Vatican by Emperor Justinian II and his wife, Sophia, in the year 570 and was intended to be set up at the Apostle's tomb. On the front are five embossed medallions. These depict: above, God the Father; in the center, the Lamb of God; beneath this, Jesus Christ; and at the sides, adorned with flowers, the noble donors. A Latin inscription on the back says that this cross—which contains the wood that Jesus Christ used to destroy the enemy of mankind— is a donation from Justinian and Sophia. In the middle of it, there is indeed a relic of the Holy Cross, and until the French occupation it was mounted in pearls. This priceless relic is used by the Vatican chapter at Good Friday Mass.